CONTENTS

P9-AEY-715

PART ONE

The Colonial Heritage of Latin America   3

 1   Ancient America   7

 2   The Hispanic Background   37

 3   The Conquest of America   53

Maps

PREFACE

THE NINTH EDITION of *A History of Latin America* offers teachers and students of Latin American history a text based on the best recent scholarship, enriched with data and concepts drawn from the sister social sciences of economics, anthropology, and sociology. Because the book is a history of Latin American *civilization*, it devotes considerable space to the way of life adopted at each period of the region's history.

To achieve its goal, this book sets Latin American history within a broad interpretive framework based on the "dependency theory." The dependency theory is the most influential theoretical model for social scientists concerned with understanding Latin America. Not all followers of the theory understand it in precisely the same way, but most probably agree with the definition of *dependency* offered by the Brazilian scholar Theotonio dos Santos: "A situation in which the economy of certain countries is conditioned by the development and expansion of another economy to which the former is subject."

Writers of the dependency school employ some standard terms that we use in this text: *neocolonialism, neoliberalism, center,* and *periphery. Neocolonialism* refers to the dependent condition of countries that enjoy formal political independence. *Neoliberalism* refers to the policies of privatization, austerity, and trade liberalization accepted willingly or unwillingly by the governments of dependent countries as a condition of approval for investment, loans, and debt relief by the International Monetary Fund (IMF) and the World Bank. (The IMF and the World Bank prefer to give such policies the innocuous-sounding name of "structural adjustment programs.") The term *center* applies to the dominant group of developed capitalist countries, and *periphery* to the underdeveloped or dependent countries.

Dependency theory has been criticized intermittently over the last seventy years by scholars who feel it does not adequately describe Latin America's historical struggle for development in the twenty-first-century global context. Those who reject the dependency approach typically favor one of a number of alternative paradigms for explaining Latin America's historical struggle for development. In particular, in the first decades following World War II, modernization theory informed and dominated discussions in the United States and Western Europe. Drawing on their own postwar national experiences, scholars espousing modernization theory assumed that "underdevelopment" and "economic backwardness" were conditions common to all societies at one time in their evolution. The key to unlocking the mystery of development, for these scholars, was to contrast conditions in the developed countries with those in undeveloped areas. This produced a prescription for social, political, cultural, and economic change that sought to bring the developmental benefits of modernity to all. Modernizationists concluded that the undeveloped world suffered from a lack of personal freedom, excessive government regulation, highly politicized states, weak civil societies, a shortage of "entrepreneurial values," and the survival of powerful "antimodern" cultural traditions that stressed cooperative communal, rather than competitive individualistic, values.

For the modernization theorists, then, Latin America's failure to develop was largely a consequence of its own internal problems and its reluctance to open itself to the forces of modernity emanating from Western Europe and the United States. Some scholars have even suggested that this failure was the product of a distinct tradition in Latin America, informed by a historic legacy of militarism, local political bosses (*caudillaje*), indigenous communalism, and insular Iberic Catholic culture. To combat these perceived deficiencies in the developmental experiences of Latin America, the modernizationists prescribed a bitter medicine that largely mirrored neoliberal recommendations to dismantle state bureaucracies, reduce budget deficits, cut spending on social services, deregulate private business, privatize national resources, provide incentives to foreign investors, promote free trade, encourage entrepreneurial education, and reduce the political power of so-called antimodern social sectors.

A rapid glance at the results of more than a decade of application of neoliberal therapy to Latin America's problems suggests that in all essential respects the area's economic and social crisis worsened and its dependency on the core capitalist powers deepened. In this book, we draw on a critical synthesis of these two intellectual traditions and emphasize both internal and external factors that have shaped Latin America's historic struggle for development. We challenge the developmentalist belief that all countries have been equally underdeveloped in their historic past and that the developed countries achieved modernity by promoting personal freedom, free trade, and unfettered foreign direct investment. The text unambiguously shows that European and U.S. modernity relied on a five-century legacy of brutal conquest, enslavement, exploitation, and unequal trade enforced alternately by military and market coercion. Moreover, unlike classical dependency theory, which emphasizes transnational social forces and institutional structures of power that seemingly rendered inconsequential all forms of popular resistance, this text documents the powerful role that internal class, racial, gender, ethnic, and interest group struggles have played in shaping the region's development.

Unlike both classical dependency and modernizationist formulations, this text's revised dependency approach also draws on recent feminist theory that defines women as the "last colony," whose shared experiences, according to feminist scholars Christine Bose and Edna Acosta-Belén, include unwaged and low-wage labor, extreme poverty, and "structural subordination and dependency." However, women, like colonial peoples more generally, have not been passive victims in the developmental process. They have been active in the spheres of both production and reproduction. As producers of material wealth in Latin America, women have played a significant, but largely neglected, historical role, working endless hours without pay in household activities that have been an essential source of private capital accumulation. For example, even an inefficient colonial workforce needed certain household services—shopping, cooking, cleaning, first aid, child-rearing, washing, elder care, and so on—to reproduce its labor on a daily basis. If poorly paid male workers in Latin America had to purchase these services that women—wives and daughters—freely provided, they would have had to demand higher wages, and employers would have had to pay these higher costs out of profits.

Historically, men largely assigned women to the family household, where they were responsible for reproduction—i.e., to rear, nurture, and educate the next generation of workers. Once freed from these constraints to seek employment in the marketplace, however, many working-class women experienced double exploitation: first, as poorly paid wage earners whose collective hard work outside the home produced great value that enriched their employers; second, as traditional unwaged household labor that sustained working-class families as the bedrock of classical capital accumulation. This text both highlights the transition of women's roles in Latin America and documents women's demand for state regulation of market activities to protect their developmental contributions in the vital areas of production and reproduction.

Finally, like classical dependency writers who originally blamed global markets for Latin America's poverty and doubted the region's developmental potential in the absence of socialism, we conclude that market expansion often has created economic growth at the expense of development. Unlike these classical dependency theorists, however, we stress the key role of popular social movements in taming markets, restraining inequities produced by their unregulated activities, and transforming them into agents of development. Contrary to modernizationists who argued that market expansion was key to development, this text shows that markets in and of themselves are not nearly as important as how they were regulated. Historical struggles, in turn, have shaped the specific nature of these regulations. In socialist Cuba, for example, the expansion of market activities since the collapse of the Soviet Union and its global trading partners had a decidedly different developmental impact than it had in neoliberal Argentina or Peru. Similarly, Brazil, Chile, and Venezuela regulated global markets differently, with correspondingly different developmental impacts.

More to the point, after 2002, Latin Americans elected a wave of progressive nationalist governments in Argentina, Bolivia, Brazil, Chile, Ecuador, Nicaragua, Paraguay, Uruguay, and Venezuela. Known as the "Pink Tide," these democratically elected governments, despite their many differences, shared a collective commitment to oppose neoliberalism and expand the state's control of market forces. The resulting combination of state regulation, outright nationalization, growing regional integration, increased Chinese market demand, relatively high international export prices, and significant expansion of state antipoverty programs started slowly to reverse the social losses experienced during the neoliberal decade of the 1990s. Our text documents these conclusions in historic detail, underlining the general collapse of the neoliberal, modernizationist model and simultaneously reinforcing the relevance of our revised dependency perspective.

Organization and Revisions

A History of Latin America is published in two volumes as well as in a complete version. Volume 1 includes Latin American history from ancient times to 1910, and Volume 2 covers Latin American history from independence to the present.

This text has developed organically in response to valuable feedback from students and faculty. Early on we decided not to try to cover the postindependence history of the twenty Latin American republics in detail and have avoided cataloging every single general who ever passed through a presidential palace. Most teachers will agree that such content can discourage students by miring them in a bog of tedious facts. Accordingly, the text limited coverage of the national period in the nineteenth century to Argentina, Brazil, Chile, and Mexico, whose histories best illustrate the major issues and trends of the period. In addition to covering these four countries, the survey of the twentieth century later broadened to include the central Andean area, with a special concentration on Peru and Cuba, the scene of a socialist revolution with continental repercussions.

The second edition added a chapter on Central America, where a revolutionary storm, having toppled the U.S.-unsupported Somoza tyranny in Nicaragua, threatened the rickety structures of oligarchical and military rule in Guatemala and El Salvador. The fourth edition recognized the political and economic importance of the Bolivarian lands of Colombia and Venezuela by including a chapter on the modern history of those countries. The seventh edition more fully integrated the discussion of the Andean and Central American regions, the Bolivarian republics, and Cuba into the text's original layout. Because teachers rarely have time to cover all the Latin American countries in their survey classes, this organization provides greater flexibility, without sacrificing historical continuity, as instructors select those nations on which students should focus. This ninth edition preserves this historical detail, which supplies a foundation for the case study approach, but revisions aim to satisfy the needs of instructors who are interested in a comparative or thematic course design.

Responding to readers' suggestions, we made significant changes to the eighth edition to facilitate its use in course designs that employ both case study and comparative approaches. Part Two included a more detailed overview that highlights the major themes covered in the chapters on nineteenth-century Latin America. It also expanded the coverage with a new chapter on the roles of slavery and emancipation in shaping the postcolonial search for independent national identities. Veteran readers of this text found material on literary traditions that reflected nineteenth- and twentieth-century cultural developments posted to a robust website that accompanies the text. Part Three likewise offered greater comparative cohesion without sacrificing the unique historical details that distinguish each country's national development.

After a more robust overview introducing major themes in the twentieth-century history of Latin America, the text offers successive chapters on the history of liberalism and populism in the Andean Republics, Argentina, Brazil, Central America, Chile, Cuba, Colombia, Mexico, and Venezuela. The focus of Chapter 12 is the Mexican Revolution, the first social revolution in the twentieth century, which decisively shaped Mexico's quest for a unified national identity and bequeathed various institutions, ideologies, and interests that later influenced populism elsewhere. Chapter 13 examines Getulio Vargas and the populist movement unleashed by Brazil's 1930 Revolution, including its historical antecedents and legacies. Chapter 14 explores the origin and evolution of the distinctive postwar populist experience in Argentina under Juan Domingo Perón and his charismatic wife Evita.

Chapter 15 analyzes the 1959 Cuban Revolution, its causes and effects, to explain how it aimed to transcend the limitations of populism and promote an authentically independent national development. As an alternative both to the failures of populism and the Cuban Revolution, Chapter 16 discusses the development of the Andean region's flirtation with military socialism and the military's role in Peru's 1968 "Revolution from Above." Chapter 17 focuses on the populist experience and its role in shaping Chile's distinctive road to national development in 1970 under the leadership of Salvador Allende, the region's first democratically elected Socialist president. Chapter 18 discusses the roles of armed revolution and prolonged popular war as historically particular struggles to promote national liberation in Central America during the 1980s. Chapter 19 concentrates on the historical sources of Venezuela's Bolivarian Revolution in the 1990s and contrasts

this with the protracted guerrilla war in Colombia, concluding that both offered different strategies for securing an elusive unified national development. Neoliberalism, yet another strategy to transcend the limitations of a failed populism, is the focus of Chapters 20 and 21, which examine respectively its historical evolution and common experiences in the 1990s and beyond. Finally, Chapter 22 explores the historical role of the United States, its regional and global objectives, and the impact of its foreign policies on Latin American national development.

The ninth edition continues the reorganization of the text that began with the eighth edition and updates the history of the region since 2008, stressing especially the roles of regional integration and the Chinese market in Latin America's recovery from the 2009 global recession. The histories of all the countries discussed in this edition have been brought up to date, and the rest of the book has been thoroughly revised to reflect current scholarship, particularly the respective roles of race, class, and gender in the region's historical development. This edition especially emphasizes such topics as the impact of neoliberal economic policies and the gathering revolt against them, the effects of the North American Free Trade Agreement, the growing urgency of environmental issues, the heightened visibility of the women's movement, and the significance of popular culture.

Website Resources

Newly available with the ninth edition is Cengage Learning's History CourseMate website with interactive learning, study, and exam preparation tools that support *A History of Latin America*. The History CourseMate website includes an integrated e-book, primary sources, quizzes, flashcards, glossary terms, and Engagement Tracker, a first-of-its-kind tool that monitors student engagement in the course. A collection of related full-color maps and video clips relevant to specific chapters of the book are also included. Learn more at www.cengagebrain.com. An online version of the Instructor's Resource Manual and a test bank are available on the Instructor website.

Acknowledgments

Although my friend and comrade Benjamin Keen has not been involved physically in revisions to this book for more than a decade, his spirit still lives in its ideas and interpretations; it will be his book forever. This edition has benefited from the careful scrutiny of the eighth edition by fellow Latin American History professors: Frank Argote-Freyre, Kean University; Eileen Ford, California State University, Los Angeles; Greg Landau, City College of San Francisco; and Angela Vergara, California State University, Los Angeles. We want to acknowledge a special debt of gratitude to Professor Asunción Lavrín, who graciously shared her photo archive on Latin American feminism. Jim Livingston of Rutgers University and Carl Swidorski of the College of Saint Rose provided special guidance and support. We wish to recall, too, the many students, graduate and undergraduate, who helped us to define our views on Latin American history through the give-and-take of classroom discussion and the reading and discussion of their papers and theses.

Benjamin Keen
Keith Haynes

INTRODUCTION

The Geographic Background of Latin American History

LATIN AMERICA, a region of startling physical contrasts, stretches 7,000 miles southward from the Mexican-U.S. border to the tip of Tierra del Fuego on Cape Horn. The widest east-west point, across Peru and Brazil, spans 3,200 miles. This diverse geography has helped produce the distinctive development of each Latin American nation.

Latin America has two dominant physical characteristics: enormous mountains and vast river systems. The often-snowcapped and sometimes volcanic mountain ranges—the three Sierra Madre ranges in Mexico and the 4,000-mile-long Andes in South America that make a western spine from Venezuela to Tierra del Fuego—form the backbone of the landmass. Nearly impassable for most of their length, these mountain ranges boast many peaks of more than 22,000 feet. The mountains have presented a formidable barrier to trade and communications in Mexico and the nations of the southern continent. The mountain ranges not only separate nations from each other but also divide regions within nations.

The enormous rivers most often lie in lightly populated areas. Three mammoth river systems (the Amazon, the Orinoco, and the Río de la Plata) spread over almost the entire South American continent east of the Andes. The size of the Amazon River basin and the surrounding tropics—the largest such area in the world—has posed another impediment to the development of transportation and human settlement, although some rivers are navigable for long distances. Only with the advent of modern technology—railroads, telegraph, telephones, automobiles, and airplanes—has geographic isolation been partly overcome, a condition that has helped create markets and forge independent states.

Latin America encompasses five climatological regions: high mountains, tropical jungles, deserts, temperate coastal plains, and temperate highlands. The first three are sparsely populated, whereas the latter two tend to be densely inhabited. With the exception of the Maya, all the great ancient civilizations arose in the highlands of the Andes and Mexico.

The varied climate and topography of South America, Mexico, and Central America have produced this highly uneven distribution of population. Three notable examples—the gargantuan Amazonian region of mostly steamy tropical forests and savannah, the vast desert of Patagonia in southern Argentina, and the northern wastelands of Mexico—support few inhabitants. In contrast to these inhospitable regions, a thin strip along Brazil's coast, the plain along the Río de la Plata estuary in Argentina, and the central plateau of Mexico contain most of the people in these countries. Thus, these nations are overpopulated and underpopulated at the same time.

In western South America, the heaviest concentration of people is found on the inland plateaus. None of its major cities—including Santiago, Chile; Bogotá and Medellín, Colombia; Quito, Ecuador; and Lima, Peru—are ports; the Pacific coast is home to few good natural harbors. By contrast, in eastern South America, the major cities—including Buenos Aires, Argentina; São Paulo–Santos, Rio de Janeiro, Bahia, and Recife, Brazil; and Montevideo, Uruguay—are situated on the Atlantic coast. The majority of people in Argentina, Brazil, and Uruguay reside on the coastal plains. Guadalajara, Mexico City, and Monterrey, Mexico's largest cities, are inland. Almost all these cities have a population of more than 1 million, with Mexico City, the largest, having more than 20 million.

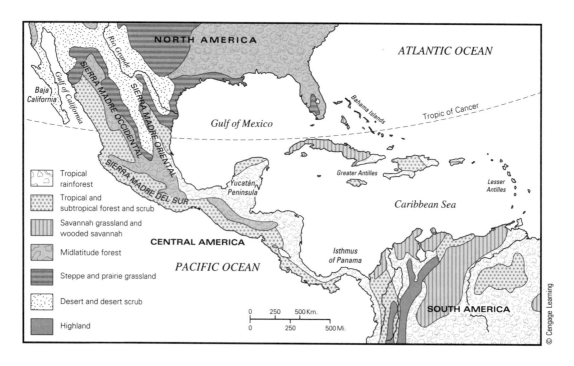

The maps on these two pages form an overall picture of the natural geographic features of
Latin America: Middle America (*above*), composed of Mexico, Central America, and the Caribbean region; and
South America (*next page*).

The number of waterways and the amount of
rainfall vary greatly from region to region. Mexico
has no rivers of importance, but Brazil contains the
huge Amazon network. Lack of rain and rivers for
irrigation in large areas makes farming impossible.
Barely 10 percent of Mexico's land is fertile enough
to farm; rainfall is so uncertain in some cultivable
areas that drought strikes often and for years at a
time. Mexico, with too little water, contrasts with
Brazil, with too much. Much of Brazil's vast territory,
however, is equally uncultivable, as its tropical soils
have high acidity and have proved infertile and incapable of sustaining agricultural crops.

On the other hand, Latin America has enormous
natural resources for economic development. Mexico and Venezuela rank among the world's largest oil
producers. Mexico may have the biggest petroleum
reserves of any nation other than Saudi Arabia. Bolivia, Ecuador, Colombia, and Peru also produce oil.
Over the centuries, Latin American nations have been

leading sources of copper (Chile and Mexico), nitrate
(Chile), silver (Mexico and Peru), gold (Brazil), diamonds (Brazil), and tin (Bolivia). Much of the world's
coffee grows on the fertile highlands of Central
America, Colombia, and Brazil. Much of the world's
cattle pasture on the plains of northern Mexico,
southern Brazil, and central Argentina. Argentina's
immense plains, the Pampas, are among the planet's
most fertile areas, yielding not only cattle but sheep,
wheat, and soy beans as well. Over the past five centuries, the coastal plains of Brazil have produced enormous amounts of sugar, but they now have
transformed the nation into the world's second largest
producer of soy beans. In addition, human ingenuity
has converted geographic obstacles into assets. Some
extensive river systems have the potential for hydro-
electric power and provide water for irrigation as
well, as has been done in Mexico's arid regions.

The historical record shows that the richness of
Latin America's resources has had a significant impact

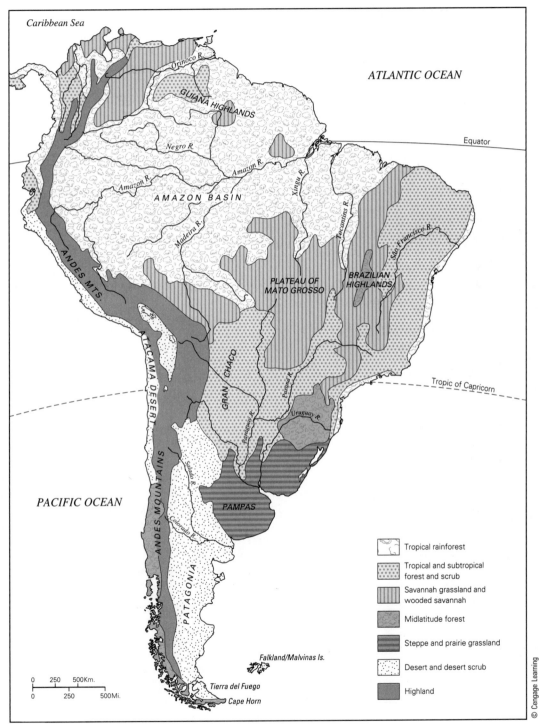

Caribbean Sea

ATLANTIC OCEAN

Orinoco R.

GUIANA HIGHLANDS

Equator

Negro R.

Amazon R.

Amazon R.

AMAZON BASIN

Xingu R.

Tocantins R.

San Francisco R.

Madeira R.

ANDES MTS.

ATACAMA DESERT

PLATEAU OF
MATO GROSSO

BRAZILIAN
HIGHLANDS

GRAN CHACO

Paraguay R.

Paraná R.

Uruguay R.

Tropic of Capricorn

PACIFIC OCEAN

ANDES MOUNTAINS

Salado R.

Colorado R.

PAMPAS

PATAGONIA

Falkland/Malvinas Is.

Tierra del Fuego

Cape Horn

0   250   500 Km.
0   250   500 Mi.

Tropical rainforest

Tropical and subtropical
forest and scrub

Savannah grassland and
wooded savannah

Midlatitude forest

Steppe and prairie grassland

Desert and desert scrub

Highland

© Cengage Learning

on the economic and political development of Europe and North America. The gold and silver of its New World empire fueled Spain's wars and diplomacy in Europe for four hundred years. Many scholars trace the origins of the Industrial Revolution in such nations as Great Britain and the Netherlands to resources extracted from Latin America by its colonial masters, Spain and Portugal.

Latin America's resources have affected economic development elsewhere, but how these resources have been developed and by whom and in which ways has profoundly changed the history of the nations in this area. Geography has perhaps narrowed historical alternatives in Latin America, but the decisions of people determined its development. Going back to the colonization by Spain and Portugal, exploitation of its peoples and its natural resources has marked Latin America's history. Imperial Spain's policy to drain its conquered lands of gold, silver, and other resources fixed the pattern for later exploiters. With European dominance came the decision to subjugate the indigenous peoples and often force them to labor under subhuman conditions in mines and on

large estates, where many died. In the more recent era, external market demand has caused foreign companies and local producers to grow bananas on the coastal plains of Central America instead of corn or other staples of the local diet. This has made export profitable, usually for North American concerns, but this land use has left many, like the Guatemalans, without sufficient food. Meanwhile, the uncontrolled expansion of capitalism in the area has led to an ecological crisis, reflected in massive deforestation, severe soil exhaustion, and growing agricultural and industrial pollution. These developments have contributed to rapid depletion of renewable resources, lack of clean water and air, and major epidemics of contagious diseases and other health problems.

The work that follows is a history of the development of Latin America's economy, politics, and society viewed primarily from the perspective of ordinary people, who endured exploitation and oppression but steadfastly resisted and continued to struggle for social justice. It is the story of the events and forces that produced the alternatives from which Latin Americans created their world.

A History of Latin America

PART ONE

7000–2300 B.C.E.	Domestication of maize, beans, and pumpkins
1500–400 B.C.E.	Development of Preclassic Olmec, Zapotec, and Chavín cultures
250–900 C.E.	Development of Classic Teotihuacán, Maya, and Mochica cultures
1100–1532	Development of Postclassic Mexica (Aztec) and Inca civilizations
1479	Treaty of Alcaçovas recognizes union of kingdoms of Castile and Aragón and guarantees Portugal a Christian monopoly of East India trade routes around Africa
1492	Expulsion of Muslim occupation of Granada and first voyage of Columbus
1519–1532	Spanish Conquest of Aztec and Inca empires
1542	New Laws of the Indies, abolishing *encomienda* and permitting enslavement of Africans
1580	Unification of Spain and Portugal and dramatic expansion of transatlantic slave trade
1603–1694	Development of independent kingdom of Palmares, a refuge for Africans and their descendants escaping Portuguese enslavement in Brazil
1700–1713	War of the Spanish Succession and rise of the Spanish Bourbon dynasty
1780	Tupac Amaru rebellion and popular resistance to Spanish colonialism in Andean world
1791–1803	Haitian Revolution, abolition of slavery, and declaration of independence from France
1808	Napoleonic invasion of Spain and Portugal, deposition of Bourbon king, installation of brother Joseph as José I, and alienation of creole aristocracy in colonial Spanish America
1810	Revolt led by Miguel Hidalgo and José María Morelos, abolition of slavery, and declaration of independence from Spain
1815–1823	Revolts led by Simón Bolívar, José de San Martín, and Agustín Iturbide, declaring political independence and calling for slavery's abolition throughout continental Spanish America but preserving remaining institutions of colonial society

2

The Colonial Heritage of Latin America

The Great City of Tenochtitlan (detail), 1945, by Diego Rivera. National Palace, Mexico City, D.F., Mexico.

FOR MOST NORTH AMERICANS, perhaps, the colonial past is a remote, picturesque time that has little relevance to the way we live now. The situation is different in Latin America. "Even the casual visitor to Latin America," says the historian Woodrow Borah, "is struck by the survival of institutions and features that are patently colonial." The inventory of colonial survivals includes many articles and practices of everyday life, systems of land use and labor, and a wealth of social relations and attitudes.

Characteristic of the Latin American scene is the coexistence and mingling of colonial and modern elements: the digging stick, the foot plow, and the handloom coexist with the tractor, the conveyor belt, the computer, and the cell phone. In Latin America, the colonial past is a harsh reality, not a nostalgic memory. It signifies economic backwardness; political arbitrariness, corruption, and nepotism; and a hierarchical social order with feelings of condescension and contempt on the part of elites toward the masses.

We begin our survey of the colonial period of Latin American history with some account of Ancient America, that long span of time during which indigenous Americans developed their cultures in virtual isolation from the Old World. This past profoundly influenced the character of the Colonial Era. By no accident, the chief capitals of the Spanish empire in America arose in the old indigenous heartlands—the Mexican and Peruvian areas—the homes of millions of industrious natives accustomed to performing tribute labor for their ruling classes. The Spaniards understood well that these people were the true wealth of the Indies. Territories with small indigenous populations remained marginal in Spanish colonial plans.

Equally decisive for the character of the colonial period was the Hispanic background. The conquistadors came from a Spain where seven centuries of struggle against Muslims had made warfare almost a way of life and had created a large *hidalgo* (noble) class that regarded manual labor with contempt. To some, like the Spanish chronicler Francisco López de Gómara, "The conquest of Indians began when the conquest of the Moors had ended, in order that Spaniards may always war against the infidels." Spain's economic backwardness and immense inequalities of wealth, which sharply limited opportunities for advancement or even a decent livelihood for most Spaniards, help explain both the desperate valor of the conquistadors and their harshness in dealing with others. Significantly, many great captains of the Conquest—Cortés, Pizarro, Valdivia, and Balboa—came from the bleak land of Estremadura, Spain's poorest province.

Another factor that may explain the peculiarly ferocious, predatory character of the Conquest was the climate of violence that existed in contemporary Spain, a clear legacy of the Reconquest and its social conditions and values. In his *Spanish Character: Attitudes and Mentalities from the Sixteenth to the Nineteenth Century*, Bartolomé Bennassar notes that assassins proliferated, as did the ancient practice of issuing writs of pardon in return for the payment of blood money—usually a small amount—for the murder of individuals of humble social status. To concede that the historic background had created this climate of violence is not to ascribe to Spaniards a unique capacity for cruelty or deviltry. We know all too well that colonial, imperialist, and civil wars are replete with atrocities and horrors of every kind. Indeed, what distinguishes Spain among the colonial powers of history is that it produced a minority of men who denounced in the face of the world the crimes of their own compatriots and did all in their power to stop what Bartolomé de Las Casas called "the destruction of the Indies."

Since the sixteenth century, defenders of Spain's colonial record have charged Las Casas and other accusers with bias and exaggeration, claiming that they created a "Black Legend" of Spanish cruelty and intolerance. In fact, every colonial power has its own Black Legend that is no legend but a dismal reality. The brutality of the Spanish Conquest is equivalent to the genocidal "Indian wars" waged by American folk heroes like General and President Andrew Jackson, who supervised the mutilation of some 800 Creek corpses, cutting off their noses to count and keep a record of the dead. Moreover, the United States brutally suppressed the 1899–1902 Filipino revolt against U.S. colonialism with massacres, use of "water torture" to elicit information, and incarceration of civilian populations in concentration camps. Gen. J. Franklin Bell, who took part in that repression, estimated that the war and war-related disease had killed more than 600,000 people in Luzon alone.

On the ruins of indigenous societies, Spain laid the foundations of a new colonial order with three distinctive characteristics. The first was the predominantly feudal character of its economic structure, social organization, and ideology. This feudal character clearly influenced Spain's "Indian" policy, which assigned to them the status of a hereditary servile class, obliged to pay tribute in goods, cash, and labor and to engage in unequal trade with their European masters. The same feudal principles assigned separate legal status to Europeans, *castas* (persons of mixed race), and blacks and regulated the conduct and lifestyle of each racial category. These feudal characteristics, admixed with some capitalist elements, formed part of Spain's (and Portugal's) legacy to independent Latin America.

Second, the colonial economy, externally dependent on the export of precious metals and such staples as sugar, cacao, tobacco, and hides, gradually were integrated into the new capitalist order that arose in northern Europe in the seventeenth and eighteenth centuries. Spain, itself increasingly dependent economically on the capitalist North, was powerless to prevent the flow of colonial treasure and commodities to its rivals through smuggling, piracy, and foreign takeover of Spanish merchant houses. In the process of insertion into the European capitalist system, the feudal colonial economy acquired some capitalist features. Thus, slavery, relatively patriarchal in Europe, acquired a peculiarly brutal character in the Caribbean colonies, with "the civilized horrors of overwork," in the words of Karl Marx, "grafted onto the barbaric horrors of slavery."

Third, Spain's colonial order was rooted in conflict between the crown and the conquistadors and their descendants. The crown feared the rise of a colonial seigneurial class and sought to rein in the colonists' ambitions; on the other hand, it relied on them for security against internal and external threats, and this disposed the crown to make major concessions to them. Against this background, a continual struggle developed, sometimes open, sometimes muffled, between the Spanish crown and the conquistadors and their descendants for control of indigenous labor and tribute. In that struggle, the colonists gradually gained the upper hand.

Spain's seventeenth-century decline contributed to this shift in the balance of power in favor of the colonists. The emergence of a hereditary colonial aristocracy rich in land and peons represented a defeat for the crown and for indigenous communities whose interests, however feebly, the crown defended. When, in the late eighteenth century, Spain's kings sought to tighten their control over the colonies, exclude creoles (American-born Spaniards) from high official posts, and institute reforms that sometimes clashed with creole vested interests, it was too late. These policies only alienated a powerful colonial elite whose members already felt a dawning sense of nationality and dreamed of the advantages of a free trade with the outside world.

A parallel development occurred during the same period in relations between Portugal and Brazil. Between 1810 and 1822, American elites, taking advantage of Spain's and Portugal's distresses, seized power in most of Spanish America and Brazil. These aristocratic rebels wanted no radical social changes or economic diversification; their interests as producers of staples for export to western Europe required the continuance of the system of large estates worked by peons or slaves. As a result, independent Latin America inherited almost intact the colonial legacy of a rigidly stratified society and an economy dependent on foreign countries for capital and finished goods.

Ancient America

1

FOCUS QUESTIONS

- How did different local environments affect cultural development in Ancient America?
- What were the distinctive characteristics of the Formative, Classic, and Postclassic periods?
- How was Maya society organized, and what explains its collapse around 900 C.E.?
- How was Aztec society organized, and how did Aztec rulers govern their empire?
- How was Inca society organized, and how did its empire compare to the Aztecs?
- What was "gender parallelism," and how did the roles of women in Ancient America compare with those of European women?

 GREAT NUMBER OF INDIGEOUS GROUPS, WHO spoke many different languages and had dramatically different ways of life, occupied America at the time of Columbus's arrival. A careful examination of their historic experiences, both before and after European conquest, provides interesting insights into the roles played by internal and external forces in shaping human development, which contemporary indigenous rights activists in Latin America have been quick to acknowledge. For at least ten thousand years, the New World existed in virtual isolation from the Old. Sporadic and transient contacts between America and Asia no doubt occurred, and some transfer of cultural traits, mainly stylistic embellishments, probably took place. The cultural development of indigenous America, however, primarily reflected relationships within each indigenous community, their often conflict-ridden relations with each other, and their interaction with the material environment.

Environment and Culture in Ancient America

During its thousands of years of isolation, America was a unique social laboratory in which indigenous communities worked out their own destinies, adapting in various ways to their special environments. By 1492 this process had produced results that suggest that the patterns of early human cultural evolution are basically similar the world over. The first Europeans found native groups in much the same stages of cultural development as those that parts of the Old World had experienced: Old Stone Age hunters and food gatherers, New Stone Age farmers, and empires as complex as those of Bronze-Age Egypt and Mesopotamia.

The inhabitants of Ancient America were blends of several Asiatic physical types. They had dark eyes, straight or wavy black hair, and yellowish or copper skin. Their remote ancestors probably had come from Asia across the Bering Strait in

9000 B.C.E.	Retreat of glaciers and crisis of hunting economy
7000–2300 B.C.E.	Domestication of subsistence plants and shift to Archaic stage that included hunting, gathering, and agriculture
2500–1500 B.C.E.	Development of Formative or Preclassic stage, involving development of agriculture and sedentary civilizations like Olmec on gulf coast of Mesoamerica
1000 B.C.E.	Population of Valley of Mexico and cultivation of maize, beans, and squash
900–500 B.C.E.	Development of Preclassic Chavín civilization on Peruvian coast and Andean highlands
0–1000 C.E.	Development of Classic civilizations like Teotihuacán and Maya in Mesoamerica and Nazca, Mochica, and Tiahuanaco in Peru
700–1000	Time of Troubles in Mesoamerica
1000–1500	Development of Postclassic civilizations like Toltec, Aztec, Chimu, and Inca
1418–1472	Climax of Texcocan civilization under King Nezahualcoyotl
1430	Aztec imperial expansion under King Itzcoatl and establishment of Triple Alliance, including Texcoco, Tenochtitlán, and Tlacopán
1438	Expansion of Inca empire under Pachacuti Inca
1502	Rise of Aztec emperor, Moctezuma II, and decline of Aztec empire

waves of migration that began perhaps as early as forty thousand years ago and continued until about 10000 B.C.E. Much controversy, however, surrounds the problem of the approximate date of the first human habitation in America. Based on the dating of so-called Folsom stone projectile points found throughout North and South America, some archaeologists argue that no firm evidence exists to refute the traditional view that such habitation began about twelve thousand years ago.

Revisionists point to discoveries, especially in Chile and Brazil, that suggest a much earlier occupation. Most recently, the arguments in favor of such an earlier occupation have been reinforced by linguistic evidence that takes account of the immense time span required for the formation of the many languages spoken in Ancient America.

Two waves of migrations appear to have taken place. The first brought extremely primitive groups who lived by gathering wild fruit, fishing, and hunting small game. A recent archaeological discovery suggests that these primitive hunters and gatherers passed through Peru about twenty-two thousand years ago. The second series of invasions brought big-game hunters who, like their predecessors, spread out through the continent. By 9000 B.C.E., these Asiatic invaders or their descendants had reached Patagonia, the southern tip of the continent.

This first colonization of America took place in the last part of the great geological epoch known as the Pleistocene, a period of great climatic changes. Glacial ages, during which blankets of ice covered extensive areas of the Old and New Worlds, alternated with periods of thaw, when temperatures rose to approximately present-day levels. Even in ice-free areas, precipitation often increased markedly during the Glacial Ages, creating lush growth of pastures and woodlands that supported many varieties of game. Consequently, large sections of America in this period were a hunter's paradise. Many large prehistoric beasts roamed over its plains and through its forests. The projectile points of prehistoric hunters have been found near the remains of such animals from one end of America to the other.

Around 9000 B.C.E., the retreat of the last great glaciation (the Wisconsin), accompanied by drastic climate changes, caused a crisis for the hunting economy. A warmer, drier climate settled over vast areas. Grasslands decreased, and the large animals that had pastured on them gradually died out. The improved techniques of late Pleistocene hunting also may have contributed to the disappearance of these animals. The hunting folk now had to adapt to their changing environment or vanish with the animals that had sustained them.

The southwestern United States, northern Mexico, and other areas offer archaeological evidence of a successful adjustment to the new conditions. Here, people increasingly found sustenance in smaller animals, such as deer and jackrabbits, and edible, wild plants, especially seeds, which were ground into a palatable meal. This new way of life eventually led to the development of agriculture. At first, agriculture merely supplemented the older pursuits of hunting and food collecting; its use hardly constituted an agricultural revolution. The shift from food gathering to food producing was more likely a gradual accumulation of more and more domesticated plants that gradually replaced the edible wild plants. Over an immensely long period, time and energy formerly devoted to hunting and plant collecting shifted to such agricultural activities as clearing, planting, weeding, gardening, picking, harvesting, and food preparation. But in the long run, agriculture, in the New World as in the Old, had revolutionary effects: People began to lead a more disciplined and sedentary life, the food supply increased, population grew, and division of labor became possible.

In caves in the Mexican highlands, archaeologists have found the wild plants that gradually were domesticated; among the more important were pumpkins, beans, and maize. Domestication of these plants probably occurred between 7000 and 2300 B.C.E. Among these achievements, none was more significant than the domestication of maize, the mainstay of the great cultures of Ancient America. Manioc (a starchy root cultivated in the tropics as a staple food) and the potato (in Peru) joined the list of important domesticated plants between 5000 and 1000 B.C.E.

From its place or places of origin, agriculture swiftly spread over the American continents. By 1492, maize was under cultivation from the northern boundary of the present-day United States to Chile, but not all indigenous peoples adopted agriculture as a way of life. Severe climatic conditions forced some, like those who inhabited the bleak wastes of Tierra del Fuego at the far tip of South America, to either hunt and collect food or starve. Others, like the prosperous, sedentary peoples of the Pacific northwest coast, who lived by waters teeming with fish and forests filled with game, had no reason to abandon their good life in favor of agriculture.

Where agriculture became the principal economic activity, its yield depended on such natural factors as soil fertility and climate and on the farming techniques employed. Forest people, usually employing the slash-and-burn (swidden) method of cultivation, cut down and burned trees or brush, and planted maize or other staples in the cleared area with a digging stick. Because this method soon exhausted the soil, they had to leave it fallow and clear a new plot. After this process of clearing the soil had gone on long enough, the whole village had to move to a new site or adopt a dispersed pattern of settlement that would allow each family group sufficient land for its needs. Slash-and-burn agriculture thus had a structural weakness that sharply limited the cultural development of those who employed it. The success of the Maya suggests that a strong, controlling authority could at least temporarily overcome the defects of this method: Their brilliant civilization arose in a tropical forest environment on a base of slash-and-burn farming directed by a powerful priesthood. Abundant evidence, however, now exists that, from very early times, more intensive methods of agriculture supplemented slash-and-burn farming.

A more productive agriculture developed in the rugged highlands of Middle America, in the Andean altiplano, and on the desert coast of Peru. In such arid or semiarid country, favored with a temperate climate and a naturally rich soil, residents tilled the land more easily and preserved its fertility longer with digging-stick methods. Most important, they increased food production with the aid of irrigation, which led to larger populations and a greater division of labor. The need for cooperation and regulation on irrigation projects favored the rise of strong central governments and the extension of their authority over larger areas. The Aztec and Inca empires arose in natural settings of this kind.

Finally, diverse human groups inhabited the American continents on the eve of the Spanish Conquest, and their subsistence base largely shaped the complexity of their social organization, which followed three stages of general cultural evolution: tribes, chiefdoms, and states. The simplest or most primitive, the *band* and *tribal* levels, usually correlated with difficult environments (dense forests; plains; or extremely wet, dry, or frigid areas) that sharply limited productivity. They typically included small, egalitarian groups who relied on hunting, fishing, and foraging; a shifting agriculture; or a combination of these activities. Hunting and gathering groups typically were nomadic, migrating within a given territory in a cyclical pattern according to the seasonal availability of game and edible plants. Groups that supplemented hunting, fishing, and gathering with slash-and-burn agriculture were semisedentary. The often-precarious nature of the subsistence base tended to keep band and tribal population densities low and to hinder the development of a division of labor. The social unit on this level was an autonomous band or a village; a loose association of bands or villages, linked by ties of kinship, real or fictitious, formed a tribe. Social stratification was unknown; all members of the group had access to its hunting and fishing grounds and its land. Village and tribal leaders or chiefs owed their authority to their prowess in battle or other outstanding abilities; the exercise of their authority was limited to the duration of a hunt, a military operation, or some other communal activity.

Typical of these egalitarian societies were many Brazilian tribes of the Amazon basin. A frequent feature of their way of life was constant intertribal warfare whose purpose was to capture rival warriors alive, imprison them for weeks or months, organize ritual executions, and then cook and eat their flesh to gain spiritual strength and perpetuate the tribal feud. The sixteenth-century French philosopher Michel de Montaigne, who read about their customs in travel accounts and met some Brazilian Indians brought to France, greatly valued their democratic spirit and freedom from the familiar European contrasts of extreme poverty and wealth. He used these impressions to draw an influential literary portrait of the noble savage, the innocent cannibal who represents a type of moral perfection free from the vices of civilization.

The *chiefdom*, the second category of indigenous social organization, represented an intermediate level. Most commonly, the subsistence base of the chiefdom was intensive farming, which supported a dense population that dwelled in large villages. A hierarchy of subordinate chiefs, ruled from an elite center by a paramount chief, deprived these villages of their traditional autonomy. Kinship terms defined hierarchy in chiefdom social organization. Genealogical nearness to the paramount chief determined an individual's rank. The paramount chief, who enjoyed a sacred status and was attended by a large retinue of officials and servants, siphoned off the group's surplus production by requiring tribute payment and forced donations; he used much of this surplus for selective redistribution to officials, retainers, and warriors, thereby enhancing his own power. Warfare between chiefdoms was common and likely played a decisive role in their origin and expansion through the absorption of neighboring villages. Warfare leading to the capture and enslavement of labor also contributed to the growth of incipient social stratification.

Numerous chiefdoms existed in ancient America on the eve of the Spanish Conquest, with the largest number in the Circum-Caribbean area (including Panama, Costa Rica, northern Colombia, and Venezuela; and the islands of Hispaniola, Puerto Rico, Jamaica, and Cuba). The Cauca Valley of Colombia alone contained no fewer than eighty chiefdoms.

The complex, densely populated Chibcha or Muisca chiefdoms, located in the eastern highlands of Colombia, may illustrate this level of social and political integration. They rested on a subsistence base of intensive agriculture and fishing, and hunting was an important supplementary activity. The agricultural techniques most likely included terracing and ridged planting beds (raised above wet basin floors to control moisture), as well as slash-and-burn methods. In addition to maize, these chiefdoms cultivated potatoes, *quinoa* (a hardy grain resembling buckwheat), and a wide variety of other plants. The crafts—pottery, weaving, and metallurgy—were highly developed. Their magnificent gold work ranks among the finest such work in Ancient America.

At the time of the Spanish Conquest, two rival chiefdoms, centered at Bogotá and Tunja, respectively, dominated most of the Muisca territory; the area's population was about 1.5 million. The Muisca lived in large villages of several hundred to several thousand people. Surrounded by a palisade, each village consisted of pole-and-thatch houses. The society was divided into commoners and elites, and membership in both sectors entailed differential rights and obligations. Commoners owed tribute in goods and labor for the support of the chiefs and nobles, who controlled the distribution and consumption of surplus production.

The chiefdom marks the transition to the next and highest stage of organization, sometimes called *civilization* or, more simply, the *state* level of social and political integration. The dividing line between the two stages, especially in the case of larger and more complex chiefdoms, is difficult to draw because the state reflected an expansion and deepening of tendencies already present in the chiefdom. A growth of division of labor and specialization was indicated by the formation of artisan groups who no longer engaged in farming, the rise of a priesthood in charge of religious and intellectual activities, the rise of a distinct warrior class, and a bureaucracy entrusted with the administration of the state. Intensified social stratification and corresponding ideological changes accompanied this transition, which also weakened or dissolved the kinship ties that, in fact or in theory, had united the paramount chief and the elite with the commoners. Thereafter, a true class structure arose, with a ruling group claiming a separate origin from the commoners whose labor supported it. At the head of the state stood a priest-king or emperor who sometimes was endowed with divine attributes.

The state level of organization required a technological base of high productivity, usually an in-

tensive agriculture that made large use of irrigation, terracing, and other advanced techniques. The state differed from the chiefdom in its larger size and population, the increased exchange of goods between regions—sometimes accompanied by the emergence of a professional merchant class—and the rise of true cities. In addition to being population, administrative, and industrial centers, these cities were cult centers that often featured a monumental architecture not found in chiefdoms. The Aztec, Maya, and Inca societies offer the best-known examples of the state level of organization.

What were the decisive factors in the qualitative leap from the chiefdom to the state in Ancient America? Some regard warfare leading to territorial conquest as the prime mover in this process; others believe that the state arose primarily as a coercive mechanism to resolve internal conflict between economically stratified classes. Others stress the importance of religious ideology in promoting centralized control by elites over populations and their resources. All these factors played a part in the process of state formation.

Certain environmental conditions were more favorable than others for the formation of early states, especially of their highest form, the empire. Indeed, such states likely could not have arisen in the grassy plains of North America, whose hard sod was impervious to digging sticks. Nor were they likely in the Amazonian rain forests that were unsuitable for farming methods other than transient slash-and-burn clearings.[1] Specialists often refer to the favored region that combined the necessary environmental conditions for the rise of states and empires as *Nuclear America*.

POPULATIONS IN 1492

Research conducted by anthropologists and historians has spawned a rapid growth of information on Ancient America and more frequent comparisons between these complex ancient civilizations and

---

1. At various sites along the shores of the Amazon, archaeologists found evidence of complex societies with elaborate pottery, raised fields, and large statues of chiefs. None of these ancient Amazonian societies appear to have evolved beyond the chiefdom level, and questions remain regarding their origin and the size of their populations.

such advanced Old World cultures as ancient Egypt and Mesopotamia. Recent studies of Ancient America's population history have contributed to the rising respect for its cultural achievement. If we assume, as many social scientists do, that population density correlates with a certain technological and cultural level, then a high estimate of the indigenous population in 1492 is in some measure a judgment of its social achievement and of the colonial societies that arose on its ruins.

The subject of the pre-Conquest population of the Americas, however, has produced sharp, sometimes bitter, debate. The first Spanish arrivals in the New World reported dense populations. Some early estimates of the native population of Hispaniola (modern Haiti and the Dominican Republic) ranged as high as 2 and 4 million. The famous missionary known as Motolinía, who arrived in Mexico in 1524, offered no numbers but wrote that the inhabitants were as numerous as "the blades of grass in a field." The Spanish also reported great densities for the Inca empire and Central America. In the twentieth century, scholars who assessed these early reports tended to divide into two groups. Some found them generally credible; in the 1920s, the American archaeologist H. J. Spinden and the German archaeologist Karl Sapper, taking account of indigenous technology and resources, came up with the same overall totals of 40 to 50 million for the whole New World. Others, like the U.S. anthropologist A. L. Kroeber and the Argentine scholar Angel Rosenblat, concluded that this technology could not support the densities cited by the early sources and that the Spaniards either consciously or unconsciously had exaggerated the number of people they found to enhance their own achievements as conquerors or missionaries. Kroeber produced a hemispheric estimate of 8.4 million; Rosenblat raised this figure to nearly 13.4 million.

Beginning in the 1940s, three professors at the University of California, Woodrow Borah, Sherburne Cook, and Lesley B. Simpson, opened a new line of inquiry into the demographic history of Ancient America with a remarkable series of studies that focused on ancient Mexico. Using a variety of records and sophisticated statistical methods, the Berkeley school projected backward from a base established from Spanish counts for tribute purposes and arrived at a population figure of 25.3 million for central Mexico on the eve of the Conquest.

Later, Cook and Borah extended their inquiries into other areas. Particularly striking are their conclusions concerning the population of Hispaniola in 1492. Previous estimates of the island's population had ranged from a low of 600,000 to the 3 to 4 million proposed by the sixteenth-century Spanish friar Bartolomé de Las Casas, but scholars had long regarded those high figures as the exaggerations of a "Black Legend" enthusiast. After a careful study of a series of statements and estimates on the aboriginal population of Hispaniola made between 1492 and 1520, Cook and Borah not only confirmed the reliability of Las Casas's figures but offered an even higher probable range of 7 to 8 million.

Aside from Borah's suggestion in 1964 that the population of America in 1492 may have been "upwards of 100 million," the Berkeley school did not attempt to estimate the pre-Columbian population of the continent as a whole. The U.S. anthropologist Henry Dobyns, however, did undertake such a systematic effort. Assuming that the indigenous population declined by roughly 95 percent after contact with the Europeans, primarily as a result of new diseases to which they had no acquired immunity, Dobyns estimated a pre-Conquest population of 90 to 112 million; of this figure he assigned 30 million each to central Mexico and Peru.

The findings and methods of the Berkeley school and Dobyns provoked strong dissent; two notable dissenters from those high findings were William T. Sanders and David Henige. In general, however, the evidence of the last half-century of research in this field quite consistently pointed to larger populations than were accepted previously. One effort to generalize from this evidence, taking account both of the findings of the Berkeley school and those of its critics, was that of William T. Denevan, who postulated a total population of 57.3 million—a far cry from Kroeber's 1939 estimate of 8.4 million.

Scholars have also attempted to establish long-range population trends in Ancient America. These scholars generally agree that overall, in Woodrow Borah's words, "American Indians had relatively few diseases and, aside from natural disasters such as floods or droughts causing crop failures, seem to have enjoyed especially good health." Until 1492, their isolation protected them from the unified pool of diseases like smallpox, measles, and typhus that had formed in the Old World by the time of the Renaissance. What the long-range perspective may have been, assuming no European contact, is problematic. In many areas, indigenous peoples had developed a system that combined hunting-gathering and shifting slash-and-burn agriculture, often based on the corn-beans-squash triad, that was sustainable and inflicted little damage on the ecosystem. The Taino of the West Indies had developed a sophisticated form of agriculture that relied on permanent fields of *conucos* (knee-high mounds), in which they planted cassava, sweet potato, and various beans and squashes. This method slowed erosion and, according to historical geographer Carl Sauer, "gave the highest returns of food in continuous supply by the simplest methods and modest labor." Little evidence exists of any population pressure on food resources in such areas. Conversely, historical demographers found evidence of an approaching crisis in the Aztec empire; Borah gloomily observed, "By the close of the fifteenth century, the Indian population of central Mexico was doomed even had there been no European conquests." Moreover, scholars now agree that population pressure on scant resources may have played a major part in the collapse of the classic Maya civilization of Central America. The evidence includes signs of chronic malnutrition, high infant mortality, and a decline of population from perhaps 12 million to a remnant of about 1.8 million within 150 years. Deforestation, loss of surface water, and overcultivation of worn-out soils, among other factors, likely contributed to the crisis.

Nuclear America

Mexico and Peru were the centers of an extensive, high-culture area that included central and southern Mexico, Central America, and the Andean zone of South America. This was the heartland of Ancient America, the home of its first agricultural civilizations. Archaeological evidence of early village life and the basic techniques of civilization—agriculture, pottery, weaving—appeared in almost every part of this territory.

In recent decades, this region was the scene of major archaeological discoveries. Excavations in the Valley of Mexico, southern Mexico and its gulf coast, the high plateau of Bolivia, and the desert sands of coastal Peru all have uncovered the remains of splendid temples, mighty fortresses, large cities and towns, and pottery and textiles of exquisite artistry. Combining the testimony of the spade with that provided by historical accounts, specialists have attempted to reconstruct the history of Nuclear America within a framework that includes a sequence of stages based on the technology, social and political organization, religion, and art of a given period. Specialists commonly call these stages *Archaic, Formative* or *Preclassic, Classic,* and *Postclassic.* This scheme is tentative in detail, with much chronological overlap between stages and considerable variation in the duration of some periods from area to area.

The *Archaic* stage began about nine thousand years ago when a gradual shift from food gathering and hunting to agriculture began in many parts of Nuclear America. This incipient agriculture, however, did not cause revolutionary changes in these societies. For thousands of years, people continued to live in much the same primitive fashion as before. Social groups were small and probably semi-nomadic. Weaving was unknown, but simple pottery appeared in some areas toward the end of the period.

Between 2500 and 1500 B.C.E., a major cultural advance in various regions of Nuclear America opened the *Formative,* or *Preclassic,* period. Centuries of haphazard experimentation with plants led to the selection of improved, high-yield varieties. These advances ultimately produced an economy solidly based on agriculture and sedentary village life. Maize and other important domesticated plants were brought under careful cultivation, irrigation came into use in some areas, and a few animals were domesticated. By the end of the period, pottery and weaving were highly developed. Increased food production enabled villagers to support a class of priests who acted as intermediaries between people and gods. More abundant food also released labor for the construction of ceremonial sites—mounds of earth topped by temples of wood or thatch.

The social unit of the Formative period was a village community that was composed of one or more kinship groups, but by the end of the period, small chiefdoms that united several villages developed. Because land and food were relatively plentiful and populations were small, warfare must have been infrequent. Religion centered on the worship of water and fertility gods; human sacrifice was probably absent or rare.

The advances of the Formative period culminated in the Classic period, which began around the opening of the Common Era and lasted until approximately 1000 C.E. The term *Classic* refers to the flowering of material, intellectual, and artistic culture that marked this stage. No basic changes in technology took place, but the extension of irrigation works in some areas caused increases in food production and freed labor for construction and technical tasks. Population also increased, and in some regions genuine cities arose. Architecture, pottery, and weaving reached an impressive level of style. Metallurgy flourished in Peru, as did astronomy, mathematics, and writing in Mesoamerica (central and southern Mexico and adjacent upper Central America). The earlier earth mounds gave way to huge stone-faced pyramids, elaborately ornamented and topped by great temples. The construction of palaces and other official buildings nearby made each ceremonial center the administrative capital of a state ruled by a priest-king. Social stratification developed, with the priesthood as the main ruling class. The growing incidence of warfare in the late Classic period (perhaps caused by population pressure, with greater competition for land and water) brought more recognition and rewards to successful warriors. Religion became an elaborate polytheism served by a large class of priests.

Typical cultures of the Classic period were the Teotihuacán civilization of central Mexico, the Monte Albán culture in southwestern Mexico, and the lowland Maya culture of southern Yucatán and northern Guatemala. The Olmec civilization of the Mexican gulf lowlands displayed some Classic features but fell within the time span usually allotted to the Formative period. In Peru, the brilliant Mochica and Nazca civilizations of the coast best represented the period. The available evidence suggests that the Classic stage was limited to Mesoamerica, the central Andean area (the highlands and coasts of Peru and Bolivia), and the Ecuadorian coast.

The Classic Era ended abruptly in both the northern and southern ends of Nuclear America. Shortly before or after 1000 C.E., civil war or foreign invasion led to the abandonment or destruction of most of the great Classic centers in Mesoamerica and Peru. Almost certainly, the fall of these civilizations came as the climax of a longer period of decline. Population pressure, soil erosion, and peasant revolts caused by excessive tribute demands are among the explanations for the collapse of the great Classic city-states and kingdoms.

A Time of Troubles, of obscure struggles and migrations of peoples, followed these disasters. Then new civilizations arose on the ruins of the old. The *Postclassic* stage, from about 1000 to 1500 C.E., seems to have repeated on a larger, more complex scale the rise-and-fall pattern of the previous era. Chronic warfare, reflected in the number of fortifications and fortified communities, and an increased emphasis on urban living were distinguishing features of this stage. Another was the formation of empires through the subjugation of a number of states by one powerful state. The dominant state appropriated a portion of the production of the conquered people, primarily for the benefit of its ruling classes. The Aztec and Inca empires typified this era.

No important advances in technology occurred in the Postclassic period, but in some regions, the network of irrigation works spread. The continuous growth of warfare and the rise of commerce sharpened economic distinctions between nobles and commoners, between rich and poor. The warrior class replaced the priesthood as the main ruling class. Imperialism also influenced the character of religion, enhancing the importance of war gods and human sacrifice. The arts and crafts showed some decline from Classic achievements, with a tendency more toward standardization and mass production of textiles and pottery in some areas.

After reaching a peak of power, the empires displayed the same tendency toward disintegration as had their Classic forerunners. The Tiahuanaco civilization and the Inca empire in Peru may have represented two cycles of empire growth, whereas the first true Mexican imperial cycle, that of the Aztec conquests, had not ended when the Spaniards conquered America.

Three high civilizations, the Maya of Central America, the Aztecs of Mexico, and the Incas of Peru, have held the center of attention to the virtual exclusion of the others. This partiality is understandable: We know more about these peoples and their ways of life. The Aztec and Inca civilizations still flourished at the coming of the Spaniards, and some conquistadors wrote vivid accounts of what they saw. The colorful story of the conquest of Mexico and Peru and the unhappy fate of their emperors Moctezuma (Montezuma) and Atahualpa have also served to focus historical and literary attention on the Aztecs and the Incas. Unfortunately, the fame and glamor that surrounded these peoples obscured the achievements of their predecessors, who laid the cultural foundations on which the Maya, Aztecs, and Incas built.

EARLY AMERICAN CIVILIZATIONS

As early as 1000 B.C.E., the inhabitants of the Valley of Mexico lived in small villages set in the midst of their maize, bean, and squash fields. They cultivated the land with slash-and-burn methods, produced simple but well-made pottery, and turned out large numbers of small clay figures that suggest a belief in fertility goddesses. By the opening of the Old World's Christian Era, small, flat-topped mounds had appeared, evidence of a more formal religion and directing priesthood.

Much earlier (perhaps spanning the period 1500 to 400 B.C.E.), there arose the precocious and enigmatic Olmec civilization of the gulf coast lowlands, whose influence radiated widely into the central Mexican plateau and Central America. The origins, development, and disappearance of the Olmec culture remain a mystery.

Important elements of the Olmec civilization were its ceremonial centers, monumental stone carving and sculpture, hieroglyphic writing, and calendric system. The principal Olmec sites are La Venta and Tres Zapotes, in the modern state of Veracruz. Discovery of Olmec culture and evidence of the wide diffusion of its art style have made untenable the older view that Maya civilization was the first in Mesoamerica. It seems likely that Olmec culture was the region's mother civilization.

The technical, artistic, and scientific advances of the Formative period made possible the climactic cultural achievements of the Classic Era. In Mexico's central highlands, the Classic period opened in splendor at Teotihuacán, some twenty-eight miles from Mexico City, where mighty pyramids named for the Sun and the Moon arose and towered over clusters of imposing temples and other buildings. The stone sculpture used to decorate the temples and the marvelous grace and finish of the cement work and fresco painting are testaments to the high development of the arts among the Teotihuacáns. The ancient water god, later known to the Aztecs as Tlaloc, seems to have been Teotihuacán's chief deity, but the feathered serpent with jaguar fangs, later known as Quetzalcóatl and identified with both water and fertility, appeared prominently in the greatest temple. War and human sacrifice did not appear until a relatively late phase. Priests in benign poses and wearing the symbols of their gods dominate the mural paintings.

This great ceremonial center at Teotihuacán was sacred ground that only the priestly nobility and their servants most likely inhabited. Farther out were the residential quarters where officials, artisans, and merchants lived. Teotihuacán had a population of at least 125,000. On the outskirts of the city, which covered an area of seven square miles, lived a large

In the ceremonial center of the great city-state of Teotihuacán, the Avenue of the Dead linked the "Citadel"—the royal palace compound—to the Pyramids of the Sun and Moon. With a population estimated between 125,000 and 200,000, it was the world's sixth-largest city in 600 C.E.

rural population that supplied the metropolis with its food. An intensive agriculture, using canal irrigation and terracing on hillslopes, likely formed the economic foundation of the Teotihuacán civilization. Despite the predominantly peaceful aspect of its religion and art, Teotihuacán seemed to be not only a major trading center but also a military state that directly controlled regions as remote as highland Guatemala.

Other centers of Classic culture in Mesoamerica were contemporary with, but overshadowed by, Teotihuacán. To the southwest, at Monte Albán in the rugged mountains of Oaxaca, the Zapotecs erected a great ceremonial center that was also a true city. One of their achievements, probably of Olmec origin, was a complicated system of hiero-glyphic writing. In the same period, the Maya Classic civilization flowered in the Petén region of northern Guatemala.

The Maya of Central America

Among Ancient American civilizations, the Maya were preeminent in cultural achievement. Certainly, no other group ever demonstrated such extraordinary abilities in architecture, sculpture, painting, mathematics, and astronomy. Inhabiting a region that consisted of portions of modern-day southeastern Mexico, almost all of Guatemala, the western part of Honduras, all of Belize, and the western half of El Salvador, the Maya civilization attained its highest development in the tropical

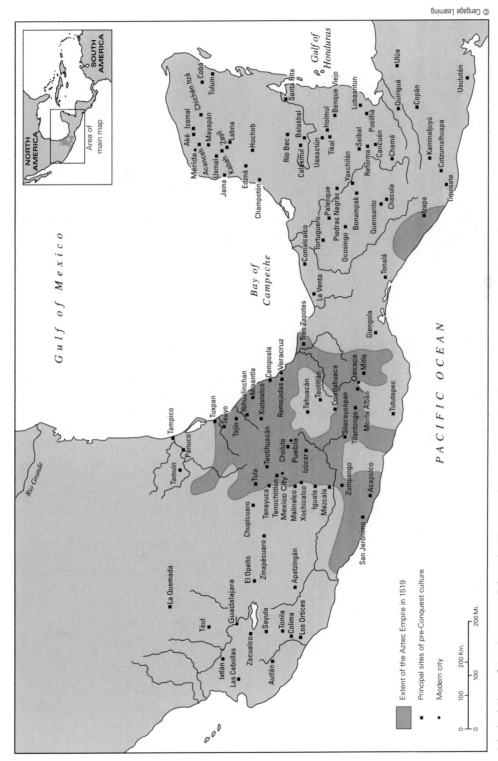

Principal Sites of Pre-Conquest Culture in Mesoamerica

forest lowland area whose core is the Petén region of Guatemala, at the base of the Yucatán Peninsula. This was the primary center of Maya Classic civilization from about 250 to 900 C.E.[2] The region was rich in wild game and building materials (limestone and fine hardwoods). In almost every other respect, it offered immense obstacles to the establishment of a high culture. To clear the dense forests for planting and control weeds with only the primitive implements available at the time were arduous tasks. No metal existed, the water supply was unreliable, and communication facilities were poor. Yet, here the Maya built some of their largest ceremonial centers.

The contrast between the forbidding environment and the Maya achievement led some authorities to speculate that Maya culture was a transplant from some other, more favorable area. Archaeological discoveries of long Preclassic sequences at lowland sites made this view obsolete. Abundant linguistic and archaeological evidence also suggests that the lowland Maya were descendants of groups who lived in or near the Olmec area before 1000 B.C.E. and who brought with them the essential elements of Mesoamerican civilization. In time, they incorporated these elements into their own unique achievements in the sciences, art, and architecture.

Just as puzzling as the rise of the Maya lowland culture in such an inhospitable setting is the dramatic decline that led to a gradual cessation of building activity and eventual abandonment of the ceremonial centers after 800 C.E. Specialists have advanced many explanations for this decline, including soil exhaustion because of slash-and-burn farming, invasion of cornfields by grasslands from the same cause, failure of the water supply, peasant revolts against the ruling priesthood, and the disruptive effects of the fall of Teotihuacán, which had close commercial and political ties with the Maya area. None of these explanations by itself, however, appeared completely satisfactory.

Recently a more complex explanation of the Classic Maya collapse emerged. According to this theory, the cessation of political and commercial contacts with Teotihuacán after about 550 C.E. led to a breakdown of centralized authority—perhaps previously exerted by Tikal, the largest and most important ceremonial center of the southern lowlands—and increased autonomy of local Maya elites. These elites expressed their pride and power through the construction of increasingly elaborate ceremonial centers that added to the burdens of commoners. Growing population size and density strained food resources and forced the adoption of more intensive agricultural methods. These, in turn, increased competition for land that led to a growth of warfare and militarism. Improved agricultural production relieved population pressures for a time and made possible the late Classic flowering (600 to 800 C.E.), marked by a revival of ceremonial center construction, architecture, and the arts. Renewed population pressures, food shortages, and warfare between regional centers, perhaps aggravated by external attacks, led to a severe cultural and social decline in the last century of the Classic period. The buildup of pressure—so runs the theory—resulted in what anthropologist Norman Hammond calls "a swift and catastrophic collapse accompanied by widespread depopulation through warfare, malnutrition, and disaster, until those who survived were again able to achieve a stable agricultural society at a much lower level of population density and social organization."

No such decline occurred in northern Yucatán, a low, limestone plain covered in most places with dense thickets of thorny scrub forest. Occupied by the Maya in numbers equal to the south, this area was the site of great ceremonial centers complete with steep pyramids, multistoried palaces, and large quadrangles. Into this area, in about 900 C.E., poured invaders from the central Mexican highlands, probably Toltec emigrants from strife-torn

---

2. Archaeological discoveries, however, periodically revolutionize the dates traditionally assigned to the Maya Classic period. The newly discovered city of Nakbé in the dense tropical forest of northern Guatemala, which contains extensive stone monuments and temples, dates from 600 to 400 B.C.E., pushing the Classic Era back into the time span commonly assigned to the Formative or Preclassic period.

Tula. Toltec armies overran northern Yucatán and established their rule over the Maya, governing from the temple city of Chichén Itzá. The invaders introduced Toltec styles in art and architecture, including colonnaded halls, warrior columns, and the reclining stone figures called Chac Mools. An increased obsession with human sacrifice also reflected Toltec influence. After 1200 C.E., Maya cultural and political influence revived with the abandonment of Chichén Itzá, and power passed to the city-state of Mayapan, a large, walled town from which Maya rulers dominated much of the peninsula, holding tribal chiefs and their families as hostages to exact tribute from surrounding provinces. But, in the fifteenth century, virtually all centralized rule disappeared. A successful revolt overthrew the tyranny of Mayapan and destroyed the city in 1441. By this time, Maya civilization was in full decline. By the arrival of the Spaniards, all political unity or imperial organization in the area had disappeared.

Maya Economy and Society

Archaeological discoveries radically revised notions about the subsistence base of the ancient Maya. Until recently, the prevailing view assumed the primary role of maize in the diet and the almost exclusive reliance on the slash-and-burn system of agriculture. Because this system excluded the possibility of such dense populations as existed at Teotihuacán and other Mesoamerican Classic or Postclassic centers, the traditional interpretation assumed a dispersed peasant population whose houses—typically one-room, pole-and-thatch structures—were scattered widely or grouped in small hamlets across the countryside between the ceremonial and administrative centers. These centers, which contained temples, pyramids, ritual ball courts, and other structures, lacked the character of true cities; scholars believed that only the Maya elites—a few priests, nobles, and officials and their attendants—lived in them. On the other hand, the rural population, who lived among their *milpas* (farm plots), visited these centers only for religious festivals and other special occasions.

This traditional view began to change in the late 1950s, when detailed mapping of the area around the Tikal ceremonial precinct revealed dense suburbs that spread out behind the center for several miles. Similar dense concentrations of house clusters were later found at other major and even minor centers of the Classic period. In the words of Norman Hammond, "The wide-open spaces between the Maya centers, with their scattered bucolic farmers, suddenly became filled with closely packed and hungry suburbanites."

These revelations of the size and density of Classic Maya settlements forced a reassessment of the economic system that supported them. In addition to slash-and-burn farming, the Maya clearly practiced an intensive and permanent agriculture that included highly productive kitchen gardens with root crops as staples, arboriculture, terracing, and raised fields—artificial platforms of soil built up from low-lying areas.

The evidence of dense suburban populations around ceremonial centers like Tikal also provoked a debate about the degree of urbanism present in the Maya lowlands. The traditional view that the Classic Maya centers were virtually deserted for most of the year has become untenable. Debate continues, however, as to whether they were "cities" in the sense that Teotihuacán was clearly a city. Tikal, in the heart of the Petén, was certainly a metropolitan center with a population of perhaps fifty thousand and a countryside heavily populated over an area of some fifty square miles. Evidence also indicates some genuine urbanization in northern Yucatán during the Postclassic period, possibly a result of Toltec influence and the tendency to develop the city or town as a fortified position. Chichén Itzá, an old Classic ceremonial center, grew substantially under Toltec influence, whereas Mayapan, which succeeded Chichén Itzá as a political and military center, constituted a large urban zone encircled by a great wall.

Awareness of the large size and density of Classic Maya populations, the intensive character of much of their agriculture, and the strict social controls that such complex conditions require also led to a reassessment of Maya social organization.

Scholars have abandoned the older view that the ruling class was a small theocratic elite who lived in empty ceremonial centers and ruled over a dispersed peasant population. Increased ability to decipher glyphs on the *stelae* (carved monuments that periodically were erected at Classic Maya centers) contributed to a better understanding of the Maya social order. Although scholars once believed that the content of these inscriptions was exclusively religious and astronomical, evidence now suggests that many of the glyphs carved on stelae, lintels, and other monuments record accessions, wars, and other milestones in the lives of secular rulers.

The new interpretation assumes a complex social order with a large distance between the classes. At the apex of the social pyramid stood a hereditary ruler who combined the political, military, and religious leadership of the state. He surrounded himself with an aristocracy or nobility, from which he drew the administrative and executive bureaucracy. Intellectual specialists such as architects, priests, and scribes probably formed another social level. Below them were the numerous artisans required for ceremonial and civil construction: potters, sculptors, stoneworkers, painters, and the like. At the bottom of the social pyramid were the common laborers and peasant farmers who supplied the labor and food that supported this massive superstructure. The weight of their growing burdens in time became unsustainable, and their discontent likely ignited revolts that brought about the ultimate collapse of the lowland Maya civilization.

Archaeological investigations have thrown new light on Classic Maya family and settlement patterns, suggesting that the Maya family was extended rather than nuclear. It probably consisted of two or more nuclear families spanning two or more generations with a common ancestor, evidence of which comes from the discovery that the residential foundations occurred in groups of three or more. Moreover, the richer furnishings of male graves and the preeminence of men in monumental art suggest male predominance, leading to the conclusion that descent was patrilineal—from father to son. Maya dress and diet, like its housing, reflected class distinctions. Maya clothing was typically Mesoamerican: cotton loincloths, leather sandals, and sometimes a mantle knotted about the shoulder for men and wraparound skirts of cotton and blouses with holes for the head and arms for women. The upper classes wore the same articles of clothing, only much more ornately decorated.

MAYA RELIGION AND LEARNING

The great object of Maya religion, as the Spanish bishop Diego de Landa concisely put it, was "that they [the gods] should give them health, life, and sustenance." The principal Maya divinities represented those natural forces and objects that most directly affected the material welfare of the people. The supreme god in the Maya pantheon was Itzam Na, a creator god who incorporated in himself the aspects of many other gods. He was responsible not only for creation but for fire, rain, crops, and Earth as well. Other important divinities were the sun god, the moon goddess, the rain god, the maize god, and the much-feared god of death. The Maya believed that a number of worlds had appeared successively, only to face destruction, and that this world, too, would end in catastrophe.

The Maya believed in an afterlife: an Upper World that consisted of thirteen layers and an Under World with nine. A certain god presided over each layer, with the god of death, Ah Puch, reigning over the lowest layer of the Under World. Like the Aztecs and other peoples of Middle America, the Maya worshiped and placated the gods with a variety of ritual practices that included fasting, penance by bloodletting, the burning of incense, and human sacrifice. Human sacrifice on a large scale already existed in the late Classic period, marked by growing political turbulence and strife among the lowland Maya states, but it probably increased in the Postclassic period under Toltec influence.

The Maya priests were obsessed with time, to which they assigned an occult, or magical, content. They developed a calendar that was more accurate than ours (the Gregorian calendar) in adjusting the exact length of the solar year. Maya theologians believed that time was a burden that the gods carried on their backs. At the end of a certain period, one god laid down his burden for another god to pick up and continue on the journey of time. A given day or year was lucky or unlucky depending on whether the god-bearer at the time was a benevolent or a malevolent god. Thus, the Maya calendars were primarily divinatory in character— used to predict conditions in a particular time period.

The Maya had two almanacs. One was a sacred round of 260 days that corresponded to the pattern of ceremonial life. This calendar was composed of two intermeshing and recurrent cycles of different length: one of thirteen days, recorded as numbers, and the second of twenty days, recorded as names. The name of the fourteenth day-name began with one again. A second cycle was the solar year of 365 days, divided into eighteen "months" of twenty days each, plus a final period of five unlucky days during which they banned all unnecessary activity. Completion of these two cycles coincided every fifty-two years. Stelae bearing hieroglyphic texts indicating the date and other calendric data—such as the state of the moon, the position of the planet Venus, and so on—frequently were erected at the end of the fifty-two-year cycle and at other intervals.

The Maya developed the science of mathematics further than any of their Middle American neighbors. Their units were ones, fives, and twenties, with ones designated by dots, fives by bars, and positions for twenty and multiples of twenty. Place-value numeration, based on a sign for zero, was perhaps the greatest intellectual development of Ancient America. In this system, the position of a number determined its value, making it possible for a limited quantity of symbols to express numbers of any size. Its simplicity made it far superior to the contemporary western European arithmetical system, which employed the cumbersome Roman numeration consisting of distinct symbols for each higher unit. The Arabs brought their numeration concept to Europe from India, the only other place that had invented it. Maya mathematics, however, appears to have been applied chiefly to calendrical and astronomical calculation; no record of Maya enumeration of people or objects exists.

Until recently, scholars believed that Maya hieroglyphic writing, like the mathematics, chiefly served religious and divinatory rather than utilitarian ends. We now have abundant evidence that many of the glyphs carved on the monuments are historic, recording milestones in the lives of Maya rulers. In addition to the inscriptions that appear on stone monuments, lintels, stairways, and other monumental remains, the Maya had great numbers of sacred books or codices, of which only three survive into the twenty-first century. They painted these books on folding screens of native paper made of bark. Concerned above all with astronomy, divination, and other related topics, the books revealed that Maya astronomers made observations and calculations of truly astounding complexity.

The Maya had no alphabet, strictly speaking; the majority of their characters represented ideas or objects rather than sounds. But Maya writing had reached the stage of syllabic phonetics through the use of rebus writing, in which the sound of a word was represented by combining pictures or signs of things whose spoken names resemble sounds in the word to be formed. Thus, the Maya wrote the word for drought, *kintunyaabil*, with four characters: the signs of sun or day (*kin*), stone or 360-day unit of time (*tun*), solar year (*haab*), and the affix *il*. In the 1950s, a Russian scholar advanced a theory that Maya writing was truly syllabic and so could be deciphered by matching the most frequent sound elements in modern Maya to the most frequent signs in the ancient writing, using computers to speed the process of decipherment. Scholars now generally accept the existence of purely phonetic glyphs in the Maya script, but they seem to be relatively rare in the deciphered material.

Maya writing was not a narrative used to record literature; rather, the large body of Maya myths, legends, poetry, and traditional history was transmitted orally from generation to generation. Examples of such material include the *Popol Vuh*, the so-called Sacred Book of the Quiché Maya of Guatemala. This book describes the adventures of the heroic twins Hunahpu and Xbalanque, who, after many exploits, ascended into heaven to become the sun and the moon. It reflects the thinking

e.t. archive, London/The Art Archive

Ancient murals uncovered at the Bonampak acropolis depict Mayan cultural rituals that integrated history, music, and dance. Here, dancers dressed as lobsters, birds, and crocodiles accompany musicians playing drums, gourd-maracas, and trumpets in a celebration of the debut of a royal heir to the throne.

of a post-Conquest Maya native who drew on the oral traditions of his people to write a parable about Maya life in the Spanish alphabet.

In certain types of artistic activity, the Maya surpassed all other Middle American peoples. The temples and pyramids at Teotihuacán and Tenochtitlán often were larger than their Maya counterparts but lacked their grace and subtlety. A distinctive feature of Maya architecture was the corbeled vault, or false arch. Other Middle American peoples used horizontal wooden beams to bridge entrances, producing a heavy and squarish impression. The Maya solved the same problem by having the stones on either side of the opening project farther and farther inward, bridging the two sides at the apex by a capstone. Other characteristics of the Maya architectural style were the great façades that they richly decorated with carved stone and high ornamental roof combs in temples and palaces. They frequently covered inner walls with paintings, a few of which have survived into the twenty-first century. The most celebrated of these paintings are the frescoes discovered in 1946 at Bonampak, an isolated site in the tropical forests of the northeastern corner of the Mexican state of Chiapas. They date from about 800 C.E. These frescoes completely

cover the inner walls of a small building of three rooms. They tell a story that begins with a ritual dance, goes on to portray an expedition to obtain sacrificial victims, continues with a battle scene, and ends with a human sacrifice, ceremonies, and dance. Despite the highly conventionalized and static style, the absence of perspective and shading, and the obvious errors in the human figure, it has an effect of realism that often is missing from other Mesoamerican art.

Students of the Maya frequently have testified to the admirable personal qualities of the people who, with a limited technology and in a most forbidding environment, created one of the greatest cultural traditions of all time. Bishop Diego de Landa, who burned twenty-seven Maya codices as "works of the devil," nevertheless observed that the Maya were generous and hospitable. No one could enter their houses, he wrote, without receiving offers of food and drink.

MAYA DECLINE AND TRANSFORMATION OF MESOAMERICA

By 800 C.E., a crisis spread from one Classic center to another and shook the foundations of the

Mesoamerican world. Teotihuacán, the Rome of that world, perished at the hands of invaders, who burned down the city sometime between 650 and 800 C.E. Toward the latter date, residents of the great ceremonial center at Monte Albán abandoned the site. By 800 C.E., the process of disintegration had reached the Classic Maya heartland of southern Yucatán and northern Guatemala, whose deserted or destroyed centers reverted one by one to the bush.

From this Time of Troubles in Mesoamerica (approximately 700 to 1000 C.E.), a new Postclassic order emerged, sometimes appropriately called Militarist. Whereas priests and benign nature gods may have presided over some Mesoamerican societies of the Classic Era, warriors and terrible war gods clearly dominated the states that arose on the ruins of the Classic world. In central Mexico, the sway of Teotihuacán, probably based above all on cultural and economic supremacy, gave way to strife among new states that warred with one another for land, water, and tribute.

The most important of these, successor to the power of Teotihuacán, was the Toltec empire, with its capital at Tula, about fifty miles from present-day Mexico City. Lying on the periphery of the Valley of Mexico, Tula once might have been an outpost of Teotihuacán, guarding its frontiers against the hunting tribes of the northern deserts. Following the collapse of Teotihuacán, one such group, the Toltecs, swept down from the north, entered the Valley of Mexico, and overwhelmed the pitiful survivors among the Teotihuacán people.

Toltec power and prosperity reached its peak under a ruler named Topiltzin, who moved his capital to Tula in about 980 C.E. Apparently renamed Quetzalcóatl in his capacity of high priest of the ancient god worshiped by the Teotihuacáns, Topiltzin-Quetzalcóatl reigned for nineteen years with such splendor that both he and his city became legendary. The Song of Quetzalcóatl tells of the wonders of Tula, a true paradise on Earth where cotton grew in bright colors and the soil yielded fruit of such size that small ears of corn were used not as food but as fuel to heat steam baths. The legends of ancient Mexico described the Toltecs as master artisans and creators of culture, with superhuman powers and talents. Over this Golden Age presided the great priest-king Quetzalcóatl, who thus revived the glories of Teotihuacán.

Toward the end of Quetzalcóatl's reign, Tula became the scene of an obscure struggle between two religious traditions. One worshipped Tezcatlipoca, a Toltec tribal god pictured as an all-powerful and capricious deity who demanded human sacrifice. The other revered the ancient god Quetzalcóatl, who had given maize, learning, and the arts to men and women. In a version of the Quetzalcóatl legend that may reflect post-Conquest Christian influence, the god asked the people for only the peaceful sacrifices of jade, snakes, and butterflies. This struggle found fanciful expression in the native legend that tells how the black magic of the enchanter Tezcatlipoca caused the saintly priest-king Quetzalcóatl to fall from grace and drove him into exile from Tula.

Whatever its actual basis, the Quetzalcóatl legend, with its promise that a mystical Redeemer would someday return to reclaim his kingdom, profoundly impressed the people of ancient Mexico and played its part in the destruction of the Mesoamerican world. By a singular coincidence, the year in which Quetzalcóatl promised to return was the very year in which Cortés landed at Veracruz. Belief in the legend helped immobilize indigenous resistance, at least initially.

Lesser kings, who vainly struggled to solve the growing problems of the Toltec state, succeeded Topiltzin-Quetzalcóatl. Although obscure, the causes of this crisis probably included tremendous droughts that caused crop failure and famines, perhaps aggravated by Toltec neglect of agriculture in favor of collection of tribute from conquered peoples. A series of revolutions reflected the Toltec economic and social difficulties. The last Toltec king, Hue-mac, apparently committed suicide about 1174, and the Toltec state disappeared with him. In the following year, a general dispersion or exodus of the Toltecs took place. Tula itself fell into the hands of barbarians in about 1224.

The fall of Tula, situated on the margins of the Valley of Mexico, opened the way for a general invasion of the valley by Nahuatl-speaking northern peoples. These newcomers, called Chichimecs, were analogous to the Germanic invaders who broke into the dying Roman empire. Like them, the Chichimec leaders respected and tried to absorb the superior culture of the vanquished people. They were eager to intermarry with the surviving Toltec royalty and nobility.

These invaders founded a number of succession-states in the lake country at the bottom of the Valley of Mexico. Legitimately or not, their rulers all claimed the honor of Toltec descent. In artistic and industrial development, the Texcocan kingdom, organized in 1260, easily excelled its neighbors. Texcocan civilization reached its climactic moment two centuries later during the reign of King Nezahualcoyotl (1418–1472), distinguished poet, philosopher, and lawgiver, and perhaps the most remarkable figure to emerge from the mists of Ancient America.

The Aztecs of Mexico

Among the last of the Chichimecs to arrive in the valley were the Aztecs, or Mexica, which was the name they gave themselves. The date of their departure from the north was probably about 1111 C.E. Led by four priests and a woman who carried a medicine bundle that contained the spirit of their tribal god, Huitzilopochtli, they arrived in the Valley of Mexico in about 1218 after obscure wanderings. Some scholars have questioned the traditional belief that the Aztecs were basically a hunting-and-gathering people who were only "half civilized" but had some acquaintance with agriculture. They argue that, by the time of their arrival, the Aztecs were typically Mesoamerican in culture, religion, and economic and social organization. Finding the most desirable sites occupied by others, they were forced to take refuge on the marshy lands around Lake Texcoco, where, in 1344 or 1345, they built the town of Tenochtitlán. At this time, the Aztec community included a small number of *calpulli* (kinship, landholding groups).

Huts made of cane and reeds gradually covered the patches of solid ground that formed the Aztec territory. Later, more ambitious structures of turf, adobe, and light stone followed. As the population increased, a larger cultivable area became necessary, and the Aztecs adopted their neighbors' technique of constructing *chinampas* (artificial garden beds made of earth and sediment dredged from lake beds and held in place by wickerwork). Eventually, roots would grow and grasp the lake bottom, creating solid ground. On these chinampas, the Aztecs grew maize, beans, and other products.

Aztec Imperial Expansion

For a long time, the Aztecs were subservient to their powerful neighbors in Azcapotzalco, the dominant power in the lake country in the late fourteenth and early fifteenth centuries. A turning point in Aztec history came in 1428. Led by their war chief Itzcoatl, the Aztecs joined the rebellious city-state of Texcoco and the smaller town of Tlacopan to destroy the tyranny of Azcapotzalco. Their joint victory (1430) led to the rise of a Triple Alliance for the conquest first of the valley and then of much of the Middle American world. Gradually, the balance of power shifted to the aggressive Aztec state. Texcoco became a junior partner, and Tlacopan became a satellite. The strong position of their island fortification and a shrewd policy of forming alliances and sharing the spoils of conquest with strategic mainland towns, which they later came to dominate, explained Aztec success in gaining control of the Valley of Mexico. In turn, conquest of the valley offered a key to the conquest of Middle America. The valley had the advantages of short internal lines of communication surrounded by easily defensible mountain barriers. Openings to the north, east, west, and south gave Aztec warriors easy access to adjacent valleys.

Conquest of Azcapotzalco gave the Aztecs their first beachhead on the lakeshore. Warrior-nobles who had distinguished themselves in battle controlled most of the conquered land and the peasantry who lived on it. Originally assigned for life, these lands tended to become fiefs that were held in permanent inheritance. Thus, warfare created new economic and social cleavages within Aztec society.

In the process, it eroded the original kinship basis of the calpulli, which, at least in the Valley of Mexico, lost most of its autonomy, becoming primarily a social and territorial administrative unit. Composed mostly of *macehualtín* (commoners) who owed tribute, labor, and military service to the Aztec state, the calpulli continued to be led by hereditary elite families who were completely subject to superior Aztec officials whose orders they carried out.

In the Valley of Mexico, and in other highly developed areas, the communal landownership formerly associated with the calpulli also suffered erosion because of growing population pressure that forced some members to leave, caused internal economic differentiation, and created the need to sell or rent communal land in times of famine or some other crisis. Calpulli of the original kinship, landowning type survived better in areas where the process of class stratification and state formation was less pronounced. By the time of the Spanish Conquest, however, landlessness and tenant farming were widespread over much of central Mexico, with *mayeque* (serflike peasants) forming perhaps the majority of the Aztec population. These unfree peasants enjoyed only the usufruct of the land and had to render tribute and service to the noble owner. The picture that emerges from recent studies, according to historian Rik Hoekstra, is one of a society "like medieval European society, highly complicated and locally diverse." The growing cleavage between commoners and nobles found ideological reflection in the origin myth that claimed a separate divine origin (from the god Quetzalcóatl) for the Aztec nobility.

Other ideological changes included the elevation of the tribal god Huitzilopochtli to a position of equality with, or supremacy over, the great nature gods traditionally worshiped in the Valley of Mexico; the burning of the ancient picture writings because these books slighted the Aztecs; and the creation of a new history that recognized the Aztec grandeur. These changes placed a new emphasis on capturing prisoners of war to use as sacrifices on the altars of the Aztec gods to ensure the continuance of the universe.[3]

The successors of Itzcoatl—sometimes individually and sometimes in alliance with Texcoco—extended Aztec rule over and beyond the Valley of Mexico. By the time Moctezuma II became ruler in 1502, the Triple Alliance was levying tribute on scores of towns, large and small, from the fringes of the arid northern plateau to the lowlands of Tehuantepec, and from the Atlantic to the Pacific. Within this extensive area only a few states or kingdoms, like the fierce Tarascans' state or the city-state of Tlaxcala, retained complete independence. Others, like Cholula, were left at peace in return for their benevolent neutrality or cooperation with the Aztecs. According to some controversial modern estimates, the Aztecs and their allies ruled over a population of perhaps 25 million.

The Aztecs waged war with or without cause. If a group refused to pay tribute to the Aztec ruler or if patrons of an area injured traveling Aztec merchants, it became a valid motive for invasion. Aztec merchants also prepared the way for conquest by reporting on the resources and defenses of the areas in which they traded; sometimes they acted as spies in hostile territory. The emperor honored these valiant merchants with amber lip plugs and other gifts, if they returned home safely. If their enemies discovered them, however, the consequences were horrid. "They were slain in ambush and served up with chili sauce," reports a native account.

Victory in war always had the same results: long lines of captives made the long journey to Tenochtitlán, where the Aztecs sacrificed them on

---

3. Some social scientists have attempted to explain the Aztec practice of mass human sacrifice and its accompaniment of ritual cannibalism by the lack of protein in the Aztec diet. Contradictory evidence includes the variety of animal foods available to the Aztecs and the absence of either Indian or Spanish sources that refer to the practice of cannibalism during the great famine that hastened the end of Aztec resistance to the Spanish Conquest. For the rest, the sacramental feast, which was designed so the participants could share the blessings of the god to whom they sacrificed the prisoner, was simplicity itself. The captor could not eat his captive's flesh because of an assumed mystical kinship relationship between the captor and his prisoner.

the altars of the gods. In addition, they imposed periodic tribute payments of maize, cotton mantles, cacao beans, or other products—depending on the geography and resources of the region—on the vanquished. Certain lands were also set aside to be cultivated by the captives for the support of the Aztec crown, priesthood, and state officials or as fiefs given to warriors who had distinguished themselves in battle. A steward or tribute collector,

sometimes assisted by a resident garrison, was stationed in the town. As for the rest, the conquered people usually continued to enjoy autonomy in government, culture, and customs.

Because of its nonintegrated character, which was reflected in the relative autonomy enjoyed by vanquished peoples and the light Aztec political and military presence in conquered territories, the Aztec empire traditionally has been regarded as an

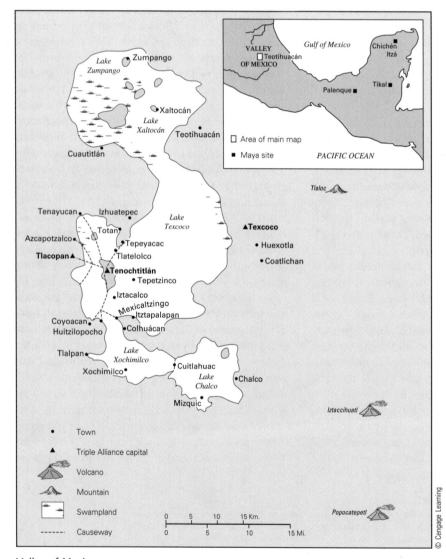

© Cengage Learning

Valley of Mexico

inferior or deficient political organization compared with the Inca empire, with its centralized administration, standing armies, massive transfers of populations, and other integrative policies. Recently, however, scholars have argued that, rather than being inferior, the Aztec imperial system represented an alternative—but no less efficient—approach to the problem of extracting surplus from tributary peoples at a minimal administrative and military cost. The Aztec army mobilized only for further conquests and the suppression of rebellions. By leaving the defeated regimes in place and avoiding direct territorial control, the Aztec state avoided the expense, which was inherent in an integrated empire, of maintaining provincial administrations, standing armies, permanent garrisons, and fortifications.

AZTEC CULTURE AND SOCIETY

The Aztec capital of Tenochtitlán had a population between 150,000 and 200,000. Like Venice, the city was an oval island connected to the mainland by three causeways that converged at the center of the city and served as its main arteries of traffic. Instead of streets, numerous canals, thronged with canoes and bordered by footpaths, provided access to the thousands of houses that lined their sides. An aqueduct in solid masonry brought fresh water from the mountain springs of Chapultepec.

On the outlying chinampas, the Aztec farmers, who paddled their produce to town in tiny dugouts, lived in huts with thatched roofs resting on walls of wattle smeared with mud. Inside each hut were a three-legged *metate* (grinding stone), a few mats that served as beds and seats, some pottery, and little more. The majority of the population—artisans, priests, civil servants, soldiers, and entertainers—lived in more imposing houses. Built of adobe or a reddish *tezontli* lava (volcanic stone), these homes were lime-washed and painted to give them a more spruce appearance. The houses of calpulli leaders, merchants, and nobles were far more pretentious.

As in housing, Aztec clothing differed according to the individual's economic and social status. For men, the essential garments were a loincloth with broad flaps at the front and back, usually decorated with fringes and tassels as well as embroidery work, and a blanket about two yards by one yard in size. This blanket hung under the left arm and was knotted on the right shoulder. Commoners wore plain blankets of maguey fiber or coarse cotton; rich merchants and nobles displayed elaborate cotton mantles that they adorned with symbolic designs. Women wore shifts, wraparound skirts of white cotton tied with a narrow belt, and loose, short-sleeved tunics. They decorated both shifts and tunics with vivid embroidery. Men wore sandals of leather or woven maguey fiber; women went barefoot.

As with dress, so it was with food: Wealth and social position determined its abundance and variety. The fare of the ordinary Aztec consisted of ground maize meal, beans, and vegetables cooked with chili. Commoners rarely ate meat, but, on festive occasions, dog meat might be served. The nobility enjoyed a far more diverse diet, however; according to a native account, these foods included many varieties of tortillas and tamales, roast turkey hen, roast quail, turkey with a sauce of small chilies, tomatoes, ground squash seeds, venison sprinkled with seeds, many kinds of fish and fruits, and such delicacies as maguey grubs with a sauce of small chilies, winged ants with savory herbs, and rats with sauce. They finished their repast with chocolate, a divine beverage that was forbidden to commoners.

Education among the Aztecs was highly formal and served the dual purpose of preparing boys and girls for their duties in the world and indoctrinating them with Aztec ideals. Boys went to school at the age of ten or twelve. Sons of commoners, merchants, and artisans attended the *Telpochcalli* (House of Youth), where they received instruction in religion, good usage, and the art of war. The *Calmecac* (Priests' House), a school of higher learning, was reserved in principle for the sons of the nobility, but some children of merchants and commoners were also admitted. Here, in addition to ordinary training, students received instruction that prepared them to be priests, public officials, and military leaders. The curriculum included what we would call rhetoric, or a noble manner of speaking—that is, the study of religious and philosophical doctrines as revealed in the divine songs of the sacred books, the arts of chronology and astrology, and training in history through the study of the *Xiuhamatl* (Books of the Years). The *tlamatinime* (sages) who taught in the Aztec schools were also concerned with the formation of "a true face and heart," the striking Nahuatl metaphor for personality. Self-restraint, moderation, devotion to duty, a stoic awareness that "life is short and filled with hardships, and all comes to an end," an impeccable civility, and modesty were among the qualities and concepts that the Aztec sages instilled in their charges.

Girls had special schools where they were taught such temple duties as sweeping, offering incense three times during the night, and preparing food for the idols; weaving and other womanly tasks; and general preparation for marriage. Education for men usually terminated at the age of twenty or twenty-two, and for girls, at sixteen or seventeen— also the ages at which marriage was contracted. The development of Aztec militarism led to some decline in women's status, and the Aztec "speeches of the elders" warned the wife that "your obligation is to obey your husband. You are to make the beverage, the food for him, and his shirt, his cape, his breeches." The model wife was a diligent housewife and a mother dedicated to the careful raising of her children. In some respects, however, the status of Aztec women was complementary rather than subordinate to that of men. Childbirth, for example, was symbolically compared to warfare: successful delivery was equated with the taking of a prisoner, and death in childbirth was equivalent to being killed in battle. Aztec women also worked as doctors, artisans, merchants, and priests.

In a society with such a complex economic and social life, disputes and aggressions inevitably arose and necessitated the development of an elaborate legal code. A hierarchy of courts included two high tribunals that met in the royal palace in Tenochtitlán. Aztec punishments were severe. Death was the penalty for murder, rebellion, wearing the clothes of the other sex, and adultery; they punished theft with slavery for the first offense and hanging for the second.

Economic life in Aztec Mexico rested on a base of intensive and extensive agriculture. Intensive irrigation was practiced in areas with reliable water sources; its most notable form was that of the chinampas. Slash-and-burn cultivation, with field rotation, was the rule in other areas, but maize and beans were the principal crops in almost every area. In the absence of large, domesticated animals as a source of manure, the Aztec regularly used "night soil" (human waste) as fertilizer in chinampa agriculture in the Valley of Mexico. To prevent contamination of the valley's two freshwater lakes by flows of water from the saline ones that harmed chinampa agriculture and to maintain the fairly constant water level that it required, they constructed an elaborate system of dikes, canals, and aqueducts during the reign of King Itzcoatl. This led to the creation of large chinampa areas that produced foodstuffs for Tenochtitlán. Productive as they were, however, they accounted for only 5 percent of the city's subsistence needs, and the salinity of the remaining lakes limited their expansion. For the balance of its food needs, therefore, Tenochtitlán had to rely on imports obtained by way of tribute and trade. An elaborate, state-controlled trade and transportation network, based on regional and metropolitan markets, the *tlameme* (professional carrier) system of portage, and an efficient canoe traffic that linked the entire lake system of the Valley of Mexico, funneled a vast quantity of foodstuffs and other bulk goods into Tenochtitlán. Manufactured goods were then exported from Tenochtitlán to its hinterlands, forming a core–periphery relationship.

The vast scale on which the exchange of goods and services was conducted in the great market of Tenochtitlán aroused the astonishment of the conquistador Cortés, who gave a detailed account of its immense activity: "Each kind of merchandise is sold in its respective street," he wrote, "and they do not mix their kinds of merchandise of any species; thus they preserve perfect order." The Aztecs lacked a unitary system of money, but cacao beans, cotton mantles, quills filled with gold dust, and small copper axes were assigned standardized values and supplemented a barter system of exchange. The Aztecs had no scales; they sold goods by count and measure. Officials patrolled the market and checked on the fairness of transactions; a merchants' court sat to hear and settle disputes between buyers and sellers.

As the preceding account implies, by the time of the Conquest, division of labor among the Aztecs had progressed to the point at which a large class of artisans no longer engaged in agriculture. The artisan class included carpenters, potters, stonemasons, silversmiths, and featherworkers. In the same category belonged such specialists as anglers, hunters, dancers, and musicians. All these specialists organized in guilds, each with its guildhall and patron god; their professions probably passed from father to son. The artist and the artisan enjoyed a position of high honor and responsibility in Aztec society. Assigning the origin of all their arts and crafts to the Toltec period, the Aztecs applied the name *Toltec* to the true or master painter, singer, potter, or sculptor.

Advances in regional division of labor and the growth of the market for luxury goods also led to the emergence of a merchant class, which organized a powerful guild. The wealth of this class and its important military and diplomatic services to the Aztec state made the merchants a third force in Aztec society, ranking only after the warrior nobility and the priesthood. The wealth of the merchants sometimes aroused the distrust and hostility of the Aztec rulers and nobility. A native account brilliantly captured this popular animosity toward the merchants: "The merchants were those who had plenty, who prospered; the greedy, the well-fed man, the covetous, the niggardly, the miser, who controlled wealth and family ... the mean, the stingy, the selfish."

The priesthood was the main integrating force in Aztec society. Through its possession of a sacred calendar that regulated the performance of agricultural tasks, it played a key role in the life of the people. The priesthood was also the repository of the accumulated lore and history of the Aztec tribe. By virtue of his special powers of intercession with the gods, his knowledge, and his wisdom, the priest intervened in every private or collective crisis of the Aztec. Celibate, austere, continually engaged in the penance of bloodletting, priests wielded enormous influence over the Aztec people.

The priesthood shared authority and prestige with the nobility, a class that had gained power through war and political centralization. In addition to many warriors, this class consisted of a large bureaucracy made up of tribute collectors, judges, ambassadors, and the like. Such officeholders were rewarded for their services by the revenue from public lands assigned to support them. Their offices were not hereditary, but the Aztec state usually conferred them on the sons of fathers who had held the same positions.

The wealth of the warrior nobility consisted chiefly of landed estates. Originally granted for life, these lands eventually became private estates that fathers bequeathed to their sons or could sell. The formerly free peasants on these lands probably became mayeque, farm workers, or tenant farmers tied to the land. With the expansion of the Aztec empire, the number of private estates grew steadily.

On the margins of Aztec society was a large class of slaves. Slavery was the punishment for a variety of offenses, including failure to pay debts, and some people voluntarily became slaves in exchange for food. Slave owners frequently brought their chattels to the great market at Azcapotzalco for sale to rich merchants or nobles for personal service or as sacrificial offerings to the gods.

The Aztec political system was a mixture of royal despotism and theocracy. Political power was concentrated in a ruling class of priests and nobles, over which presided an absolute ruler. Originally, the whole Aztec community assembled for the purpose of selecting the ruler. Later, he was chosen by a council or electoral college that the most important priests, officials, and warriors, including close relatives of the king, dominated. The council, in consultation with the kings of Texcoco and Tlacopan, selected the monarch from among the sons, brothers, or nephews of the previous ruler. A council of four great nobles assisted the new ruler. At the time of the Conquest, the emperor was the luckless Moctezuma II, who succeeded his uncle, Ahuitzotl.

Great splendor and intricate ceremonies prevailed in Moctezuma's court. The great nobles of the realm removed their rich ornaments of feather, jade, and gold before they appeared before him. Barefoot, with their eyes on the ground, they approached the basketry throne of their king. Moctezuma dined in solitary magnificence, separated by a wooden screen from his servants and the four great lords with whom he conversed.

This wealth, luxury, and ceremony revealed the great social and economic changes that had taken place in the small, despised Aztec tribe that had come to live in the marshes of Lake Texcoco less than two centuries before. The Aztec empire had reached a peak of pride and power. Yet the Aztec leaders lived in fear, as evidenced by the Aztec chronicles. The mounting demands of the Aztec tribute collectors caused revolts on the part of tributary towns. Although repressed, they broke out afresh. The haunted Aztec imagination saw portents of evil on Earth and in the troubled air. A child was born with two heads; the volcano Popocatepetl became unusually active; a comet streamed across the sky. The year 1519 approached, the year in which, according to Aztec lore, the god-king Quetzalcóatl might return to reclaim the realm from which the forces of evil had driven him centuries earlier.

The Incas of Peru

In the highlands of modern Peru in the mid-fourteenth century, a small tribe rose from obscurity to create by 1500 the mightiest empire of Ancient America. Since the time of Pizarro's discovery and conquest of Peru, Inca achievements in political and social organization have attracted intense interest. Soon after the Conquest, a debate began on the nature of Inca society that has continued until the late twentieth century. For some it was a "socialist empire"; others viewed it as a forerunner of the twentieth-century "welfare state"; and for still others, the Inca realm anticipated the totalitarian tyrannies of the twentieth century. Only recently has more careful study of evidence from colonial provincial records—including official economic and social inquiries, litigation, wills, and the like—provided a more correct picture of Inca society and banished the traditional labels.

The physical environment of the central Andean area offers a key to the remarkable cultural development of this region. In Peru, high mountains rise steeply from the sea, leaving a narrow coastal plain that is a true desert. The Humboldt Current runs north along the coast from the Antarctic, making the ocean much colder than the land so the rains fall at sea.

Short rivers that make their precipitous way down from the high snowfields compensate for this lack of rainfall. These rivers create oases at intervals along the coast and provide water for systems of canal irrigation. The aridity of the climate preserves the great natural wealth of the soil, which can be leached away in areas of heavy rainfall. The coastal waters of Peru are rich in fish, and its offshore islands, laden in Inca times with millions of tons of *guano* (excrement), made available an inexhaustible source of fertilizer for agriculture.

To be sure, the rugged highlands of modern Peru and Bolivia offer relatively little arable land, but the valleys are fertile and well watered and support a large variety of crops. Maize is grown at lower levels (up to about eleven thousand feet), potatoes and quinoa at higher altitudes. Above the agricultural zone, the *puna* (plateau) provides fodder for herds of llamas and alpacas, domesticated members of the camel family that in Inca times were an important source of meat and wool. Potentially, this environment offered a basis for large food production and a dense population.

Origins of Inca Culture

Like the Aztecs of ancient Mexico, the Incas of Peru were heirs to a cultural tradition of great antiquity. This tradition had its origin on the coast, not in the highlands. By 2500 B.C.E., a village life, based chiefly on fishing and food gathering and supplemented by the cultivation of squash, lima beans, and a few other plants, had arisen around the mouths of rivers in the coastal area. Maize, introduced into Peruvian agriculture about 1500 B.C.E., did not become important until many centuries later.

The transition from the Archaic to the Preclassic period seems to have come later and more suddenly in Peru than in Mesoamerica. After long centuries of the simple village life just described, a strong advance of culture began on the coast around 900 B.C.E. This advance seems to have been associated with progress in agriculture, especially the greater use of maize, and with a movement up the river valleys from the littoral zone, possibly because of population pressure. Between 900 and 500 B.C.E., a distinctive style in building, art, ceramics, and weaving, known as

Chavín (from the name of the site of a great cere-monial center discovered in 1946), spread along the coast and even into the highlands. The most distinctive feature of Chavín is its art style, which features a feline being, presumably a deity, whose cult spread over the area of Chavín influence.

The Classic or Florescent period that emerged in Peru at or shortly before the beginning of the Old World's Christian Era reflected further progress in agriculture, notably in the use of irrigation and fertilization. The brilliant culture called Nazca displaced the Chavín along the coast and highlands of southern Peru at this time. Its use of color distinguished Nazca pottery. Often, a pot had as many as eleven soft, pastel shades. The lovely Nazca textiles displayed an enormous range of colors.

Even more remarkable was the Mochica culture of the northern Peruvian coast. The Mochica built pyramids, temples, roads, and large irrigation canals, and they evolved a complex, highly stratified society with a directing priesthood and a powerful priest-king. Metallurgy was highly developed, as evidenced by the wide use of copper weapons and tools and the manufacture of alloys of gold, copper, and silver. As artisans and artists, however, the Mochica were best known for their red and black pottery, never surpassed in the perfection of its realistic modeling. The so-called portrait vases, apparently representing actual individuals, marked the acme of Mochica realism. The Mochica also frequently decorated their pottery with realistic paintings of the most varied kind, including erotic scenes, which are twenty-first-century collector's items. The pottery frequently depicted war scenes, suggesting chronic struggles for limited arable land and sources of water. The aggressive Mochica finally fell victim to invaders who ravaged their lands, and a time of turbulence and cultural decline came to northern Peru.

Around 600 C.E., the focus of Andean civilization shifted from the coast to the highlands. At the site called Tiahuanaco, just south of Lake Titicaca on the high plateau of Bolivia, a great ceremonial center arose that was famed for its megalithic architecture, which was constructed with great stone blocks perfectly fitted together, and for its monumental human statuary. Tiahuanaco seems to have

been the capital of a military state that eventually controlled all of southern Peru from Arequipa south to highland Bolivia and Chile.

Another people, the Huari, embarked on a career of conquest from their homeland near modern Ayacucho; their territory ultimately included both the coast and highlands as far north as Cajamarca and south to the Tiahuanaco frontier. After a few centuries of domination, the Huari empire broke up about 1000 C.E., and at about the same time, the Tiahuanaco influence also came to an end. A return to political and artistic regionalism in the southern Andean area followed the disintegration of these empires.

By 1000 C.E., a number of Postclassic states, which differed from their predecessors in their larger size, had established their control over large portions of the northern Peruvian coast. The growth of cities accompanied their rise. Each river valley had its own urban center, and an expanded net of irrigation works made support of larger populations possible. The largest of these new states was the Chimu kingdom. Its capital, Chanchan, was an immense city spread over eight square miles, with houses made of great molded adobe bricks grouped into large units or compounds. The Chimu kingdom survived until its conquest by the Inca in the mid-fifteenth century.

INCA ECONOMY AND SOCIETY

In the highlands, meanwhile, where less settled conditions prevailed, a new power was emerging. The Incas (so called after their own name for the ruling lineage) made a modest appearance in history as one of a number of small tribes that inhabited the Cuzco region in the Andean highlands and struggled with each other for possession of land and water. A strong strategic situation in the Valley of Cuzco and some cultural superiority over their neighbors favored the Incas as they began their career of conquest. Previous empires—Huari, Tiahuanaco, and Chimu—no doubt provided the Incas with instructive precedents for conquest and the consolidation of conquest through a variety of political and socioeconomic techniques. Like other imperialist nations of antiquity, the Incas had a body of myth and legend that ascribed a divine origin to their rulers and gave their warriors a comforting assurance of supernatural favor and protection.

True imperial expansion seems to have begun in the second quarter of the fifteenth century, in the reign of Pachacuti Inca, who was crowned in 1438. Together with his son Topa Inca, also a great conqueror, Pachacuti obtained the submission of many provinces by the skillful use of claims of divine aid, fair promises, threats, and brute force. Reputed to be a great organizer as well as a mighty warrior, Pachacuti is credited with many reforms and innovations, including the establishment of the territorial divisions and elaborate administrative bureaucracy that made the wheels of the Inca empire go round. By 1527, the boundary markers of the Children of the Sun rested on the modern frontier between Ecuador and Colombia to the north and on the Maule River in Chile to the south. A population of perhaps 9 million people owed allegiance to the emperor. When the Spaniards arrived, the ruler was Atahualpa, who had just won the imperial mantle by defeating his half-brother Huascar.

The Incas maintained their authority with an arsenal of devices that included the spread of their Quechua language (still spoken by five-sixths of the indigenous peoples of the central Andean area) as the official language of the empire, the imposition of a unifying state religion, and a shrewd policy of incorporating chieftains of conquered regions into the central bureaucracy. An important factor in the Inca plan of unification was the policy of resettlement, or colonization. This consisted of deporting dissident populations and replacing them with loyal *mitimaes* (colonists) from older provinces of the empire. An excellent network of roads and footpaths linked administrative centers and made it possible to send armies and messengers quickly from one part of the empire to another. Some roads were paved, and others were cut into solid rock. Where the land was marshy, the roads passed over causeways; suspension bridges spanned gorges, and pontoon bridges of buoyant reeds were used to cross rivers. The Incas had no system of writing, but they possessed a most efficient means of keeping records in a memory aid called the *quipu* (a stick or cord with a number of knotted strings tied to it).

Strings of different colors represented different articles, people, or districts; knots tied in the strings ascended in units representing ones, tens, hundreds, thousands, and so on.

The economic basis of the Inca empire was its intensive irrigation agriculture capable of supporting without serious strain not only the producers but the large Inca armies, a large administrative bureaucracy, and many others engaged in nonproductive activities. The Incas did not develop this agriculture. By the time of their rise, the original coastal irrigation systems had probably extended over all suitable areas in coastal and highland Peru. But along with their political and religious institutions, the Incas introduced the advanced practices of irrigation, terracing, and fertilization among conquered peoples of more primitive cul-

Born Kusi Yupanqui, Pachacuti Inca, whose name means "Redeemer of Worlds," succeeded his father, Inca Viracocha, as the ninth emperor of the Kingdom of Cuzco.

ture. Terracing was used widely to extend the arable area and to prevent injury to fields and settlements in the narrow Andean valleys from runoff from the steep slopes during the rainy season. Irrigation ditches—sometimes mere trenches, sometimes elaborate stone channels—conducted water to the fields and pastures where it was needed.

Agricultural implements were few and simple. They consisted chiefly of a foot plow for breaking up the ground and digging holes for planting and a hoe with a bronze blade for general cultivation. As noted, the potato and quinoa were staple crops in the higher valleys; maize was the principal crop at lower altitudes. A wide variety of plants, including cotton, coca, and beans, were cultivated in the lower and hotter valleys. A major function of the Inca state was to regulate the exchange of the products of these multiple environments, primarily through the collection of tribute and its redistribution to various groups in Inca society. The Inca state also promoted self-sufficiency by allowing members of a given community to exploit the resources of different levels of the Andean "vertical" economy.

The basic unit of Inca social organization was the *ayllu* (a kinship group whose members claimed descent from a common ancestor and married within the group). According to historian Karen Spalding, the joining of two people in marriage linked the kin of each partner, who were "henceforth expected to behave toward one another as brothers and sisters." Not only brothers and sisters born of the same parents, but also first, second, and third cousins (that is, all who could trace their ancestry back to the same great-grandfather) regarded one another as brothers and sisters, so marriage created a large, extended kinship group. The members of this group sought to aid one another in tasks beyond the capacity of a single household.

A village community typically consisted of several ayllu, who each owned certain lands assigned in lots to the heads of families. Each family head had the right to use and pass on the land to his descendants but not to sell or otherwise dispose of it. Villagers frequently practiced mutual aid in agricultural tasks, in the construction of dwellings, and in other projects of a private or public nature. The Inca rulers took over

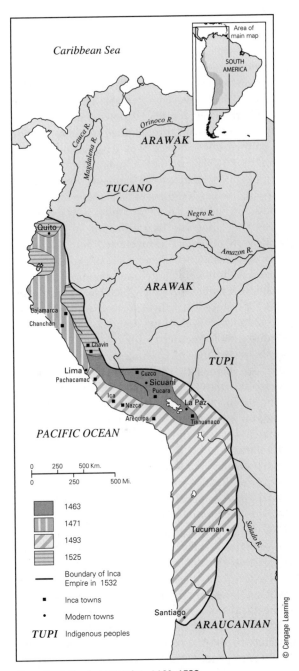

Growth of the Inca Empire, 1460–1532

this communal principle and utilized it for their own ends in the form of *corvée* (unpaid, forced labor). In the words of the anthropologist Nathan Wachtel, "The imperial Inca mode of production was based on the ancient communal mode of production which it left in place, while exploiting the principle of reciprocity to legitimate its rule."

Gender parallelism, beginning with parallel lines of descent, played a key role in ayllu kinship organization and ideology. Women regarded themselves as descendants through their mothers of a line of women; men viewed themselves as descending from their fathers in a line of men. "This organization of gender relations and kin ties through parallel descent," writes Irene Silverblatt in her remarkable study of gender relations in Andean society, *Sun, Moon, and Witches*, "was inherent in the ways Andean women and men created and re-created their social existence. The values and tone of gender parallelism were continuously reinforced in the practical activities through which they constructed and experienced their lives."

Parallel transmission ensured that women, through their mothers, enjoyed access to land, herds, water, and other resources. Gender parallelism also defined the division of labor in Andean society, with certain activities considered more appropriate for men or for women. According to Andean custom, weaving and spinning were women's work, and plowing and bearing arms were men's tasks, but all of these activities were complementary and equally important.

After the Inca conquest, however, notes Silverblatt, "The imperial ideal of Andean male-hood became the norm." "Soldier" was the title given to a male commoner when, as a married adult, he was inscribed in the imperial census rolls; "soldier's wife" was the equivalent category for a woman. Evidence exists that before the Inca conquest, women, inheriting rights from their mothers, sometimes held leadership positions on the ayllu level. However, the Inca imperial norm "attaching masculinity to political power and conquest skewed the balance of gender relations as the empire expanded, as men filled positions of authority in the Inca administration and military which were denied to

women of an equivalent social station." The Andean tradition of parallel descent allowed Inca noblewomen to claim access to their own resources, however, with rights to land in the Cuzco region passing down from noblewoman to noblewoman.

Before the Inca conquest, **curacas** (hereditary chiefs), assisted by a council of elders, governed the ayllu, with a ***jatun curaca*** (superior curaca or lord) ruling over the whole people or state. Under Inca rule, the kinship basis of ayllu organization was weakened through the planned removal of some of its members and the settlement of strangers in its midst (the system of mitimaes). A varying amount of land was taken from the villages and vested in the Inca state and the state church. In addition to working their own lands and those of their curaca, ayllu members were required to till the Inca state and church lands. The Inca government also used the forced labor of villagers to create new, arable land by leveling and terracing slopes. It often turned over this new land as private estates to curacas and Inca military leaders and nobles who had rendered conspicuous service to the Inca state. The Inca himself possessed private estates, and the descendants of dead emperors also owned estates that they used to maintain the cult of these former rulers. A new servile class, the ***yanacona***,[4] defined by Spanish sources as "permanent servants," typically worked these private estates. Each ayllu had to contribute a number of such servants or retainers, who also worked in the Inca temples and palaces and performed personal service.

In addition to agricultural labor, ayllu members had to work on roads, irrigation channels, and fortresses, as well in the mines, in a system called the ***mita*** (forced labor), which Spaniards later adopted for their own purposes. Another requirement was that villages produce specified quantities of cloth for the state to use in clothing soldiers and retainers. All able-bodied commoners between certain ages were subject to military service.

No trace of socialism or a welfare state was evident in these arrangements, which favored the Inca

4. A plural term in Quechua but treated by the Spaniards as singular.

dynasty, nobility, priesthood, warriors, and officials, not commoners. Many of the activities cited as reflecting the benevolence and foresight of the Inca state were actually traditional village and ayllu functions. One such activity was the maintenance of storehouses of grain and cloth by the community for times of crop failure. The Inca state merely took over this principle, as it had taken over the principle of cooperative labor for communal ends, and established storehouses containing the goods produced by the peasants' forced labor on state and church lands. The cloth and grain stored in these warehouses primarily clothed and fed the army, the crown artisans, the conscript labor for public works, and the officials who lived in Cuzco and other towns.

The relations between the Inca and the peasantry drew on the principle of reciprocity, expressed in an elaborate system of gifts and countergifts. The peasantry cultivated the lands of the Inca, worked up his wool and cotton into cloth, and performed various other kinds of labor for him. The Inca—the divine, universal lord—in turn permitted the peasantry to cultivate the communal lands and, in time of shortages, released to the villages the surplus grain in his storehouses. Because the imperial gifts were the products of the peasants' own labor, this "reciprocity" amounted to intensive exploitation of the commoners by the Inca rulers and nobility. We must not underestimate, however, the hold of this ideology on the Inca peasant mentality, which, buttressed by a religious worldview, regarded the Inca as responsible for defending the order and very existence of the universe.

At the time of the Conquest, a vast gulf separated the regimented and laborious life of the commoners from the luxurious life of the Inca nobility. At the apex of the social pyramid were the Inca and his relatives, composed of twelve lineages. Members of these lineages had the privilege of piercing their ears and distending the lobes with large ornaments—hence the name *orejones* (big ears) assigned to the Inca relatives by the Spaniards. The orejones were exempt from tribute labor and military service, and the same was true of the curacas, who once had been chieftains in their own right, and of a numerous class of specialists—servants, retainers, quipu keepers and other officials, and entertainers. Side by side with the Inca state, which drained off the peasants' surplus production, regulated the exchange of goods between the various regions, and directed vast public works, there arose the incipient feudalism of the Inca nobility and curacas. Rich gifts of land, llamas, and yanacona rewarded their loyalty and services to the Inca. Their growing resources enabled them to form their own local clienteles, achieve a certain relative independence from the crown, and play an important role in the disputes over the succession that sometimes followed the emperor's death.

Inca rule over the peasant masses was largely indirect, exercised through local chieftains. It probably did not seriously affect the round of daily life in the villages. The typical peasant house in the highlands was a small hut with walls of fieldstone or adobe and a gable roof thatched with grass. The scanty furniture consisted of a raised sleeping platform, a clay stove, and some clay pots and dishes. A man's clothing consisted of a breechcloth, a sleeveless tunic, and a large cloak over the shoulders with two corners tied in front; the fineness of the cloth used and the ornamentation varied according to social rank. A woman's dress was a wraparound cloth extending from beneath the arms to the ankles, with the top edges drawn over the shoulders and fastened with straight pins. An ornamented sash around the waist and a shoulder mantle completed the woman's apparel. Men adorned themselves with earplugs and bracelets; women wore necklaces and shawl pins.

On the eve of the Spanish Conquest, the Inca state appeared all-powerful, but, like the Aztec empire, this masked deep contradictions. It faced frequent revolts by conquered peoples that it suppressed with ferocious cruelty. Even the outwardly loyal curacas, former lords of independent states, chafed at the vigilant Inca control and dreamed of regaining their lost freedom.

INCA RELIGION AND LEARNING

The Inca state religion existed side by side with the much older ancestor cults and the worship of innumerable *huacas* (local objects and places). The chief of the Inca gods was a nameless creator called Viracocha and Pachayachachic (lord and instructor of the world). His cult seems to have been a philosophical religion largely confined to the priesthood and nobility. First in importance after Viracocha was the sun god, claimed by the Inca royal family as its divine ancestor. Other notable divinities were the thunder god, who sent the life-giving rain, and the Moon, wife of the Sun, who played a vital role in the regulation of the Inca festival calendar. The Inca idols were housed in numerous temples attended by priests who directed and performed ceremonies that included prayer, sacrifice, confession, and the rite of divination. Another priestly function was the magical cure of disease. A class of *mamacuna* (holy women, who had taken vows of permanent chastity) assisted the priests in their religious duties. Human sacrifice was performed on momentous occasions, such as an important victory or some great natural calamity.

Inca art was marked by a high level of technical excellence. The architecture was solid and functional, characterized by massiveness rather than beauty. Although some have described their stone sculpture, more frequent in the highlands than on the coast, as ponderous and severe, the tapestries of Inca weavers were among the world's textile masterpieces, so fine and intricate was the weaving. Inca metallurgy was also on a high technical and artistic plane. Cuzco, the Inca capital, abounded in gold objects: The imperial palace had gold friezes and panels of gold and silver, and the Temple of the Sun contained a garden with lifelike replicas of plants and animals, all made of hammered gold.

Although the Incas had no system of writing and thus no written literature, they transmitted narrative poems, prayers, and tales orally from generation to generation. These Inca hymns and prayers are notable for their lofty thought and beauty of expression. Of the long narrative poems that dealt

with Inca mythology, legends, and history, only summaries in Spanish prose remain.

A melancholy and nostalgic spirit pervades many of the traditional Inca love songs, and the same plaintiveness characterizes the few examples of their music that have been passed down. Based on the five-toned, or pentatonic, scale, this music was performed with an assortment of instruments: flutes, trumpets, and whistles; gongs, bells, and rattles; and several kinds of skin drums and tambourines. The dances that accompanied the music sometimes represented an elementary form of drama.

Spanish conquistadors destroyed the Inca political organization and dealt shattering blows to all aspects of Inca civilization, but elements of that culture survive everywhere in the central Andean area. These survivals, tangible and intangible, include the Quechua speech; the numerous indigenous communities, or ayllu, still partly based on cooperative principles; the widespread pagan beliefs and rites of the people; and, of course, the monumental ruins of Sacsahuaman, Ollantay-tambo, Machu Picchu, Pisac, and Cuzco itself. Inca civilization also lives on in the writings of Peruvian historians, novelists, and public officials, who evoke the vanished Inca greatness and praise the ancient virtues of their people. For many Peruvians, the great technical achievements and social engineering of the Incas, ensuring a modest well-being for all, offer proof of the inherent capacity of their native peoples and a prospect of what the poverty-ridden, strife-torn Peru of the twenty-first century may yet become.

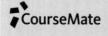 Go to the CourseMate website at **www.cengagebrain.com** for primary sources, additional study tools, and review materials—including audio and video clips—for this chapter.

The Hispanic Background

2

FOCUS QUESTIONS

- How did conquest affect the development of the Iberian Peninsula in the ancient world?
- What were the Castilian institutions, traditions, and values that shaped the future of Latin America?
- How did the Reconquest shape Castile's economic, social, and political structures?
- What were the positive and negative aspects of the reign of Ferdinand and Isabella?
- What were the policies of the Hapsburg dynasty, and how did they affect the empire's decline?
- What were the causes and significance of the Comunero revolt?

ROM VERY EARLY TIMES, conquest was a major theme of Iberian history. The prehistoric inhabitants of the peninsula, whose unknown artists produced the marvelous cave paintings of Altamira, were overrun by tribes vaguely called Iberians and by the Celts, who are believed to have come from North Africa and central Europe, respectively, probably before 1000 B.C.E. New waves of invasion brought the Phoenicians, Greeks, and Carthaginians, commercial nations that established trading posts and cities on the coast but made no effort to dominate the interior. Still later, the Iberian Peninsula became a stake of empire in the great struggle for commercial supremacy between Rome and Carthage that ended with the decisive defeat of the latter in 201 B.C.E. For six centuries thereafter, Rome was the dominant power in the region.

Unlike earlier invaders, the Romans attempted to occupy the lands and establish their authority over the native people, on whom they imposed their language, governing institutions, and even the name: *Hispania*. From Latin, made the official language, sprang the various dialects and languages still spoken by Hispanic peoples today. Roman law replaced the customary law of the Celts, Iberians, and other native groups. Native tribal organization was destroyed through forced changes of residence, concentration in towns, and the establishment of Roman colonies that served as agencies of pacification and assimilation. Agriculture, mining, and industry developed, and these Roman colonies carried on an extensive trade in wheat, wine, and olive oil with Italy. Roman engineers constructed great public roads and aqueducts, some of which are still in use. Romans brought with them their educational institutions and literary culture, and a number of Roman citizens, including the satirical poet Martial, the epic poet Lucan, and the philosopher Seneca, who were either born or residing in the peninsular colonies, made notable contributions to Latin literature.

Early in the fifth century C.E., as a result of the decline of Roman military power, a number of barbarian peoples of Germanic origin invaded. By the last half of the century, one group of invaders, the Visigoths, had gained mastery over most of the peninsula. As a result of long contact with the

201 B.C.E.	Rome defeats Carthage and dominates Iberian Peninsula for six centuries
484 C.E.	Visigothic invasion and establishment of capital at Toledo
711	Islamic Umayyad invasion and occupation of Iberia
1212–1248	Christian Reconquest successively captures Andalucia, Córdoba, and Sevilla (Seville)
1479	Treaty of Alcaçovas unites Christian Kingdoms of Castile and Aragón under Queen Isabela and King Ferdinand
1492	"Catholic sovereigns" conquer last remaining Muslim Kingdom of Granada and authorize Christopher Columbus's first voyage to the Americas
1504	Queen Isabela dies, followed twelve years later by Ferdinand's death
1519–1556	First king of the Hapsburg dynasty, Charles I (Charles V of the Holy Roman empire) ascends to the throne of Castile and Aragón
1520–1521	Comunero rebellion challenges Hapsburg rule
1556–1598	Charles' son, Philip II, succeeds to the throne of Castile and Aragón
1580	Union of Kingdoms of Portugal, Castile, and Aragón
1700	Death of Charles II, last of the Hapsburg sovereigns, and the origin of the War of the Spanish Succession

empire, the Visigoths already had assimilated Roman culture, which continued through contact with the Hispano-Romans. The Visigothic kingdom was Christian. Its speech became Latin with a small admixture of Germanic terms, and in administration, it followed the Roman model. But the succession to the kingship followed Germanic tradition in being elective, a frequent source of great internal strife.

The Medieval Heritage of Iberia's Christian Kingdoms

The divisions among the Goths, caused by struggles over kingship, played into the hands of a rising new Muslim power that emerged from Arabia and swept across the North African plains. In 711 C.E. the armies of the Umayyad caliphate crossed the straits and decisively defeated Roderic, the last Gothic king. Within a few years, the entire Iberian Peninsula, except for the remote region north of the Cantabrian Mountains, fell into Muslim hands. But the Muslims' hold on the bleak uplands of one Christian kingdom, Castile, was never strong; they preferred the fertile plains and mild climate of southern Spain, which they called Al-Andalus, the land of Andalusia.

The Umayyads, who were heir to the accumulated cultural wealth of the ancient Mediterranean and Asian worlds, enriched this heritage with their own magnificent contributions to science, arts, and letters. With its capital located at Córdoba, the Umayyad dynasty transformed the Iberian world into an economic and intellectual showplace from which fresh knowledge and ideas flowed into Christian lands. Agriculture gained from the introduction of new methods of irrigation, water-lifting devices, and new crops like sugar, saffron, cotton, silk, and citrus fruits. Industry expanded through the introduction of such products as paper and glass, hitherto unknown to the Christian kingdoms. Muslim metalwork, pottery, silk, and leatherwork were esteemed throughout Europe. Many Muslim rulers were patrons of literature and learning; the scholar-king Al-Haquem II built up a library said to have numbered four hundred thousand volumes.

As a rule, the Umayyad conquerors did not insist on the conversion of the vanquished Christians, preferring to give them the option of accepting the Islamic faith or paying a special poll tax. This relatively tolerant Muslim rule was favorable to economic and cultural advance. Jews, who had suffered severe persecution under the Christian Visigoths, enjoyed official protection and made major contributions to medicine, philosophy, and Talmudic studies. The condition of the peasantry probably

With the aid of Iberian Jews oppressed by Christian kings, Islamic forces conquered the peninsula in the eighth century and inaugurated a period of peaceful coexistence that, even after the Christian Reconquest, left a lasting multicultural imprint on Spanish art, architecture, music, and literature.

improved, for the conquerors distributed the vast estates of the Visigothic lords among the serfs, who paid a certain portion of the produce to the Muslim lords and kept the rest for themselves. But in later centuries, during the Almoravid occupation, these trends were reversed; great landed estates again arose, taxation increased, and severe persecution of Jews and *Mozárabes* (Christians who had adopted Arab speech and customs) drove many to flee to Christian territory.

Despite its noble achievements, the Umayyad dynasty rested on insecure foundations. First, its extraordinary success in expanding the caliphate had created unimaginable conflicts that exhausted scarce resources and slowed its imperial advance after the tenth century. Second, the Muslim world was torn by fierce political and religious feuds over control of the empire. Some Muslims scorned the Umayyads as blasphemers for their reluctance to follow the "messengers of God" and their desire to concentrate power in the hands of kings. On the Iberian Peninsula, these internal differences were compli-cated by conflicts between the Umayyads and Almoravids, North African Berbers who were recent converts to Islam and more fanatically devout than their teachers. By the mid-eleventh century, the caliphate of Córdoba had broken into a large number of *taifas* (states) that constantly warred with one another. These discords enabled the petty Christian kingdoms that had arisen in the north to survive, grow strong, and eventually launch a general advance against the Muslims. In the west, the kingdom of Portugal, having achieved independence from Castile by the mid-twelfth century, attained its historic boundaries two centuries later. In the center, the joint realm of León and Castile pressed its advance, and, to the east, the kingdom of Aragón steadily expanded at the expense of the disunited Muslim states.

The Reconquest began as a struggle of Christian kings and nobles to regain their lost lands and serfs; only later did it assume the character of a religious crusade. Early in the ninth century, the tomb of St. James, supposedly found in the peninsula's northwestern lands, became the center of the famous pilgrimage of Santiago de Compostela and gave the Christian kingdoms a warrior patron saint who figured prominently in the Reconquest and the conquest of the New World. But the career of the famous Cid (Ruy Díaz de Vivar), to whom his Muslim soldiers gave the title "Lord," illustrates the absence of religious fanaticism in the first stage of the struggle. True to the ideals of his time, the Cid placed feudal above religious loyalties and, as a vassal of the Muslim kings of Saragossa and Valencia, fought Muslim and Christian foes alike. When he captured Valencia for himself in 1094, he allowed the Muslims to worship freely and retain their property, requiring only the payment of tributes authorized by the Koran.

The Umayyads vainly sought to check the Christian advance by calling on the newly converted, fanatically religious Almoravids of North Africa to come to their aid. The Christian victory at Las Navas de Tolosa (1212) in Andalusia over a large Almoravid army marked a turning point in the Reconquest. Ferdinand III of Castile captured Córdoba, the jewel of Muslim Iberia, in 1236, and the surrender of Sevilla in 1248 gave him control of the mouth of the Guadalquivir River and communication with the sea. By the time of Ferdinand's death in 1252, the Muslim territory had been reduced to the small kingdom of Granada. The strength of its position, protected by steep mountains and impassable gorges, and the divisions that arose within the Christian camp gave Granada two and a half more centuries of independent life.

CASTILE

Although the twentieth-century Spanish fascists under Francisco Franco sought to legitimize their contemporaneous quest for power by identifying with the historic achievements of their fifteenth-century ancestors, no unified nation-state called Spain existed on the Iberian Peninsula until 1947. Instead, it consisted of a variety of more or less independent Christian kingdoms that engaged in a brutal contest among themselves and with their Muslim occupiers, first to dominate the Mediterranean world and then to control the world beyond the seas. Castile, the largest and most powerful of these kingdoms, played a leading role in the Reconquest. The great movement left an enduring stamp on the Castilian character. Centuries of struggle against the Muslim occupation made war almost a Castilian way of life and created a large class of warrior-nobles, who regarded manual labor with contempt. In the Castilian scale of values, the military virtues of courage, endurance, and honor were paramount, and both nobles and commoners accepted these values. The lure of plunder, land, and other rewards drew many peasants and artisans into the armies of the Reconquest and diffused militarist and aristocratic ideals throughout Castilian society. To these ideals the crusading spirit of the Reconquest, especially in its later phase, added a strong sense of religious superiority and mission.

The Reconquest also shaped the character of the Castilian economy. As the Muslims fell back, vast tracts of land came into the possession of the crown. The kings assigned the lion's share of this land to the nobility, the church, and the three military orders of Calatrava, Alcántara, and Santiago. As a result, Castile, especially the area south of Toledo

(New Castile), became a region of enormous estates and a wealthy, powerful aristocracy.

The Reconquest also ensured the supremacy of sheep raising over agriculture in Castile. In a time of constant warfare, of raids and counterraids, the mobile sheep was a more secure and valuable form of property than land. With the advance of the Christian frontier, much new territory—frequently too arid for easy agricultural use—was opened to the sheep industry. The introduction of the merino sheep from North Africa around 1300, which coincided with a sharply increased demand in northern Europe for wool, gave a marked stimulus to sheep raising in Castile. By the late thirteenth century, the **Mesta** (a powerful organization of sheep raisers) had established themselves. In return for large subsidies to the crown, this organization received extensive privileges, including the right to move great flocks of sheep across Castile from summer pastures in the north to winter pastures in the south, with frequent injury to the farmlands and woods in their path. The great nobles dominated the sheep industry as well as agriculture. Their large rents and the profits from the sale of their wool gave them an economic, social, and military power that threatened the supremacy of the king.

The Castilian towns represented the only counterpoise to this power. The advance of the Reconquest and the need to consolidate its gains promoted municipal growth. To attract settlers to the newly conquered territory, the king gave generous **fueros** (charters of liberties) to the towns that sprang up one after another. These charters endowed the towns with administrative autonomy and vast areas of land that extended their jurisdiction into the surrounding countryside. The towns were governed by **alcaldes** (elected judicial officials) and **regidores** (members of the town council). The economic expansion of the thirteenth and fourteenth centuries and the growth of the wool trade, above all, made the Castilian towns bustling centers of industry and commerce. The wealth of the towns gave them a peculiar importance in the meetings of the consultative body, the **cortes** (parliament). Because the nobles and the clergy were exempt from taxes, the king had to request funds from the towns' deputies, who, in exchange for their assent to taxation, typically required royal redress of town grievances previously presented in the form of petitions for justice. In the words of historian Joseph F. O'Callaghan, "Unless the king or the regents promised to govern rightly, they could not expect the cortes to agree blindly to a levy of taxes."

The Castilian towns had their time of splendor, but in the final analysis, the middle class remained small and weak, and it was overshadowed by the enormous power of the great nobles. Aware of their weakness, the towns joined their forces in *hermandades* (military associations that resisted the aggressions of the nobles and sometimes of the king). But the posture of the towns essentially was defensive. Without the aid of the king, they could not hope to impose their will on the aristocracy.

As Muslim power waned, the great nobles turned from fighting the infidel to battling the king, the towns, and one another. In the course of the fourteenth and fifteenth centuries, the nobles gained the upper hand in their struggle with the king, usurping royal lands and revenues and often transforming the monarch into their pawn. The degradation of the crown reached its lowest point in the reign of Henry IV (1454–1474), when the central government and public order almost broke down completely. Beneath this anarchy, however, the continued expansion of economic life inspired a growing demand for a strong monarchy that could establish peace and order.

ARAGÓN

The medieval history of the smaller, less populous kingdom of Aragón differed in important ways from that of Castile. The king of Aragón ruled over three states—Aragón, Valencia, and Catalonia—each regarded as a separate *reino* (kingdom) and each having its own Cortes. The upland state of Aragón was the poorest and least developed of the three. Valencia was the home of a large Muslim peasant population that was subject to a Christian landowning nobility. Catalonia played the dominant role in the union, and its great city of Barcelona had given Aragón its dynasty and most of its

revenues. A thriving industry and powerful fleets had made Barcelona the center of a commercial empire based on the export of textiles. Catalán arms had also won Sardinia and Sicily for the crown of Aragón. In Aragón, therefore, the ruling class was not the landed nobility, which was relatively poor, but the commercial and industrial oligarchy of Barcelona. The constitutional system of Aragón reflected the supremacy of this class by giving legislative power to the Cortes of Catalonia and by providing special watchdog committees of the Cortes, which guarded against any infringement of the rights and liberties of the subjects.

In the fourteenth and fifteenth centuries, Barcelona's prosperity declined because of the ravages of the Black Death, agrarian unrest in the Catalán countryside, struggles between the merchant oligarchy and popular elements in Barcelona, and, above all, the loss of traditional Catalán markets to Genoese competitors. This economic decline sharpened internal Catalán struggles, in which the crown joined the side of the popular elements. The result was the civil war of 1462–1472, which ended in a qualified victory for King John II, but it completed the ruin of Catalonia. The weakness of Aragón on the eve of its union with Castile ensured Castilian leadership of the united kingdoms.

The chain of events that led to the union of Castile and Aragón began with the secret marriage in 1469 of Isabella, sister of Henry IV of Castile, and Ferdinand, son of John II of Aragón. This match was the fruit of complex intrigues in which the personal ambitions of the young couple, the hostility of many Castilian nobles to their king, and the desire of John II to add Castile to his son Ferdinand's heritage all played their part. On the death of Henry IV in 1474, Isabella proclaimed herself queen of Castile with the support of a powerful faction of Castilian nobles and towns that declared that Henry's daughter Juana was illegitimate, a claim that led to a dynastic war in which Portugal supported Juana. By 1479, the struggle had ended in Isabella's favor, John II had died, and Ferdinand had succeeded to his dominions. Ferdinand and Isabella now became joint rulers of Aragón and Castile, but the terms of their marriage contract carefully subordinated Ferdinand to Isabella

Reunion des Musées Nationaux/Art Resource, New York

Isabella and Ferdinand transformed Spain into one of the strongest European kingdoms of the fifteenth century.

in the government of Castile and excluded Isabella from the administration of Aragón. Nonetheless, the union of Castile and Aragón, under Castilian leadership, marked a decisive advantage in what became a remarkable career of domestic progress and imperial expansion.

Ferdinand and Isabella: The Catholic Sovereigns

RESTORATION OF ORDER

The young monarchs faced an urgent problem of restoring peace and order in their respective kingdoms. Catalonia was still troubled by struggles between feudal lords and serfs who were determined to end their legal servitude. Ferdinand intervened and proposed a solution that was relatively favorable to the peasantry. His ruling of Guadalupe (1486) ended serfdom in Catalonia and enabled fifty thousand peasants to become small landowners. He made no effort, however, to reform Aragón's archaic constitutional system, which set strict limits on royal power. As a result, Castile and Aragón, despite their newfound unity, continued to move along divergent political courses.

The task of restoring order was greater in Castile. The age of anarchy under Henry IV had transformed cities into battlefields and parts of the countryside into a desert. To eradicate the evils of banditry and feudal violence, Isabella counted above all on the support of the towns and the middle classes. The Cortes of Madrigal (1476) forged a solid alliance between the crown and the towns for the suppression of disorder. Their instrument was the *Santa Hermandad*, a police force paid for and manned principally by the towns but under the direct control of the crown. The efficiency of this force and the severe and prompt punishments meted out by its tribunals gradually restored peace in Castile.

But Isabella's program went beyond this immediate goal. She proposed to bend to the royal will all the great institutions of medieval Castile: the nobility, the church, and the towns themselves. The Cortes of Toledo of 1480 reduced the power of the grandees (nobles of the first rank) in various ways. An Act of Resumption compelled them to return to the crown about half the revenues they had usurped since 1464. Another reform reorganized the Council of Castile, the central governing agency of the kingdom. This reform reduced the grandees who had dominated the old royal council to holders of empty dignities. It vested effective responsibility and power in *letrados* (officials usually possessed of legal training), who were drawn from the lower nobility, the middle class, and *conversos* (converted Jews).

The establishment of a hierarchy of courts and magistrates that ascended from the *corregidor* (the royal officer who watched over the affairs of a municipality) through the *cancillerías* (the high law courts of Castile) up to the Council of Castile, both the highest court and the supreme administrative body of the country, also curbed aristocratic power. At all levels, the crown asserted its judicial primacy, including the right of intervention in the feudal jurisdiction of the nobility. Lasting success in these endeavors, however, required the crown to rely on more than its coercive power, which alone never could secure its borders or sustain its authority over a recalcitrant population. As historian Jack Owens impressively argues, aristocrats and commoners alike only recognized the crown's "absolute royal authority" when they believed that its judicial institutions rendered fair judgments.

The vast wealth of the military orders made them veritable states within the Castilian state, and the crown was determined to weaken their power by gaining control of them. When the grand mastership of Santiago fell vacant in 1476, Isabella personally appeared before the dignitaries of the order to insist that they confer the headship on her husband; they meekly assented. When the grand masterships of Calatrava and Alcántara fell vacant, they too were duly conferred on Ferdinand. By these moves, the crown gained new sources of revenue and patronage.

The towns had served the crown well in the struggle against anarchy, but in the past two centuries, their democratic traditions had declined, and many had fallen under the control of selfish oligarchies. Some, like Sevilla, had become battlefields of aristocratic factions. These disorders provided Isabella with pretexts for resuming the policy, which her predecessors had initiated, of intervening in municipal affairs by introducing corregidores into the towns. These officials combined administrative and judicial functions and steadily usurped the roles of the alcaldes and regidores. Ferdinand and Isabella also carried forward another practice begun by their predecessors: They required the crown to appoint the offices of alcalde and regidor in towns with royal charters instead of permitting their election by the householders. *Villas de señorío* (towns under noble or ecclesiastical jurisdiction) functioned under the traditional system but with the right of royal intervention if necessary.

A decline in the importance of the Cortes accompanied the taming of the towns. An important factor in this decline was the large increase in revenues from royal taxes, such as the **alcabala** (sales tax), which freed the crown from excessive dependence on the grants of the Cortes. The increased supervision of the crown over the municipalities also decreased the likelihood of resistance by their deputies in the Cortes to royal demands. The Sovereigns summoned the Castilian Cortes only when they needed money, but when the treasury was full or when peace prevailed, the king and queen ignored them.

RELIGIOUS AND ECONOMIC REFORMS

In their march toward absolute power, the monarchs did not hesitate to challenge the church. Under their pressure, the weak popes of this period yielded to them the right of **patronato real** (the right of appointment to all major ecclesiastical benefices in the Castilian realms). Although, unlike Henry VIII of England, Ferdinand and Isabella never despoiled the church of its vast landed possessions, they did drain off for themselves a part of the ecclesiastical wealth by taking one-third of all the tithes paid to the Castilian church and the proceeds from the sale of indulgences.

To ensure the loyalty of the church and to make it an effective instrument of royal policy, the Sovereigns had to purge it of abuses that included plural benefices, absenteeism, and concubinage. The pious Isabella found a strong ally in the work of reform in a dissident faction of the regular clergy (those belonging to a monastic order or religious community). This group, whose members called themselves Observants, protested against the worldliness of their colleagues and demanded a return to the strict simplicity of the primitive church. The struggle for reform began within the Franciscan order under the leadership of the ascetic Francisco Jiménez de Cisneros, whom Isabella appointed archbishop of Toledo in 1495, and then spread to the other orders. It grew so heated that four hundred Andalusian friars moved to North Africa and became Muslims rather than accept the new rule. The dispute ended in the complete victory of the Observants over their more easygoing brethren.

Isabella was less successful in efforts to reform the secular (or nonmonastic) clergy, but here too an improvement took place. The great ecclesiastical offices ceased to be a monopoly of the aristocracy. Isabella preferred to select prelates from the lower nobility and the middle class, taking account of the morals and learning of the candidates. The Isabelline religious reform had a special meaning for the New World: It ensured that the Faith would be carried to the Indies by an elite force of clergy who often were distinguished for their zeal, humanity, and learning.

The Sovereigns also gave attention to the need for economic reform. They attempted to promote Castilian industry and commerce by protectionist measures. They forbade the export of gold and silver, sporadically barred the import of cloth that competed with native products, and encouraged Italian and Flemish artisans to settle in Castile. They promulgated navigation acts that gave preference to domestic shipping and subsidies to domestic shipbuilding. They suppressed all the internal tolls that had been established in Castile since 1464 and tried to standardize weights and measures. Under Isabella's predecessors, a serious depreciation of the currency had taken place. To restore the credit of the coinage, Isabella suppressed all private mints and struck her own coinage that had the same value as foreign coins. All these measures contributed to an economic expansion and consequently to a rapid increase of crown revenues, from 885,000 *reales* (Spanish unit of currency) in 1474 to 26,283,334 reales in 1504.

Despite their basically pragmatic outlook, the Sovereigns had broad intellectual and artistic interests. To their court they summoned Italian humanists like Alessandro Geraldini, Lucio Marineo Siculo, and Peter Martyr de Anghera to tutor their children and the sons of the greatest houses of Castile. Enlightened prelates like Archbishop Jiménez de Cisneros founded new schools and universities to rival the famed University of Salamanca. Castile produced some distinguished practitioners of the

new learning, such as Antonio de Nebrija, grammarian, historian, and lexicographer, who in 1492 published and presented to Isabella a Castilian grammar—the first grammar of any modern European language. The vitality of the Castilian language and life found expression in a realistic masterpiece: the novel *La Celestina* (1499) by Fernando de Rojas. Meanwhile, Castilian architecture and sculpture developed its own style, known as plateresque, an ornamental blend of Islamic arabesques, flowers, foliage, and Renaissance motifs.

FOREIGN POLICY

The restoration of domestic peace enabled the Sovereigns to turn their attention to questions of foreign policy. For the Castilian Isabella, the conquest of Granada came first. Hardly had their authority firmly been restored when the Sovereigns demanded of the Granadan ruler the tribute paid by his predecessors to Castile. Abdul Hassan replied that his mints now coined steel, not gold. The wealth of the Granadan kingdom and its mountainous terrain enabled the Almoravids to hold out for ten years. But Castile's superior military power, especially the formidable new arm of artillery, finally broke the Muslim resistance. In January 1492, Granada surrendered to Ferdinand and Isabella, on whom Pope Alexander VI bestowed the title "The Catholic Sovereigns" in honor of their crusading piety.

Whereas Isabella's heart was set on the conquest of Granada, Ferdinand, heir to Aragón's Mediterranean empire and the traditional rivalry between France and Aragón, looked eastward to Aragón's borders with France and to Italy. He achieved most of his goals after Isabella's death in 1504. Employing an adroit blend of war and diplomacy, he obtained the return of two Aragonese provinces lost to France by previous rulers, the incorporation of the kingdom of Naples into the Aragonese empire, and the checkmating of French designs in Italy. In the course of Ferdinand's Italian wars, his commanders, especially the "Great Captain" Gonzalo de Córdoba, created a new-style army that was equipped with impressive firepower and strong offensive and defensive weapons. The new system, first tested in Italy, established the military supremacy of Castile and Aragón in Europe. Before his death, Ferdinand rounded out his conquests with the acquisition of Navarre (1512), which gave the united kingdoms a strongly defensible frontier with France. Although his royal successors officially continued to govern the sovereign kingdoms of Castile, Aragón, Navarre, and so on, their European rivals thereafter increasingly called this new power emerging from the Iberian Peninsula by its Roman name: *Hispania* or Spain.

The Catholic Sovereigns rendered major services to their people. They tamed the arrogant nobility, defeated the forces of Islam, and united the feuding Christian kingdoms in the pursuit of common goals. They encouraged the growth of trade and industry and showed themselves to be intelligent patrons of learning and the arts. Their prudent diplomacy gave Castile a place among the first powers of Europe. In the same period, America was discovered under Castilian auspices, the Caribbean became a Castillian lake, and by the end of their reign, the kingdom's explorers and adventurers were on the verge of discovering the great Indian empires of Mexico and Peru. Naturally, the monarchs who presided over such victories became for succeeding generations the objects of a national cult and legend.

REAPPRAISAL OF FERDINAND AND ISABELLA'S POLICIES

For modern historians, the fame of the Catholic Sovereigns has lost some of its luster. These historians charge Ferdinand and Isabella with mistaken policies that nullified much of the sound part of their work. One of these errors was a definite bias in favor of the economic and social interests of the aristocracy. If the nobility lost most of its political power under Ferdinand and Isabella, nothing of the kind happened in the economic sphere. Concentration of land in noble hands actually increased during their reign. The Cortes of 1480, which forced the nobility to surrender about half the lands and revenues usurped from the crown since 1464, explicitly authorized the nobles to retain the vast holdings acquired before that date. A policy of assigning a lion's share of the territory reconquered from the Muslims to the grandees also favored the growth of land monopoly. After the War of Granada, moreover, the great nobles used their private armies and increased political influence to expand their territories and seigneurial control. This "aristocratic offensive" met with little resistance from the crown. As a result, by 1500, about 2 or 3 percent of the population owned 95 percent of the land.

This land monopoly reduced the great majority of the Castilian peasants to the condition of tenants heavily burdened by rents, seigneurial dues, tithes, and taxes. Although serfdom in the strict sense apparently had disappeared from most parts of Castile by 1480 and the Castilian peasant was legally free to leave his village and move elsewhere, the nobility still owned virtually all the land. Thus, the peasant's "liberty" was, as the Spanish historian Jaime Vicens Vives has called it, the liberty "to die of hunger."

The royal policy of favoring sheep raising over agriculture was equally harmful to Castile's long-range economic interests. Like their predecessors, the Sovereigns were influenced by the taxes and export duties paid by the sheep farmers and by the inflow of gold in payment for their wool. As a result, they granted extensive privileges to the sheep raisers' guild, the Mesta. The climax of these favors was a 1501 law that reserved in perpetuity for pasture all land on which the migrant flocks had ever pastured. This measure barred vast tracts of land in Andalusia and Estremadura from agricultural cultivation. The privilege granted the shepherds to cut trees for fuel, fencing, or pasturage contributed heavily to deforestation and soil erosion. Moreover, the overflow of sheep from their legal passage caused much damage to crops and soil. In a time of growing population, these policies and conditions inevitably produced serious food deficits. Chronic shortages climaxed in a devastating food crisis in the early sixteenth century.

Modern historians also question the traditional view that Spanish industry made spectacular advances under the Catholic Sovereigns. These historians claim

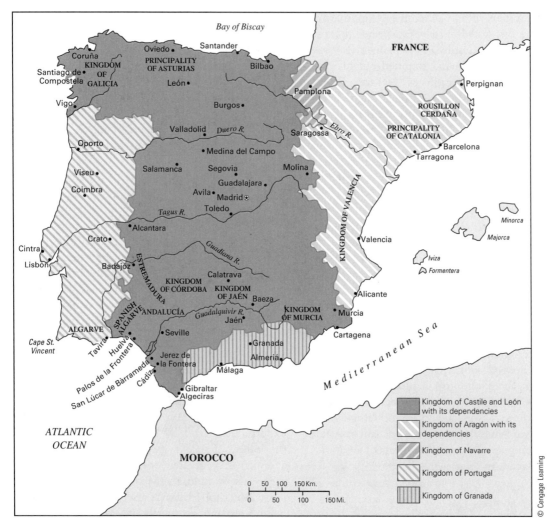

Spain in the Time of Christopher Columbus

that the only true industries of the period were the iron industry of the Basque provinces and the cloth industry of the Castilian central zone, which received a strong stimulus from the discovery of America and the opening of American markets. The resulting industrial prosperity lasted until shortly after the middle of the sixteenth century, but the level of industrial production never reached that of England, the Low Countries, or Italy. The abject poverty of the peasantry, which composed 80 percent of the population, sharply limited the effective market for manufactured goods. Shortages of capital and skilled labor also acted as a brake on industrial expansion.

Other obstacles to industrial growth were the excessive costs of transport by mule train and oxcarts across the rugged peninsula and the customs barriers that continued to separate the Christian kingdoms, nor were the paternalistic measures of the Sovereigns invariably helpful to industry. Through Ferdinand's influence, a guild system modeled on the rigid Catalán model was introduced into the Castilian towns. In this, the Sovereigns did Castilian industry no service, for they fastened the straitjacket of guild organization on it precisely at the time when the discovery and colonization of America promised to enrich the realm. The influx of American gold and silver and the resulting economic upsurge challenged Castilian industry to transform its techniques, lower costs, increase output and quality, and thereby establish its economic as well as political supremacy in Europe.

No policy of the Sovereigns has come under harsher attack than their anti-Semitic measures. During the early Middle Ages, Jews formed an influential and prosperous group in Castile. Down to the close of the thirteenth century, a relatively tolerant spirit prevailed in the Christian kingdoms. Relations among Jews, Christians, and Muslims were so close and neighborly as to provoke protests by the church. In the fourteenth century, these relations began to deteriorate. Efforts by the clergy to arouse hatred of Jews and popular resentment of such specialized Jewish economic activities as usury and tax collecting, which caused severe hardship for peasants and other groups, contributed to this process. The rise of anti-Semitism led to the adoption of repressive legislation by the crown and to a wave of attacks on Jewish communities. To save their lives, many Jews accepted baptism and eventually formed a numerous class of *conversos* (converts).

The converts soon achieved a marked prosperity and influence as tax farmers, court physicians, counselors, and lawyers. Wealthy, unhampered by feudal traditions, intellectually curious, and intensely ambitious, the conversos incurred the hostility not only of peasants but also of the church and many nobles and burghers. Whether heretics or not, they posed a threat to the feudal order based on landed wealth, hereditary status, and religious orthodoxy. The envy and hostility they aroused explained why the Sovereigns—one of whom (Ferdinand) had Jewish blood in his veins, and relied heavily on Jewish and converso advisers—established the Inquisition and expelled the Jews from their kingdom. When the crown had tamed the nobility and the towns, and when it had acquired large new sources of revenue, its dependence on the Jews and conversos weakened. The sacrifice of

The Granger Collection, New York

Even as they continued secretly to observe their religious and cultural traditions, Jews publicly converted to Christianity to avoid the torture and burning depicted in this 1475 woodcut, which shows the Spanish Inquisition at work in Granada.

the Jews and conversos sealed the alliance among the absolute monarchy, the church, and the nobility.

The conversos first felt the blows of religious persecution with the establishment of the Inquisition in Castile in 1478. The task of this tribunal was to detect, try, and punish heresy, and its special target was the conversos, many of whom the tribunal suspected of secretly adhering to Judaism. Because of the Inquisition's activities, some two thousand conversos were burned at the stake; a hundred and twenty thousand fled abroad. As certain Castilian towns pointed out in memorials that protested the establishment of the Inquisition, the purge caused a great flight of conversos and their capital, which had a disastrous effect on the economy.

The Jews had a breathing space of twelve years during the costly War of Granada, for they were among the largest contributors to the royal finances. The surrender of Granada, however, sealed their fate. The conquest of a rich territory and an industrious Islamic population, which ended the drain of the war, meant that the Jews were no longer financially indispensable. After some hesitation, the Sovereigns yielded to anti-Semitic pressure and, on March 30, 1492, signed the edict giving the Jews the choice of conversion or expulsion.

The destruction or flight of many conversos and the expulsion of the Jews certainly contributed to the dreary picture presented by the kingdom's economy at the close of the sixteenth century. The purge of the conversos eliminated from Castilian life its most vital merchant and artisan elements, the groups that in England and Holland were preparing the ground for the Industrial Revolution. The flight of converso artisans dealt local industry a heavy blow and was directly responsible for royal edicts (1484) that invited foreign artisans to settle in Castile with an exemption from taxes for ten years.

The anti-Semitic policies of the Sovereigns also harmed science and thought in general. The Inquisition helped to blight the spirit of free inquiry and discussion in Castile at a time when the Renaissance was giving an extraordinary impulse to the play of European intellect in all fields. The Sovereigns, who laid the foundations of imperial greatness in so short a time, bear much of the responsibility for its premature decline. But the contradictions in their policies, the incorrect decisions that nullified much of the sound part of their work, resulted from more than personal errors of judgment; they reflected the structural weakness and backwardness of Castilian society as it emerged from seven centuries of struggle against the Muslim occupation.

The Hapsburg Era: Triumph and Tragedy

Isabella's death in 1504 placed all of the Iberian Peninsula except Portugal under the rule of Ferdinand. Isabella's will named her daughter Juana as successor, with the provision that Ferdinand should govern in case Juana proved unable to. Because Juana's growing mental instability made her unfit to govern, Ferdinand assumed the regency. Juana's husband, Philip the Handsome of Burgundy, supported by a number of Castilian nobles, challenged Ferdinand's right to rule Castile, but Philip's sudden death in 1506 left Ferdinand undisputed master of the kingdom. Ferdinand himself died in 1516. To the Castilian throne ascended his grandson Charles, eldest son of Juana and Philip. Through his maternal grandparents, Charles inherited Castile, Naples and Sicily, and the Castilian possessions in Africa and America. Through his paternal grandparents, Marie of Burgundy and the Holy Roman Emperor Maximilian, he also inherited the territories of the house of Burgundy, which included the rich Netherlands and the German possessions of the house of Hapsburg.

THE REIGN OF CHARLES

The Catholic Sovereigns, whatever their errors, had attempted to foster the kingdom's economic development and its partial unity; their prudent diplomacy set for itself limited goals. They had advanced toward absolute monarchy discreetly, respecting both the sensitivities of their peoples and those traditions that did not stand in the way of their designs.

A solemn youth with the characteristic jutting underjaw of the Hapsburgs, Charles (first of that name in Castile and fifth in the Holy Roman empire) had been born and reared in Flanders and spoke no Spanish. Reared at the court of Burgundy in a spirit of royal absolutism, he had a different notion of kingship. On his arrival in Castile, he immediately alienated his subjects by his haughty manner and by the greed of his Flemish courtiers, whom he placed in all key positions. He aroused even greater resentment by attempting to make the Castilians pay the bill for his election as Holy Roman emperor to succeed his grandfather Maximilian. Having achieved his ambition by expending immense sums of money, which placed him deeply in debt to the German banking house of Fugger, Charles hurried off to Germany.

For Castilians, the election appeared to mean an absentee king and heavier tax burdens. Popular wrath burst forth in the revolt of the Castilian towns, or communes, in 1520–1521. The Revolt of the *Comuneros* (commoners) was the first bourgeois revolution in Europe, but it began as an essentially conservative movement. The rebels demanded that Charles return to Castile and make his residence there, that the drain of money abroad end, and that he appoint no more foreigners to offices in the kingdom. Many nobles supported the rebellion at this stage, although the grandees remained neutral or hostile. But the leadership of the revolution soon fell into more radical hands. Simultaneously, a revolt of the artisans and middle classes arose in Valencia against the great landowners. Because of these developments, the Comunero movement lost almost all aristocratic support. In April 1521, the Comunero army suffered a total defeat, and the revolt began to fall apart. In July 1522, Charles returned to Castile with four thousand German troops at his side. The last effort of the Castilian people to turn back the political clock, to prevent the final success of the centralizing and absolutist policies initiated by the Catholic Sovereigns, had failed.

For a time, at least, the dazzling successes of Charles V in the New and Old Worlds reconciled Castilians to the new course. They rejoiced over the conquests of Cortés and Pizarro and the victories of their invincible infantry in Europe. They set to dreaming of El Dorados, universal empires, and a universal church. The poet Hernando de Acuña gives voice to the kingdom's exalted mood:

One Fold, one Shepherd only on the earth . . .
One Monarch, one Empire, and one Sword.

War dominated Charles's reign—war against France, against the Protestant princes of Germany, against the Turks, even against the pope, whose holdings in central Italy were threatened by his expansionist plans. Actually, only one of these wars vitally concerned the kingdom's interests: the struggle with the Turkish empire, whose growing naval power endangered Aragón's possessions in Italy and Sicily and even threatened the kingdom's coasts with attack. Yet Charles, absorbed in the Protestant problem and his rivalry with France, pursued this struggle against the infidels less consistently than the others; in the end, it declined into a mere holding operation.

The impressive victories of Castilian arms on land and sea had few tangible results; Charles, embroiled in too many quarters, was unable to take full advantage of his successes. In 1556, Charles renounced the throne in favor of his son, Philip. Charles had failed in all his major objectives. The Protestant heresy still flourished in the north. The Turks remained solidly entrenched in North Africa, and their piratical fleets prowled the Mediterranean. Charles's project of placing Philip on the imperial throne had broken on the opposition of German princes, Protestant and Catholic, and of Charles's own brother Ferdinand, who wished to make the title of Holy Roman emperor hereditary in his own line. Charles's other dream of bringing England into the empire by marrying Philip to Mary Tudor collapsed when Mary died in 1558.

Meanwhile, commoners in the growing empire groaned under a crushing burden of debts and taxes, with Castile bearing the main part of the load. German and Italian merchant-princes and bankers, to whom an ever-increasing part of the royal revenue was pledged for loans, took over important segments of the Castilian economy. The Fuggers assumed the administration of the estates of the military orders and the exploitation of the mercury mines of Almadén. Their rivals, the Welsers, took over the Galician mines and received the American province of Venezuela as a fief whose inhabitants they barbarously exploited. To find money for his fantastically expensive foreign enterprises, Charles resorted to extraordinary measures: He extracted ever-larger grants from the Cortes of Castile and Aragón; he multiplied royal taxes; and he appropriated remittances of American treasure to private individuals, compensating the victims with *juros* (bonds). When his son Philip came to the throne in 1556, the kingdom was bankrupt.

THE REIGN OF PHILIP II AND THE REMAINING HAPSBURGS

The reign of Philip (1556–1598) continued in all essential respects the policies of his father, with the same general results. Spain won brilliant military victories, which Philip failed to follow up from lack of funds or because some new crisis diverted his attention to another quarter. His hopes of dominating France by playing on the divisions between Huguenots and Catholics were frustrated when the Protestant Henry of Navarre entered the Catholic Church, a move that united France behind Henry and forced Philip to sign the Peace of Vervins with him. The war against the Turks produced the great sea victory of Lepanto (1571), which broke the Turkish naval power, but when Philip's reign ended, the Turks remained in control of most of North Africa. In the prosperous Netherlands, the richest jewel in his imperial crown, Philip's policies of religious repression and absolutism provoked a great revolt that continued throughout his reign and imposed a terrible drain on the Spanish treasury. War with England flowed from the accession of the Protestant Elizabeth to the throne, from her unofficial support to the Dutch rebels, and from the encroachments of English corsairs and smugglers in American waters.

The crushing defeat of the Invincible Armada in 1588 dealt a heavy blow to the empire's self-confidence and virtually sealed the doom of Philip's crusade against the heretical north. Philip succeeded in another enterprise, the annexation of the kingdom of Portugal (1580), which gave Spain considerably more naval strength and a long Atlantic seaboard to use in a struggle against the Protestant north. But Philip failed to exploit these strategic opportunities, and Portugal, whose colonies and ships now became fair game for Dutch and English seafarers, grew increasingly discontent with a union whose disadvantages exceeded its gains.

At his death in 1598, Philip II left an empire in which the forces of disintegration were at work but that was still powerful enough militarily and territorially to be feared and respected. Under his successors, Spain entered a rapid decline, the first signs of which became visible in the area of diplomacy and war. The truce of 1609 with the Dutch, which

tacitly recognized Dutch independence, was an early sign of waning Spanish power. The famous defeat of the infantry at the battle of Rocroi (1643) revealed the obsolescence of Spanish military organization and tactics, marking the end of the kingdom's military preponderance on the Continent. By the third quarter of the century, Spain, reduced to the defensive, had been compelled to sign a series of humiliating treaties by which it lost the Dutch Netherlands, part of Flanders, Luxembourg, and a string of lesser possessions.

The crisis existed at home as well as abroad. Efforts to make other Christian kingdoms bear part of the burdens of the wars in which Castile had been so long engaged caused resentment and resistance. The able but imprudent favorite of Philip IV, Count Olivares, aroused a storm with his efforts to billet troops in Catalonia and otherwise make Catalonia contribute to the Castilian war effort at the expense of the ancient fueros, or privileges, of the principality. In 1640, a formidable revolt broke out; it continued for twelve years and shattered the economy of Catalonia. In the same year, Portugal, weary of a union that brought more losses than gains, successfully revolted against Castilian rule. Lesser insurrections took place in Biscay, Andalusia, Sicily, and Naples.

THE WANING ECONOMY AND SOCIETY

A decline in the quality of Castile's rulers no doubt contributed to its political decline, but the crumbling economic foundations on which the empire rested virtually guaranteed it. By the 1590s, the Castilian economy had begun to crack under the strain of costly Hapsburg adventures in foreign policy. Philip II several times resorted to bankruptcy to evade payments of debts to foreign bankers. His successors, lacking Philip's resources, inflated the currency, which caused a flight of gold and silver abroad, until the national currency consisted largely of copper. But the development that contributed most to the kingdom's economic crisis was a drastic decline in the inflow of American treasure in the middle decades of the seventeenth century. In the decade from 1591 to 1600, revenues from the American colonies totaled about 135 million *pesos*

(Spanish colonial unit of currency), but half a century later, they declined to 19 million pesos in the decade from 1651 to 1660 (the complex causes of this decline are discussed in Chapter 4).

By 1621, signs of economic decline were everywhere. Sevilla had only four hundred looms producing silk and wool, down from sixteen thousand a century earlier. Toledo had fifty woolen manufacturing establishments in the sixteenth century; it had only thirteen by 1665. The plight of agriculture showed itself in a chronic shortage of foodstuffs, sometimes approaching famine conditions, and in the exodus of peasants from the countryside. Castile became a land of deserted villages. In the period from 1600 to 1700, it also suffered an absolute loss of population, from about 8 million to 6 million. The ravages of epidemics, aggravated by near-famine conditions; the expulsion of the **Moriscos** (converted Muslims) between 1609 and 1614; and emigration to the Indies all contributed to this heavy loss.

The economic decline caused a contraction of the kingdom's artisan and merchant class, strengthened the domination of aristocratic values, and fostered the growth of parasitism. In the seventeenth century, ambitious young people looked above all to the church and the court for an assured living. In 1626, Castile had nine thousand monasteries; at the end of the century, about two hundred thousand monks and priests existed in a population of 6 million. The nobility formed another large unproductive class. At the end of the century, according to one calculation, Spain had four times as many nobles as France with its much larger population. A small number of grandees—counts, dukes, and marquis—who possessed enormous wealth and immense prerogatives occupied the highest rung of the ladder of nobility. Peasants, artisans, burghers, and a great number of hidalgos—petty nobles whose sole capital often was their honor and the precious letters patent (royal public proclamations) that attested to their rank and their superiority over base **pecheros** (taxpayers)—occupied the lowest. The noble contempt for labor infected all classes. The number of vagabonds steadily grew; meanwhile, agriculture lacked enough laborers to till the land.

LITERARY AND ARTISTIC DEVELOPMENTS

Spreading into all areas of life, the **decadencia** (decadence) inspired moods of pessimism, fatalism, and cynicism. Spanish society presented extreme contrasts: great wealth and abject poverty, displays of fanatical piety and scandalous manners, and desperate efforts to revive the imperial glories of a past age by kings who sometimes lacked the cash to pay their servants and supply the royal table. The paradoxes of Spanish life, the contrast between the ideal and the real, stimulated the literary imagination. In this time, so sterile in other respects, Spain enjoyed a Golden Age of letters. As early as 1554, the unknown author of *Lazarillo de Tormes*, first of the picaresque novels, captured the seamy reality of a world teeming with rogues and vagabonds. Its hero relates his adventures under a succession of masters—a blind beggar, a stingy priest, a hungry hidalgo; he finally attains his highest hope, a sinecure as a town crier, secured for him by a priest whose mistress he had married.

The picaresque genre reached its climax in the *Guzmán de Alfarache* of Mateo de Alemán (1599), with its note of somber pessimism: "All steal, all lie.... You will not find a soul who is man unto man." The cleavage in the Castilian soul, the conflict between the ideal and the real, acquired a universal meaning and symbolism in the *Don Quijote* (1605) of Miguel Cervantes de Saavedra. The corrosive satires of Francisco Quevedo (1580–1645) gave voice to the despair of many seventeenth-century intellectuals. "There are many things here," wrote Quevedo, "that seem to exist and have their being, and yet they are nothing more than a name and an appearance."

By contrast, dramas of the Golden Age only faintly reflected the national crisis. The plays of Lope de Vega (1562–1645) were rich in invention, sparkling dialogue, and melodious verse; his gallant hidalgos, courageous and clever heroines, and dignified peasants evoked the best traditions of Castile's past with a curious disregard for the dismal present. The defeatism of late-seventeenth-century Castile, however, was reflected in the dramas of Calderón de la Barca (1600–1681), who stressed tragedy and the illusory nature of reality: "*La vida es sueño, y los sueños sueño son*" ("Life is a dream, and our dreams are part of a dream").

Alinari/Art Resource, New York

Diego Velázquez's portrait *Las Meniñas* (*The Maids of Honor*) is a culminating work of the Spanish seventeenth-century school of painting. Note the utter detachment with which Velázquez treats the members of the Royal Family, the ladies-in-waiting, and the dwarf, making no effort to enhance the dignity or beauty of one at the expense of the other.

Painting during the Golden Age, like its literature, mirrored the transition from the confident and exalted mood of the early sixteenth century to the disillusioned spirit of the late seventeenth century. The great age of painting began with El Greco (1541–1616), whose work blends naturalism, deliberate distortion, and intense emotion to convey the somber religious passion of Castile during the age of Philip II. Yet some of El Greco's portraits reflected a magnificent realism. The mysticism of El Greco was completely absent from the canvases of Diego Velázquez (1599–1660). With a sovereign mastery of light, coloring, and movement, Velázquez captured for all time the palace life of two Spanish kings, presenting with the same detachment the princes and princesses and the dwarfs and buffoons of the court.

As we shall see in Chapter 5, the seventeenth-century *decadencia* profoundly influenced the relations between Castile and its American colonies. The loosening of economic and political ties

between the mother country and the colonies, along with growing colonial self-sufficiency and self-consciousness, produced a shift in the balance of forces in favor of the colonists—a change that the empire's best efforts could not reverse.

The death of the wretched Charles II in 1700 brought the Hapsburg Era to its end. Even before that symbolic death, signs appeared of a Spanish demographic and economic revival, notably in Catalonia, which by the 1670s had made a strong recovery from the depths of the great depression. Nonetheless, a new foreign dynasty, the French-descended House of Bourbon, with the support of the kingdom's progressive elements, was about to begin a remarkable, many-sided effort at imperial reconstruction.

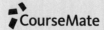 CourseMate   Go to the CourseMate website at www.cengagebrain.com for primary sources, additional study tools, and review materials—including audio and video clips—for this chapter.

The Conquest of America

3

FOCUS QUESTIONS

- What were the conditions in Europe that led to the conquest of America?
- What effects did the conquest have on the native peoples of America and the Europeans?
- What were the motives, mind-sets, and social backgrounds of the Spanish conquistadors?
- What factors explain the relative ease with which a small number of Spaniards conquered great and populous indigenous empires?
- What is the "Vision of the Vanquished," and how does this compare with conventional interpretations of the "encounter" between Europe and indigenous America?

A EUROPEAN CONTACT WITH AMERICA resulted from efforts to find a sea road to the East that would break the monopoly of Egypt and Venice over the lucrative trade in spices and other Asian products. The drain of their scanty stock of gold and silver into the pockets of Italian and Levantine intermediaries had grown increasingly intolerable to the merchants and monarchs of western Europe. Portugal took a decisive lead in the race to find a waterway to the land of spices. It had important advantages over its rivals: a long Atlantic seaboard with excellent harbors, a large class of fishermen and sailors, and an aristocracy that already had discovered it could supplement the meager revenue from land with income from trade and shipbuilding. Earlier than any other European country, Portugal became a unified nation-state under an able dynasty, the house of Avis, which formed a firm alliance with the merchant class and took a personal interest in the expansion of commerce. This alliance gave Portugal a head start in the work of discovery. The Portuguese victory of Aljubarrota (1385), gained with English support, ended for a time Castile's efforts to absorb its smaller neighbor and released Portuguese energies for an ambitious program of overseas expansion.

The Great Voyages

EXPLORATION UNDER PRINCE HENRY

The famous Prince Henry (1394–1460) initiated the era of Portuguese exploration and conquest. Henry, somewhat misleadingly known as "the Navigator" because he never sailed beyond sight of land, united a medieval crusading spirit with the more modern desire to penetrate the secrets of unknown lands and seas and reap the profits of expanded trade. In 1415 Henry participated in the capture of the Moroccan seaport of Ceuta, a great Muslim trading center from which caravans crossed the desert to Timbuktu, returning with ivory and gold obtained by barter from the blacks of the Niger basin. Possession of the African beachhead of Ceuta opened up large prospects for the Portuguese. By penetrating to the sources of Ceuta gold, they could relieve a serious Portuguese shortage of the precious metal; Henry also hoped to reach the land of the fabled Christian ruler Prester John, the legendary emperor of Abyssinia, although no one knew how far his empire extended. An alliance with this ruler, he believed, would encircle the Muslims in North Africa with a powerful league of Christian states.

1394–1460	Prince Henry initiates the era of Portuguese exploration and conquest
1402	Kingdom of Castile conquers and colonizes the Canary Islands
1415	Portuguese capture the Muslim trading center at Ceuta on the northern coast of Africa
1425	Portuguese colonize Madeira Islands off the coast of Africa
1481	Portuguese King João establishes trading center at Elmina that specializes in slaves, ivory, gold, and black pepper
1492	Christopher Columbus sails westward en route to India and instead lands in the Americas, initiating successive conquests of Hispaniola, Jamaica, Puerto Rico, and Cuba
1497	Portuguese under the command of Vasco da Gama circumnavigate the Cape of Good Hope and establish a commercial presence in East Africa
1500	Pedro Cabral accidentally lands on the coast of Brazil and claims its lands for the Portuguese crown
1519	Hernán Cortés lands at Veracruz en route to the conquest of the Aztec empire at Tenochtitlán
1533	Francisco Pizarro takes advantage of a civil war between Inca kings, Atahualpa and Huáscar, to defeat the Inca empire at Cusco
1533–1572	Inca king Manco leads indigenous resistance to Spanish conquest and occupation of Inca lands
1542	Proclamation of New Laws of the Indies to reduce conquistador power, increase the authority of the monarchy, and abolish indigenous slavery leads to open rebellion led by Gonzalo Pizarro

Efforts to expand the Moroccan beachhead, however, made little progress. If the Portuguese could not penetrate the Muslim barrier that separated them from the southern sources of gold and the kingdom of Prester John, could they not reach these goals by sea? In 1419, Henry set up a headquarters at Sagres on Cape St. Vincent, the rocky tip of southwest Portugal. Here he assembled a group of expert seamen and scientists. At the nearby port of Lagos, he began the construction of stronger and larger ships, equipped with the compass and the improved astrolabe. Beginning in 1420, he dispatched several ships to explore the western coast of Africa. Each captain was required to enter in his log data concerning currents, winds, and calms and to sketch the coastline. An eminent converso mapmaker, Jehuda Crespes, used these data to produce more detailed and accurate charts.

The first decade of exploration resulted in the discovery of the Madeiras and the Azores, but progress southward was slow; the imaginary barriers of a flaming torrid zone and a green sea of darkness made sailors excessively cautious. Passage in 1434 around Cape Bojador, the first major landmark on the West African coast, proved these fears groundless. Before Henry's death in 1460, the Portuguese had pushed as far as the Gulf of Guinea, and they had begun a lucrative trade in gold dust and slaves captured in raids or bought from coastal chiefs. Henry's death slowed the progress of exploration, but the advance down the African coast continued, under private auspices and as an adjunct to the slave trade, the first bitter fruit of European overseas expansion. In 1469 a wealthy merchant, Fernão Gomes, secured a monopoly of the trade to Guinea (the name then given to the whole African coast), on the condition that he explore farther south at the rate of one hundred miles a year. Complying with his pledge, Gomes sent his ships eastward along the Gold, Ivory, and Slave Coasts and then southward almost to the mouth of the Congo.

THE SEA ROUTE TO THE EAST

Under the energetic John II, who came to the throne in 1481, the crown resumed control and direction of the African enterprise. At Elmina, on the Gold Coast, John established a fort that became a center of trade in slaves, ivory, gold dust, and a coarse black pepper, as well as a base for further exploration. Henry had dreamed of finding gold and Prester John, but King John was more concerned with the project of reaching India by rounding Africa. In 1483 an expedition commanded by Diogo Cão discovered the mouth of the Congo River and sailed partway up the mighty stream. On a second voyage in 1484, Cão pushed as far south as Cape Cross in southwest Africa. The Portuguese monarch sensed that victory was near. In 1487 a fleet headed by Bartholomeu Dias left Lisbon with orders to pass the farthest point reached by Cão and, if possible, to sail around the tip of Africa. After he had cruised farther south than any captain before him, a providential gale blew Dias's ships in a wide sweep around the Cape of Good Hope and to landfall on the coast of East Africa. He had solved the problem of a sea road to the Indies and returned to Lisbon to report his success to King John.

The route to the East lay open, but domestic and foreign problems distracted John's attention from the Indian enterprise. He died in 1495 without having sent the expedition for which he had made elaborate preparations, but his successor, Manuel I, known as the Fortunate, carried out John's plan. In 1497, a fleet of four ships, commanded by the tough, surly nobleman Vasco da Gama, sailed from Lisbon on a voyage that inaugurated the age of European colonialism in Asia. After rounding the Cape, da Gama sailed into the Indian Ocean and up the coast of East Africa. At Malinda, in modern Kenya, he hired an Arab pilot, who guided the fleet to Calicut, the great spice trade center on the west coast of India. Received with hostility by the dominant Arab traders and with indifference by the local Indian potentate, who scorned his petty gifts, the persistent da Gama managed to load his holds with a cargo of pepper and cinnamon and returned to Lisbon in 1499 with two of the four ships with which he had begun his voyage. A new fleet, commanded by Pedro Álvares Cabral, was quickly outfitted and sent to India. Swinging far west in the south Atlantic, Cabral made landfall on the coast of Brazil in early 1500 and sent one ship back to Lisbon to report his discovery before continuing to India. He returned to Portugal with a cargo of spices and tales of scuffles with Arab merchants, who were determined to resist the Portuguese intruders.

The great soldier and administrator Afonso de Albuquerque, who set out in 1509, completed the work begun by da Gama. He knew the only way to squeeze out the Egyptian and Venetian competition and gain a total monopoly of the spice trade was by conquering key points on the trade routes of the Indian Ocean. Capture of Malacca on the Malay Peninsula gave the Portuguese control of the strait through which East Indian spices entered the Indian Ocean. Capture of Muscat and Ormuz barred entrance to the Persian Gulf and closed that route to Europe to other nations' ships. Although the Portuguese strategy was not completely successful, it diverted to Lisbon the greater part of the spice supply.

For a time, Portugal basked in the sun of an unprecedented prosperity. But the strain of maintaining its vast Eastern defense establishment was too great for Portugal's limited manpower and financial resources, and expenses began to outrun revenues. To make matters worse, because of Spanish pressure, King Manuel decreed the expulsion of all unbaptized Jews in 1496. Thus, Portugal lost the only native group that was financially capable of exploiting the investment opportunities offered by the Portuguese triumph in the East. Florentine and German bankers quickly moved in and diverted most of the profits of the Eastern spice trade abroad. Lisbon was soon only a depot, and cargoes that arrived there from the East were shipped almost immediately to Antwerp or Amsterdam, which were better situated as centers of distribution to European customers. In time, Dutch and English rivals snatched most of the Asiatic colonies from Portugal's failing hands.

THE ADVANCE INTO THE ATLANTIC

Certain groups of islands in the eastern Atlantic—the Canaries, Madeiras, Azores, and Cape Verdes—attracted the early attention of Portugal and Spain. These islands played a strategic role in the colonization of America, providing steppingstones and staging areas for the Atlantic crossing. Moreover, their conquest and colonial economic organization set the pattern for Iberian policies in the New World.

The Madeira island group, colonized in 1425, became the most important Portuguese colony in the eastern Atlantic. Madeira's soil and climate were suitable for growing sugar, the most lucrative cash crop of the time, and, with Genoese financial and technical aid, sugar production spread in Madeira, using slaves from the Canary Islands and later Africa. By 1460, Madeira had its first sugar mill, and by 1478 it was the largest sugar producer in the Western world. The Portuguese applied the same successful formula—the combination of sugar and African slave labor—in their colonization of Brazil.

Europeans had known the Canaries since the early fourteenth century, but their definitive conquest by Castile began in 1402. The islanders, **Guanches** (a herding and farming people organized in mutually hostile tribes), resisted fiercely, and the conquest was not complete until about 1497. Less than two centuries after the conquest of the Canaries began, the Guanches, who once numbered between 50,000 and 100,000, were extinct, chiefly because of mistreatment and disease. The conquest of the Canaries foretold similar developments in the Caribbean.

Like the Madeiras, the Canaries became a laboratory for testing political and economic institutions that the Spanish later transferred to the Americas. Although the lordship of the islands was vested in the crown, the monarchs made *capitulaciones* (agreements) with individual *adelantados* (captains) who were authorized to conquer specific regions and granted large governing powers and other privileges. These agreements resembled the contracts made with military leaders during the Reconquest and with Columbus, Francisco Pizarro, and other great captains during the conquest of America.

Like the Madeiras, the Canaries also became a testing ground for a plantation system based on sugar and slave labor. By the early sixteenth century, twenty-nine sugar mills were in operation. The character of the Canaries as a way station

between Europe and America for sugar production is borne out by the transfer from the Canaries to the Caribbean of sugar-processing techniques and the method of using cuttings to plant sugar cane.

THE VOYAGES OF COLUMBUS

The search for a sea road to the Indies inspired more than one solution. If some believed that the route around Africa offered the answer to the Eastern riddle, others favored sailing due west across the Atlantic. This view had the support of an eminent authority, the Florentine scientist Paolo Toscanelli, who in 1474 advised the Portuguese to try the western route as "shorter than the one which you are pursuing by way of Guinea." His letter came to the attention of an obscure Italian seafarer, Christopher Columbus, who had been reflecting on the problem, and it confirmed his belief that such a passage from Europe to Cipangu (Japan) and Cathay (China) would be easy. This conception rested on a gross underestimate of the Earth's circumference and an equal overestimate of the size and eastward extension of Asia. Because all educated Europeans believed the world was round, that question never entered into the dispute between Columbus and his opponents. The main issue was the extent of the ocean between Europe and Asia, and on this point, the opposition was right.

For Columbus the idea of reaching the East by sailing west acquired all the force of an obsession. A figure of transition from the dying Middle Ages to the world of capitalism and science, a curious combination of mystic and practical man, Columbus believed that God Himself had revealed to him "that it was feasible to sail from here to the Indies, and placed in me a burning desire to carry out this plan."

About 1484, Columbus, who then resided in Lisbon, offered to make a western voyage of discovery for John II, but a committee of experts who listened to his proposal advised the king to turn it down. Undismayed by his rebuff, Columbus next turned to Castile. After eight years of discouraging delays and negotiation, Isabella—in a last-minute change of mind—agreed to support the "Enterprise of the Indies." The capitulación (contract) made by the queen with Columbus named him admiral, viceroy, and governor of the lands he should discover and promised him a generous share in the profits of the venture.

On August 3, 1492, Columbus sailed from Palos with three small ships, the *Pinta*, the *Santa María*, and the *Niña*, manned not by the jailbirds of legend but by experienced crews under competent officers. The voyage was remarkably prosperous, with fair winds the whole way out, but the great distance beyond sight of land began to worry some of the crew. By the end of September, the crew of the *Santa María*, Columbus's flagship, became disgruntled. According to Columbus's son Ferdinand, some sailors proposed to heave the admiral overboard and return to Spain with the report that he had fallen in while watching the stars. Columbus managed to calm his crew, and soon floating gulfweed and bosun birds gave signs of land. On October 12, they made landfall at an island in the Bahamas that Columbus named San Salvador.

Cruising southward through the Bahamas, Columbus came to the northeast coast of Cuba, which he took for part of Cathay. An embassy sent to find the Great Khan failed in its mission but returned with reports of a hospitable reception by natives who introduced the Spaniards to the use of "certain herbs the smoke of which they inhale," an early reference to tobacco. Columbus next sailed eastward to explore the northern coast of an island (present-day Dominican Republic and Haiti), which he named Española (Hispaniola). Here the discovery of some alluvial gold and gold ornaments, which the natives bartered for Spanish trinkets, cheered the Spaniards.

From Hispaniola, on whose coast Columbus lost his flagship, he returned to Spain to report his supposed discovery of the Indies. The Sovereigns received him with signal honors and ordered him immediately to prepare a second expedition to follow up his discovery. In response to Portuguese charges of encroachment on an area in the Atlantic reserved to Portugal by a previous treaty with Cas-

tile, Ferdinand and Isabella appealed for help to Pope Alexander VI, himself a Spaniard. The pontiff complied by issuing a series of bulls in 1493 that assigned to Castile all lands discovered or to be discovered by Columbus and drew a line from north to south a hundred leagues west of the Azores and Cape Verdes; the area west of this line was to be a Spanish sphere of exploration. To John II, this demarcation line seemed to threaten Portuguese interests in the south Atlantic and the promising route around Africa to the East. Yielding to Portuguese pressure, Ferdinand and Isabella signed in 1494 the Treaty of Tordesillas, which established a boundary 270 leagues farther west. Portugal obtained exclusive rights of discovery and conquest east of this line; Castile gained the same rights to the west.

Columbus returned to Hispaniola at the end of 1493 with a fleet of seventeen ships carrying twelve hundred people, most of them artisans and peasants, with a sprinkling of "caballeros, hidalgos, and other men of worth, drawn by the fame of gold and the other wonders of that land." The settlers soon gave themselves up to gold hunting and preying on indigenous peoples. A foreigner of obscure origins, Columbus lacked the powers and personal qualities needed to control this turbulent mass of fortune hunters.

After founding the town of Isabella on the north coast of Hispaniola, Columbus sailed again in quest of Cathay. He coasted down the southern shore of Cuba almost to its western end. The great length of the island convinced him that he had reached the Asiatic mainland. To extinguish all doubts, he made his officers and crews take a solemn oath, "on pain of a hundred lashes and having the tongue slit if they ever gainsaid the same," that Cuba was the mainland of Asia. In 1496, he returned to Spain to report his discoveries and answer charges sent by disgruntled settlers to the court. He left behind his brother Bartholomew, who removed the settlement from Isabella to a healthier site on the south shore and named the new town Santo Domingo.

The first two voyages had not paid their way, but the Sovereigns still had faith in Columbus and outfitted a third fleet in 1498. On this voyage, he landed at Trinidad and the mouths of the Orinoco. The mighty current of sweet water discharged by the great river made Columbus conclude that he was on the shores of a continent, but his crotchety mysticism also suggested that the Orinoco was one of the four rivers of Paradise and had its source in the Garden of Eden.

Columbus arrived in Hispaniola to find chaos. The intolerable demands of the greedy Castilian adventurers had provoked the peaceable Taino natives to the point of war. The Spaniards, disappointed in their hopes of quick wealth, blamed the Columbus brothers for their misfortunes and rose in revolt under a leader named Roldán. To appease the rebels, Columbus issued pardons, granted land, and distributed native slaves. Meanwhile, acting on a stream of complaints against Columbus, the Sovereigns had sent out an agent, Francisco de Bobadilla, to supersede Columbus and investigate the charges against him. Arriving at the island, the irascible Bobadilla seized Columbus and his brother and sent them to Spain in chains. Although Isabella immediately disavowed Bobadilla's arbitrary actions, Columbus never again exercised the functions of viceroy and governor in the New World.

Still gripped by his great illusion, Columbus continued to dream of finding a western way to the land of spices. He made one more voyage, the most difficult and disastrous of all. He was now convinced that between the mainland on which he recently had landed and the Malay Peninsula shown on ancient maps, a strait existed that would lead into the Indian Ocean. In 1502, he sailed in search of this strait and a route to southern Asia. From Hispaniola, where Spanish authorities refused him permission to land, he crossed the Caribbean to the coast of Central America and followed it south to the Isthmus of Panama. At this point, he believed he was ten days' journey from the Ganges River. In Panama, he found some gold, but the hoped-for strait continued to elude him. He finally departed for Hispaniola with his two remaining ships but was forced to beach the worm-riddled craft on Jamaica, where he and his men were marooned for a year awaiting the arrival of a relief ship. In November

1504, Columbus returned to Europe. Broken in health, convinced of the ingratitude of princes, he died in 1506 a rich but embittered man.

THE DISCOVERY OF AMERICA IN HISTORICAL PERSPECTIVE

The five-hundredth anniversary of Columbus's 1492 voyage to America produced an outpouring of writings seeking to throw new light on that momentous event. Debate still rages over the prodigious consequences of Columbus's legacy and how we should remember it. The Spanish chronicler Francisco López de Gómara, filled with imperialist pride, had no doubts on that score. In 1552 he wrote, "The greatest event since the creation of the world (excluding the incarnation of Him who created it) is the discovery of the Indies." But the radical Italian philosopher Giordano Bruno, who was burned for heresy in 1600, strongly dissented, assailing Columbus as one of those "audacious navigators" who only "disturbed the peace of others ... increased the vices of nations, spread fresh follies by violence, and ... taught men a new art and means of tyranny and assassination among themselves."

Until recently, however, few Europeans and Americans questioned the splendor and value of Columbus's achievement. In the nineteenth century, they viewed his voyages as a harbinger and cause of the great movement of Western economic expansion and global domination that was then under way. Celebrations of Columbus were especially exuberant in the United States, where a mystical link appeared between that event and the spectacular rise of the great republic of the West. In this period, Columbus became an almost mythic hero, a larger-than-life figure who overcame all the obstacles placed in his path by prejudiced and ignorant adversaries to complete his providential task.

Until well into the twentieth century, this view of the "Discovery" as an event that should inspire unalloyed pride and satisfaction was rarely challenged. Only the immense political and economic changes caused by World War II and the anticolonial revolutions unleashed by the conflict led to a new way of looking at the "Discovery" and its repercussions. That new frame of reference, commonly known as "The Vision of the Vanquished," takes as its point of departure the impact of Columbus's voyages not on Europe but rather on the peoples and cultures of the Americas. Awareness of the ethnocentric, Eurocentric connotations of the term *discovery* has even led many scholars to replace it with the more neutral term *encounter* (**encuentro** in Spanish). America, after all, was not an empty continent when the first Europeans arrived; its true "discoverers" were the people who had crossed over from Asia by way of the Bering Strait many thousands of years before. But the word *encounter,* with its suggestion of a peaceful meeting of peoples and cultures, hardly fits the grim reality of the European invasion of indigenous America, so we shall continue to use *discovery*, for lack of a better word.

"The Vision of the Vanquished" initiated a more balanced assessment of the discovery of America and its consequences. For the native peoples of America, the Discovery and its sequel, the Conquest, were an unmitigated disaster. The combination of new diseases to which they had no acquired immunity, their brutal exploitation, and the resulting social disorganization and loss of will to live led to perhaps the greatest demographic catastrophe in recorded history, with an estimated loss of between 90 and 95 percent of the native population between 1492 and 1575.

The Discovery and the Conquest also cut short the independent development of brilliant civilizations like the Aztec and Inca empires, which, many scholars believe, had not exhausted their possibilities for further cultural advance and flowering. Finally, the Discovery initiated a process of ecological devastation in the New World through the introduction of European animals, plants, and agricultural practices that transformed long-stable ecosystems. Columbus began the process on Hispaniola by introducing the extensive Spanish system of farming with plows and cattle ranching, producing rapid soil erosion and deforestation. The process begun by Columbus continues to this day, as evidenced by the rapid destruction of Latin America's

rain forests. This, too, is part of the "Columbian legacy."

The impact of the Discovery on Europe and its long-term development was much more positive. That impact, as noted long ago by Adam Smith and Karl Marx, is clearest in the realm of economics. Historians may debate the impact of American precious metals on Europe's sixteenth-century "price revolution" or the contribution of the slave trade to the "primitive accumulation" of capital in Europe. It is beyond dispute, however, that the combination of these and other events flowing from the discovery of America gave an immense stimulus to Europe's economic modernization and the rise of *capitalism*, which in turn hastened and facilitated its domination of the rest of the globe.

The intellectual impact of the Discovery on Europe is more difficult to measure, but it seems indisputable that the expansion of geographic horizons produced by the discovery of America spurred an expansion of mental horizons and the rise of new ways of viewing the world that significantly contributed to intellectual progress. One of the first casualties of the great geographic discoveries was the authority of the ancients and even of the church fathers. Thus, the Spanish friar Bartolomé de Las Casas (1484–1566), writing on the traditional belief in uninhabitable zones, managed in one paragraph to demolish the authority of Saint Augustine and the ancients, who, "after all, did not know very much."

The discovery of America and its peoples also produced disputes about their origins and nature that led to the founding of anthropology. The desire to prove the essential humanity and equality of these indigenous Americans inspired some sixteenth-century Spanish missionaries to make profound investigations of their culture. One of the greatest of these friar-anthropologists was, again, Bartolomé de Las Casas, one of whose works is an immense accumulation of ethnographic data used to demonstrate that indigenous Americans fully met the requirements laid down by Aristotle for the good life. Las Casas, resting his case above all on experience and observation, offered an environmentalist explanation of cultural differences and regarded with scientific detachment such deviations from European standards as human sacrifices and ritual cannibalism.

Reflections on the apparent novelty and strangeness of some indigenous ways, and the efforts of friar-anthropologists to understand and explain those ways, also led to the development of a cultural relativism that, like the rejection of authority, represented a sharp break with the past. Las Casas, for example, subjected the term *barbarian* to a careful semantic analysis that robbed it, as applied to advanced cultures like the Aztec or the Inca, of most of its sting. Michel de Montaigne, who avidly read accounts of indigenous American customs, observes in his famous essay on native Brazilians, "Of Cannibals," "I think there is nothing barbarous and savage in this nation, from what I have been told, except that each man calls barbarian whatever is not his own practice."

The discovery of America and its peoples also inspired Europeans who were troubled by the social injustices of Renaissance Europe to propose radical new schemes of political and economic organization. In 1516, for example, Thomas More published *Utopia*, which portrayed a pagan, socialist society whose institutions were governed by justice and reason, so unlike the states of contemporary Europe, which More described as a "conspiracy of the rich" against the poor. More's narrator, who tells about the Utopians and their institutions, claims to be a sailor who made three voyages with Amerigo Vespucci. The principal source of More's ideas about the evils of private property and the benefits of popular government appears to be a key passage about indigenous customs and beliefs in Vespucci's *Second Letter*:

Having no laws and no religious doctrine, they live according to nature. They understand nothing of the immortality of the soul. There is no possession of private property among them, for everything is in common. They have no king, nor do they obey anyone. Each is his own master. There is no administration of justice, which is unnecessary to them.

But if the Discovery had a beneficial impact on European intellectual life, reflected in the new rejection of authority, the growth of cultural relativism, and the impulse it gave to unorthodox social and political thought, it also reinforced the negative European attitudes of racism and ethnocentrism. The great Flemish mapmaker Abraham Ortelius gave clear expression to these attitudes in his 1579 world atlas. To the map of Europe, Ortelius attached a note proclaiming Europe's historic mission of world conquest, in process of fulfillment by Spain and Portugal, "who between them dominate the four parts of the globe." Ortelius declared that Europeans had always surpassed all other peoples in intelligence and physical dexterity, thus qualifying them to govern the other parts of the globe.

Other Europeans disagreed. Bartolomé de Las Casas proclaimed that "all mankind is one," and Michel de Montaigne furiously denounced European savagery, proposing that a "brotherly fellowship and understanding" was the proper relationship between Europeans and the peoples of the New World. However, these views were not typical of contemporary European thinking on the subject. Colonial rivals might condemn Spanish behavior toward indigenous Americans, but they usually agreed in regarding them as tainted with vices and as "poor barbarians."

The perspective of "The Vision of the Vanquished" and new approaches in historical research combine to give us a better understanding of the man Columbus and his dealings with the people he wrongly called "Indians." A curious blend of medieval mystic and modern entrepreneur, Columbus revealed the contradictions in his thought by his comment on gold: "O, most excellent gold! Who has gold has a treasure with which he gets what he wants, imposes his will on the world, and even helps souls to paradise." In *Conquest of America*, Tzvetan Todorov subjects the ideology of Columbus (which represented the ideology of the European invaders) to a careful and subtle dissection that reveals other contradictions. Sometimes Columbus viewed the "Indians" as "noble savages," and sometimes, depending on the occasion, he saw them as "filthy dogs." Todorov explains that both myths

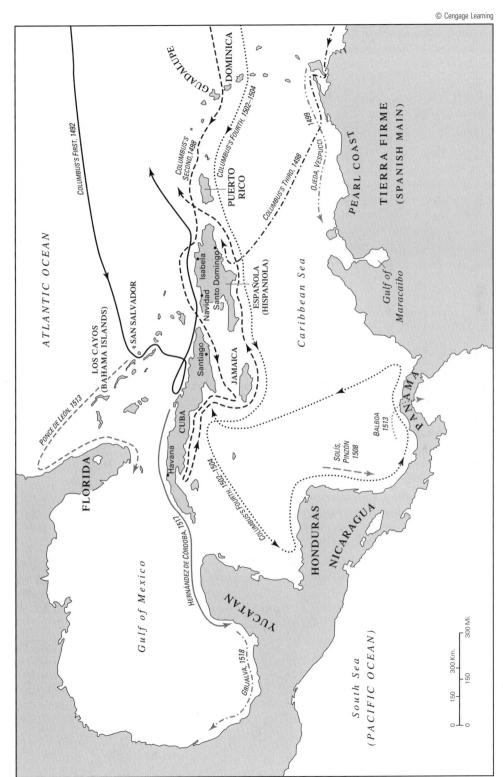

Early Spanish Voyages in the Caribbean

rest on a common base: scorn for "Indians" and refusal to admit them as human beings with the same rights as himself. In the last analysis, Columbus regarded indigenous peoples as objects, not human beings, which he clearly revealed in a September 1498 letter to the Spanish monarchs:

> We can send from here in the name of the Holy Trinity, all the slaves and brazilwood that can be sold. If my information is correct, one could sell 4,000 slaves that would bring at least twenty millions.... And I believe that my information is correct, for in Castile and Aragon and Italy and Sicily and the islands of Portugal and Aragon and the Canary Islands they use up many slaves, and the number of slaves coming from Guinea is diminishing.... And although the Indian slaves tend to die off now, this will not always be the case, for the same thing used to happen with the slaves from Africa and the Canary Islands.

In fact, Columbus early on conceived the idea of supplementing the search for a western route to the Indies and for gold with the enslavement of indigenous Americans and their sale in Castile. To make the idea more palatable to the Spanish monarchs, he proposed to limit the slave hunting to a supposed "cannibal" people: the Caribs. When the Tainos of Hispaniola rose in revolt against their intolerable treatment, it provided another legal justification for their enslavement. Between 1494 and 1500, Columbus sent some two thousand "Indians" to the slave markets of Castile. Contrary to legend, Queen Isabella approved the majority of these shipments.

Columbus, of course, viewed this slavery from the background of a merchant adventurer who was familiar with the conduct of Portugal's African slave trade, in which other Genoese merchants were deeply involved. He lived at a time when slavery, under certain conditions, was almost universally regarded as licit and proper. His callous lack of con-

cern for the life and death of the enslaved did not make him a monster. If he ardently desired gold, it was not from vulgar greed alone. To be sure, as the Spanish scholar Juan Gil observes, he was "fascinated by the tinkle of maravedis."[1] He bargained hard with the Spanish monarchs for the highest possible share of profits from his discoveries, and despite his lamentation in his last years about his poverty and even the lack of a roof over his head, he died a millionaire. But Columbus had another side. He viewed gold as a means to promote the universal triumph of Christianity, urged his royal masters to use the revenues from the Indies for a crusade to wrest the Holy Land from Muslim hands, and offered himself to head the crusader host. Within Columbus raged a constant struggle between the medieval mystic who believed the world would end in 155 years and the Renaissance man filled with a drive to achieve power, titles, wealth, and fame.

To assess the significance of Columbus's achievement properly, one must accept that he was the instrument of historic forces of which he was unaware, forces of transition from the dying Middle Ages to the rising world of capitalism, whose success rested on conquest and the creation of a global market. That process in turn required an ideological justification, a proud conviction of the superiority of white Europeans over all other peoples and races. Columbus's work in the Caribbean represents the first tragic application of that ideology in the New World. If not the father of colonialism, he was at least one of its fathers, and he bears part of the responsibility for the devastating effects of that system of domination.

BALBOA AND MAGELLAN

Others followed in the wake of Columbus's ships and gradually made known the immense extent of the mainland coast of South America. In 1499, Alonso de Ojeda, accompanied by the pilot Juan de la Cosa and the Florentine Amerigo Vespucci,

1. A Spanish coin.

sailed to the mouths of the Orinoco and explored the coast of Venezuela. Vespucci took part in another voyage in 1501–1502 under the flag of Portugal. This expedition, sent to follow up the discovery of Brazil by Pedro Álvares Cabral in 1500, explored the Brazilian coast from Salvador da Bahia to Rio de Janeiro before turning back. Vespucci's letters to his patrons, Giovanni and Lorenzo de' Medici, reveal an urbane, cultivated Renaissance figure with a flair for lively and realistic description of the fauna, flora, and inhabitants of the New World. Published and circulated widely in the early 1500s, his letters told of a nonexistent voyage in 1497 and gave him the fame of being the first European to set foot on the South American continent. A German geographer, Martin Waldseemuller, decided to honor Vespucci by assigning the name "America" to the area of Brazil in a map of the newly discovered lands. The name caught on and soon was applied to the whole of the New World.

A growing shortage of indigenous labor and the general lack of economic opportunities for new settlers on Hispaniola incited Spanish slave hunters and adventurers to conquer the remaining Greater Antilles. Puerto Rico, Jamaica, and Cuba were occupied between 1509 and 1511. In the same period, efforts to found colonies on the coast of northern Colombia and Panama failed disastrously, and the remnants of two expeditions were united under the energetic leadership of the conquistador Vasco Núñez de Balboa to form the new settlement of Darien on the Isthmus of Panama. Moved by local tales of a great sea, south of which lay a land overflowing with gold, Balboa led an expedition across the forests and mountains of Panama to the shores of the Pacific. He might have gone on to make contact with the Inca empire of Peru if he had not aroused the jealousy of his terrible father-in-law, the "two-legged tiger," Pedrarias Dávila, sent out by Charles V in 1514 as governor of the isthmus. Charged with treason and desertion, Balboa was tried, condemned, and beheaded in 1519.

After Balboa had confirmed the existence of the Pacific Ocean, subsequent European voyages searched for a waterway through or around the American continent to connect with the East. Ferdinand Magellan, a Portuguese who had fought in India and the East Indies, was convinced that a short passage to the East existed south of Brazil. Failing to interest the Portuguese king in his project, Magellan turned to Spain, with greater success. The resulting voyage of circumnavigation of the globe from 1519 to 1522, the first in history, represented an immense navigational feat and greatly increased Europe's stock of geographic knowledge. Aside from the acquisition of the Philippines for Spain, however, Magellan's exploit had little practical value, for his new route to the East was too long to have commercial significance. The net result was to enhance the value of America in Spanish eyes. Disillusioned with the dream of easy access to the riches of the East, Spain turned with concentrated energy to the task of extending its American conquests and to the exploitation of the human and natural resources of the New World.

The Conquest of Mexico

EARLY CONTACT WITH MOCTEZUMA

A disturbing report reached the Aztec capital of Tenochtitlán in 1518. Up from the coast of the Gulf of Mexico hurried the tribute collector Pinotl to inform King Moctezuma of the approach from the sea of winged towers bearing men with white faces and heavy beards. Pinotl had communicated with these men by signs and had exchanged gifts with their leader. Before departing, the mysterious visitors had promised (so Pinotl interpreted their gestures) to return soon and visit Moctezuma in his city in the mountains.

Aztec accounts agree that the news filled Moctezuma with dismay. Could the leader of these strangers be the redeemer-god Quetzalcóatl, returning to reclaim his lost kingdom? According to one Aztec source, Moctezuma exclaimed, "He has appeared! He has come back! He will come here, to the place of his throne and canopy, for that is what he promised when he departed!"

The "winged towers" were the ships of the Spanish captain Juan de Grijalva, sent by Governor

Diego Velázquez of Cuba to explore the coasts that the slave-hunting expedition of Francisco Hernández de Córdoba (1517) had discovered. Córdoba had landed at the peninsula of Yucatán, which was inhabited by Maya peoples, whose cotton cloaks and brilliant plumes, stone pyramids, temples, and gold ornaments revealed a native culture far more advanced than any the Spaniards had hitherto encountered. Córdoba met with disastrous defeat at the hands of the Maya and returned to Cuba to die of his wounds. He brought back enough gold and other signs of wealth, however, to encourage Velázquez to outfit a new venture, which he entrusted to his compatriot Juan de Grijalva.

Grijalva sailed from Santiago in April 1518 and, following Córdoba's route, reached the limits of Moctezuma's empire, where natives waving white flags greeted him and invited his ships by signs to draw near. Here the Aztec official Pinotl boarded Grijalva's flagship, and later returned to Tenochtitlán to deliver a report that caused much consternation. A lively trade developed, with Aztecs bartering gold for Spanish green beads. Grijalva was now convinced that he had come to a wealthy kingdom filled with many large towns. Near the present port of Veracruz, Grijalva sent Pedro de Alvarado back to Cuba with the gold that he had acquired by barter. Alvarado was to report to Velázquez what Grijalva had accomplished, request authority to found a colony, and seek reinforcements. Grijalva himself sailed on with three other ships, perhaps as far as the river Pánuco, which marked the northern limits of the Aztec empire. Then he turned back and retraced his course, arriving in Cuba in November 1518.

Cortés-Quetzalcóatl

Velázquez was already planning a third expedition to conquer the Mexican mainland. He passed over Grijalva and chose as leader of the expedition the thirty-four-year-old Hernando Cortés, a native of Medellín in the Spanish province of Estremadura. Cortés was born in 1485 into an hidalgo family of modest means. At the age of fourteen, he went to Salamanca, seat of a great Spanish university, to prepare for the study of law, but he left some years later to pursue a military career. He had to choose between Italy, the great battlefield of Europe, where Spanish arms were winning fame under the great captain Gonzalo de Córdoba, and the Indies, land of gold, Amazons, and El Dorados. In 1504, at the age of nineteen, he embarked for Hispaniola.

Soon after arriving on the island, Cortés participated in his first military exploit: the suppression of a revolt of Arawaks made desperate by Spanish mistreatment. His reward was an **encomienda** (a grant of indigenous tribute and labor). In 1511, he served under Velázquez in the easy conquest of Cuba. The following year he became alcalde of the newly founded town of Santiago in Cuba. In 1518, he persuaded Velázquez to give him command of the new expedition to the Mexican mainland, but at the last moment, the distrustful governor decided to recall him. Cortés simply disregarded Velázquez's messages, however, and in February 1519, he sailed from Cuba with a force of some six hundred men. Because Velázquez had not completed negotiations with the emperor Charles for an agreement authorizing the conquest and settlement of the mainland, Cortés's instructions permitted him only to trade and explore.

Cortés's fleet first touched land at the island of Cozumel, where they rescued a Spanish castaway, Jerónimo de Aguilar, who had lived among the Maya for eight years. In March 1519, Cortés landed on the coast of Tabasco, defeated local natives in a sharp skirmish, and secured from them, along with pledges of friendship, the Mexican girl Malinche,[2] who was to serve him as interpreter,

---

2. After the achievement of Mexican independence, her conspicuous services to Cortés and the Conquest made her name a byword, a synonym for selling out to foreigners, and for many Mexicans it continues to have that meaning today. In fairness to Malinche, however, it should be understood that no Mexican nationality or sense of unity among the various ethnic groups that inhabited Mesoamerica existed at the time. A talented young woman who apparently possessed extraordinary linguistic skills, Malinche found herself thrown against her will into a dangerous situation. Her best hope of survival, writes Frances Karttunen, was to serve Cortés, and she "served him unwaveringly. Rather than the embodiment of treachery, her consistency could be viewed as an exercise in total loyalty."

adviser, and mistress. In April, Cortés dropped anchor near the site of modern Veracruz. He had contrived a way to free himself from Velázquez's irksome authority. In apparent deference to the wishes of a majority of his followers, who claimed that conquest and settlement would serve the royal interest better than mere trade, Cortés founded the town of Villa Rica de la Vera Cruz and appointed its first officials, into whose hands he surrendered the authority he had received from Velázquez. These officials then conferred on Cortés the title of captain general with authority to conquer and colonize the newly discovered lands. Cortés thus drew on Spanish medieval traditions of municipal autonomy to vest his disobedience in a cloak of legality.

Some days later, Moctezuma's ambassadors appeared in the Spanish camp.[3] The envoys brought precious gifts, the finery of the great gods Tlaloc, Tezcatlipoca, and Quetzalcóatl. Reverently, they arrayed Cortés in the finery of Quetzalcóatl. On his face they placed a serpent mask inlaid with turquoise, with a crossband of quetzal feathers and a golden earring hanging down on either side. On his breast, they fastened a vest decorated with quetzal feathers; about his neck, they hung a collar of precious stones with a gold disc in the center. In his hand, they placed a shield with ornaments of gold and mother-of-pearl and a fringe and pendant of quetzal feathers. They also set before him sandals of fine, soft rubber, black as obsidian.

The Aztec account relates that the god was not satisfied. "Is this all?" Cortés is said to have asked. "Is this your gift of welcome? Is this how you greet people?" The stricken envoys departed and re-

turned with gifts more to the god's liking, including a gold disc in the shape of the sun, as big as a cartwheel, an even larger silver pendant in the shape of the moon, and a helmet full of gold nuggets.

The envoys reported to Moctezuma what they had heard and seen, supplementing their accounts with painted pictures of the gods and their possessions. They described the firing of a cannon, done on Cortés's order to impress the Aztec emissaries:

> A thing like a ball of stone comes out of its entrails; it comes out shooting sparks and raining fire. The smoke that comes out with it has a pestilent odor, like that of rotten mud.... If the cannon is aimed against a mountain, the mountain splits and cracks open. If it is aimed against a tree, it shatters the tree into splinters.

Vividly, they described other weapons, the armor, and the mounts of the Spaniards.

Of the terrible war dogs of the Spaniards, the envoys said:

> Their dogs are enormous, with flat ears and long dangling tongues. The color of their eyes is burning yellow; their eyes flash fire and shoot off sparks. Their bellies are hollow, their flanks long and narrow. They are tireless and very powerful. They bound here and there, panting, with their tongues hanging out. And they are spotted like an ocelot.

Moctezuma's envoys assured Cortés that they would serve him in every way during his stay on the coast but pleaded with him not to seek a

3. In relating the conquest of Mexico, we have often given the Aztec version of events, with all its fantastic elements, as told in the *Florentine Codex*, compiled by the great missionary-scholar Bernardino de Sahagún, because it offers a remarkable insight into the Aztec mentality and reaction to the Conquest. In that version, the legend that foretold the return of the god-king Quetzalcóatl plays a prominent role; initially, at least, the conquistador Cortés appears to have been identified with the god himself or with his emissary. Recently, however, some skeptical scholars have suggested that the legend is a post-Conquest native rationalization of the Aztec defeat or a combined Spanish-Aztec creation, or even a pure invention of Cortés, who twice cites a version of the legend as told by Moctezuma. This skeptical point of view strikes us as ahistorical. History records numerous legends that foretell the return of redeemer-gods or kings. If medieval Germans could believe in the return of the emperor Frederick Barbarossa, and if Renaissance Portuguese could believe in the return of King Sebastian, why could not the Aztecs believe in the return of the god-king Quetzalcóatl?

The famed Mexican muralist Diego Rivera depicted the horrors of slavery, oppression, and genocide that Hernan Cortés and the Spanish Conquest imposed on indigenous people to accumulate wealth and expand the Spanish empire.

meeting with their king. This pleading was part of Moctezuma's pathetic strategy to ply Cortés-Quetzalcóatl with gifts in the hope that he could dissuade him from advancing into the interior to reclaim his lost throne. Suavely, Cortés informed the ambassadors that he had crossed many seas and journeyed from distant lands to see and speak with Moctezuma and could not return without doing so.

THE MARCH TO TENOCHTITLÁN

Aware of the tributary towns' bitter discontent with Aztec rule, Cortés decided to play a double game. He encouraged the Totonacs of the coast to seize and imprison Moctezuma's tax collectors but promptly obtained their release and sent them to the king with expressions of his regard and friendship. He then sent a ship to Spain with dispatches for the emperor Charles, in which he sought to obtain approval for his actions by describing the great extent and value of his discoveries. To gain the emperor's good will, Cortés persuaded his men to send Charles his **quinto** (royal fifth) and all the treasure received from Moctezuma. Then to stiffen the resolution of his followers by cutting off all avenues of escape, he scuttled and sank all his remaining ships on the pretext that they were not seaworthy. Finally, Cortés and his small army began the march on Mexico-Tenochtitlán.

Advancing into the sierra, Cortés entered the territory of the tough Tlaxcalans, traditional enemies of the Aztecs. The Spaniards had to prove in battle the superiority of their weapons and their fighting capacity before they obtained an alliance with this powerful nation. Then Cortés marched on Cholula, an ancient center of Classic cultural traditions and the cult of Quetzalcóatl. Here, claiming that the Cholulans were conspiring to attack him, Cortés staged a mass slaughter of the Cholulan nobility and warriors after they had assembled in a great courtyard. When news of this event reached Tenochtitlán, terror spread throughout the city.

The Spaniards continued their inexorable advance:

> They came in battle array, as conquerors, and the dust rose in whirlwinds on the roads. Their spears glinted in the sun, and their pennons fluttered like bats. They made a loud clamor as they marched, for their coats of mail and their weapons clashed and rattled. Some of them were dressed in glistening iron from head to foot; they terrified everyone who saw them.

By now, Moctezuma's fears and doubts had reduced him to a hopelessly indecisive state of mind. He wavered between submission and resistance, between the conviction that the Spaniards were gods and half-formed suspicions that they were less than divine. He sent new envoys, who brought rich gifts to Cortés but urged him to abandon his plan of visiting the Aztec capital. Moctezuma's naive efforts to bribe or cajole the terrible strangers proved futile. In the bitter words of an Aztec account of the Spanish conquest, they "longed and lusted for gold," and "hungered like pigs for gold." Nothing short of armed force would deter them. As Moctezuma's doom approached, his own gods turned against him. The young god Tezcatlipoca stopped a group of sorcerers and soothsayers sent by the king to cast spells over the Spaniards and then conjured up a vision of Mexico-Tenochtitlán burning to the ground. His forces spent, Moctezuma ended by welcoming

Cortés at the entrance to the capital as a rightful ruler returning to his throne. The Aztec king completed his degradation by allowing Cortés and a few comrades to kidnap him from his palace and take him to live as a hostage in the Spanish quarters.

The Aztec nation had not said its last word. In Cortés's absence from the city—he had set off for the coast to face an expedition sent by Governor Velázquez to arrest him—his lieutenant Pedro de Alvarado ordered an unprovoked massacre of the leading Aztec chiefs and warriors as they celebrated with song and dance a religious festival in honor of Huitzilopochtli. The result was a popular uprising that forced the Spaniards to retreat to their own quarters. This was the situation that Cortés, having won over most of the newcomers and defeated the rest, found when he returned to Tenochtitlán to rejoin his comrades. His efforts to pacify the Aztecs failed. The Aztec council deposed the captive Moctezuma and elected a new chief, who launched heavy attacks on the invaders. As the fighting raged, Moctezuma died, either stoned by his own people as he appealed for peace, according to Spanish accounts, or strangled by the Spaniards, according to Aztec sources. Fearing a long siege and famine, Cortés evacuated Tenochtitlán at a heavy cost in lives. The surviving Spaniards and their indigenous allies at last reached friendly Tlaxcala.

Strengthened by the arrival of Spanish reinforcements from Cuba and by thousands of indigenous enemies of the Aztec empire, Cortés again marched on Tenochtitlán in December 1520. A ferocious struggle began in late April 1521. On August 23, after a siege in which the Aztecs fought for four months with extraordinary bravery, their last king, Cuauhtémoc, surrendered amid the laments of his starving people. Cortés took possession of the ruins that had been the city of Tenochtitlán.

THE AFTERMATH OF CONQUEST

From the Valley of Mexico, the process of conquest extended in all directions. Pedro de Alvarado conquered Guatemala and Cortés subdued Honduras. In 1527, Francisco de Montejo began the conquest of Yucatán, but as late as 1542, the Maya rose in a desperate revolt that was crushed with great slaughter. Meanwhile, expeditions from Darien subjugated indigenous Nicaraguans. Thus did the two streams of Spanish conquest, both originating in Hispaniola, come together again.

For a brief time, Cortés was the undisputed master of the old Aztec empire, renamed the "Kingdom of New Spain." He made grants of encomienda to his soldiers, reserving for himself the tributes of the richest towns and provinces. The crown rewarded his services by granting him the title of marquis of the Valley of Oaxaca and the tributes of twenty-three thousand vassals; he lived in almost kingly style, dining "with minstrels and trumpets." But royal distrust of the great conquerors soon asserted itself, and the crown removed him from his office of governor, vested his authority in an *audiencia* (high court), pending the appointment of a viceroy, and closely scrutinized the legality of his actions. In 1539, he returned to Spain and served with distinction in the expedition against Algiers in the following year, but the king ignored and snubbed him. Filled with bitterness, he retired to live in seclusion in Sevilla. He died in 1547, leaving his title and estates to his eldest legitimate son, Martín Cortés.

The Conquest of Peru

The conquest of Mexico challenged other Spaniards to match the exploits of Cortés and his companions. The work of discovering a golden kingdom rumored to lie beyond the "South Sea" was begun by Balboa but was cut short by his death at the hands of Pedrarias Dávila. In 1519, Dávila founded the town of Panama on the western side of the isthmus, and this town became a base for explorations along the Pacific coast. Three years later, Pascual de Andagoya crossed the Gulf of San Miguel and returned with more information concerning a land of gold called Biru.

Pizarro and Atahualpa

Dávila entrusted a southward voyage to Francisco Pizarro, an illiterate, impoverished soldier, of whom little was known. Pizarro recruited two partners for the Peruvian venture: Diego de Almagro, an adventurer of equally obscure origins, and Hernando de Luque, a priest who acted as financial agent for the trio. Two preliminary expeditions, fitted out from Panama in 1524 and 1526, yielded enough finds of gold and silver to confirm the existence of the elusive kingdom. Pizarro now left for Spain to obtain royal sanction for the enterprise of Peru. He returned to Panama with the titles of captain general and adelantado (commander), accompanied by his four brothers and other followers. Almagro, dissatisfied with the allotment of titles and other rewards in the royal contract, accused Pizarro of slighting his services to the king. Although they resolved the quarrel, it sowed the seeds of a deadly feud.

In December 1531, Pizarro again sailed from Panama for the south with a force of some two hundred men and landed several months later on the Peruvian coast. On arrival, the Spaniards learned that civil war was raging in the Inca empire. Atahualpa, son of the late emperor Huayna Capac by a secondary wife, had risen against another claimant of the throne: his half-brother, Huascar. Atahualpa defeated Huascar in a war marked by great slaughter and made him prisoner. Atahualpa was advancing toward the imperial capital of Cuzco when messengers brought him news of the arrival of white strangers. After an exchange of messages and gifts between the leaders, the two armies advanced to a meeting at the town of Cajamarca, high in the mountains.

Perhaps in direct imitation of Cortés, Pizarro proposed to win a quick and relatively bloodless victory by seizing the Inca Atahualpa, through whom he may have hoped to rule the country, much as Cortés had done with Moctezuma. In one important respect, however, the Peruvian story differs from that of Mexico. If Moctezuma's undoing was his passive acceptance of the divinity of the invaders, Atahualpa's mistake was to underestimate the massed striking power of the small Spanish force. He mistakenly believed that the swords were no more dangerous than women's weaving battens, that the firearms were capable of firing only two shots, and that the horses were powerless

Atahualpa, last of the independent Incan emperors, grandly displayed his regal power with golden objects, including vestments, earrings, and headband.

Brooklyn Museum of Art, Museum Purchase

at night. This last delusion apparently led to his delayed entry into Cajamarca at dusk, instead of noon, as Pizarro had expected.

When Atahualpa and his escort appeared for the rendezvous in the square of Cajamarca, he found it deserted, for Pizarro had concealed his men in some large buildings that opened onto the square. Then the priest Vicente de Valverde came forward, accompanied by an interpreter, to harangue the bewildered Inca concerning his obligations to the Christian God and the Spanish king until the angry emperor threw down a Bible that Valverde had handed him. At a signal from Pizarro, his soldiers, supported by cavalry and artillery, rushed forward to kill hundreds and take the Inca prisoner. "It was a very wonderful thing," wrote a Spanish observer, "to see so great a lord, who came in such power, taken prisoner in so short a time."

Atahualpa vainly begged for his freedom by offering to fill his spacious cell higher than a man could reach with gold objects as the price of his ransom. Pizarro accepted the offer, and hundreds of llama-loads of gold arrived from all parts of the empire until they had filled the room to the stipulated height. But Pizarro had no intention of letting the emperor go; he remained in "protective custody," a puppet ruler who was to ensure popular acceptance of the new order. Soon, however, the Spaniards began to suspect that Atahualpa was becoming the focal point of a widespread conspiracy against them and decided that he must die. They charged him with treason and condemned him to death by burning, a sentence commuted to strangling on his acceptance of baptism.

After the death of the Inca, the Spaniards marched on the Inca capital of Cuzco, which they captured and pillaged in November 1533. A major factor in the success of this and later Spanish campaigns was the military and other assistance given by the late Huascar's branch of the Inca royal family and by curacas who, seeing an opportunity to regain their lost independence and power, rallied to the Spanish side after the capture of Atahualpa. The Spanish melted the gold and silver looted from Cuzco, together with Atahualpa's enormous ransom of gold, and divided it among the soldiers. Hernando Pizarro, Francisco's brother, traveled to Spain with Emperor Charles's share of the plunder. Hernando's arrival with his load of gold and silver caused feverish excitement, and a new wave of Spanish fortune hunters sailed for the New World. Meanwhile, Francisco Pizarro had begun construction of an entirely new Spanish capital, Lima, the City of the Kings, conveniently near the coast for communication with Panama.

POST-CONQUEST TROUBLES

After Atahualpa's death, Pizarro posed as the defender of the legitimate Inca line and proclaimed Huascar's brother Manco as the new Inca emperor, but Manco was not content to play the role of a Spanish puppet. A formidable insurrection, organized and led by Manco, broke out in many parts of the empire. A large army laid siege to Cuzco for ten months but failed by a narrow margin to take the city. Defeated by superior Spanish weapons and tactics and by food shortages in his army, Manco retreated to a remote stronghold in the Andean mountains. There, he and his successors maintained a kind of Inca government-in-exile until 1572, when a Spanish military expedition entered the mountains, broke up the imperial court, captured the last Inca, Tupac Amaru, and beheaded him in a solemn ceremony at Cuzco.

The Inca siege of Cuzco had barely been broken when fighting began between a group of the conquerors headed by the Pizarro brothers and a group led by Diego de Almagro over possession of the city of Cuzco. Defeated in battle, Almagro suffered death by strangling but left behind a son and a large group of supporters to brood over their poverty and supposed wrongs. Twelve of them, contemptuously dubbed by Pizarro's secretary "the knights of the cape" because they allegedly had only one cloak among them, planned and carried out the assassination of the conqueror of Peru in June 1541. But their triumph was of short duration. Charles V sent a judge, Vaca de Castro, to advise Pizarro on the government of his province. Assuring himself of the loyalty of Pizarro's principal captains, Vaca de Castro made war on Almagro's son, defeated his army on the "bloody plains of Chupas," and promptly had him tried and beheaded as a traitor to the king.

That was not, however, to be the end of the troubles. Early in 1544, a new viceroy, Blasco Núñez Vela, arrived in Lima to proclaim the edicts known as the New Laws of the Indies. These laws regulated Indian tribute, freed indigenous slaves, and forbade forced labor. They evoked outraged cries and appeals for their suspension from the Spanish landowners in Peru. When the crown failed to heed these pleas, the desperate conquistadors rose in revolt and found a leader in Gonzalo Pizarro, brother of the murdered Francisco.

The first phase of the great revolt in Peru ended auspiciously for Gonzalo Pizarro with the defeat and death of the viceroy Núñez Vela in a battle near Quito. Pizarro now became the uncrowned king of the country. The rebel leader owed much of his initial success to the resourcefulness and demoniac energy of his eighty-year-old field commander and principal adviser, Francisco de Carbajal. To these qualities, Carbajal added an inhuman cruelty that became legendary in Peru.

After his victory over the viceroy, Carbajal and other advisers urged Pizarro to proclaim himself king of Peru, but Pizarro, a weaker man than his iron-willed lieutenant, hesitated to avow the revolutionary meaning of his actions. The arrival of a smooth-tongued envoy of the crown, Pedro de la Gasca, who announced suspension of the New Laws and offered pardons and rewards to all repentant rebels, caused a trickle of desertions from Pizarro's ranks that soon became a flood.

Finally, the rebellion collapsed almost without a struggle, and its leaders were executed. Before the civil wars in Peru had run their course, four of the Pizarro "brothers of doom" and the Almagros, father and son, had met violent deaths; the rebels had assassinated a viceroy; and numberless others had lost their lives. Peace and order did not return to the country until the administration of Viceroy Francisco de Toledo, who assumed his responsibilities in 1569, a quarter-century after the beginning of the great civil wars.

How a Handful of Spaniards Won Two Empires

The Spanish Conquest raises a question: How did small groups of Spaniards, which initially numbered only a few hundred men, conquer the Aztec and Inca empires that had populations in the millions, large armies, and militarist traditions of their own? With relative ease, the Spaniards conquered the Aztecs and the Incas, peoples who were organized on the state level, lived a sedentary life based on intensive agriculture, and were ruled by emperors to whom they gave complete obedience. On the other hand, tribes of marginal culture, such as the nomadic Chichimecs of the northern Mexican plains or the Araucanians of Chile, who practiced a simple shifting agriculture and herding, were indomitable; the Araucanians continued to battle Spanish invaders and their descendants for hundreds of years until 1883.

Reflecting on the contrast between the swift fall of the Inca empire and the failure of the Spaniards to conquer the "uncivilized tribes" of the Colombian jungles, a sixteenth-century Spanish soldier and chronicler of uncommon intelligence, Pedro Cieza de León, found a simple explanation. The social and economic organization of the tribes allowed native people to flee before a Spanish advance and soon rebuild village life elsewhere. In contrast, the mass of the Inca population, docile subjects, accepted their emperor's defeat as their own and quickly submitted to the new Spanish masters. For these people, flight from the fertile valleys of the Inca to the deserts, bleak plateaus, and snowcapped mountains that dominate the geography of the region would have been unthinkable.

Although Cieza's comments are insightful, they do not satisfactorily explain the swift fall of these great empires. At least four other factors contributed to that outcome:

1. Spanish firearms and cannon, although primitive by modern standards, gave the invaders a decided superiority over Aztecs and Incas armed with bows and arrows, wooden lances and darts, slings, war clubs with stone or bronze heads, and wooden swords tipped with obsidian points. Even more decisive for the Spanish was the horse, an animal unknown to both Aztecs and Incas, who at least initially regarded it with awe. The Spanish cavalryman, armed with lance and sword, clad in armor and chain mail, had a striking force comparable to that of the modern tank. A small Spanish squadron of cavalry repeatedly routed a much larger number of Aztec and Inca warriors.

2. Diseases, notably smallpox, unwittingly introduced by the invaders, became effective Spanish allies. To give one instance, smallpox raged in Tenochtitlán during the Spanish siege of the city, killing King Cuitlahuac and many Aztec soldiers and civilians, and thereby contributed to its fall.

3. The Spaniards were Renaissance men with a secular outlook, whereas their adversaries represented a much more archaic worldview in which ritual and magic played a large role. Certainly, religious zeal inspired the conquistadors, but for them, war was a science or art based on centuries of European study and practice of military strategy and tactics. For the Aztecs and the Incas, war had a large religious component. The Aztec method of waging war, for example, emphasized capturing Spaniards alive for sacrifice to their gods instead of killing them on the spot. Aztec and Inca warfare also included elaborate ceremonies and conventions that required giving proper notice to a people targeted for attack. The Spaniards did not limit themselves with such conventions.[4]

4. Internal division was a major factor in the swift collapse of these empires. Hatred of the Aztecs by tributary peoples or unvanquished peoples like the Tlaxcalans explains why they formed a majority of Cortés's forces during the last struggle for Tenochtitlán. In what is now Peru, the conflict between two claimants of the Inca throne and their followers played directly into Pizarro's hands. Also, the Inca empire was a mosaic of states, some quite recently incorporated into the empire, and the former lords or curacas of these states, eager to regain their independence, rallied to the Spanish side. All too late, they discovered that they had exchanged one oppressor for a worse one.

Thus, these sophisticated, highly organized empires fell to the Spaniards because of the superior armament and decimating diseases brought by the latter, the differing worldviews of the two peoples, and the internal divisions within the empires themselves.

---

4. One exception was the **Requerimiento** (or Requirement), a document designed to satisfy Spanish royal conscience. It contained Spanish demands that must be read before making war. For the farcical use of this document, see Chapter 4.

The Quest for El Dorado

FAILURES IN NORTH AMERICA

The Spanish conquest radiated in all directions from the West Indies and the two new centers of Mexico and Peru. While the Spanish launched ships on the waters of the Pacific to search for the Spice Islands, land expeditions roamed the interior of North and South America in quest of new golden kingdoms.

The North American mainland attracted the attention of Spanish gold hunters and slave hunters based in the West Indies. In 1513, Ponce de León, governor of Puerto Rico, sailed west and claimed a subtropical land to which he gave the name La Florida. His subsequent efforts to colonize the region ended with his death. In the 1520s, another expedition, ineptly led by Pánfilo de Narváez, met with disaster in the vast, indefinite expanse of La Florida. Only four survivors of the venture, among them its future chronicler, the honest and humane Alvar Núñez Cabeza de Vaca, reached Mexico safely after a long, circuitous trek over the plains of Texas.

Cabeza de Vaca's tales of adventure, with their hints of populous cities just beyond the horizon, inspired the conquistador Hernando de Soto, a

In this mural, *Cuauhtémoc contra el mito,* David Alfaro Siqueiros immortalizes Cuauhtémoc, the last Aztec emperor to die resisting the Spanish Conquest. For many Mexicans, Cuauhtémoc became a symbol of rebellion and national resistance to foreign intervention and oppression.

veteran of the conquest of Peru, to try his fortune in La Florida. In 1542, after three years of unprofitable wanderings and struggles with peoples indigenous to the great area between modern-day South Carolina and Arkansas, de Soto died in the wilderness of a fever.

Upon their arrival in Mexico in 1536, Cabeza de Vaca and his three companions regaled their compatriots with strange tales. A certain Fray Marcos, however, told an even stranger story. He claimed to have traveled in the far north, where he saw one of the Seven Cities of the mythical golden realm of Cibola. These stories persuaded Viceroy Antonio de Mendoza in 1540 to send an expedition northward commanded by Francisco Vásquez de Coronado. For two years, Spanish knights in armor pursued the elusive realm of gold through the future states of Arizona, New Mexico, Colorado, Oklahoma, Kansas, and possibly Nebraska. Disillusioned by the humble reality of the Zuñi pueblos of Arizona, the apparent source of the Cibola myth, Coronado pushed east in search of still another El Dorado, this time called Quivira. Repelled by the immensity of the Great Plains, the Spanish intruders left no trace of their passage and returned home bitterly disappointed with their failure to find treasure.

FRUSTRATIONS IN SOUTH AMERICA

The golden will-o'-the-wisp that lured Spanish knights into the deserts of the Southwest also beckoned to them from South America's jungles and mountains. From the town of Santa Marta, founded in 1525 on the coast of modern Colombia, an expedition led by Gonzalo Jiménez de Quesada set out in 1536 on a difficult journey up the Magdalena River in search of gold and a passage to the Pacific. They suffered incredible hardships before they finally emerged onto the high plateau east of the Magdalena inhabited by the Chibcha. Primarily farmers, skillful in casting gold and copper ornaments, the Chibcha lived in palisaded towns and were ruled by a chieftain called the Zipa. After defeating them in battle, Jiménez de Quesada founded in 1538 the town of Santa Fé de Bogotá, future

capital of the province of New Granada. The immense treasure in gold and emeralds looted from the Chibcha fired Spanish imaginations and inspired fantasies about yet other golden kingdoms. The most famous of these legends was that of El Dorado (the Golden Man).

The dream of spices also inspired the saga of Spanish conquest. Attracted by accounts of an eastern land where cinnamon trees grew in profusion, Gonzalo Pizarro led an expedition in 1539 from Quito in modern Ecuador across the Andes and down the forested eastern mountain slopes. Cinnamon was found, but in disappointingly small quantities. To encourage the Spanish intruders to move on, local natives told tall tales of rich kingdoms somewhere beyond the horizon, and the treasure hunters dutifully plunged deeper into the wilderness. Gonzalo's lieutenant, Francisco de Orellana, sent with a party down a certain stream in search of food, found the current too strong to return, and went on to enter a great river whose course he followed in two makeshift boats for a distance of eighteen hundred leagues, eventually emerging from its mouth to reach Spanish settlements in Venezuela. On the banks of the great river, Orellana fought natives whose women joined the battle. For this reason, he gave the river its Spanish name of Amazonas, an illustration of the myth-making process among the Spaniards of the Conquest.

In the southern reaches of the continent, which possessed little gold or silver, new agricultural and pastoral settlements arose. In 1537, Pizarro's comrade and rival, Diego de Almagro, made a fruitless march across the rugged Andean altiplano and the sun-baked Chilean desert in search of gold and returned bitterly disappointed. Two years later, Pizarro authorized Pedro de Valdivia to undertake the conquest of the lands to the south of Peru. After crossing the desert of northern Chile, Valdivia reached the fertile Central Valley and founded the town of Santiago. In constant struggle with Araucanians, Valdivia laid the foundations of an agricultural colony based on the servile labor of other, more pacific native peoples. He was finally captured and killed by the Araucanians during an expedition southward in 1553.

In the same period (1536), the adelantado Pedro de Mendoza brought twenty-five hundred colonists in fourteen ships and founded the town of Buenos Aires on the estuary of the Río de la Plata. But its famished inhabitants soon abandoned Buenos Aires and moved almost a thousand miles upstream to the newly founded town of Asunción in Paraguay. There, a genial climate, an abundance of food, and a multitude of docile Guaraní people created more favorable conditions for Spanish settlement. Asunción became the capital of Paraguay and all the Spanish territory in southeastern South America.

THE CONQUISTADORS

The conquest of America lured a wide variety of adventurers. Professional soldiers, some with backgrounds of service in the Italian wars and some with pasts they wanted to forget, made up some of this group. The old conquistador Gonzalo Fernández de Oviedo had such men in mind when he warned the organizers of expeditions against "fine-feathered birds and great talkers ... [who] will either slay you or sell you or forsake you when they find that you promised them more in Spain than you can produce." In one of his *Exemplary Tales*, Cervantes describes the Americas as "the refuge and shelter of the desperate men of Spain, sanctuary of rebels, safe-conduct of homicides." No doubt, men of this type contributed more than their share of the atrocities that stained the Spanish Conquest, but the background of the conquistadors varied greatly, running the whole gamut of the Spanish social spectrum. Most were commoners, but some were marginal hidalgos, poor gentlemen who wished to improve their fortunes. Of the 168 men who captured Atahualpa at Cajamarca in 1532, thirty-eight were hidalgos and ninety-one were plebeians, with the background of the rest unknown or uncertain. According to James Lockhart, who has studied the men of Cajamarca, fifty-one members of the group were definitely literate and about seventy-six "almost certainly functioning literates." The group included nineteen artisans, twelve notaries or clerks, and thirteen "men of affairs."

Of the Spanish kingdoms, Castile provided the largest contingent, with natives of Andalusia predominating in the first, or Caribbean, phase of the Conquest; men from Estremadura, the poorest region of Spain, made up the largest single group in the second, or mainland, phase. Cortés, Pizarro, Almagro, Valdivia, Balboa, Orellana, and other famous conquistadors all came from Estremadura. Foreigners were not absent from the Conquest. Oviedo assures us that men had come "from all the other nations of Asia, Africa, and Europe."

By the 1520s, an institution inherited from the Spanish Reconquest, the *compaña* (warrior band), whose members shared in the profits of conquest according to certain rules, had become the principal instrument of Spanish expansion in the New World. At its head stood a military leader who usually possessed a royal capitulación, which vested him with the title of adelantado and with the governorship of the territory to be conquered. Sometimes these men were wealthy in their own right and contributed large sums or incurred enormous debts to finance the expedition. Italian, German, and Spanish merchant capitalists and royal officials grown wealthy through the slave trade or other means provided much of the capital needed to fit out ships, acquire horses and slaves, and supply arms and food.

The warrior band was in principle a military democracy, with the distribution of spoils carried out by a committee elected from among the entire company. After subtracting the quinto and the common debts, they divided the remaining booty into equal shares. In the distribution of Atahualpa's treasure were 217 such shares, each worth 5,345 gold pesos, a tidy sum for that time. Particular shares varied with the individual's rank and contribution to the enterprise. The norm was one share for a *peón* or foot soldier, two for a *caballero* or equestrian (one for the rider, another for the horse), and more for a captain.

Despite its democratic aspect, the captains, large investors, and royal officials dominated the enterprise of conquest and took the lion's share for themselves. Some of the men were servants or slaves of the captains and investors, and their shares went entirely or in part to their employers or masters. In other cases, conquistadors had borrowed or bought on credit to outfit themselves, and the greater part of their earnings went to their creditors. Contemporary accounts complain of the predatory ways of some captains, who sold supplies to their men in time of need at profiteering prices. At a later stage of each conquest came the distribution of encomiendas. Artisans and other plebeians received encomiendas after the conquest of Mexico and Peru; later, however, only the leaders and hidalgo members of expeditions received such grants.

Many conquistadors were hard, ruthless men, hard in dealing with each other and harder still with indigenous peoples. The conquistador and chronicler Gonzalo Fernández de Oviedo, an ardent imperialist, nonetheless wrote that some conquistadors were "depopulators or destroyers of the new lands." The harshness of the conquistador reflected the conditions that formed his character: the climate of violence in Spain as it emerged from seven centuries of warfare against the Moor, the desperate struggle of most Spaniards to survive in a society divided by great inequalities of wealth, and the brutalizing effects of a colonial war.

Not all conquistadors fit this negative pattern, however. Some were transformed by their experiences, learned humility and respect for indigenous values, or even came to concede the moral superiority of the "Indian" over the Spaniard. This was the lesson that Alvar Núñez Cabeza de Vaca learned in the course of his immense eight-year trek from the gulf coast of Texas to Mexico. In his account of his adventures, he presented Spaniards as savages and "Indians" as humane and civilized. Another conquistador, Pedro Cieza de León, the "prince of chroniclers," had high praise for Inca civilization, criticized the cruelties of the Conquest, and clearly sympathized with the ideas of Las Casas. Yet another conquistador, Alonso de Ercilla, author of the finest Spanish epic poem of the sixteenth century, La Araucana, which dealt with the struggle of the Araucanians of Chile against the Spaniards, praised and even glorified the Araucanians, who appear throughout the poem as a heroic people determined to be free. The victorious Spaniards, however, are portrayed as cowardly, greedy, and selfish.

Of the trinity of motives (God, Gold, and Glory) commonly assigned to the Spanish conquistador, the second was certainly uppermost in the minds of most. "Do not say that you are going to the Indies to serve the king and to employ your time as a brave man and an hidalgo should," observes Oviedo in an open letter to would-be conquerors. "For you know the truth is just the opposite: you are going solely because you want to have a larger fortune than your father and your neighbors." Pizarro puts it even more plainly in his reply to a priest who urged the need for spreading the Faith: "I have not come for any such reasons. I have come to take away from them their gold." The conquistador and chronicler of the conquest of Mexico, Bernal Díaz del Castillo, ingenuously declares that the conquerors died "in the service of God and of His Majesty, and to give light to those who sat in darkness—and also to acquire that gold which most men covet."

Most conquistadors dreamed of eventually returning to Spain with enough money to found a family and live in a style that would earn them the respect and admiration of their neighbors. Only a minority, chiefly large merchants and *encomenderos*, acquired the capital needed to fulfill this ambition, and not all of them returned to Spain. The majority, lacking encomiendas or other sources of wealth, remained and often formed ties of dependency with more powerful Spaniards, usually encomenderos in whose service they entered as artisans, military retainers, or overseers of their encomiendas or other enterprises. After 1535, more and more would-be conquistadors came to the Americas, while the opportunities for joining profitable conquests diminished. As a result, the problem of a large number of unemployed and turbulent Spaniards caused serious concern to royal officials and to the crown itself.

Most conquistadors and other early Spanish settlers in the Indies were single, young males, with a sprinkling of married men who had left their wives at home while they sought their fortunes. Aside from an occasional mistress or camp follower, few Spanish women accompanied the expeditions.

Once the fighting had stopped, however, a few Spanish women crossed the Atlantic. Some were wives who came to rejoin their husbands (the laws, generally unenforced, stated that, to avoid deportation to Spain, a married man must have his wife living with him); others were mothers, sisters, or nieces of the settlers. Marriages with indigenous women were not uncommon; even hidalgos were happy at the opportunity to marry a wealthy noblewoman like Moctezuma's daughter, Tecuixpo (Isabel Moctezuma), who was wed to three Spanish husbands in turn. After mid-century, however, most Spaniards of all social levels tended to marry Spanish women, either immigrants or those born in the Indies. By the last quarter of the century, the Spanish family and household, based on strong clan and regional loyalties, had been reconstituted.

Of the thousands of bold captains and their followers who rode or marched under the banner of Castile to the conquest of America, few lived to enjoy the fruits of their valor, sufferings, and cruelties. "I do not like the title of adelantado," writes Oviedo, "for actually that honor and title is an evil omen in the Indies, and many who bore it have come to an evil end." Of those who survived the battles and the marches, a few received the lion's share of spoils, land, and labor; the majority remained in modest or even worse circumstances and were frequently in debt. The conflict between the haves and the have-nots among the conquerors contributed significantly to the explosive, tension-ridden state of affairs in the Indies in the decades following the Conquest.

LOPE DE AGUIRRE—AN UNDERDOG OF THE CONQUEST

That conflict was a major ingredient in the devil's brew of passions that produced three decades of murderous civil wars and revolts among the Spaniards in Peru after the fall of the Inca empire. The defeat of the great revolt of Gonzalo Pizarro in 1548 brought no lasting peace to Peru, for it left seething with discontent the many adventurers who had flocked from all parts of the Indies to join the struggle against Pizarro. These men had hoped to win fitting rewards for their services to the crown. Instead, Pizarro's wily conqueror, La Gasca, added to the encomiendas of the rich and powerful friends who had abandoned Pizarro and come over to the royal side. The sense of betrayal felt by many rank-and-file conquistadors was expressed by Pero López, who charged that La Gasca had left "all His Majesty's servants poor, while he let many of His Majesty's foes keep all they had and even gave them much more."

The Viceroy Cañete clearly defined the economic essence of the problem in a letter he wrote to Emperor Charles V in 1551; he reported that only 480 encomiendas existed in Peru, whereas the number of Spaniards was eight thousand. Including the jobs that the colonial administration could provide, only one thousand Spaniards could "have food to eat." Cañete's only solution to rid Peru of the plague of unemployed conquistadors was to send them off on new conquests, "for it is well known that they will not work or dig or plow, and they say that they did not come to these parts to do such things." The emperor agreed; permission for new conquests, he wrote the viceroy in December 1555, would serve "to rid and cleanse the country of the idle and licentious men who are there at present and who would leave to engage in that business." Accordingly, Charles revoked a decree of 1549, issued at the urging of Las Casas, which prohibited new conquests.

The career of the famous Lope de Aguirre, "the Wanderer," casts a vivid light on the psychology and mentality of the disinherited conquistador host. A veteran conquistador, Aguirre was fifty, lame in one leg because of wounds, and had spent a quarter-century in a fruitless search for fortune in the Indies when the rumor of a new El Dorado in the heart of the Amazon wilderness caused feverish excitement in Peru. Whether or not the legendary realm existed, it provided a convenient means of solving a potentially explosive social problem. In 1559, Viceroy Andrés Hurtado de Mendoza authorized Pedro de Ursúa to lead an expedition to search for the province of "Omagua and Dorado." Lope de Aguirre, accompanied by his young mestiza daughter, formed part of the expedition when it sailed down the Huallaga River, a tributary of the Amazon, in quest of the new golden realm. Ursúa proved to be a poor leader, and unrest, aggravated by intolerable heat, disease, and lack of food, soon grew into a mutiny whose ringleader was Lope de Aguirre. Ursúa was murdered and, although the rebels raised a Spanish noble named Fernando de Guzmán to be their figurehead "prince," Aguirre soon became the expedition's undisputed leader.

He had devised an audacious new plan that had nothing to do with the quest for El Dorado. It called for the conquest of Peru, removal of its present rulers, and rewards for old conquistadors like himself

> for the labors we have had in conquering
> and pacifying the native Indians of those
> kingdoms. For although we won those
> Indians with our persons and effort, spilling
> our blood, at our expense, we were not
> rewarded.... Instead the Viceroy exiled us
> with deception and falsehood, saying that
> we were coming to the best and most
> populous land in the world, when it is in
> fact bad and uninhabitable.

Having constructed two large boats on the banks of the Amazon, the expedition sailed off down the great river, bound for the conquest of Peru. Aguirre's distrust of Guzmán soon led to the killing of the "lord and Prince of Peru" and his mistress and followers. By the time Aguirre and his men entered the Atlantic in July 1561, other killings had reduced the number of Spaniards from 370 to 230. Sailing past the shores of Guiana, they seized the island of Margarita and killed its governor. In September, he landed on the coast of Venezuela, captured the town of Valencia, and proclaimed a "cruel war of fire and sword" against King Philip II of Spain. By now, however, the alarm had gone out in all directions, and overwhelming royal forces were moving against him. His small army, already much diminished by his summary executions of suspected traitors, began to melt away because of growing desertions. On October 27, 1561, after a number of his most trusted followers had fled to the royalist camp, Aguirre ran his sixteen-year-old daughter through with his sword to save her, he said, from going through life as the daughter of a rebel. Shortly after, he fell victim to harquebus shots fired by two of his former soldiers.

Some weeks before his death, Aguirre had written King Philip a remarkable letter that offers a conquistador's vision of the Conquest and the world it created. In stark contrast to the heroic vision of the great captains like Cortés, however, Aguirre described the Conquest's underdogs, bitter over their betrayal by the great captains, the viceroys, cunning letrados (officials with legal training) or judges like La Gasca, and their king. Aguirre insisted that he was of Old Christian descent and of noble blood but admitted that he was born of "middling parents," basically admitting that he was one of the many poor hidalgos who came to the Indies in search of fame and fortune.

Aguirre recounted the services that he and his comrades had rendered to the crown and fiercely attacked the king's ingratitude:

> Consider, King and Lord, that you cannot
> justly take any profits from this land, where
> you risked nothing, until you have properly rewarded those who labored and
> sweated there in your service.... Few kings
> go to hell, because there are so few of you,
> but if there were many none would go to
> heaven. I hold it for certain that even in
> hell you would be worse than Lucifer, for
> your whole ambition is to quench your
> insatiable thirst for human blood.

Despite this blasphemously revolutionary sentiment, Aguirre expressed the horror that he and his comrades felt for the Lutheran heresy and assured the king that, sinners though they were, they accepted completely the teachings of the Holy Mother Church of Rome. But Aguirre denounced the scandalous dissolution and pride of the friars in the Indies. "Their whole way of life here is to acquire material goods and sell the sacraments of the church for a price. They are enemies of the poor—ambitious, gluttonous, and proud—so that even the meanest friar seeks to govern and rule these lands."

Aguirre was also harsh in his comments on the royal officials in Peru. He noted that each royal *oidor* (judge) received an annual salary of 4,000 pesos plus 8,000 pesos of expenses, yet at the end of three years of service, each had saved 60,000 pesos and acquired estates and other possessions to boot. Moreover, they were so proud that "whenever we run into them they want us to drop on our knees and worship them like Nebuchadnezzar." Aguirre advised the king not to entrust the discharge of his royal conscience to these judges, for they spent all their time planning marriages for their children, and their common refrain was "[t]o the left and to the right, I claim all in my sight."

Aguirre closed his revealing letter by wishing King Philip good fortune in his struggle against the Turks and the French and all others "who wish to make war on you in those parts. In these, God grant that we may obtain with our arms the reward rightfully due us, but which you have denied." He signed himself, "son of your loyal Basque vassals and rebel till death against you for your ingratitude, Lope de Aguirre, the Wanderer."[5]

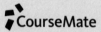 Go to the CourseMate website at www.cengagebrain.com for primary sources, additional study tools, and review materials—including audio and video clips—for this chapter.

5. Thanks to Professor Thomas Holloway of the University of California at Davis for calling attention to the peculiar interest of the Aguirre episode and for allowing the use of his translation of Aguirre's letter to Philip II.

The Economic Foundations of Colonial Life

FOCUS QUESTIONS

- What was Spain's policy on indigenous peoples, and how did it affect the colonial economy and political conflicts among the crown, the clergy, and the colonial elites?

- What factors shaped the evolution of colonial labor systems from *encomienda* and slavery, to *repartimiento* or *mita*, to theoretically free labor or debt servitude?

- What factors shaped the transition from *encomienda* to the *hacienda* and mining as the bases of Spanish colonial economic activity?

- What were the characteristic features of the colonial economy that identified it as capitalist or feudal?

- What were the main features of the Spanish commercial system, and how did its structural weaknesses affect smuggling and piracy?

ROM THE FIRST DAYS of the Conquest, the Spanish government faced the problem of harmonizing the conquistadors' demand for cheap labor, which they frequently used in a wasteful and destructive manner, with the crown's interest in preserving a large, tribute-paying indigenous population. The first decades of colonial experience demonstrated that indigenous peoples, left to the tender mercies of the colonists, might either become extinct, as actually happened on the once densely populated island of Hispaniola, or rise in revolts that could threaten the very existence of the Spanish empire in America. The crown naturally regarded these alternatives with distaste.

The crown also feared that Spanish colonists' monopolistic control of indigenous lands and labor might lead to the rise of a class of feudal lords who were independent of royal authority, a development the Spanish kings were determined to prevent. The church also had a major interest in this problem. If the *indígenas* (indigenous peoples) died out because of Spanish mistreatment, the great task of saving pagan souls would remain incomplete and the good name of the church would suffer. Besides, who then would build churches and monasteries and support the servants of God in the Indies?

The dispute over indigenous policy immediately assumed the dramatic outward form of a struggle of ideas. For reasons deeply rooted in Spain's medieval past, Spanish ideas about the sixteenth century were strongly legalistic and scholastic. At a time when scholasticism[1] was dying out in other Western lands, it retained great vitality in Spain as a philosophic method and as an instrument for the solution of private and public problems. The

---

1. A system of theological and philosophical doctrine and inquiry that predominated in the Middle Ages. It relied chiefly on the authority of the church fathers and of Aristotle and his commentators.

1503	Establishment of *Casa de Contratación* (House of Trade) to license and regulate all commercial traffic with the Indies, collect import and export duties, and collect the royal share of all precious metals and stones
1511	Father Antonio de Montesinos denounces Spanish exploitation of indigenous peoples on Advent Sunday
1512–1513	King Ferdinand decrees Laws of Burgos that sanctioned and regularized the *encomienda* on the island of Hispaniola
1519–1605	Indigenous populations fall from 25 million in Central Mexico to 1 million (with similar experience in Peru)
1521	Destruction of experimental colony on the coast of Venezuela radicalizes Father Bartolomé de Las Casas, who calls for suppression of all encomiendas and abolition of indigenous servitude
1542	New Laws of the Indies prohibit indigenous enslavement, regulate tribute, and declare that existing encomiendas will lapse on the death of the holder
1550–1700	Labor conscription, known as *repartimiento* or *mita*, increasingly replaces encomienda as principal source of Spanish wealth; hacienda or plantation agriculture stresses export production of sugar, cacao, tobacco, and other raw materials
1550–1650	Expansion of colonial Latin American mining industry
1562–1580	John Hawkins, Sir Francis Drake, and English empire challenge the closed Spanish American empire
1570–1811	Rise and decline of the Manila Galleon, commercial trade between Asia and colonial Latin America
1580–1650	Union of Spain and Portugal under Philip II and dramatic expansion of transatlantic trade in enslaved Africans
1670	England and Spain sign Treaty of Madrid, which requires British to aid in the suppression of Caribbean piracy in return for Spanish recognition of British sovereignty in West Indies
1697	Spain and France sign Treaty of Ryswick, formally recognizing French sovereignty in St. Domingue

sixteenth century legal need "to discharge the royal conscience," to make the royal actions conform to the natural and divine law, helps explain Spanish preoccupation with the doctrinal foundations of its policy. What was the nature of the indígenas? What was their cultural level? Were they the slaves by nature that Aristotle described, a race of subhumans whom the Spaniards properly conquered and forced into servitude? What rights and obligations did the papal donation of America to the Spanish monarchs confer on them? Summoned by the monarchs to answer these and similar questions, jurists and theologians waged a battle of books in which they bombarded each other with citations from Aristotle, the church fathers, and medieval philosophers. Less frequently, they supported their positions with materials based on direct observation or written accounts of indigenous life.

Tribute and Labor in the Spanish Colonies

Behind these subtle disputations over Spain's obligations to the indígenas, however, raged a complex struggle over the question of who should control their labor and tribute, the foundations of the Spanish empire in America. The main parties to this struggle were the crown, the church, and the colonists.

THE ENCOMIENDA AND SLAVERY

Hispaniola was the first testing ground of Spain's policy. Calling it "Hell on Hispaniola," Samuel Eliot Morison aptly summarized the situation created on the island by the arrival of Columbus's second expedition. Eager to prove to the crown the value of his "discoveries," Columbus compelled the natives to bring in a daily tribute of gold dust. When the hard-pressed Arawaks revolted, he hunted them down and sent hundreds to Spain as slaves. Later, yielding to the demands of rebellious settlers, Columbus distributed Arawaks among them, with the grantees enjoying the right to use the forced labor of the natives.

This temporary arrangement, formalized in the administration of Governor Nicolás de Ovando and

In sharp contrast to Spanish art that depicted the heroic civilizing influence of conquest and colonization, this Mayan codex emphasized Spanish barbarism and the pivotal role of enslaved Mayan labor in the colonial economy.

sanctioned by the crown, became the encomienda. This system had its origin in the Spanish medieval practice of granting to leading warriors jurisdiction over lands and people captured from the Moors. The encomienda assigned to a colonist responsibility for indigenous people who were to serve him with tribute and labor. He in turn assumed the obligation to protect them, pay for the support of a parish priest, and help defend the colony. In practice, the encomienda in the West Indies proved a hideous slavery. Largely because of this mistreatment, the indigenous population of Hispaniola dwindled from several million to 29,000 within two decades. This decline was not the result of epidemic disease, for no epidemics were recorded in the Antilles before 1518.

The first voices raised against this state of affairs belonged to a company of Dominican friars who arrived in Hispaniola in 1510. Their leader was Father Antonio de Montesinos, who on Advent Sunday, 1511, ascended the church pulpit to threaten the island's Spaniards with damnation for their offenses against the natives. The angry colonists and the Dominicans soon carried their dispute to the court. In response, King Ferdinand approved the Laws of Burgos (1512–1513), which merely sanctioned and regularized the existing situation.

This agitation raised the larger question of the legality of Spain's claim to the Indies. To satisfy the royal conscience, a distinguished jurist, Dr. Juan López de Palacios Rubios, drew up a document, the *Requerimiento*, which the conquistadors were required to read before making war on indigenous peoples. This curious manifesto called on the natives to acknowledge the supremacy of the church and the pope and the sovereignty of the Spanish monarchs over their lands by virtue of the papal donation of 1493, on pain of suffering war and enslavement. Not until they had rejected those demands, which interpreters were to make known to them, could the Spanish legally wage war against them. Some conquistadors took the Requirement lightly, mumbling it into their beards before an attack or reading it to captured natives after a raid; the chronicler Oviedo relates that Palacios Rubios himself laughed heartily when told of the strange use these captains made of the document.

Bartolomé de Las Casas, the former ***encomendero*** (encomienda owner) who had repented of his ways and later turned friar, now joined the struggle against indigenous slavery and the doctrines of Palacios Rubios. Of the Requirement, Las Casas said that, upon reading it, he could not decide whether to laugh or weep. Las Casas argued that the Pope had granted America to the crown of Castile solely for the purpose of conversion; it gave the Spanish crown no temporal power or possession in the Indies. The indígenas had rightful possession of their lands by natural law and the law of nations. All Spanish wars and conquests in the New World were illegal. According to Las Casas, Spain must bring Christianity to indigenous peoples by the only method "that is proper and natural to men … namely, love and gentleness and kindness."

Las Casas hoped for a peaceful colonization of the New World by Spanish farmers who would live side by side with the natives, teach them to farm and live in the European way, and gradually bring into being an ideal Christian community. A series of disillusioning experiences, including the destruction of an experimental colony on the coast of Venezuela (1521), turned Las Casas's mind toward more radical solutions. His final program called for the suppression of all encomiendas, liberation of the indígenas from all forms of servitude except a small voluntary tribute to the crown in recompense for its gift of Christianity, and the restoration of their ancient states and rulers, the rightful owners of those lands. Over these states the Spanish king would preside as "Emperor over many kings" to fulfill his sacred mission of bringing them to the Catholic faith and the Christian way of life. The instruments of that mission should be friars, who would enjoy special jurisdiction over indigenous peoples and protect them from the corrupting influence of lay Spaniards. Although Las Casas's proposals appeared radical, they in fact served the royal aim of curbing the power of the conquistadors and preventing the rise of a powerful colonial feudalism in the New World. Not humanitarianism but self-interest, above all, explains the partial official support that Las Casas's reform efforts received during the reign of Charles V (1516–1556).

This question became crucial with the conquest of the rich, populous empires of Mexico and Peru. The most elementary interests of the crown demanded that its representatives should not repeat the West Indian catastrophe in the newly conquered lands. In 1523, Las Casas appeared to have won a major victory. King Charles sent Cortés an order forbidding the establishment of encomiendas in New Spain (the name given to the former Aztec empire), because "God created the Indians free and not subject." Cortés, who already had assigned encomiendas to himself and his comrades, did not enforce the order. Backed by the strength and needs of his hard-bitten soldiers, he argued so persuasively for the encomienda system as necessary for the welfare and security of the colony that the crown revoked the royal order. Encomienda tribute and labor, supplemented by slaves captured in war, continued to be the main source of income for the colonists until the middle of the sixteenth century.

THE NEW LAWS OF THE INDIES AND THE ENCOMIENDA

Despite its retreat in the face of Cortés's disobedience, the crown renewed its efforts to bring indigenous tribute and labor under royal control. Cautiously, it moved to curb the power of the conquistadors and established the second *audiencia* (high court) of New Spain in 1531–1532 after a stormy period of rule by the first "gangster" audiencia, which devoted itself to despoiling Cortés and mercilessly oppressing the natives. Taking the first steps in the regulation of tribute and labor, the second audiencia moderated the tribute paid by many indigenous towns, provided for registration of tribute assessments, and forbade, in principle, the use of natives as carriers without their consent. The climax of royal intervention came with proclamation of the New Laws of the Indies (1542). These laws appeared to doom the encomienda. They prohibited the enslavement of native peoples, ordered the release of slaves to whom legal title could not be proved, barred compulsory personal service by indígenas, regulated tribute, and declared that existing encomiendas were to lapse on the death of the holder.

In Peru, the New Laws provoked a great revolt; in New Spain, they caused a storm of protest by the encomenderos and a large part of the clergy.

Under this pressure the crown again retreated. It reaffirmed the laws forbidding indigenous slavery and forced labor, but also recognized the right of inheritance by the heir of an encomendero and even extended it by stages to a third, fourth, and sometimes even a fifth life. Thereafter, or earlier in the absence of an heir, the encomienda reverted to the crown. In the natural course of events, the number of encomiendas steadily diminished and that of crown towns increased.

By about 1560, the encomienda had been "tamed." Royal intervention had curbed the power of the encomenderos and partially stabilized the tribute and labor situation, at least in areas near the colonial capitals. The audiencias now assessed tribute in most places and, on appeal from indigenous villages, made a continuing effort to adjust it to the fluctuations of population and harvests. The institution of *visita* (inspection of an indigenous town) and *cuenta* (the count) was responsible for making such adjustments. To determine an indigenous town's per capita quota, the visita sought information concerning its resources or capacity to pay. The cuenta, made at the same time, gave the number of tribute payers. About 1560, the annual tribute paid to the king or to an encomendero by each married tributary in New Spain was usually one silver peso and four-fifths of a bushel of maize or its equivalent in other produce.

This mechanism of assessment and copious protective legislation did not bring significant or enduring relief to indigenous peoples. Padding of population counts and other abuses by encomenderos and other interested parties were common. More important, recounts and reassessments consistently lagged behind the rapidly shrinking number of tribute payers, with the result that the survivors had to bear the tribute burdens of those who had died or fled. In addition, after Philip II (1556) ascended the throne, the dominant motive of Spain's policy became the increase of royal revenues to relieve the crown's desperate financial crisis. Native groups who were hitherto exempt from tribute lost their favored status, and the crown progressively raised the tribute quota. Because of these measures and the gradual reversion of encomiendas

to the crown, the amount of royal tribute collected annually in New Spain rose from about 100,000 pesos to well over 1 million pesos between 1550 and the close of the eighteenth century. (These figures do not take into account the impact of the considerable rise in prices on the tribute's value during the same period.)

For the colonists, however, the encomienda steadily declined in economic value. They lost the right to demand labor from their tributaries (1549), and they lost their fight to make the encomienda perpetual. The heaviest blow of all to the encomendero class was the catastrophic decline of the native population in the second half of the sixteenth century. In central Mexico, it dropped from perhaps 25 million in 1519 to slightly over 1 million in 1605. On the central coast of Peru, by 1575, the tributary population seems to have fallen to 4 percent of what it had been before the Conquest. For reasons that remain unclear, the rates of population decline in both Mexico and Peru appear to have been considerably higher on the coast than in the highlands. Diseases—especially those of European origin, against which the natives had no acquired immunity—such as measles, smallpox, typhus, and malaria were the major direct cause of this demographic disaster. However, overwork, malnutrition, severe social disorganization, and the resulting loss of the will to live underlay the terrible mortality associated with the great epidemics and even with epidemic-free years. In Peru, the great civil wars and disorder of the period from 1535 to 1550 undoubtedly contributed materially to depopulation.

As the number of their tributaries fell, the encomenderos' income from tribute dropped proportionately, whereas their expenses, which included the maintenance of a steward to collect tribute, support of a parish priest, and heavy taxes, remained steady or even increased. As a result, many encomenderos, as well as other Spaniards without encomiendas, began to engage in the more lucrative pursuits of agriculture, stock raising, and mining. The decline of the indigenous population, which sharply reduced the flow of foodstuffs and metals, stimulated a rapid growth of *haciendas* (Spanish estates) that produced grain and meat.

Thus, in central Mexico by the 1570s, and in the northern and central Andean highlands by the end of the sixteenth century, the encomienda had lost its original character of an institution based on the use of native labor without payment. Its importance as a source of revenue to Spanish colonists had greatly diminished, and the progressive reversion of individual encomiendas to the crown placed it in the way of extinction. These changes, however, did not take place everywhere. In areas that lacked precious metals, where agricultural productivity was low, and consequently little danger existed that the colonists might acquire excessive power, the crown permitted encomenderos to continue exploiting the forced labor of the natives. This was the case in Chile, where the encomienda based on personal service continued until 1791; in Venezuela, where it survived until the 1680s; and in Paraguay, where it still existed in the early 1800s. The crown also allowed the encomienda as a labor system to continue in such areas of New Spain as Oaxaca and Yucatán.

In Paraguay, the encomienda assumed a peculiar form that reflected the culture and social organization of its Guaraní people. After a failed attempt to colonize Argentina, the Spaniards who moved into the vicinity of the present-day city of Asunción found a population that lived in villages, each having four to eight communal buildings. Each building housed a patrilineal lineage composed of several families, which were frequently polygynous. With no hereditary chiefly class, the chiefs' tenure depended above all on their personal qualities, and there was no political organization above the village level. The Spaniards won the friendship of the Guaraní by helping them defeat their warlike neighbors, the nomadic hunting groups of the Chaco desert, and were rewarded with presents of food and women. In effect, the Spaniards became a class of headmen in Guaraní society. Because women played a key role in Guaraní agriculture and social organization, their culture required the relatives of the women who became Spanish concubines to provide the Spaniards with labor services as part of their kinship obligations. The lineage or household thus became the basis of the Paraguayan

encomienda—the name with which the Spaniards formalized their control of the groups of concubines and their relatives who surrounded and served them. Because the Spaniards could increase their access to labor by adding to the number of their concubines, official efforts to stop the colonists from invading native villages to get them or from trading women for horses or dogs proved ineffective. Efforts to limit the number of days the Guaraní had to work for the Spaniards were equally ineffective.

This arrangement was the ***encomienda originaria***, and it continued to the end of the colonial period. In 1556, the crown established a second encomienda, the ***encomienda mitaya***, alongside the original one. It allocated Guaraní men who lived within a 139-mile radius of Asunción to Spaniards, with the number of tributaries varying according to the rank or merits of the grantee. In Paraguay, unlike in the central areas of the empire, there was no payment for labor or specified amounts of tribute in goods or money. By 1688, because of the ravages of disease, the effects of ***mestizaje*** (miscegenation), and flight, colonial records identified only 21,950 Guaraní held in encomienda. By 1778, the number had dwindled to hundreds. Consequently, the ***mestizo*** (mixed-race) descendants of Spanish fathers began to supplement the few surviving Guaraní with black slaves, paying for them with the proceeds from the export of yerba mate, the area's chief staple and the source of a tea still greatly prized in southern South America. By 1782, blacks outnumbered Guaraní in the area.

REPARTIMIENTO, YANACONAJE, AND FREE LABOR

In the key areas of central Mexico and the Andean highlands, however, a new system, the ***repartimiento***, replaced forced labor under the encomienda after 1550. Under this system, all adult male indígenas were required to give a certain amount of their time in rotation throughout the year to work in Spanish mines and workshops, on farms and ranches, and on public works. The crown hoped this would regulate the use of an ever-diminishing pool of native labor and give access to such labor to both encomenderos and the growing number of Spaniards without encomiendas. The indígenas received a token wage for their work, but the repartimiento, like the encomienda, was essentially disguised slavery. The Spanish imprisoned, fined, and physically punished those who avoided service and community leaders who failed to provide the required quotas.

In Peru, where the condition of indigenous peoples seems to have been generally worse than in New Spain, the repartimiento (here known as the *mita*) produced especially disastrous effects. Under this system, developed by Viceroy Francisco de Toledo in the 1570s, all able-bodied native men in the provinces subject to the mita were required to work for six-month periods, one year in seven, at Potosí or other mining centers, or were assigned to other Spanish employers. The silver mines of Potosí and the Huancavelica mercury mine were notorious deathtraps for laborers under the mita. In Peru and Bolivia, the mita remained an important source of labor in mining and agriculture up to the end of the colonial period.

In the Andean area, another institution borrowed from Inca society supplemented the repartimiento: the system of *yanaconas* (indigenous peoples bound to personal service). This system separated indígenas from their communities and forced them to reside on Spanish lands and serve Spaniards as personal servants. Like European serfs, the yanaconas belonged to the estate and were subject to sale along with the land. By the end of the sixteenth century, the number of yanaconas on Spanish haciendas was almost equal to the number of natives who lived in their own communities.

Although the repartimiento offered a temporary solution to the critical labor problem, many Spanish employers found it unsatisfactory because it did not provide a dependable and continuing supply of labor. From an early date, mine owners and *hacendados* (large landowners) in New Spain turned increasingly to the use of wage labor. The heavy weight of tribute and repartimiento obligations on a diminishing native population and Spanish usurpation of indigenous communal lands induced many to accept an hacendado's invitation to become farm laborers who would work for wages, mostly paid in kind. Some traveled back and forth to work from their communities, whereas others became resident peons on the haciendas. Yet relatively high wages lured others to the northern silver mines.

When the crown abolished the agricultural repartimiento in central Mexico in 1630, it provoked little or no protest because most landowners relied on wage labor. The mining repartimiento, however, continued in New Spain. It still functioned intermittently in the eighteenth century but had little importance because the mines of New Spain operated mainly with contractual labor. In Peru and Bolivia, wage labor was less important because the mita—supplemented by *yanaconaje* (semi-servile indigenous labor)—was the dominant labor system and provided a mass of cheap workers for the high-cost silver mines. However, as many as forty thousand free indigenous miners (known as *mingas*) were employed at the Potosí mines in the seventeenth century.[2] From the first, this wage labor was associated with debt servitude. The second half of the seventeenth century saw the growth of the system of repartimiento or *repartimiento de mercancías*,[3] the compulsory purchase by indigenous villages of goods from district governors (corregidores, *alcaldes mayores*). In combination with their other burdens, repartimiento was a powerful inducement for them to accept advances of cash and goods from Spanish hacendados; the tribute payment usually was included in the reckoning. A native so indebted had to work for his employer until the debt was paid. Despite its later evil reputation, peonage, whether or not enforced by debts, had definite advantages. It

2. In the early seventeenth century, the growing shortage of indigenous labor, resulting from the ravages of epidemic disease and the flight from communities subject to the mita, gave rise to a new system; deliveries of silver, collected from native communities and raised through the operation of economic enterprises supervised by curacas, replaced the delivery of mita labor. Mine owners used this silver to cover minga costs and to hire minga substitutes for *mitayos* (mita labor) not received in person.

3. The term repartimiento also referred to the periodic conscription of natives for labor useful to the Spanish community.

usually freed indígenas from the recurrent tribute and repartimiento burdens of their community and offered security in the form of a plot of land they could work for themselves and their families. But if the hacienda offered escape from intolerable conditions, it aggravated the difficulties of those who remained on their ancestral lands. The hacienda expanded by legal or illegal means at the expense of the indigenous *pueblo* (town), absorbing whole towns and leaving others without enough land for their people when the long population decline finally ended in the first half of the seventeenth century and a slow recovery began. The hacienda also lured laborers from the pueblo, making it difficult for indigenous towns to meet their tribute and repartimiento obligations. Between the two *repúblicas* (commonwealths), the *república de indios* and the *república de españoles*, as Spanish documents frequently called them, stretched a gulf of hostility and distrust.

The importance of debt servitude as a means of securing and holding labor varied according to the availability of wage labor. It predominated in northern Mexico, where such labor was scarce, but it was less important in central Mexico, where workers were more abundant. Some recent studies stress that debt peonage was "more of an inducement than a bond," with the size of advances reflecting the bargaining power of labor in dealing with employers, and that hacendados sometimes made no special effort to recover their peons who had fled without repayment of loans. However, the evidence for such relative lack of concern about fugitive peons comes chiefly from late-eighteenth-century Mexico, when labor was increasingly abundant. For earlier, labor-scarce periods, much evidence exists of strenuous efforts to compel indígenas to remain on estates until they had repaid their debts. Indeed, hacendados and officials sometimes likened Mexican peons to European serfs who were bound to their estates, with the right to their services passing with the transfer of the land from one owner to another.

Widely used in agriculture and mining, debt servitude assumed its harshest form in the numerous *obrajes* (workshops), which produced cloth and other goods, that sprang up in many areas in the sixteenth and seventeenth centuries. Early on, the "free" labor of natives ensnared by a variety of devices supplemented convict labor, assigned to employers by Spanish judges. Unscrupulous Spaniards often lured natives into these workshops with offers of liquor or a small sum of money and, once inside the gates, forbid their escape. "In this way," wrote a seventeenth-century observer,

> they have gathered in and duped many married Indians with families, who have passed into oblivion here for twenty years, or longer, or their whole lives, without their wives or children knowing anything about them; for even if they want to get out, they cannot, thanks to the great watchfulness with which the doormen guard the exits.

BLACK SLAVERY

Side by side with the disguised slavery of repartimiento and debt servitude existed black slavery. For a variety of reasons, including that Spaniards and Portuguese were accustomed to keeping black slaves, the beliefs that blacks were the descendants of the biblical Ham and bore his curse, and that they were better able to support the hardships of plantation labor, Spanish defenders of the "Indian" did not display the same zeal on behalf of enslaved Africans.

In fact, the rapid development of sugar-cane agriculture in the West Indies in the early 1500s brought an insistent demand for black slave labor to replace the vanishing natives. A lucrative slave trade arose, chiefly carried on by foreigners under a system of *asiento* (a contract between an individual or company and the Spanish crown). The high cost of slaves tended to limit their use to the more profitable plantation cultures or to domestic service in the homes of the wealthy. Large numbers lived on the coasts of Venezuela and Colombia, where they produced such crops as cacao, sugar, and tobacco, and in the coastal valleys of Peru, where they labored on sugar and cotton plantations, but smaller concentrations existed in every part of the Indies. In

Chapter 5, we shall consider the much-disputed question of whether enslavement of Africans in Hispanic America was "milder" than in other European colonies.

All colonial labor systems rested in varying degrees on servitude and coercion. Although contractual labor gradually emerged as the theoretical norm, all these labor systems coexisted throughout the colonial period. For example, the crown legally abolished indigenous slavery in 1542, but it continued in frontier areas on various pretexts into the eighteenth century. Which labor system dominated at a given time and place depended on such factors as the area's natural resources, the number of Europeans in the area and the character of their economic activities, the size and cultural level of its indigenous population, and the crown's economic and political interests. Finally, in the course of the sixteenth and seventeenth centuries, the labor pool gradually expanded with the addition of mestizos, free blacks and mulattos, and poor whites. Because most of these people were exempt from encomienda and repartimiento obligations, they usually worked for wages and enjoyed freedom of movement, but like the indígenas, they were subject to control through debts. In Chapter 7, we shall discuss eighteenth-century changes in the labor system.

The Colonial Economy

The Conquest disrupted the traditional subsistence-and-tribute economy of indigenous communities. War and disease took a heavy toll of lives, to the detriment of production. In some areas, Spanish attacks destroyed the complex irrigation networks established and maintained by centralized native authorities. The Conquest also transformed the character and tempo of economic activity. When the frenzied scramble for treasure had ended with the exhaustion of the available gold and silver objects, the encomienda became the principal instrument for the extraction of wealth from the vanquished. The peoples of the Aztec and Inca empires were accustomed to paying tribute in labor and commodities to their rulers and nobility. However, the tribute demands of the old ruling classes, al-

though apparently increasing on the eve of the Conquest, had been limited by custom and by the capacity of their ruling groups to utilize tribute goods. The greater part of such tribute was destined for consumption or display, not for trade. The demands of the new Spanish masters, on the other hand, were unlimited. Gold and silver were their great objects; if they could not obtain these directly, the encomenderos proposed to obtain them by sale in local or distant markets of their tribute goods. Driven by visions of infinite wealth, the Spaniards took no account of indigenous tribute traditions and exploited them mercilessly. A compassionate missionary, writing in 1554, complained that before the Conquest the native peoples in his part of Mexico

> never used to give such large loads of *mantas* [pieces of cotton cloth], nor had they ever heard of beds, fine cotton fabrics, wax, or a thousand other fripperies like bed sheets, tablecloths, shirts, and skirts. All they used to do was cultivate the fields of their lords, build their houses, repair the temples, and give of the produce of their fields when their lords asked for it.

CORTÉS AS A BUSINESSMAN

The business career of Hernando Cortés illustrates the large variety and scale of the economic activities of some encomenderos. By 1528, Cortés was already worth 500,000 gold pesos. Part of this wealth represented his share of the loot taken in Tenochtitlán and other places during and immediately after the Conquest. However, his chief source of income was his encomienda holdings. He assigned himself the richest tribute areas in the former Aztec empire. At the time of his death in 1547, although the crown had drastically reduced many of his encomiendas and lowered tribute assessments, he still received 30,000 gold pesos annually from this source. He received large quantities of gold dust, textiles, maize, poultry, and other products from encomienda towns. The pueblo of Cuernavaca (near Mexico City) alone gave as part of its annual tribute cloth worth 5,000 gold pesos. Cortés's

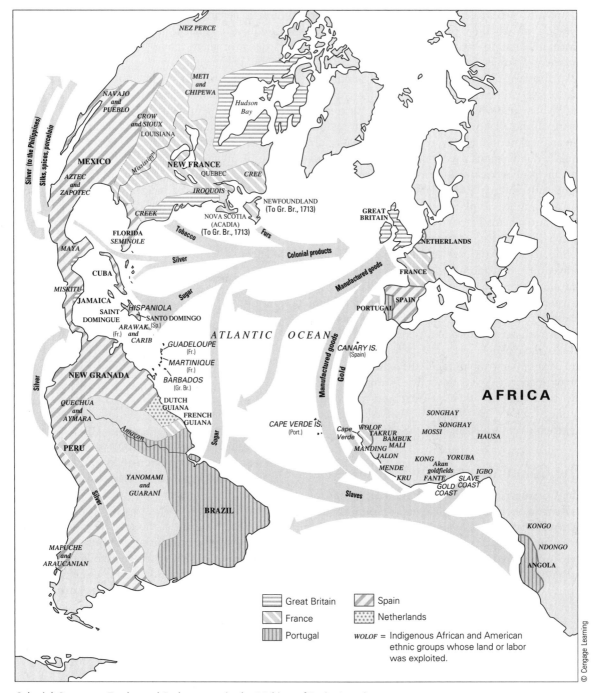

Colonial Conquest, Trade, and Enslavement in the Making of Latin America

agents sold the tribute cloth and other products to traders, who retailed them in Mexico City and other Spanish towns. Cortés had his own extensive real estate holdings in Mexico City. On or near the central square, he erected shops, some of which he used for his own trading interests and some that he rented out.

Cortés was an empire builder in the economic as well as the political sense of the word. He invested the capital he acquired from encomienda tribute and labor in many enterprises. Mining attracted his special attention. In the Oaxaca and Michoacán districts, he had gangs of indigenous slaves, more than a thousand in each, panning gold; many of these slaves died from hard labor and inadequate food. In 1529, these mining areas brought him 12,000 pesos in gold annually. In addition to his own mining properties, Cortés held others, such as silver mines in the Taxco area of Mexico, in partnerships. In such cases, his investment usually consisted of goods, livestock, encomienda, or black slave labor.

After encomienda tribute, agriculture and stock raising were Cortés's largest sources of income. He had large landholdings in various parts of Mexico, some acquired by royal grant, others usurped from native peoples. He employed encomienda labor to grow maize on his land. His fields near Oaxaca alone produced ten to fifteen thousand bushels a year. Part of this grain he sold in the Spanish towns and at the mines; part went to feed his gangs of slaves at the gold washings. Cortés also raised great numbers of cattle and hogs, which were butchered in his own slaughterhouses. Near Tehuantepec, he had herds of more than ten thousand wild cattle, which supplied hides and tallow for export to Panama and Peru.

The restless Cortés also was a pioneer in the development of the Mexican sugar industry. By 1547, his plantations produced more than three hundred thousand pounds of sugar annually, most of which he sold to agents of European merchants for export. If he was not the first to experiment with silk raising in New Spain, as he claimed, he certainly went into the business on a large scale, planting thousands of mulberry trees with native

labor paid in cash or cacao beans. In this venture, however, he suffered heavy losses. Nonetheless, the variety and extent of Cortés's business interests suggest how misleading is the familiar portrait of the conquistador as a purely feudal type devoted only to war and plunder, disdainful of all trade and industry.

THE GROWTH OF THE HACIENDAS

Among the first generation of colonists, large-scale enterprises such as those of Cortés were rare. The typical encomendero was content to occupy a relatively small land grant and draw tribute from natives who continued to live and work in large numbers on their ancestral lands. The major shift from reliance on encomienda tribute to the development of Spanish commercial agriculture and stock raising came after 1550 in response to the massive indigenous population decline and the crown's restrictive legislation, which combined to deprive the encomienda of much of its economic value. Acute food shortages in the Spanish towns created new economic opportunities for Spanish farmers and ranchers. Simultaneously, this population decline left vacant large expanses of land, which Spanish colonists hastened to occupy for wheat raising or, more commonly, for sheep or cattle ranges.

By the end of the sixteenth century, the Spanish-owned hacienda was responsible for the bulk of agricultural commercial production and pressed ever more aggressively on the shrinking native sector of the colonial economy. Spanish colonists used various methods to "free" land from indigenous occupation: purchase, usurpation, and *congregación* (forced concentration of natives in new communities, ostensibly to facilitate control and Christianization). Although Spain's declared policy was to protect community land, the numerous laws forbidding encroachment on such land failed to halt the advance of the hacienda. The power of the hacendados, whose ranks included high royal officials, churchmen, and wealthy merchants, usually carried all before it.

In the seventeenth century, the crown, facing an acute, chronic economic crisis, actually encouraged usurpation of indigenous lands by adopting the device of *composición* (settlement), which legalized the defective title of the usurper through payment of a fee to the king. Native communities, Spanish, and mestizo small farmers all saw their lands devoured by the advancing hacienda. A striking feature of this process was that hacendados sometimes acquired land primarily to obtain day laborers and peons by depriving them of their fields or to eliminate competition from small producers. The establishment of a *mayorazgo* (entailed estate) ensured the perpetuation of the consolidated property in the hands of the owner's descendants, but this feudal device required approval by the crown and payment of a large fee and benefited only a small number of wealthy families.

A more common strategy for consolidation and preservation of holdings was marriage within the extended family, often between cousins. In the majority of cases, however, this and other strategies for ensuring the longevity of family estates were less than successful. Spanish inheritance laws that required the equal division of estates among heirs, economic downturns, and lack of investment capital because of large expenditures for conspicuous consumption and donations to the church were some of the factors that made for an unstable landed elite and a high turnover rate in estate ownership. Historian Susan Ramírez studied the collective biography of colonial elite families who lived in north coastal Peru over a period of three hundred years. She found that, contrary to tradition, this elite was "unstable, open, and in constant flux," with most families lasting no more than two or three generations. The historian Lucas Alamán, himself a member of Mexico's former colonial elite, alluded to this instability at the top, citing a Mexican proverb: "The father a merchant, the son a gentleman, the grandson a beggar."

The tempo of land concentration varied from region to region according to its resources and proximity to markets. In the Valley of Mexico, for example, great haciendas held the bulk of the land by the end of the colonial period. Native commoners and chiefs, on the other hand, retained much of the land in the province of Oaxaca, which had limited markets for its crops. Recent studies of the colonial hacienda stress the large variations in hacienda size and productivity from one region to another. This variety in size and productivity reflects the great regional divergencies in productive potential—determined by proximity to water and quality of soil—and in access to labor and markets, among other variables, in the vast Spanish empire in America.

Despite the long-term trend toward land concentration, a class of mostly mixed-race small farmers of uncertain size gradually arose. In Mexico, such small farmers, typically mestizos, came to be known as *rancheros*, and they were interspersed among the native villages and commercial estates of the central and southern highlands. Some were former *mayordomos* (foremen) of large landowners from whom they rented or leased unused portions of their estates, generally raising products for sale in local markets. Their limited resources and dependence on large landowners made their situation precarious; in prosperous times of rising land values, their wealthy neighbors often swallowed up their small properties. Less frequently, successful rancheros expanded their holdings and themselves joined the ranks of the landed elite.

SPANISH AGRICULTURE IN THE NEW WORLD

Spanish agriculture differed from indigenous land use in significant ways. First, it was extensive, cultivating large tracts with plows and draft animals, in contrast to the intensive native digging-stick agriculture. Second, Spanish agriculture was predominantly commercial, producing commodities for sale in local or distant markets, in contrast to the subsistence character of traditional agriculture. Through the need to pay tribute and other obligations in cash, the indigenous farmer came under increasing pressure to produce for the market. But, as a rule, the hacendado's superior resources made it difficult for him to compete except in times of abundant harvests, and he tended to fall back to the level of subsistence agriculture, whose meager yield he sometimes supplemented by labor for the local hacendado.

Spanish colonial agriculture early produced wheat on a large scale to sell in urban centers like Mexico City, Lima, Veracruz, and Cartagena. Haciendas also produced maize for the sizable local consumers' market in Mexico City and Lima. Sugar, like wheat, was one of Europe's agricultural gifts to America. Spaniards brought it from the Canary Islands to Hispaniola, where it soon became the foundation of the island's prosperity. By 1550, more than twenty sugar mills processed cane into sugar and shipped it in great quantities to Spain. "The sugar industry is the principal industry of those islands," wrote José de Acosta at the end of the sixteenth century, "such a taste have men developed for sweets." From the West Indies, sugar quickly spread to Mexico and Peru. After silver mining, sugar refining, with its large capital outlays for equipment and black slaves, was the largest-scale enterprise in the Indies.

The irrigated coastal valleys of Peru produced wine and olives, as well as sugar, in quantity. The silk industry had a brief period of prosperity in Mexico but soon declined in the face of labor shortages and competition from Chinese silk brought in the Manila galleons from the Philippines to the port of Acapulco. Spain's sporadic efforts to discourage the production of wine, olives, and silk, regarded as interfering with Spanish exports of the same products, seem to have had little effect. Other products cultivated by the Spaniards on an extensive plantation basis included tobacco, cacao, and indigo. Cochineal, a blood-red dye made from the dried bodies of insects parasitic on the nopal cactus, also was a unique Mexican and Central American export, highly valued by the European cloth industry.

Spain made a major contribution to American economic life with the introduction of various domestic animals—chickens, mules, horses, cattle, pigs, and sheep. The mules and horses revolutionized transport, gradually eliminating the familiar spectacle of long lines of native carriers loaded down with burdens. Horses and mules became vital to the mining industry for hauling and turning machinery. Cattle and smaller domesticated animals greatly enlarged the food resources of the conti-

nent. Meat was indispensable to the mining industry, for only a meat diet could sustain the hard work of the miners. "If the mines have been worked at all," wrote a Spanish judge in 1606, "it is thanks to the plentiful and cheap supply of livestock." In addition to meat, cattle provided hides for export to Spain and other European centers of leather manufacture, as well as hides and tallow (used for lighting) for the domestic market, especially in the mining areas. Sheep raisers found a large market for their wool in the textile workshops that arose in many parts of the colonies.

In a densely settled region like central Mexico, the explosive increase of Spanish cattle and sheep had catastrophic consequences. A horde of animals swarmed over the land, often invading not only the land vacated by the dwindling native population but the reserves of land needed by their system of field rotation. Cattle trampled the indigenous crops, causing untold damage; torrential rains caused massive erosion on valley slopes close-cropped by sheep. By the end of the sixteenth century, however, the Mexican cattle industry had achieved stability. Exhaustion of virgin pasturelands, mass slaughter of cattle for their hides and tallow, and official efforts to halt grazing on native harvest lands had produced a marked reduction in the herds. The problem further abated in the seventeenth century because of the cumulative transfer of these lands in the Central Valley to Spaniards who established haciendas that produced *pulque* (a fermented drink popular with the natives) and wheat. Gradually, the cattle ranches and sheep herds moved to new, permanent grazing grounds in the sparsely settled, semiarid north.

An equally rapid increase of horses, mules, and cattle took place in the vast, rich *pampas* (grasslands) of the Río de la Plata (modern Argentina). Their increase in this area of almost infinite pasturage soon outstripped potential demand and utilization, and herds of wild cattle became a common phenomenon in La Plata, as in other parts of Spanish America. Barred by Spanish law from seaborne trade with the outside world, the inhabitants of this remote province, lacking precious metals or abundant native labor, relieved their poverty by illegal commerce with Dutch and other foreign traders, who carried their hides and tallow to Europe. In addition, they sent mules and horses, hides, and tallow to the mining regions of Upper Peru (Bolivia).

Another center of the cattle industry was the West Indies. José de Acosta wrote in 1590 that

> the cattle have multiplied so greatly in Santo Domingo and in other islands of that region that they wander by the thousands through the forests and fields, all master-less. They hunt these beasts only for their hides; whites and Negroes go out on horseback, equipped with a kind of hooked knife, to chase the cattle, and any animal that falls to their knives is theirs. They kill it and carry the hide home, leaving the flesh to rot; no one wants it, since meat is so plentiful.

COLONIAL MINING AND INDUSTRY

Mining, as the principal source of royal revenue in the form of the quinto (the royal one-fifth of all gold, silver, or other precious metals obtained in the Indies), received the special attention and protection of the crown. Silver, rather than gold, was the principal product of the American mines. Spain's proudest possession in the New World was the great silver mine of Potosí in Upper Peru; discovered in 1545, its flow of treasure attained gigantic proportions between 1579 and 1635. A few years later, the Spanish opened the rich Mexican silver mines of Zacatecas and Guanajuato in 1548 and 1558, respectively. In the same period, Spaniards found important gold placers (sand or gravel deposits containing eroded particles of the ore) in central Chile and in the interior of New Granada (Colombia).

At first silver processing involved the simple and inexpensive technique of smelting, in which heavy iron hammers and stamping mills broke up the ore, which they fired in furnaces using charcoal or other fuel. However, smelting was labor intensive and heavily dependent on adequate supplies of fuel, which created serious problems for an Andean mining center like Potosí, located high above the

timberline, or the Mexican center of Zacatecas, situated in a semiarid area far from the densely populated central zone from which it needed to draw its workforce. Thus, in 1556, the introduction of the patio or amalgamation process, which used mercury to separate the silver from the ore, gave a great stimulus to silver mining. The chief source of mercury for Potosí silver was the Peruvian Huancavelica mine, whose health hazards and wretched working conditions made labor there "a thing of horror." Mexican silver was processed chiefly with mercury from the Almaden mine in Spain.

Lack of capital to finance technical improvements required by the gradual exhaustion of veins and increasing depth of mines, flooding, and other problems, combined with the high cost of mercury (a crown monopoly), caused a precipitous decline in silver production at Potosí after 1650. The rise of new Peruvian centers like Oruro and Cerro de Pasco, however, partially offset this decline. In Mexico, production levels fluctuated, with output declining in some old centers like Zacatecas and rising in new ones like Parral, but here the long-range trend for the seventeenth century seems to have been upward. Notwithstanding earlier historians' claims that an acute labor shortage caused by the catastrophic fall of the native population was the root cause of a supposed decline in silver production in New Spain, it now appears that mine owners in general had no difficulty filling their labor needs. After 1650, in both Peru and Mexico, silver mining shifted from large centers like Potosí and Zacatecas to small, dispersed, and mobile mining camps. In the same period, many mine owners abandoned the amalgamation process, based on scarce and costly mercury, in favor of smelting. Because the quantity of mercury a mine owner purchased gave royal officials a fairly accurate measure of silver production, by using the smelting process, the mine owner could cut his costs and also evade payment of all or a part of the quinto, the *alcabala* (sales tax), and other taxes to the detriment of the royal treasury. Great quantities of such untaxed, illegal silver circulated at home or went to Europe or Asia to pay for smuggled goods. The loss of royal control over the quality and destination of a large

The Art Archive/Science Academy Lisbon/Dagli Orti

Theodore de Bry's 1590 engraving graphically depicts the exploitation of enslaved labor in the mines of Potosí, whose wealth provided an extraordinary stimulus to European economic development.

part of silver production aggravated the chronic colonial problem of coin shortage and unreliability,[4] causing increased resorts to barter and substitute money on the local level and adding to the difficulty of long-distance trade.

The transformation of the silver mining industry in the seventeenth century had other consequences. One was the disruption of the commercial and agricultural networks that had arisen to provide the great mining centers with grain, hides, tallow, and work animals. The resulting contraction of commercial agriculture and stock raising gave rise in some areas, like northern New Spain, to a characteristic institution of the period, the self-sufficient great hacienda. It typically housed an extended, elite family, over which a patriarch presided—monarch of all he surveyed, ruling his own little world with its workforce, church, jail, workshops, storehouses, and private army.

Scholars continue to debate whether the seventeenth century was a time of crisis and depression

---

4. By way of example, in the mid-seventeenth century the *alcalde provincial* of Potosí, in collusion with officials and technicians of the Potosí mint, adulterated with copper the silver coins that went into circulation. The fraud, says Peruvian historian Luis Millones, had "enormous repercussions," causing a loss of 200,000 ducats to the royal treasury and an immediate steep rise in prices.

for colonial Spanish America—the dominant view a few decades ago—or one of growing colonial autonomy, both economic and political—a view now favored by many students. An argument cited by the supporters of the thesis of a colonial economic crisis was the spectacular decline in silver remittances to Spain after 1630. Recent studies of the accounts of colonial treasuries, however, suggest that the decision of Spanish officials to retain large quantities of silver in America to cover local administrative and defense needs caused much of this decline. Another cause of the decline was a growing colonial self-sufficiency that, combined with a vast increase in smuggled goods, sharply reduced the demand for higher priced Spanish goods. By the opening of the seventeenth century, Mexico, Peru, and Chile had become self-sufficient in grains and partly so in wine, olive oil, ironware, and furniture. The moribund state of Spanish industry in the seventeenth century contributed to its loss of American markets.

Then, in 1985, a French scholar, Michel Morineau, published a book that radically changed the terms of the debate on the colonial "economic crisis." Based on Dutch commercial journals that recorded the arrival of colonial precious metals and merchandise in European ports, he showed that contraband shipments of colonial silver and gold in the same period to northern European ports offset the decline in remittances of precious metals to Spanish ports. The sum of contraband shipments and legal remittances to Spain revealed that the volume of colonial precious metals shipped to Europe in the seventeenth century did not decline. Therefore, the thesis of a colonial "economic crisis" based on that assumption falls of its own weight.

The debate continues, but the evidence regarding colonial economic trends was at best mixed and contradictory, making it difficult to determine how real the assumed seventeenth-century "depression" was. In New Spain, for example, proceeds from the alcabala (sales tax), a significant indicator of the state of the economy, increased until 1638 and declined only slightly thereafter. If a seventeenth-century depression did occur, its impact was uneven, with some regions and sectors of the economy rising and others falling. Thus, after the cacao industry of Central America collapsed, together with its native population, there arose a brisk trade in cacao between Venezuela and Mexico. In short, no evidence of a decline in overall levels of production and domestic trade exists. As regards foreign trade, Morineau's findings suggest the contrary is true.

The Spaniards had found a flourishing handicrafts industry in the advanced culture areas of Mexico, Central America, and Peru. Throughout the colonial period, the majority of the natives continued to supply most of their own needs for pottery, clothing, and household goods. In the Spanish towns, craft guilds modeled on those of Spain arose in response to the high prices for all Spanish imported goods. To avoid competition from indigenous, black, and mestizo artisans, who quickly learned the Spanish crafts, the Spanish-controlled guilds incorporated them but prohibited them from becoming masters. The chronic shortage of skilled labor, however, soon made all such racial restrictions meaningless. These guilds attempted to maintain careful control over the quantity and quality of production in industries that served the needs of the colonial upper class.

The period up to about 1630 saw a steady growth of obrajes, many of which produced cheap cotton and woolen goods for popular consumption. Most of these were private enterprises, but indigenous communities operated some to meet their tribute payments. A number of towns in New Spain (Mexico City, Puebla, and Tlaxcala, among others) were centers of this textile industry. Other primitive factories produced such articles as soap, chinaware, and leather. The population increase of the late seventeenth century may have also stimulated the growth of manufacturing. Little evidence indicates that sporadic Spanish legislative efforts to restrict the growth of colonial manufacturers were successful.

Commerce, Smuggling, and Piracy

THE COLONIAL COMMERCIAL SYSTEM

Spain's colonial commercial system was restrictive, exclusive, and regimented in character, in conformity with the mercantilist standards of that day.

The Royal Council of the Indies vested control over all colonial trade in the *Casa de Contratación* (House of Trade), established in 1503 in Seville. This agency licensed and supervised all ships, passengers, crews, and goods passing to and from the Indies. It also collected import and export duties and the royal share of all precious metals and stones brought from the Indies, licensed all pilots, and maintained a *padrón real* (standard chart) to which all charts issued to ships in the Indies trade had to conform. It even operated a school of navigation that trained the pilots and officers needed to sail the ships in the transatlantic trade.

Until the eighteenth century, the Hapsburg crown restricted commerce with the colonies to the wealthier merchants of Seville and Cádiz, who organized a guild that exercised great influence in all matters relating to colonial trade. With the aim of preventing contraband trade and safeguarding the Seville monopoly, trade was concentrated in three American ports: Veracruz in New Spain, Cartagena in New Granada, and Nombre de Dios on the Isthmus of Panama. The Seville merchant oligarchy and corresponding merchant groups in the Indies, particularly the merchant guilds in Mexico City and Lima, deliberately kept the colonial markets understocked. In general, they played into each other's hands at the expense of the colonists, who were forced to pay exorbitant prices for all European goods acquired through legal channels. Inevitably, the system generated colonial discontent and stimulated the growth of contraband trade.

With the object of enforcing the closed-port policy and protecting merchant vessels against foreign attack, a fleet system gradually emerged and became obligatory in the sixteenth century. Perfected in the middle of the century, it called for two fleets, each numbering fifty or more ships, to sail annually under armed convoy. One left in the spring for Veracruz, taking with it ships bound for Honduras and the West Indies; the other sailed in August for Panama and convoyed ships for Cartagena and other ports on the northern coast of South America. Veracruz supplied Mexico and most of Central America; they carried Portobelo goods across the isthmus and shipped them to Lima, the

distribution point for Spanish goods to places as distant as Chile and Buenos Aires. Having loaded their returns of silver and colonial produce, the fleets were to rendezvous at Havana and sail for Spain in the spring, before the onset of the hurricane season. In the seventeenth century, because of Spain's economic decadence and the growing volume of contraband trade, fleet sailings became increasingly irregular.

In the 1570s, Mexican merchants pioneered an immensely lucrative trade between Acapulco and Manila. The annual voyage of the Manila galleon exchanged Mexican silver, which was in great demand in China, for silks, porcelains, and spices. A foreign observer estimated that the Mexican merchants who dominated the trade doubled the money they spent on it every year. From Acapulco to Manila, the ship ran with the trade wind for a space of eight to ten weeks. The return passage, however, in a region with unreliable winds and frequent typhoons, could take from four to seven months, and, according to historian J.H. Parry, on the longer voyages, the ravages of "hunger, thirst, and scurvy could reduce a ship to a floating cemetery." Spanish officials disliked the trade because it drained off bullion, most of which came from Peru, and because it flooded Peru with Chinese silks that reduced the demand for Spanish textiles. But the demand for silk was so insatiable and the supply so inadequate that considerable quantities went by pack train across Mexico to Veracruz and from there were shipped again to Spain. As with the transatlantic trade, Spain sought to regulate and limit trade with Asia, limiting the size of ships in 1593 to 300 tons and allowing only two ships to sail in any one year. The Manila galleon made its last voyage in 1811.

Danger and difficulty attended the long voyage to the Indies from the time a ship left Seville to thread its careful way down the shoal-ridden Guadalquivir to the Mediterranean. Hunger and thirst, seasickness and scurvy at sea, and yellow fever and malaria in tropical harbors like Veracruz and Portobelo were familiar afflictions. Storms at sea took a heavy toll of ships; foreign pirates and privateers posed a chronic threat. Because of competition from foreign smugglers and the crown's frequent confiscation of silver, with tardy or inadequate compensation, gluts of goods in the colonial markets often reduced merchants' profits to the vanishing point.

Spanish industry, handicapped by its guild organization and technical backwardness, could not supply the colonies with cheap and abundant manufactures in return for colonial foodstuffs and raw materials, as required by the implied terms of the mercantilist bargain. Indeed, it was not in the interest of the merchant monopolists of Seville and Cádiz, who thrived on a regime of scarcity and high prices, to permit an abundant flow of manufactures to the colonies. Prices to the colonial consumer were also raised by a multitude of taxes: the *avería* (convoy tax), the *almojarifazgo* (import duty), and the alcabala. Inevitably, the manufacturers and merchants of the advanced industrial nations of northern Europe sought to enter by force or guile the large and unsatisfied Spanish American markets. The ambitious monarchs of those lands scoffed at Spain's claim of dominion over all the Western Hemisphere except that portion that belonged to Portugal. They defied Spanish edicts forbidding foreigners to navigate American waters or trade on American coasts on pain of destruction of ships and crews. The ironic query said to have been addressed by Francis I of France to the kings of Spain and Portugal summed up the foreign viewpoint: "Show me, I pray you, the will of our father Adam, that I may see if he has really made you his only universal heirs."

SIR FRANCIS DRAKE, PIRACY, AND PLUNDER

England soon emerged as the principal threat to Spain's empire in America. The accumulation of capital and development of manufacturing under the fostering care of the Tudor kings produced an explosion of English commercial energies in the reign of Queen Elizabeth I. The Old World did not provide sufficient outlets for these erupting energies, and England's merchant adventurers eagerly turned to America. The historic slave-trading voyage of John Hawkins to the West Indies in 1562 opened England's drive to break into the closed Spanish American markets. Half honest trader, half corsair, Hawkins came to the Indies heavily armed and ready to compel the colonists to trade with him at cannon point, but he showed himself scrupulously honest in his business dealings with the Spaniards, even to the point of paying the royal license and customs dues. Hawkins owed the success of his first two American voyages to the needs of the Spanish settlers, who were ready to trade with a Lutheran heretic or the devil himself to satisfy their desperate need for slave labor and European wares. To cover up these violations of Spanish law, the venal local officials made a thin pretense of resistance. But, by 1567, that pretense had worn too thin, the Spanish government had taken alarm, and angry orders went out to drive away the English smugglers. Stiffening Spanish resistance culminated in the near-destruction of Hawkins's trading fleet by a Spanish naval force at Veracruz in 1568.

Only two of the English ships managed to get away: one commanded by Hawkins and one by his cousin, Francis Drake. Four years later, Drake left England with four small ships, bound for the Isthmus of Panama. In actions marked by audacity and careful planning, he stormed and plundered the town of Nombre de Dios, escaping at dawn. Later, he made the most lucrative haul in the history of piracy by capturing the pack train carrying Peruvian silver from the Pacific side of the isthmus to Nombre de Dios. In 1577, Drake set sail again on an expedition that had the secret sponsorship and support of Queen Elizabeth. Its objects, according to Drake, were to "singe the King of Spain's beard" by seizing his treasure ships and ravaging his colonial towns; to explore the whole Pacific coast of America, taking possession of the regions beyond the limits of Spanish occupation; and to display English maritime prowess by means of a second circumnavigation of the globe. The expedition of 1577 led by Francis Drake achieved these goals. In the 1580s, Drake made other voyages of reprisal against Cartagena, St. Augustine, and Santo Domingo. It is small wonder that the name Drake became a word of fear to the inhabitants of colonial coastal towns.

However, piracy began to decline after the signing of the Treaty of Madrid in 1670 between England and Spain, by which the British government agreed to aid in the suppression of the corsairs in return for Spanish recognition of its sovereignty over the British West Indian islands. French buccaneers, however, continued to be active until the signing of the Treaty of Ryswick in 1697, by which Spain formally recognized French possession of St. Domingue.

The injury that pirates and privateers inflicted on Spanish prosperity and prestige, great as it was, paled in comparison to the losses caused by the less spectacular operations of foreign smugglers. Contraband trade steadily increased in the course of the sixteenth and seventeenth centuries. European establishments in Jamaica, St. Domingue, and the Lesser Antilles became bases for contraband trade with the Spanish colonies. Buenos Aires was another funnel through which Dutch and other foreign traders poured immense quantities of goods that reached markets as distant as Peru. By the end of the seventeenth century, French companies, operating behind the façades of Spanish merchant houses in Seville and Cádiz, dominated even the legal trade with the Indies.

John Campbell, a shrewd Englishman, identified the major source of Spain's misfortunes: its economic weakness. The Spaniards, he remarked, were stewards for the rest of Europe:

> Their galleons bring the silver into Spain, but neither wisdom nor power can keep it there; it runs out as fast as it comes in, nay, and faster.... At first sight this seems to be strange and incredible; but when we come to examine it, the mystery is by no means impenetrable. The silver and rich commodities which come from the Indies come not for nothing (the king's duties excepted) and very little of the goods or

manufactures for which they come, belong to the subjects of the crown of Spain. It is evident, therefore, that the Spanish merchants are but factors, and that the greatest part of the returns from the West Indies belong to those foreigners for whom they negotiate.

Spanish economists of the seventeenth century understood the causes of Spain's plight. Their writings offered sound criticisms of the existing state of affairs and constructive proposals for reform. However, their arguments were powerless to change the course of Spanish policy, dictated by small mercantile and aristocratic cliques whose special interests and privileges were wholly incompatible with the cause of reform.

THE FRAMEWORK OF THE COLONIAL ECONOMY

Was the colonial economy capitalist, feudal, or something in between? Scholars have hotly debated this issue. Some, who believe that production for the market is the defining feature of capitalism, argue that Latin America has been capitalist since 1492.[5] Others deny the relevance of the concepts of **feudalism** and capitalism, taken from a European context, to a unique colonial reality. Most students, however, will admit the presence of capitalist, feudal, and even more archaic elements, such as the pre-Columbian indigenous communities based on communal land tenure, in the colonial economy. Spain tried, though not consistently, to preserve and protect that ancient corporate landowning system because it gave the crown direct control over native labor and tribute, which it then could allocate to the colonial elite in accord with its own policies and interests. That collective landowning system suffered severe erosion in the course of the colonial period because of the expansion of the Spanish agricultural sector, but at its

---

5. A leading exponent of the "Latin America-has-been-capitalist-all-along" view is André Gunder Frank (see Frank's *Capitalism and Underdevelopment in Latin America*, 1969). That view has come under heavy fire from scholars who define capitalism, first and foremost, as a mode of production based on wage labor that has lost its own means of production. See, for example, Colin Mooers, *The Making of Bourgeois Europe* (1991), pp. 5–17.

close it still maintained a large presence in many areas.

The feudal or semifeudal elements in the colonial economy included labor systems based in varying degrees on servitude and coercion, the nonmonetary character of many economic transactions,[6] and the technical backwardness of industry and agriculture. Together, these reflected the very low level of investment in production and contrasted with the high levels of expenditure for conspicuous consumption, the church, and charity. Regulations, such as those that forbade indígenas to wear European clothes or to own land privately, seriously hampered the development of a market economy and were clearly a legacy of Spanish feudalism.

This predominantly feudal character of the colonial economy reflected Spain's own backwardness. Indeed, in the course of the colonial period, Spain became in certain ways more feudal, more seigneurial. Part of the reason is that most of the wealth that flowed from the Indies to Spain paid for costly wars and diplomacy, supported a parasitic nobility, and imported goods from northern Europe, leaving little for development. Spain's dependence on colonial tribute and colonial trade monopoly inevitably strengthened the dominant aristocratic ideology and discouraged the rise of a dynamic entrepreneurial class. In fact, the passion for noble titles infected many members of the small middle class, who hastened to abandon their trades and invest their wealth in a mayorazgo. If the nobility had lost their feudal power to the crown on the national level, they nonetheless benefited, says John Lynch, "by the extension of their economic power, a process in which the crown itself was a willing ally." They also retained their feudal powers in their own districts, where they levied feudal dues, appointed local officials, and meted out justice. Indeed, under the last, weak Hapsburg kings, the nobility regained much of their old political

power. "By the late seventeenth century," writes Henry Kamen, "Spain was probably the only west European country to be completely and unquestionably under the control of the titled aristocracy." This aristocratic hegemony was a recipe for economic decay and collapse. We shall see that Spanish efforts in the eighteenth century to reverse these trends were too little and too late.

The colonial economy also contained some capitalist elements. Although based on such noncapitalist labor systems as slavery and debt peonage, the gold and silver mines, and the haciendas, ranches, and plantations that produced sugar, hides, cochineal, indigo, and other commodities for external markets were fully integrated into the expanding world market. These enterprises reflected the price fluctuations and other vicissitudes of that market and promoted the accumulation of capital in England and other lands of rising capitalism, not in Spain. Some capitalist shoots appeared in the colonies as well, notably in the great mining centers, sugar mills, and workshops that had achieved some development of wage labor and division of labor.

The development of colonial capitalism remained embryonic, however, stunted by the overwhelming weight of feudal relationships and attitudes and the continuous siphoning of its wealth to Spain, itself increasingly an economic satellite of the more advanced capitalist countries of northwest Europe. The double character of the colonial plantation—often self-sufficient and nonmonetary in its internal relations but oriented externally toward European markets—reflected the dualism of the colonial economy.

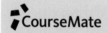 Go to the CourseMate website at **www.cengagebrain.com** for primary sources, additional study tools, and review materials—including audio and video clips—for this chapter.

---

6. As late as the mid-eighteenth century, according to historian John Coatsworth, perhaps 10 percent of New Spain's internal trade depended on silver coins as a medium of exchange, and storekeepers everywhere resorted to tokens in trading.

State, Church, and Society

FOCUS QUESTIONS

- What were the major features of the colonial political system and the institutions through which it operated?
- Why was the Spanish crown unable to enforce much colonial legislation?
- What was the relation between church and state, and how did it affect the reformed clergy, divisions within the church, and the clergy's moral decline?
- What was the colonial structure of class and caste, and how did it reflect the social construction of race?
- What were the status of colonial women, sexual behavior within the colonial structure, and changing views regarding free choice in marriage decisions?

T HE POLITICAL ORGANIZATION of the Spanish empire in America reflected the centralized, absolutist regime by which Spain governed itself. By the time of the Conquest of America, Castilian parliamentary institutions and municipal rights and exemptions had lost most of their former vitality. The process of centralization begun by the Catholic Sovereigns reached its climax under the first two Hapsburgs. In Castile, a ponderous administrative bureaucracy arose, capped by a series of royal councils appointed by and directly responsible to the king. Aragón stubbornly resisted royal encroachments on its *fueros* (charters of liberties) and retained a large measure of autonomy until the eighteenth century. Even in Castile, however, Hapsburg absolutism left largely intact the formal and informal power of the great lords over their peasantry. In Aragón, in whose soil feudal relations were more deeply rooted, the arrogant nobility claimed a broad seigneurial jurisdiction, including the right of life and death over its serfs, as late as the last decades of the seventeenth century. This contrast between the formal concentration of authority in the hands of royal officials and the actual exercise of supreme power on the local level by great landowners was to characterize the political structure of independent Spanish America as well.

Political Institutions of the Spanish Empire

FORMATION OF COLONIAL ADMINISTRATION

The pattern of Spain's administration of its colonies formed in the critical period between 1492 and 1550. The final result reflected the steady growth of centralized rule in Spain itself and the application of a trial-and-error method to the problems of colonial government. To Columbus, Cortés, Pizarro, and other great expeditionary leaders, the Spanish kings granted sweeping political powers that made these men almost sovereign in the territories they had won or proposed to subdue. Once the importance of these conquests became clear, however, royal jealousy of the great conquistadors was quick to show itself. The crown soon revoked their authority or strictly limited it, and they transferred to America the institutions that had facilitated centralization of political control in Spain. By the

1524	Council of the Indies is chartered as a separate agency responsible for Spanish imperial administration of its American colonies
1535	King Charles decrees the creation of the Viceroyalty of New Spain, with Viceroy Antonio de Mendoza responsible for governing Spanish territories in the Americas
1542	Charles decrees creation of the Viceroyalty of Peru to govern all the territories claimed by Spain in South America
1556	Philip II ascends the Spanish throne and eliminates principal power of Dominican friars to enforce decrees protecting indigenous communities by denying absolution rights to Spaniards who violated decrees
1569	Philip II inaugurates the first Spanish Inquisition in the American colonies
1570	Francisco de Toledo becomes viceroy of Peru and consolidates royal authority by defeating Inca Tupac Amaru and fractious Spanish colonial encomenderos
1572	The Society of Jesus establishes itself in the Americas and effectively functions as an autonomous colony exploiting indigenous labor
1580– 1640	Philip unites the thrones of Spain and Portugal, expanding the reach of the Spanish Inquisition and the number of Africans sold into slavery in the Americas
1624	Massive insurgency of mestizos and indigenous people in Mexico City, protesting famine and "Evil Government"
1667	Sor Juana Inés de la Cruz enters the convent to preserve her freedom from patriarchal authority and pursue her passion for literature, becoming widely known as the "Tenth Muse"
1680	Pueblo Revolt massacres mission friars in New Mexico territories and inaugurates enduring resistance to Spanish Reconquest
1681	Charles II compiles the Laws of the Indies, which combines major decrees like the Laws of Burgos, the New Laws of 1542, and Ordinances Concerning Discoveries, with lesser decrees that regulated the settlement of pueblos, missions, and presidios

mid-sixteenth century, the political organization of the Indies had assumed the definitive form it retained, with slight variations, until late in the eighteenth century.

The Council of the Indies, originally a standing committee of the all-powerful Council of Castile but chartered in 1524 as a separate agency, stood at the head of the Spanish imperial administration almost to the end of the colonial period. Although the crown appointed great nobles and court favorites to the council, its membership, especially in the seventeenth century, consisted predominantly of lawyers. Under the king, whose active participation in its work varied from monarch to monarch, it was the supreme legislative, judicial, and executive institution of government. One of its most important functions was the nomination to the king of all high colonial officials. It also framed a vast body of legislation for the Indies—the famous Laws of the Indies (1681)—which combined decrees of the most important kind with others of a trivial character. Although conscientious and highly capable officials frequently staffed the council in the early Hapsburg period, the quality of its personnel tended to decline under inept seventeenth-century princes. Nonetheless, historians owe the council a particular debt for its initiative in seeking to obtain detailed information on the history, geography, resources, and population of all the colonies. The *relaciones* (reports) that incorporated this information represent a rich mine of materials for students of colonial Spanish America.

THE ROYAL AGENTS

The principal royal agents in the colonies were the viceroys, the captains general, and the *audiencias* (the high court). The viceroys and captains general had essentially the same functions, differing only in the greater importance and extent of the territory assigned to the jurisdiction of the former. Each was the supreme civil and military officer in his realm, having in his charge such vital matters as the maintenance and increase of the royal revenues, defense, indigenous welfare, and a multitude of other responsibilities. At the end of the Hapsburg Era, in 1700, there were two great American viceroyalties: (1) the viceroyalty of New Spain, with its capital at Mexico City, which included all the Spanish possessions north of the Isthmus of Panama; and (2) that of Peru, with its capital at Lima, which embraced all of Spanish South America except for the coast of Venezuela. Captains general, theoretically subordinate to the viceroys but in practice virtually independent of them, governed large subdivisions of these vast territories. Audiencias governed **presidencias** (other administrative subdivisions). Their judge-presidents acted as governors, but military authority usually rested with the viceroy. Overlapping and shifting of jurisdiction was common throughout the colonial period and formed the subject of frequent disputes among royal officials.

A colonial viceroy, regarded as the very image of his royal master, enjoyed an immense delegated authority, which grew because of the distance that separated him from Spain and because of the frequently spineless or venal nature of lesser officials. He might be a lawyer or even a priest, but he was most commonly a representative of one of the great noble and wealthy houses of Spain. A court modeled on that of Castile, a numerous retinue, and the constant display of pomp and circumstance bore witness to his exalted status. In theory, the laws and instructions issued by the Council of the Indies limited the viceroy's freedom of action, but a sensible recognition of the need to adapt the laws to existing circumstances gave him a vast discretionary power. The viceroy employed the formula *obedezco pero no cumplo*—"I obey but do not carry out"—to set aside unrealistic or unenforceable legislation.

The sixteenth century saw some able and even distinguished viceroys in the New World. The viceroy Francisco de Toledo (1569–1581), the "supreme organizer of Peru," was certainly an energetic, hardworking administrator who consolidated Spanish rule and imposed royal authority in Peru. His resettlement program and his institution of *mita* (the system of forced labor in the mines), however, profoundly disrupted indigenous social organization and took a heavy toll of lives. In New Spain, such capable officials as Antonio de

Mendoza (1530–1550) and his successor, Luis de Velasco (1550–1564), wrestled with the problems left by the Conquest. They strove to curb the power of the conquistadors and to promote economic advance; sometimes they also tried, to a limited degree, to protect the interests of indígenas. But the predatory spirit of the colonists, royal distrust of excessive initiative on the part of high colonial officials, and opposition from other sectors of the official bureaucracy largely thwarted their efforts. In the seventeenth century, in an atmosphere of growing financial crisis, corruption, and cynicism at the Spanish court, the quality of the viceroys inevitably declined. In 1695, by way of illustration, the crown sold its viceroyships of Peru and Mexico, in effect, to the highest bidders.

An **audiencia** (the highest court of appeal in its district) assisted each viceroy or captain general in the performance of his duties; it also served as the viceroy's council of state. The joint decisions of viceroy and audiencia, taken in administrative sessions, had the force of law, giving the audiencia a legislative character roughly comparable to that of the Council of the Indies in relation to the king. Although the viceroy had supreme executive and administrative power, he was not legally obliged to heed the advice of the audiencia. Still, its immense prestige and its right to correspond directly with the Council of the Indies made it a potential and actual check on viceregal authority. The crown, ever distrustful of its colonial officers, thus developed a system of checks and balances that ensured ample deliberation and consultation on all important questions, but it also encouraged indecision and delay.

In addition to hearing appellate cases and holding consultative meetings with their viceroy or captain general, **oidores** (royal judges) made regular tours of inspection of their respective provinces with the object of making a searching inquiry into economic and social conditions, treatment of the natives, and other matters of interest to the crown. Although viceroys and oidores earned good incomes by colonial standards, the style of life their positions demanded was expensive, and the viceroy or oidor who did not take advantage of his office to enrich himself could expect to return to Spain poor.

Viceroyalties and Audiencias in Sixteenth-Century Spanish America

Provincial Administration

Provincial administration in the Indies was entrusted to royal officials who governed districts of varying size and importance from their chief towns and who usually held the title of corregidor or alcalde mayor. The viceroy appointed some, and the crown appointed others. They possessed supreme judicial and political authority in their districts and represented the royal interest in the *cabildos* (town councils). Certain civil and criminal cases could be appealed from the municipal magistrates to the corregidor, and from him to the audiencia. An *asesor* (legal

counsel) assisted the corregidor in the trial of judicial cases, if he had not trained as a lawyer.

Corregidores were of two kinds. Some presided over Spanish towns, and others, *corregidores de indios*, administered indigenous pueblos, or towns, that paid tribute to the crown. One of the principal duties of the corregidor de indios, who was usually appointed for three years, was to protect the natives from fraudulent or extortionate practices, but ample testimony exists that the corregidor was himself the worst offender in this respect. Native *caciques* (chiefs) often were his accomplices in these extortions. Perhaps the worst abuses of his

In the early seventeenth century, Felipe Guaman Poma de Ayala, a self-educated indigenous writer, chronicled the corruption and impunity of corregidores, who "feared neither justice nor God." They used their power to amass private fortunes by exploiting impoverished indigenous people, torturing their caciques, and stealing the wealth that indigenous communities produced.

authority arose in connection with the practice of repartimiento or repartimiento de mercancías, the requirement that indigenous peoples purchase goods from the corregidor. Ostensibly designed to protect the natives from the frauds of private Spanish traders, the corregidor's exclusive right to trade with indígenas became an instrument for his own speedy enrichment at the expense of the natives.

The crown employed an arsenal of regulations to ensure good and honest performance on the part of public officials. It forbade viceroys and oidores to engage in trade, to own land within their jurisdictions, or to accept gifts or fees; they even faced many restrictions in their social life. All royal officials, from the viceroy down, faced a **residencia** (judicial review) of their conduct at the end of their term of office. This took the form of a public hearing at which all who chose could appear before the judge of residence to present charges or testify for or against the official in question. At the end of the process, the judge found the official guilty or innocent of part or all of the charges and handed down a sentence that he could appeal to the Council of the Indies. Another device, the **visita** (an investigation of official conduct), usually was made unannounced by a **visitador** (royal auditor), who was specially appointed for this purpose by the crown or, in the case of lesser officials, by the viceroy in consultation with the audiencia. As a rule, the visita was no more effective than the residencia in preventing or punishing official misdeeds.

The only political institution in the Indies that satisfied to some degree local aspirations for self-rule was the town council, known as the cabildo or **ayuntamiento**. Any suggestion, however, that the cabildo had some kind of democratic character has no basis in fact. At an early date, the crown assumed the right to appoint the **regidores** (councilmen) and **alcaldes** (magistrates). Under Philip II and his successors, the king routinely sold these posts to the highest bidder, with a right of resale or bequest, on the condition that the successful bidder pay a certain portion of the value to the crown as a tax at each transfer. In some towns, however, cabildo members elected their successors.

Throughout the colonial period, according to historian Susan E. Ramírez, the municipal councils were closed, self-perpetuating oligarchies of rich landowners, mine owners, and merchants, who "ran the council as an exclusive club." These men frequently received no salaries for their duties and used their positions to award themselves municipal lands and native labor and, in general, to serve the narrow interests of their class. Their official tasks included supervision of local markets, distribution of town lands, and local taxation. They also elected the alcaldes, who administered justice as courts of first instance. Vigilantly supervised by the provincial governor, or corregidor, who frequently intervened in its affairs, the cabildo soon lost the autonomy of the early days. Yet despite its undemocratic character, inefficiency, and waning prestige and autonomy, the cabildo was not without potential significance. As the only political institution that represented the *creoles* (American-born Spaniards), the cabildo was destined to play an important part in the coming of the nineteenth-century wars of independence.

These officials and agencies represented only a small part of the apparatus of colonial government. A large number of *escribanos* (secretaries) attended to the paperwork of the various departments. As a rule, they collected no salaries but fees for their services reimbursed their expenses. Police officers, collectors of the royal fifth, alcaldes with special jurisdiction, and the like were abundant. Under Charles V, control of such offices often lay in the hands of high Spanish officials, who sold them to individuals who proposed to go to the Indies to exploit their fee-earning possibilities. Beginning with Philip II, many of these offices were withdrawn from private patronage and sold directly by the crown, usually to the highest bidder. In the second half of the seventeenth century, the sale of offices by the crown or the viceroy spread from fee-earning positions to higher, salaried posts. As a rule, the beneficiaries of such transactions sought to return to Spain rich, having made the highest possible profit on their investment. Consequently, corruption in this period became structural in government. Colonial officials, high and low, abused their trusts in innumerable and ingenious ways.

If the royal authority was more or less supreme in the capitals and the surrounding countryside, the same was not true of more distant and isolated regions. In such areas, royal authority was remote, and the power of the great landowners was virtually absolute. On their large, self-sufficient estates, landowners dispensed justice in the manner of feudal lords, holding court and imprisoning peons in their own jails; they raised and maintained their own private armies; and they generally acted as monarchs of all they surveyed. Sometimes these powerful individuals combined their de facto military and judicial power with an official title, which made them representatives of the crown in their vicinities. Spain's growing economic and political weakness in the late seventeenth century, which loosened the ties between the mother country and its colonies, favored this decentralization of power.

INEFFECTIVENESS OF MUCH SPANISH COLONIAL LAW

The frequent violation of Spanish colonial law was a fact of colonial political life. In considerable part, this situation reflected the dilemma of royal officials faced with the task of enforcing laws that the powerful colonial elites, with whom they generally had close social and economic ties, bitterly opposed. This dilemma found its most acute expression in the clash between the crown's legislative desire to regulate indigenous labor—the real wealth of the Indies—and the drive of colonial elites for maximum profits. Consequently, local elites systematically flouted these protective laws. The crown often closed its eyes to the violations, not only because it wished to avoid confrontation with powerful colonial elites, but also because those laws sometimes conflicted with the crown's own narrow, short-range interests (its need for revenue to finance wars and diplomacy and to support a parasitic nobility).

Thus, we can see the contradiction between that protective legislation, so often cited by defenders of Spain's work in America, and the reality of indigenous life and labor in the colonies. In a report to Philip II, Alonso de Zorita, a judge who retired to an honorable poverty in 1566 after nineteen years of administrative activity in the Indies, wrote the following:

> The wishes of Your Majesty and his Royal Council are well known and are made very plain in the laws that are issued every day in favor of the poor Indians and for their increase and preservation. But these laws are not obeyed and not enforced, wherefore there is no end to the destruction of the Indians, nor does any one care what Your Majesty decrees.

Not all colonial legislation was so laxly enforced, however. Many exploitative or discriminatory laws still existed, requiring indígenas to pay tribute and perform forced labor for token wages, permitting the forced sale of goods to them at fixed prices, and limiting their landownership to a low maximum figure while allowing the indefinite growth of Spanish estates.

How can we explain the longevity of Spanish rule over its American colonies, so distant from a European country that grew steadily weaker in the course of the seventeenth century? The answer does not lie in Spain's military power, because Spain maintained few troops in the Indies until the eighteenth century. Much of the durability of Spanish rule seems to lie in a royal policy of making the large concessions needed to gain and maintain the loyalty of colonial elites. The political apparatus of viceroys, audiencias, corregidores, and the like played a decisive role in implementing this royal program. The frequent failure to enforce protective legislation, the strict enforcement of the exploitative laws, the *composiciones* (settlements that legalized usurpation of native lands through payment of a fee to the king), and the toleration of great abuses by colonial oligarchs illustrate the policy. To be sure, alongside this unwritten pact between the crown and the colonial elite for sharing power and the fruits of exploitation of indigenous, black, and mixed-race people in the Indies went a royal effort to restrain the colonists' power and ambitions. Until the eighteenth century, however, this effort did not go far enough to threaten the existing arrangements.

The Church in the Indies

The Spanish church emerged from the long centuries of struggle against the Muslims with immense wealth and an authority second only to that of the crown. The Catholic Sovereigns, Ferdinand and Isabella, particularly favored the clergy and the spread of its influence as a means of achieving national unity and royal absolutism. The Spanish Inquisition, which they founded, had political as well as religious uses, and under their great-grandson Philip II it became the strongest support of an omnipotent crown. While the Spanish towns sank into political and then into economic decadence, and the great nobles were reduced to the position of a courtier class aspiring for favors from the crown, the church steadily gained in wealth and influence. Under the last Hapsburgs, the church threatened the supremacy of its royal master. It remained for the enlightened Bourbon kings of the eighteenth century to curb in some measure the excessive power of the church.

Royal control over ecclesiastical affairs, both in Spain and in the Indies, rested solidly on the institution of the **patronato real** (royal patronage). As applied to the colonies, this consisted of the absolute right of the Spanish kings to nominate all church officials, collect tithes, and found churches and monasteries in America. Under diplomatic pressure from King Ferdinand, Pope Julius II had accorded this extraordinary privilege to Spain's rulers in 1508, ostensibly to assist in converting New World heathens. The Spanish monarchs regarded the patronato real as their most cherished privilege and reacted sharply to all encroachments on it.

THE SPIRITUAL CONQUEST OF AMERICA

Beginning with Columbus's second voyage, one or more clergymen accompanied every expedition that sailed for the Indies, and they came in swelling numbers to the conquered territories. The friars formed the spearhead of the second religious invasion that followed on the heels of the Conquest. The friars who came to America in the first decades after the Conquest were, overall, an elite group. They were products of one of the periodic revivals of asceticism and discipline in the medieval church, especially of the reform of the orders instituted in Spain by the Catholic Sovereigns and carried out with implacable energy by Cardinal Cisneros. This vanguard group of clergy frequently combined with missionary zeal a sensitive social conscience and a love of learning. The admirable qualities of the indígenas, their simplicity and freedom from the greed and ambitions of Europeans, frequently impressed the missionaries. According to Vasco de

Quiroga, royal judge and later bishop of the province of Michoacán in Mexico:

> Anything may be done with these people, they are most docile, and, proceeding with due diligence, may easily be taught Christian doctrine. They possess innately the instincts of humility and obedience, and the Christian impulses of poverty, nakedness, and contempt for the things of this world, going barefoot and bareheaded with the hair long like apostles; in fine, with very tractable minds void of error and ready for impression.

Millenarian[1] and utopian ideals strongly influenced many members of the reformed clergy who came to the Indies in the first decades after the Conquest. Inspired by the vision of many native souls waiting for salvation, they dreamed of a fruitful fusion of indigenous and Spanish cultures under the sign of a Christianity returned to its original purity. Such men as Juan de Zumárraga, first bishop and archbishop of Mexico; Vasco de Quiroga; and Bartolomé de Las Casas were profoundly influenced by the humanist, reformist ideas of Erasmus and by Thomas More's *Utopia*. Indeed, Quiroga proposed to the Spanish crown the establishment of indigenous cities, organized on the lines of More's ideal commonwealth. Here, training in the Christian religion and culture would reinforce, preserve, and perfect the natives' natural virtues. When the crown ignored his proposals, Quiroga used his own resources to found the pueblos or refuges of Santa Fe in Michoacán. In these communities, Quiroga established collective ownership of property, systematic alternation between agricultural and craft labor, the six-hour working day, work for women, the distribution of the fruits of collective labor according to need, and the shunning of luxuries and of all occupations that were not useful. Quiroga's dream of establishing islands of charity and cooperative life in a sea of exploitive

encomiendas and haciendas was doomed to eventual failure, but to this day, the indígenas of Michoacán revere the name and memory of "Tata Vasco."

These attitudes of reformist clergy inevitably placed them on a collision course with the encomenderos and other lay Spaniards who sought the unchecked exploitation of native peoples and commonly described them as **perros** (dogs). To be sure, not all the religious saw eye to eye on this issue. Some, like the famous Franciscan Toribio de Benavente (better known by his Nahuatl name of Motolinía), may be called realists or moderates. These clergy believed that the encomienda, carefully regulated to safeguard indigenous welfare, was necessary for the prosperity and security of the Indies. Others, mostly Dominicans whose leader was Bartolomé de Las Casas, believed that the encomienda was incompatible with the welfare of the natives andmust be put in the way of extinction.

As we read in Chapter 4, during the reign of Charles V—who feared the rise of a colonial feudalism based on the encomienda—the Lascasian wing of the clergy won certain victories, capped by the passage of the New Laws of the Indies (1542). By their militant efforts to secure the enforcement of these laws, Las Casas and his disciples incurred the mortal enmity of the encomenderos, who repeatedly threatened them. A group of men, led by the governor's son, assassinated the Dominican bishop Antonio de Valdivieso of Nicaragua in 1550 because he tried to enforce the New Laws that abolished indigenous slavery. These and other courageous defenders of indígenas, like Bishop Juan del Valle in Colombia and Fray Domingo de Santo Tomás in Peru, were forerunners of the progressive current in the post-Vatican II Catholic Church. The ideology of Las Casas, with its demand that the Spaniards "cease to be caballeros by grace of the blood and sweat of the wretched and oppressed," seems to anticipate Latin American liberation theology and its "preferential option for the poor."

---

1. **Millenarianism** is the medieval doctrine, based on a prophecy in the Book of Revelation and widely held by the reformed clergy, that Christ would return to Earth to reign for a thousand years of peace and righteousness, to be followed by the Last Judgment at the end of the world.

Institut Amattler d'Art Hispanic, Barcelona

Bartolomé de Las Casas condemned the racist attitudes of the conquistadors and defended indigenous culture against the scorn of Europeans. His teachings emphasized the dignity of all people.

Despite the partial victories won by Las Casas during the reign of Charles V, this movement entered a decline when Philip II took the throne in 1556. Thereafter, various royal decrees forbade denial of absolution to Spaniards who had violated these protective laws—an important weapon employed by Las Casas and his coreligionists. Philip instructed the Church to concern itself only with questions of worship and preaching, leaving problems in the economic and social relations between Spaniards and native peoples to the civil authorities. Because those authorities as a rule were ready to comply with the wishes of encomenderos, great landowners, and other ruling-class groups, the descendants of the conquistadors finally obtained the direct, unchallenged dominion over indígenas for which their forebears had struggled. The encomienda (although in decline), the repartimiento or mita, and even slavery (legalized on various pretexts) remained the basic institutions in colonial Spanish America. This new political climate reinforced a growing belief in the constitutional inferiority of indigenous peoples, based on the Aristotelian theory of natural slavery, a theory that Las Casas and virtually all other Spanish theologians had previously condemned.

The first missionaries in the Indies did not regard their defense of the natives against enslavement and exploitation as separate from their primary task of conversion; they reasoned that for conversion to be effective, the prospective converts must survive the shock of Conquest, multiply, and live better under the new religion than the old one. Despite the clandestine opposition of surviving pagan priests and some native nobility, the friars converted prodigious numbers of natives, who, willingly or unwillingly, accepted the new and more powerful divinities of the invaders. In Mexico, the Franciscans claimed to have converted more than a million people by 1531; the energetic Motolinía asserted that he had converted more than fifteen hundred in one day! Where persuasion failed, pressures of various kinds, including force, obtained conversions. The Church charged natives who had been baptized and relapsed into idolatry with heresy and punished them brutally; some nobles were hanged or burned at the stake. To facilitate the missionary effort, the friars studied the native languages and wrote grammars and vocabularies that are still of value to scholars.

The religious, especially the Franciscans, also assigned a special importance to the establishment of schools in which indigenous upper-class youth might receive instruction in the humanities, including Latin, logic, and philosophy, as well as Christian doctrine. The most notable of these centers was the Franciscan Colegio de Santa Cruz in Mexico. Before it declined in the 1560s, because of lay hostility or lack of interest and the waning fervor of the friars themselves, the school had produced a harvest of graduates who often combined enthusiasm for European culture with admiration for their own pagan past. These men were invaluable to the missionaries in their effort to reconstruct the history, religion, and social institutions of the ancient civilizations.

Although some of the early friars undertook to destroy all relics of the pagan past—idols, temples, picture writings—the second generation of missionaries believed that they could not successfully combat paganism without a thorough study and understanding of the old pre-Conquest way of life. In Mexico, a genuine school of ethnography arose to inventory the rich content of pre-Columbian cultures. If the primary and avowed motive of this effort was to arm the missionary with the knowledge needed to discover the concealed presence of pagan rites and practices, intellectual curiosity and delight in the discovery of the material, artistic, and social achievements of these vanished empires also played a part.

The work of conversion, by the subsequent admission of the missionaries themselves, was less than wholly successful. In Mexico, concludes historian Louise M. Burkhart, the Aztecs "were able to become just Christian enough to get by in the colonial social and political setting without compromising their basic ideological and moral orientation." Here the result of the missionary effort was generally a fusion of old and new religious ideas, in which the cult of the Virgin Mary sometimes merged with the worship of pagan divinities. Writing half a century after the conquest of Mexico, the Dominican Diego Durán saw a persistence of paganism in every aspect of indigenous life: "in their dances, in their markets, in their baths, in the songs which mourn the loss of their ancient gods." In the same period, the great scholar-missionary Sahagún complained that they continued to celebrate their ancient festivals, in which they sang songs and danced dances with concealed pagan meanings. In Peru, the work of conversion was even less successful. "If the Indians admitted the existence of a Christian god," writes Nathan Wachtel, "they considered his influence to be limited to the Spanish world, and looked themselves for protection to their own gods." To this day, native peoples in lands like Guatemala and Peru perform ceremonies from the Maya and Inca period.

The friars also had to battle divisions within their own camp. Violent disputes arose among the orders over the degree of prebaptismal instruction required by indigenous converts, with the Dominicans and Augustinians demanding stiffer standards than the Franciscans. Other disputes arose as to which order should have jurisdiction over a particular area or pueblo. A more serious conflict arose between the secular and the regular clergy. Parish priests normally performed the pastoral and sacramental duties, but the regular clergy also performed them in America. Special papal legislation (1522) had granted these functions to the regulars, a concession made necessary by the small number of seculars who came to the Indies in the early years. After mid-century, however, their number increased, and the bishops increasingly sought to create new parishes staffed by seculars. These seculars sought to replace the regulars in the spiritual direction of converts. The friars resisted by every means at their disposal, but they fought a losing battle.

Another source of division within the church was rivalry between American-born and peninsular clergy for control of the higher positions, especially in the orders. Threatened with loss of those positions in provincial elections by the growing creole majority in the seventeenth century, the peninsulars (European-born Spaniards) sought and obtained decrees that mandated alternation of offices between themselves and creoles.

THE MORAL DECLINE OF THE CLERGY AND THE MISSIONARY IMPULSE

To the factors that contributed to the decline of the intellectual and spiritual influence of the orders, one must add the gradual loss of a sense of mission and of morale among the regular clergy. Apostolic fervor inevitably declined as the work of conversion in the central areas of the empire approached completion; many of the later arrivals among the clergy preferred a life of ease and profit to one of austerity and service. By the last decades of the sixteenth century, complaints against the excessive number of monasteries and their wealth became more frequent. The principal sources of this wealth were legacies and other gifts from rich donors: For a rich man not to provide for the church in his will was a matter of scandal. A common procedure used to endow churches, convents, or other religious institutions was to assume a *censo* (mortgage) on the landowner's estate for a fixed amount on which he or she agreed to pay the beneficiary an annual interest of 5 percent. According to historian Leslie Bethell, this method of expressing piety was so widely used that in New Spain "at the end of the eighteenth century it was said that there was no hacienda which was not burdened with one or more censos." Another procedure, which served both the donor's piety and family interest, was establishing a chantry to celebrate in perpetuity memorial masses for his or her soul. By designating a family member as chaplain, the donor ensured that control of the income from the endowment would remain in the family. These procedures, which continually drained money from the income of estates, writes Mexican historian Enrique Florescano, "helped to destabilize the already precarious haciendas and ranches ... leaving the religious institutions, in effect, as the real landowners and beneficiaries of rural income."

The resources the church acquired became inalienable in the form of mortmain, or perpetual ownership. When invested in land and mortgages, this wealth brought in more wealth. The enormous economic power of the church gave it a marked advantage over competitors and enabled it to take advantage of weaker lay property owners, especially in times of recession. The last important order to arrive in Spanish America, the Society of Jesus (1572), was also the most fortunate in the number of rich benefactors and the most efficient in running its numerous enterprises, which it used to support its excellent system of *colegios* (secondary schools) and its missions.

Inevitably, this concern with the accumulation of material wealth weakened the ties between the clergy and the humble masses whose spiritual life they were supposed to direct. As early as the 1570s, complaints about the excessive ecclesiastical fees and clerical exploitation of native labor were voiced. A viceroy of New Spain, the Marqués de Monteclaros, assured King Philip III in 1607 that indigenous peoples suffered the heaviest oppression at the hands of the friars and that one native paid

more tribute to his parish priest than twenty paid to His Majesty. Hand in hand with a growing materialism went an increasing laxity of morals. Concubinage became so common among the clergy of the later colonial period that it seems to have attracted little official notice or rebuke. By the last decades of the colonial period, the morals of the clergy had declined to a condition that the Mexican historian Lucas Alamán, himself a leader of the clerical party in the period of independence, could describe only as scandalous. From this charge one, in general, must exclude the Jesuits, noted for their high moral standards and strict discipline; of course, men of excellent character and social conscience existed among both the secular and regular clergy.

The missionary impulse of the first friars survived longest on the frontier, "the rim of Christendom." Franciscans first penetrated the great northern interior of New Spain, peopled by hostile Chichimecs, "wild Indians." Franciscans accompanied the Oñate expedition of 1598 into New Mexico and dominated the mission field until the end of the colonial period; they also served in such distant outposts of Spanish power as Florida and Georgia. After the expulsion of the Jesuits from the Indies in 1767, the Franciscans took their place directing missionary work in California.

The mission was one of three closely linked institutions—the other two being the *presidio* (garrison) and the civil settlement—designed to serve the ends of Spanish imperial expansion and defense on the northern frontier. The mission's purpose was to gather the native converts into self-contained religious communities, train them to till the land, herd cattle, and practice various crafts until they became fully Christianized and Hispanicized. The presidios provided military protection for the neighboring missions and ensured a cooperative attitude on the part of indigenous novices. Finally, attracted by the lure of free land, Spaniards of modest means would throng to the area and form civil settlements that would become bustling centers of life and trade. By all these means, the Spanish sought to push back and pacify the frontier, and to protect it against foreign encroachment.

This three-pronged attack on the wilderness was not successful. Certain tribes on the northern frontier, such as the powerful Apaches of Arizona, New Mexico, and Texas and the Comanches of Texas, resisted mission life. The missionaries had greater success among such sedentary peoples as the Pueblo of New Mexico, the Pima and Opata of Sonora in northwest Mexico, and the Hasinai of east Texas. Even among these peaceful communities, however, revolts and desertions were frequent. In 1680 the supposedly Christianized Pueblos of New Mexico revolted, slaughtered the friars, and maintained a long, tenacious resistance against Spanish efforts at Reconquest. The rise of native leaders who proclaimed that the old gods and way of life were best often sparked wholesale desertions. Mistreatment by soldiers in nearby presidios and the terror inspired by Apache and Comanche raiding parties also provoked frequent flight from the missions.

The civil settlements proved no more successful. By the end of the colonial period, only a few scattered towns remained along the northern frontier, and the continuous raids made life and property so insecure that, in New Mexico, settlers who petitioned for permission to leave outnumbered recruits coming to the area. Ultimately, the whole task of defending Spanish claims fell on a chain of presidios that stretched approximately along the present border between the United States and Mexico. Successive military defeats compelled Spanish troops to take refuge behind the security of the high presidio walls. In the end, fierce indigenous resistance forced Spain to adopt a policy of neutralizing the Apaches and Comanches by periodic distribution of gifts to them. When the outbreak of the wars of independence stopped the flow of gifts, however, they again took to the warpath, driving by the useless line of presidios into the interior of Mexico.

The most notable instance of successful missionary effort, at least from an economic point of view, was that of the Jesuit establishments in Paraguay, where, favored by a genial climate and fertile soil, the Jesuits established more than thirty missions; these formed the principal field of Jesuit activity in America. Strict discipline, centralized organization, and absolute control over the labor of thousands of docile Guaraní, producing large surpluses, enabled the Jesuits to turn their missions into highly profitable business enterprises. They shipped great quantities of such goods as cotton, tobacco, and hides down the Paraná River to Buenos Aires for export to Europe. Rather than "Christian socialism," the Jesuit mission system looked more like "theocratic capitalism."

Jesuit rule in Paraguay and Jesuit mission activity everywhere in the colonies ended when a royal decree expelled the order from the colonies in 1767. Among the motives for this action were the conflict between the nationalistic church policy of the Bourbons and Jesuit emphasis on papal supremacy, suspicions of Jesuit meddling in state affairs generally, and the belief that the Jesuit mission system constituted a state within a state. The expulsion of the Jesuits from Paraguay resulted in intensified exploitation of the Guaraní by Spanish officials and landowners. Within a generation, the previously thriving Jesuit villages were in ruins.

THE INQUISITION IN THE NEW WORLD

The Inquisition formally entered the Indies when Philip II established the tribunals of the Holy Office in Mexico and Lima in 1569. Before that time, clergy vested with inquisitorial powers had performed its functions. Its great privileges, its independence of other courts, and the dread with which Spanish generally regarded the charge of heresy made the Inquisition an effective check on "dangerous thoughts," whether religious, political, or philosophical. The great mass of cases tried by its tribunals, however, had to do with offenses against morality or minor deviations from orthodox religious conduct, such as blasphemy.

Spain's rulers, beginning with Queen Isabella, forbade Jews, Muslims, *conversos* (New Christians), and persons penanced by the Inquisition from going to the Indies. Many conversos, however, hoping to improve their fortunes and escape the climate of suspicion and hostility that surrounded them in Spain, managed to settle in the Indies, coming as seamen or servants of licensed passengers, or sometimes even with licenses purchased from the crown.

Some attained positions of wealth and authority. Toward the end of the sixteenth century, many conversos settled in New Spain and Peru. Many came from Portugal, where a strong revival of Inquisitorial activity after the country's annexation by Spain (1580) was taking place. One who came to New Spain was Luis de Carvajal, who rose to be captain general and governor of the northern kingdom of New León. Carvajal was a sincere Catholic, but his son and other relatives were fervent practicing Jews, mystics who urged other members of the large converso community of New Spain to return to Judaism. Denounced to the Inquisition as relapsed heretics, it tried them, condemned them to death, and carried out the sentences at a great **auto-da-fé** (public sentencing) in Mexico City in 1595. In 1635, the Lima Inquisition struck at the city's converso community, sending some to the stake; all suffered confiscation of goods. It is evidence of the wealth of the Lima conversos, mostly rich merchants, historian Judith Laikin Elkin argues, that the Lima office of the Inquisition, having confiscated their property, "emerged as the wealthiest in the world."

As in Spain, the Inquisition in the Indies relied largely on denunciations by informers and employed torture to secure confessions. Also like Spain, the damage done by the Inquisition was not limited to the snuffing out of lives and the confiscation of property but included the creation of an atmosphere of fear, distrust, and rigid intellectual conformity. The great poet Sor Juana Inés de la Cruz alludes to this repressive atmosphere when she mentions her difficulties with "a very saintly and guileless prelate who believed that study was a matter for the Inquisition." Indigenous peoples, originally subject to the jurisdiction of inquisitors, later escaped their control because the Church regarded them as recent converts with limited mental capacity and thus not fully responsible for their deviations from the Faith. However, they remained subject to trial and punishment by an episcopal inquisition.

THE CHURCH AND EDUCATION

The church enjoyed a virtual monopoly of colonial education at all levels. The primary and secondary schools maintained by the clergy, with few exceptions, were open only to children of the Spanish upper class and the indigenous nobility. Poverty condemned to illiteracy the overwhelming majority of the natives and mixed castes. Admission to the universities, which numbered about twenty-five at the end of the Colonial Era, was even more restricted to youths of ample means and "pure" blood.

The universities of Lima and Mexico City, both chartered by the crown in 1551, were the first permanent institutions of higher learning. Patterned on similar institutions in Spain, the colonial university faithfully reproduced their medieval organization, curricula, and methods of instruction. Indifference to practical or scientific studies, slavish respect for the authority of the Bible, Aristotle, the church fathers, and certain medieval scholars, as well as a passion for hairsplitting debate of fine points of theological or metaphysical doctrine, were among the features of colonial academic life. Theology and law were the chief disciplines; until the eighteenth century, science was a branch of philosophy, taught from the *Physics* of Aristotle.

A strict censorship of books (all publication in Spain and the colonies required the approval of the Royal Council) limited the spread of new doctrines in colonial society. Although the laws prohibiting the entry of works of fiction into the Spanish colonies were completely ineffective, this tolerance did not extend to heretical or subversive writings. The records of the colonial Inquisition revealed many tragic cases of imprisonment, torture, and even death for individuals who were charged with the possession and reading of such literature. At least until the eighteenth century, when the intellectual iron curtain that surrounded Spanish America began to lift, inquisitorial censorship effectively shielded the people of the colonies from literature of an unorthodox religious or political tendency.

Yet, within the limits imposed by official censorship and their own backgrounds, colonial scholars still made impressive contributions, especially in the fields of indigenous history, anthropology, linguistics, and natural history. The sixteenth century was the Golden Age of these studies in Spanish

America. In Mexico, a large group of missionaries, especially members of the Franciscan order, carried out long, patient investigations of the native languages, religion, and history. With the aid of native informants, Friar Bernardino de Sahagún compiled the monumental *General History of the Things of New Spain,* a veritable encyclopedia of information on all aspects of Aztec culture; scholars have only begun to mine the extraordinary wealth of ethnographic materials in Sahagún's work. Another Franciscan, usually known by his native name of Motolinía (Friar Toribio de Benavente), wrote the *History of the Indians of New Spain,* an invaluable guide to native life before and after the Conquest. Basing his work on Aztec picture writings and a chronicle that no longer exists, and written by an Aztec noble in his own language, Father Diego Durán wrote a history of ancient Mexico that preserves both the content and spirit of Aztec epics and legends. The Jesuit José de Acosta sought to satisfy Spanish curiosity about the natural productions of the New World and the history of the Aztecs and Incas in his *Natural and Moral History of the Indies.* His book, simply and pleasantly written, displays a critical spirit that was rare for its time. It achieved immediate popularity in Spain and was quickly translated into all the major languages of western Europe.

Indigenous or mestizo nobles, actuated by a variety of motives, wrote some influential historical works; interest and pride in their native heritage joined with a desire to prove the important services rendered by their forebears to the Conquest and the validity of their claims to noble titles and land. Products of convent schools or colegios, they usually combined Christian piety with nostalgic regard for the departed glories of their ancestors. A descendant of the kings of Texcoco, Fernando de Alva Ixtlilxochitl, wrote a number of historical works that show a mastery of European historical method. These works combine a great amount of valuable information with a highly idealized picture of Texcocan civilization.

Another writer of the early seventeenth century, the mestizo Garcilaso de la Vega, son of a Spanish conquistador and an Inca princess, gives in his *Royal Commentaries of the Incas,* together with much valuable information on Inca material culture and history, an idyllic picture of Peruvian life under the benevolent rule of the Inca kings. His book, written in a graceful, fluent Spanish, is more than just a history text; it is a first-class work of art. No other Spanish history was as popular in Europe as Garcilaso's *Royal Commentaries*; its favorable image of Inca civilization continues to influence our view of ancient Peru to the present.

A precious work, richly informative about social conditions in Peru before and after the Conquest, and illustrated with the author's own delightfully naive drawings, is the *New Chronicle* by the seventeenth-century Aymara noble Felipe Waman Puma de Ayala, whose manuscript did not surface until the early twentieth century. Waman Puma states that he left his home "to know the needs of, and to redeem the poor Indians, for whom there is no justice in this kingdom" and that he hoped Philip III would read his work. Waman Puma's painful effort to express himself in the unfamiliar Castilian tongue, the passionate rush of words interspersed with Quechua terms, and the melancholy and disillusioned tone of the work testify to the author's sincerity and the reality of the abuses he denounced.

SCIENCE, LITERATURE, AND THE ARTS

The second half of the seventeenth century saw a decline in the quantity and quality of colonial scholarly production. This was the age of the baroque style in literature, which subordinated content to form and meaning to ornate expression; it stressed wordplay, cleverness, and pedantry. Yet two remarkable men of this period, Carlos Sigüenza y Góngora in Mexico and Pedro de Peralta Barnuevo in Peru, foreshadowed the eighteenth-century Enlightenment by the universality of their interests and their concern with the practical uses of science. Sigüenza—mathematician, archaeologist, and historian—attacked the ancient but still dominant superstition of astrology in his polemic with the Jesuit priest Kino over the nature of comets. He also defied prejudice by providing in his will for the dissection of his body in the interests of science.

Peralta Barnuevo, cosmographer and mathematician, made astronomical observations that he published in Paris in the *Proceedings* of the French Royal Academy of Sciences, to which he was elected corresponding member; he also superintended the construction of fortifications in Lima. Yet this able and insatiably curious man of science also sought refuge in a baroque mysticism, and in one of his last works, he concluded that true wisdom, the knowledge of God, was not "subject to human comprehension."

Colonial literature, with some notable exceptions, was a pallid reflection of prevailing literary trends in the mother country. The isolation from foreign influences, the strict censorship of all reading matter, and the limited audience for writing of every kind made literary creation difficult. The discouraged Mexican poet, Bernardo de Balbuena, thus called the province of New Spain "a narrow and dwarfed world." To make matters worse, colonial literature in the seventeenth century succumbed to the Spanish literary fad of *Gongorismo* (so called after the poet Luis de Góngora), the cult of an obscure, involved, and artificial style.

Amid a flock of "jangling magpies," as one literary historian describes the Gongorist versifiers of the seventeenth century, appeared the incomparable songbird, known to her admiring contemporaries as "the Tenth Muse": Sor Juana Inés de la Cruz, the remarkable nun and poet who assembled in her convent one of the finest mathematical libraries of the time. However, Sor Juana could not escape the pressures of her environment. Rebuked by the bishop of Puebla for her worldly interests, she ultimately gave up her books and scientific interests and dedicated the remainder of her brief life to religious devotion and charitable works.

Sor Juana brilliantly defended the rights of women to education and intellectual activity, and she attacked the prevailing irrationality in the double standard that haunted the sexual conduct of men and women. "Foolish men," she asks in one of her sonnets, "why do you want them [women] to be good when you incite them to be bad?" Sor Juana's work challenged the official ideology and idealized vision of colonial life propounded by

church and state. Satire and mockery, often carried to extremes of grotesque distortion, were the weapons used by colonial critics to expose the hollowness of the ruling ideology, the gap between the idealized vision and the seamy reality of colonial life. They drew much of their inspiration from the rich traditions of the Spanish picaresque novel and satirical poetry that subjected the follies and frailties of Spanish society to pungent criticism. Naturally, because of the strict censorship of published works, colonial satire circulated principally in manuscript form, and the satirists often took measures to conceal their identities.

The first known Spanish American writer of satire was the peninsular-born Mateo Rosas de Oquendo, whose "Satire about the Things That Happened in Peru in 1598" was devoted to exposing Lima's social ills, the wealth that flaunted itself in the colonial capital, and the "sea of misery" that was the life of the mass of ordinary people. In another poem, a mock epic that described a viceroy's handling of the defense of the viceroyalty against English pirates, Rosas reduced a celebration of the victory of the Spanish fleet over a single English ship to "a lot of cackling over a single egg." His conclusion, sums up Julie Greer Johnson, was that the ruling aristocracy shared "the same basic attributes of ugliness, corruption, and hypocrisy" of the lower classes, differing only in their manifestations. According to Greer Johnson, "Anarchy and fraud prevail at court just as they do on the street, and money again controls lives, this time by buying power and influence."

In the same satirical tradition is the work *El Carnero* (the meaning of the word has not been firmly established), a history of the first century of Spanish colonization in New Granada begun late in life by Juan Rodríguez Freile, an impoverished creole landowner, and not completed until 1638. The ironic tone of the work, says Greer Johnson, reflects "the creole resentment and frustration of being considered a second-class Spaniard, the result of his American birth, and of being treated more like the colonized than the colonizers." Reversing the approach of official chroniclers of the Conquest and Spain's work in America, Rodríguez Freile

Sor Juana Inés de la Cruz, sometimes called the greatest Spanish American poet of the colonial period, entered a convent when she was eighteen years old and died at the age of forty-four. Sor Juana wrote both secular and religious poetry, but she was most admired for her love poems.

Juan del Valle y Caviedes, who arrived in Peru from Spain between 1645 and 1648, is commonly considered the best colonial satirist and second only to Sor Juana Inés de la Cruz as a poet. Evidently, because of his unfortunate experiences as a patient, Lima's physicians became the principal targets of his savage mockery, but he also subjected Lima's women, nobility, and other social types to ferocious verbal attack. In his collection of poems, *Diente del Parnaso* (*Tooth of Parnassus*), incompetent medical practice is presented as a full-scale conspiracy against patients by members of the profession, who were described as troops led by their general, Death. By equating seventeenth-century Peruvian doctors with sixteenth-century conquerors and then with modern pirates—a growing threat to the colony—Caviedes gave a subversive tinge to his irony, placing "conquerors, doctors, and pirates on the same plane for their part in causing death and destruction in the Western Hemisphere." Still more audaciously, he actually named some of Lima's best-known "malpractitioners," who are introduced by Death during a roll call of his troops. One was Francisco Bermejo y Roldán, the **protomedicato** (chief physician) of Peru; Caviedes mocked the title, calling him the **protoverdugo** (chief executioner) and charged that he took advantage of his female patients by prescribing "injections that were administered in the front."

The Structure of Class and Caste

The Spanish social order that arose in the Indies on the ruins of the old indigenous societies drew from Iberian aristocratic or feudal principles. Race, occupation, and religion were the formal criteria that determined an individual's social status. All mechanical labor was degrading, but large-scale trade (as opposed to retail trade) was compatible with nobility, at least in the Indies. Great emphasis was placed on **limpieza de sangre** (purity of blood), meaning above all descent from "Old Christians," without mixture of converso or **Morisco** (Muslim) blood. Spaniards jealously guarded and sometimes manufactured proofs of such descent.

questioned the "justification for the Conquest, the effectiveness of colonization, and even the character of the conquering Spaniard." Government officials appear as bumbling fools who "literally tripped over one another in the performance of their duties." Rodríguez Freile appears as the "omniscient narrator" who passes judgment on a long succession of crimes and follies but is capable of laughing at himself, even admitting to "having pursued the Golden Alligator like the conquerors who sought the illusive El Dorado."

Bradley Smith Collection/Laurie Platt Winfrey, Inc.

By the eighteenth century, a kind of hierarchy of rank emerged to distinguish the various races and racial mixtures. A trace of black blood legally sufficed to deprive an individual of the right to hold public office or enter the professions, among other rights and privileges. The same taint attached to the great mass of mestizos. True, the Laws of the Indies assigned perfect legal equality to those of legitimate birth, but to the very end of the colonial period, the charters of certain colonial guilds and schools excluded all mestizos, without distinction.

The lack of solid demographic information and major disagreements among historians about the size of pre-Conquest populations make estimates of Spanish America's population in 1650, and of the relative numerical strength of the racial groups that made up that population, strictly conjectural. It appears, however, that by that date, or even earlier, the long decline of the indigenous population had ended and a slow recovery had begun. It also appears that the European element in the population had grown more rapidly, but *castas* (mixed-race peoples), the great majority of whom were born out of wedlock, grew the fastest.

Spanish law and custom ranked all these racial groups in a descending order of worth and privilege, with Europeans on top, followed by the castas, indígenas, and blacks. This formal ranking did not necessarily correspond to the actual standing of individuals of different racial makeup in society, but it provided the colonial ruling groups with an ideological justification for their rule. It also created a conflict society par excellence that pitted natives against blacks, caste against caste, and inflated poor Spaniards with a sense of their superiority over all other groups. This hindered the forging of unity among the exploited masses and thus maintained an oppressive social order. The idea of "race" in Latin America, as elsewhere, was socially constructed to rationalize and preserve the power of a tiny elite.

THE RULING CLASS

In practice, racial lines were not strictly drawn. In the Indies, white skin was a symbol of social superiority, roughly the equivalent of **hidalguía**

(a title of nobility in Spain), but it had no cash value. Not all whites belonged to the privileged economic group. Colonial records testify to the existence of a large class of "poor whites"—vagabonds, beggars, or worse—who disdained work and frequently preyed on the indígenas. A Spaniard of this group, compelled by poverty to choose his mate from the castas, generally doomed his descendants to an inferior economic and social status. However, the mestizo or mulatto son of a wealthy Spanish landowner or merchant, if acknowledged and made his legal heir, could pass into the colonial aristocracy. If traces of indigenous or African descent were too strong, the father might reach an understanding with the parish priest, who had charge of baptismal certificates. It also was possible for a wealthy mestizo or mulatto to purchase from the crown a document establishing his legal whiteness. Wealth, not gentle birth or racial purity, was the distinguishing characteristic of the colonial aristocracy. Granted this fact, it remains true that the apex of the colonial pyramid was composed overwhelmingly of whites.

This white ruling class was itself divided by group jealousies and hostilities. The Spaniards brought to the New World their regional rivalries and feuds—between Old Castilians and Andalusians, between Castilians and Basques—and in the anarchic, heated atmosphere of the Indies, these rivalries often exploded into brawls or even pitched battles. But the most abiding cleavage within the upper class was the division between the Spaniards born in the colonies, called creoles, and the European-born Spaniards, called peninsulars, or referred to by such disparaging nicknames as **gachupín** or **chapetón** (tenderfoot). Legally, creoles and peninsulars were equal; indeed, when it came to filling offices, Spanish law called for preference to the descendants of conquistadors and early settlers. In practice, the creoles suffered from a system of discrimination that, during most of the colonial period, virtually denied them employment in high church and government posts and large-scale commerce.

The preference shown for peninsulars over creoles sprang from various causes, among them the greater access of Spaniards to the court, the fountainhead of all favors, and royal distrust of the creoles. By the second half of the sixteenth century, the sons or grandsons of conquistadors were complaining of the partiality of the crown and its officials toward unworthy newcomers from Spain. The creoles viewed with envenomed spite these Johnny-come-latelies, who often won out in the scramble for *corregimientos* and other government jobs. A Mexican poet, Francisco de Terrazas, expressed the creole complaint in rhyme:

> Spain: to us a harsh stepmother you have been, A mild and loving mother to the stranger, On him you lavish all your treasures dear, With us you only share your cares and danger.[2]

The resulting cleavage in the colonial upper class grew wider with the passage of time. Both groups developed an arsenal of arguments to defend their positions. Peninsulars often justified their privileged status by reference to the alleged indolence, incapacity, and frivolity of the creoles, which they sometimes solemnly attributed to the American climate or other environmental conditions. The creoles responded in kind by describing the Europeans as mean and grasping parvenus. The growing wealth of the creoles from mines, plantations, and cattle ranches only sharpened their resentment at the discrimination from which they suffered.

The Mestizo: An Ambiguous Status

The mestizo arose from a process of racial mixture that began in the first days of the Conquest. In the post-Conquest period, when Spanish women were scarce, the crown and the church viewed marriages between indigenous peoples and Spaniards with some favor; mixed marriages were not uncommon in those years. However, this attitude soon changed as the crown, for its own reasons, adopted a policy of systematic segregation. By the first quarter of the seventeenth century, the authoritative writer on Spain's colonial legislation, Juan Solórzano Pereira,

could write, "Few Spaniards of honorable position will marry Indian or Negro women." Consequently, the great mass of mestizos had their origin in irregular unions. The stigma of illegitimacy, unredeemed by wealth, doomed the majority to the social depths. Some became peons, resembling natives in their way of life; others swelled the numerous class of vagabonds, and still others enrolled in the colonial militia. Mestizos also contributed to the formation of the *rancheros* (small farmers) and formed part of the lower middle class of artisans, overseers, and shopkeepers. Without roots in either indigenous or Spanish society, scorned and distrusted by both, it is small wonder that the low-class mestizo acquired a reputation for violence and instability.

Indigenous Peoples: A Separate Nation

By contrast with the mestizo, no ambiguity marked the position of indígenas in Spanish law and practice. They constituted a separate nation, the república de indios, which also constituted a hereditary tribute-paying caste. The descendants of indigenous rulers and hereditary nobility, however, received special consideration, partly from Spanish respect for the concept of *señor natural* (the natural or legitimate lord) and partly because they played a useful role as intermediaries between the Spanish rulers and native tribute payers. The crown allowed these nobles to retain all or part of their patrimonial estates, and they enjoyed such special privileges as the right to ride horses, wear European dress, and carry arms.

Ample evidence exists that members of the indigenous aristocracy were among the worst exploiters of their own people. In Mexico, where in Aztec times a semifeudal order already existed and serf-like peasants formed a large part of the population, some Aztec lords took advantage of the fluid conditions created by the Conquest to usurp communal lands, impose excessive rents on their tenants, and force the commoners to work for them. In both Mexico and Peru, their new role as

---

2. Francisco de Terrazas, *Poesías*, ed. Antonio Castro Leal (Mexico, 1941), p. 87. From *The Aztec Image in Western Thought* by Benjamin Keen, p. 90. Copyright © 1971 by Rutgers University, The State University of New Jersey. Reprinted by permission of Rutgers University Press.

tribute collectors and labor recruiters for the Spaniards offered the native elites large opportunities for wheeling and dealing with corregidores, encomenderos, and priests at the expense of commoners. For example, chiefs and corregidores might falsify the tribute lists and share the resulting profits, or they might conceal the true number of workers available for mita or repartimiento labor and employ the hidden workers on their own estates. In Peru, where traditional bonds of kinship, ritual, and mutual dependence still powerfully linked **kurakas** (headmen) to ayllu (a kinship group in the Andean region) commoners, most kurakas at first likely sought to maintain a balance among complying with the new rulers' demands for labor and tribute, protecting their ayllus against excessive Spanish exactions, and defending their own interests. Gradually, however, adapting to the new commercial climate, they began to exploit commoners to feather their own nests.

Many kurakas became hacendados in their own right; by the end of the sixteenth century, says Peruvian historian Luis Millones, some kurakas controlled such large, complex enterprises, producing a variety of products for the Peruvian internal market, that they had to hire Spanish employees to assist them. Native peasant women, writes Irene Silverblatt, were primary targets of kuraka exploitation because they were especially vulnerable to loss of land and water rights. The seventeenth-century Inca chronicler Waman Puma de Ayala claimed that no matter how terribly colonial authorities and native elites robbed poor peasant men, "they robbed poor peasant women much more." He also accused the kurakas of illegally exploiting the labor of women in their jurisdiction and abusing them sexually, just as Spanish officials, encomenderos, and priests did.

The result of these trends pitting kurakas against ayllu commoners, writes Steve Stern, was the creation of "a more strained, suspicious relationship in which conflict, coercion, and economic power acquired added importance." In 1737, for example, community members of San Pedro de Tacna brought suit against their kuraka for illegally expropriating communal lands; they claimed he was forcing them off communal property to facilitate creation of an *aji* (chili pepper)-producing estate. In their testimony, writes Silverblatt, "witness after witness remarked that the kuraka's primary targets were peasant women."

In part, at least, what Charles Gibson says about Mexico was no doubt also true of Peru: The inordinate demands and aggressions of Mexican caciques and Peruvian kurakas against the commoners represented "a response to strain, an effort to maintain position and security" in the face of Spanish encroachments on the lands and perquisites of the native nobility. By the late sixteenth century, however, a considerable portion of the native aristocracy, especially the **principales** (minor nobility), was in full decline, apparently more rapid and general in Mexico than in Peru. Many Aztec nobles lost their retainers through flight or because of Spanish legislation that converted former servile classes (like the mayeques) into free tribute-payers. In both Mexico and Peru, Spanish refusal to recognize the noble status of many principales reduced them to the condition of tribute-payers. One cause of the nobility's ruin was Spanish invasion of their lands, to which they responded with costly but often futile litigation; another was their responsibility for the collection of tribute from the commoners. When the number of tribute-payers declined because of an epidemic or some other circumstance, the cacique or kuraka had to make up the arrears or go to jail. To make good the deficit, he might have to sell or mortgage his lands or risk the anger of commoners by imposing an extra tribute assessment.[3]

---

3. A revealing example of the trouble that his responsibility for collection of tribute might cause an indigenous governor is cited by Robert Haskett in his very informative *Indigenous Rulers: An Ethnohistory of Town Government in Colonial Cuernavaca* (1991). In 1694 the governor of Cuernavaca, Don Antonio de Hinojosa, sought sanctuary in the town's Franciscan monastery because he owed nearly 4,000 pesos (a staggeringly large sum for that time and place) in unpaid tribute assessments. Maneuvers by Don Antonio and his family to prevent the sequestration and auction of his estate were unsuccessful, and, because the sale did not completely erase his tribute debt, later Cuernavaca governors inherited it. Don Antonio died in the monastery in 1697 or 1698. His final years, observes Haskett, "saw the destruction of an estate carefully built up by his ancestors through marriage, inheritance, purchase, and perhaps usurpation."

Down to the close of the colonial period, a group of thoroughly Hispanicized cacique or kuraka families existed who, in addition to serving as intermediaries between Spanish elites and their native communities, managed to enrich themselves as landowners and entrepreneurs, ultimately becoming full members of the propertied class. In late-eighteenth-century Mexico, for example, the cacique of Panohuayan in Amecameca owned "the hacienda of San Antonio Tlaxomulco and other properties producing wheat and maguey and yielding an income of thousands of pesos per year." According to Charles Gibson,

> Like any Spanish hacendado, the cacique received payments from Indians who cut wood and grazed animals on his property. His great house was equipped with Spanish furniture, silver dining service, and rich tapestries. He possessed a private arsenal of guns, pistols, and steel and silver swords. His stables and storehouse and other possessions compared favorably with those of wealthy Spaniards.

In eighteenth-century Peru, the famous kuraka José Gabriel Condorcanqui (Tupac Amaru) represented this small class of wealthy indigenous or mestizo nobles. Lilian Fisher writes that he lived like a Spanish nobleman, wearing

> a long coat and knee-breeches of black velvet, a waistcoat of gold tissue worth seventy or eighty duros (dollars), embroidered linen, silk stockings, gold buckles at his knees and on his shoes, and a Spanish beaver hat valued at twenty-five duros. He kept his hair curled in ringlets that extended nearly down to his waist.

His source of wealth included the ownership of three hundred mules, which he used to transport mercury and other goods to Potosí and other places, and a large cacao estate.

In contrast to the privileged treatment accorded to indigenous rulers, the great majority of commoners suffered under crushing burdens of tribute, labor, and ecclesiastical fees. Viewed as a constitutionally inferior race and thus as perpetual wards of the Spanish state, they repaid the Spanish tutelage with the obligation to pay tribute and give forced labor. **Gente sin razón** ("people of weak minds") was a phrase commonly applied to native peoples in colonial documents. Their juridical inferiority and status as wards found expression in laws (universally disregarded) forbidding them to make binding contracts or to contract debts in excess of five pesos and in efforts to minimize contact between them and other racial groups. These and many other restrictions on indigenous activity had an ostensibly protective character. Nonetheless, an enlightened Mexican prelate, Bishop Manuel Abad y Queipo, argued that these so-called privileges did them little good and in most cases a lot of harm:

> Shut up in a narrow space of six hundred rods, assigned by law to the Indian towns, they possess no individual property and are obliged to work the communal lands.... Forbidden by law to commingle with the other castes, they are deprived of the instruction and assistance that they should receive from contact with these and other people. They are isolated by their language, and by a useless, tyrannical form of government.

He concludes that these ostensible privileges were "an offensive weapon employed by the white class against the Indians, and never serve to defend the latter."

Native commoners, however, did not form a single undifferentiated mass of impoverished, exploited people, for there existed a small minority who found paths to successful careers in the new colonial order. These included the skilled crafts and transport, which were in high demand. Artisans quickly entered such "Hispanic" occupations as silversmithing, masonry, stonecutting, carpentry, and the like. In late-sixteenth-century Peru, says Steve Stern, "an independent Indian craftsman could earn a very respectable income. In two months, a stonecutter could fashion a stone wheel worth sixty pesos." **Arrieros** (muleteers) could earn some 80 to 160 pesos a year. Some accumulated enough wealth to acquire landholdings for commercial production of grains, vegetables, and other products. To protect themselves against expropriations (periodic official inspections of indigenous communal land could result in redistribution of "surplus" land to Spanish petitioners), these farmers acquired individual title under Spanish law, which protected the owner from the legal confiscation to which communal land was subject. Commoners also successfully resisted Spanish exploitation by gaining exemption from heavy tribute and repartimiento obligations, which made it difficult to accumulate the money needed to invest in land or other enterprises. In addition to recognized caciques and kurakas, the exempted classes included independent women heads of households, artisans, officials of indigenous cabildos, and lay assistants of Catholic priests.

These achievements of that small minority of successful commoners, however, came with a price. Writing about late-sixteenth-century Peru, Steve Stern observes that

> the tragedy of Indian success lay in the way it recruited dynamic, powerful, or fortunate individuals to adopt Hispanic styles and relationships, thereby buttressing colonial domination. The achievements of native individuals, in the midst of a society organized to exploit indigenous peoples, educated Indians to view the Hispanic as superior, the Andean as inferior.

Most indigenous people lived in their own towns, some of pre-Hispanic origin, or in other new towns created by a process of resettlement of dispersed populations called "reductions" or "congregations." To serve the ends of Spanish control and tribute collection, the crown reorganized these towns on the peninsular model, with municipal governments patterned on those of Spanish towns. The organization of indigenous local government in New Spain and Peru differed. In New Spain, the indigenous cabildo, which in the mid-sixteenth century gradually replaced the pre-Conquest system of government by hereditary native rulers, included regidores or councilmen,

alcaldes who tried minor cases, and a **gobernador** (governor) who was responsible for the collection and delivery of tribute to the corregidor or the encomendero. Spanish colonial law required periodic election of these and other municipal officers, but it generally restricted voting to a small group of elite males. Candidates, as a rule, came from an even smaller number of hereditary aristocratic families, with the selection of officers usually the result of discussion and consultation with an assembly of elders, leading to final consensus. Election disputes were not unknown, however, and generally reflected factional divisions within the elite. Women, although barred from voting or holding office, sometimes played an active part in these disputes, as illustrated by the case of Josefa María Francisca. In the 1720s, she was a leader of one faction in the Mexican town of Tepoztlán, and she already had gained notoriety as a principal litigant in a stubborn effort to exempt Tepoztlán natives from the dreaded mining repartimiento. The rival faction accused Josefa of setting "a dangerous example by openly encouraging people to join her in 'endless lawsuits.'"

In Peru, Viceroy Francisco de Toledo imposed a structure of local government with two levels of authority. Here the key figure in the indigenous cabildo was the alcalde or mayor (a community had one or two alcaldes, depending on the number of households), who had general charge of administration and was assisted by one or two regidores and other officials. All these officials were to be replaced yearly by election, and none could succeed himself. Regarded as creatures of the Spanish state, these officials commanded little respect from the local community, for "the new power structure imposed by the Spaniards," says Karen Spalding, "cut across the traditional Andean hierarchy based on age and inherited position." Toledo distrusted the traditional Andean elite, the kurakas, but could not dispense with them, and he finally codified their status as a provincial nobility, supported by salaries paid out of tribute money and the labor service of their communities. Kurakas held important posts in the new officialdom and often served as allies and agents of the all-powerful Spanish corregidores, priests, and encomenderos. However, their personal liability for such community obligations like mita and tribute placed them at risk of having to sell their estates or losing their wealth through confiscation by corregidores.

The indigenous town typically included one or more neighborhood or kinship groups (calpulli in Mexico, ayllu in the Andean region), each with its hereditary elders who represented their community in intergroup disputes, acted as intermediaries in arranging marriages, supervised the allotment of land to the group's members, and otherwise served their communities. A certain degree of Hispanicization of commoners took place, reflected above all in religion but also in the adoption of various tools and articles of dress and food. The barriers erected by Spain between the two communities and the fixed hostility with which they regarded each other, however, prevented any complete acculturation. In response to the aggressions and injustices inflicted on it by Spaniards, the indigenous community drew into itself and fought stubbornly to preserve not only its land but also its cultural identity, speech, social organization, and traditional dances and songs. After the kinship group, the most important instrumentality for the maintenance of collective identity and security was the *cofradia* (religious brotherhood), whose members were responsible for the maintenance of certain cult activities.

The Conquest and its aftermath inflicted not only heavy material damage on indigenous society but serious psychological injury as well. Spanish accounts frequently cite the lament of native elders over the loss of the severe discipline, strong family ties, and high moral standards of the pre-Conquest regimes. The Spanish judge Zorita quotes approvingly the remark of one elder that with the coming of the Spaniards to Mexico "all was turned upside down; … liars, perjurers, and adulterers are no longer punished as they once were because the *principales* (nobles) have lost the power to chastise delinquents. This, say the Indians, is the reason why there are so many lies, disorders, and sinful women."

Blacks, Mulattos, Zambos: The Lowest Class

Blacks, mulattos, and *zambos* (African and indigenous peoples) occupied the bottom rungs of the colonial social ladder. By the end of the sixteenth century, Europeans had enslaved some seventy-five thousand Africans and transported them into the Spanish colonies under the system of **asiento** (monopolistic concession). The infamous Middle Passage (the journey of enslaved Africans across the Atlantic) was a thing of horror. The Jesuit Alonso de Sandoval, who had charge of conversion of slaves and who wrote a book on the subject, left this harrowing description of the arrival of a cargo of slaves in the port of Cartagena in New Granada:

> They arrive looking like skeletons; they are led ashore, completely naked, and are shut up in a large court or enclosure … and it is a great pity to see so many sick and needy people, denied all care or assistance, for as a rule they are left to lie on the ground, naked and without shelter.… I recall that I once saw two of them, already dead, lying on the ground on their backs like animals, their mouths open and full of flies, their arms crossed as if making the sign of the cross … and I was astounded to see them dead as a result of such great inhumanity.

By the end of the eighteenth century, Europeans had enslaved some 9.5 million Africans and brought them to the Americas. Especially dense concentrations occurred in Brazil and in the Caribbean area, where plantation economies dominated. Historians have hotly disputed the relative mildness or severity of Latin American treatment of enslaved Africans and their descendants. Recent studies generally support the view that the tempo of economic activity was decisive in determining the intensity of slave exploitation and the harshness of plantation discipline. Certainly, manumission of slaves was more frequent in the Hispanic than in the English, Dutch, or French colonies, but the unprofitability of slavery under certain conditions likely contributed to this result more than cultural traditions. Whatever the reasons, by the close of the colonial period, enslaved Africans and their descendants formed a minority of the total black and mulatto population. Whatever their treatment, slaves retained the aspiration for freedom. Fear of slave revolts haunted the Spanish ruling class, and slaves frequently fled from their masters. Some of them formed independent communities in remote jungles or mountains that successfully resisted Spanish punitive expeditions.

This stubborn attachment of the enslaved to freedom, reflected in frequent revolts, flights, and other forms of resistance, suggests that the debate over the relative mildness or severity of black slavery in Latin America evades the main issue: the dehumanizing character of even the "mildest" form of slavery. Brought from Africa by force and violence, cut off from their kindred peoples, the uprooted Africans were subjected in their new environment to severe deculturation. For reasons of security, slave owners preferred to purchase slaves of diverse ethnic origins, language, and religious beliefs, and deliberately promoted ethnic disunity among them. The economic interest of the planters dictated that the great majority of the imported slaves should be young, between the ages of fifteen and twenty. This contributed to the process of deculturation, for very few of the older blacks, the repositories of ethnic lore and traditions in African societies, came in the slaveships.

The scarcity of women (the proportion of females in the slave population on Cuban plantations between 1746 and 1822 ranged from 9 to 15 percent) distorted the lives of the slaves, creating a climate of intense sexual repression and family instability. The church might have insisted on the right of the slave to proper Christian marriage and the sanctity of the marriage, but not until the nineteenth century was the separate sale of husbands, wives, and children forbidden in the Spanish colonies. The right of the master to sell or remove members of an enslaved male's family and his free sexual access to enslaved women made it difficult if not impossible for the enslaved to have normal family lives. The world of the slave plantation, which resembled a prison rather than a society, left to independent Latin America a bitter heritage of racism, discrimination, and backwardness, problems that in most Latin American countries still await full solution.

Because of harsh treatment, poor living conditions, and the small number of women in the slave population, its rate of reproduction was very low. Miscegenation between white masters and enslaved women, on the other hand, produced a steady growth of the mulatto population. Free blacks and mulattos made important contributions to the colonial economy, both in agriculture and as artisans of all kinds. Spanish law also required free blacks and mulattos to pay tribute.

LIFE IN THE CITY AND ON THE HACIENDA

In addition to indigenous communities, social life in the Spanish colonies had two major centers: the colonial city and the hacienda, or large landed estate. Unlike its European counterpart, the colonial city as a rule did not arise spontaneously as a center of trade or industry but rather developed in planned fashion to serve the ends of Spanish settlement and administration of the surrounding area. Sometimes the Spanish built it on the ruins of an ancient capital, as in the case of Mexico City. More often, the cities developed on a site chosen for strategic or other advantages, as in the case of Lima. By contrast with the usually anarchical layout of Spanish cities, the colonial town typically followed the gridiron plan, with a large central plaza flanked by the cathedral, the governor's *palacio*, and other public buildings. From this central square originated long, wide, and straight streets that intersected to produce uniform, rectangular blocks. This passion for regularity reflected both the influence of Renaissance neoclassical works on architecture and the regulatory zeal of the crown. In sharp contrast to the carefully planned nucleus of the colonial city was the disorderly layout of the surrounding native **barrios** (slum districts) inhabited by a large native and mestizo population that provided the Spanish city with cheap labor and combustible material for the riots that shook the cities in times of famine or other troubles.

Into the capitals flowed most of the wealth produced by the mines, plantations, and cattle ranches of the surrounding area. In these cities, the rich colonial mine owners and landowners lived in houses, whose size and proximity to the center reflected the relative wealth and social position of

This sixteenth-century portrait, painted by the indigenous artist André Sánchez Gallque, depicts Don Francisco de Arobe, the black ruler of an Ecuadorian province, who surrendered to Spanish forces in 1597. Within a decade, however, local rebellions continued to challenge Spanish rule.

their owners. They displayed their wealth by the magnificence of their homes, furnishings, dress, and carriages, and by the multitude of their servants and slaves. By the end of the sixteenth century, Mexico City had acquired fame for the beauty of its women, horses, and streets; the riches of its shops; and the reckless spending, gaming, and generosity of its aristocracy. The poet Bernardo de Balbuena, in a long poem devoted to "La Grandeza Mexicana" ("The Grandeur of Mexico City"), wrote of

> That lavish giving of every ilk, Without a
> care how great the cost Of pearls, of gold,
> of silver, and of silk.

By the close of the seventeenth century, Mexico City had a population estimated to number 200,000.

Lima, founded in 1534, proud capital of the viceroyalty of Peru, and Potosí, the great Peruvian mining center whose wealth became legendary, were two other major colonial cities. By 1650, when its wealth had already begun to decline,

Potosí, with a population of 160,000 inhabitants, was the largest city in South America.

Before the eighteenth century, when changes in government and manners brought greater stability, violence was prevalent in the colonial city. Duels, assassinations, even pitched battles between different Spanish factions were frequently mentioned in official records and private diaries. From time to time, the misery of the masses in the native and mixed-race wards exploded in terrifying upheavals. In 1624, the mobs of Mexico City, goaded by famine and a decree of excommunication issued by the archbishop against an unpopular viceroy, rose with cries of "Death to the evil government" and "Long live the church." They vented their wrath in widespread destruction and looting. In 1692, similar circumstances caused an even greater explosion, which ended in many deaths, the sacking of shops, and the virtual destruction of the viceroy's palace and other public buildings.

The hacienda constituted another great center of colonial social life. We must again stress the major variations in size, productive potential, labor systems, and other aspects of the colonial hacienda. Changing economic trends brought frequent changes in the size, products, and ownership of these enterprises, with large haciendas sometimes broken up into smaller units, and vice versa. The trend in the course of the colonial period was toward concentration of landownership in fewer hands, usually at the expense of small landowners. Because of the "polymorphic" nature of the colonial hacienda, however, the following description of its social life was more characteristic of "traditional" haciendas found in certain areas of Mexico and Peru, and not of haciendas everywhere.

On the haciendas lived those creole aristocrats who could not support the expense of a city establishment or whose estates were in remote provinces or frontier areas. By the end of the seventeenth century, the hacienda in many areas had become a largely self-sufficient economic unit, combining arable land, grazing land for herds of sheep and cattle, timberland for fuel and construction, and even workshops for the manufacture and repair of the implements used on the hacienda. The hacienda often was a self-contained social unit, with a church or chapel usually served by a resident priest, a store from which workers could obtain goods charged against their wages, and even a jail to house disobedient peons. In the hacendado's large, luxuriously appointed house often lived not only his immediate family but numerous relatives who laid claim to his protection and support.

The hacienda often contained one or more indigenous villages whose residents had once owned the land on which they now lived and worked as virtual serfs. They lived in one-room adobe or thatch huts whose only furniture often was some sleeping mats and a stone used for grinding maize (called *metate* in New Spain). Unlike the independent indigenous communities, which continued to resist the landowners' aggressions with strategies ranging from revolts to prolonged litigation, the resident peons usually had learned to make the appropriate responses of resigned servility to the master. The hacienda, with its characteristic economic and social organization, represented the most authentic expression of the feudal side of colonial society.

MARRIAGE, SEXUALITY, AND THE STATUS OF WOMEN

Male domination generally characterized marital and familial relationships in elite society. Fathers had the customary right to arrange marriages for their daughters, and men imposed a double standard of sexual morality that enjoined strict chastity or fidelity for wives and daughters without corresponding restrictions on husbands and sons. Both the church—the guardian of public morality—and the state—concerned with the economic and political consequences of marriage—sought to supervise and control this standard. Throughout the sixteenth and seventeenth centuries, the church tended to support the right of children to select their marriage partners, while conceding the right of parents to have a say in the matter. In the second half of the eighteenth century, however, when large property interests grew in importance and influence, the state and then the church gradually adopted positions that supported parental objections to marriage between "unequal" partners because they were prejudicial to the family's "honor."

Although the royal decree of 1778 on the subject sanctioned parental opposition to only one kind of "inequality"—that arising from interracial unions—the interpretation placed on it by high colonial courts made clear that they regarded a wealthy mulatto family as the equal of a wealthy Spanish family. "A mulatto or a descendant of mulattoes," writes Patricia Seed, "was unequal to a Spaniard only if he was poor. The trend in decision making was that economic differences tied to racial differences, rather than racial disparity alone, constituted substantial social disparity." This issue of "inequality," of course, rarely arose in the top elite, for whom the selection of marriage partners almost invariably reflected a desire to conserve or strengthen the fortunes of the aristocratic families involved.

The concept of sexual honor also underwent some change in the same period. Previously, when a young woman lost her "honor" because of premarital sexual activity and sued for restitution of that honor through marriage or other compensation, the church tended to hold the man responsible and require him to marry her or compensate her for her loss. In the middle of the eighteenth century, however, aristocratic parents often argued that the girl's sexual activity made her—but not him—"unequal," thereby creating a bar to marriage. "This new concept of gender-related honor," says Patricia Seed, "framed an elaborate double standard that allowed young men to take the honor of young women without damage to their reputations or matrimonial consequences, but at the same time condemned women for the identical action."

Despite the emphasis placed by the Hispanic code of honor on virginity and marital fidelity, many colonial women, including members of the elite, disregarded conventional morality and church laws by engaging in premarital and extramarital sex. Sexual relations between betrothed couples were common. Elite women who bore children out of wedlock had available a number of strategies to cover up their indiscretions and legitimate their offspring. The many lower-class women who transgressed in this way lacked the means and perhaps the will to recover their lost "honor." Illegitimacy appears to have been pervasive in colonial cities in the seventeenth and eighteenth centuries. Illegitimacy, signifying the lack of honor, could be a bar to holding public office and obstruct access to higher positions in the church, the military, and the civil service. The protection of wealthy relatives and access to education, however, could mitigate or remove the taint of illegitimacy. The chronicler Garcilaso de la Vega (1539–1616) took pride in being the natural son of a noble conquistador, and Sor Juana Inés de la Cruz (1651–1695) found her out-of-wedlock birth no obstacle to achieving a brilliant literary career.

The contrast between the formal code of sexual honor and the actual sexual conduct of colonial men and women was especially striking in a plantation area like Venezuela, where the large-scale existence of slavery and the enormous power of the great landowners tended to loosen the restraints of law and convention on such conduct. In 1770, Bishop Martí of Venezuela made a visita of his diocese. To evaluate the moral health of his subjects, he invited the people of each town he visited to speak to him in confidence about their own sins and those of their neighbors. Martí's detailed record of these reports and his own investigations and judgments give an impression of sexuality run rampant. "Over fifteen hundred individuals stood accused, primarily of sexual misdeeds," writes Kathy Waldron; "nearly ten percent of the clerics in the province came under attack; and even the governor of Maracaibo was denounced. The accusations included adultery, fornication, concubinage, incest, rape, bigamy, prostitution, lust, homosexuality, bestiality, abortion, and infanticide."

The economic, social, and physical subordination of colonial women to men (prevailing church doctrine accepted a husband's right to beat disobedient or erring wives, only in moderation) is an undisputed fact. However, male domination was to some extent limited by the Hispanic property law, which required equal division of estates among heirs and gave women the right to control their dowries and inheritances during and beyond marriage. Some colonial women operated as entrepreneurs independently of their husbands; women often became executors of their husbands' wills and frequently managed a husband's business after his death. Two specialists in the field, Asunción Lavrín and Edith Couturier, conclude that colonial women enjoyed more economic independence than had been supposed: "there was repression; but repression was not the whole reality, and ... it did not wholly impair women's ability of expression."

Convent life provided an especially important means for achieving self-expression and freedom from male domination and sexual exploitation for elite and middle-class women. It was common for one or more daughters of an elite family to enter a convent. In the seventeenth century, thirteen Lima convents held more than 20 percent of the city's women.[4] The convents were self-governing

---

4. The high cost of marriage dowries, frequently mentioned by colonial observers, continued the influx of middle-class and elite women into convents. In a letter to the king, requesting the establishment of a convent, the cabildo of Buenos Aires noted that "in order to marry off a daughter with a modicum of decency one needs much more fortune than for two daughters to become nuns."

Talented girls like Isabel Flores de Oliva, later named Saint Rose of Lima, the first female saint in the Americas, sought artistic and intellectual independence in the convent.

Dolci, Carlo/The Bridgeman Art

institutions that gave women the opportunity to display their capacity for leadership in administration and resource management; like other church bodies, convents invested their wealth in mortgages on urban and rural properties. They also enabled women to develop skills in politicking, for convents could be the scenes of stormy factional struggles for control. "The convents," says Octavio Paz in his biography of the great poet Sor Juana Inés de la Cruz, "experienced the rebellions, quarrels, intrigues, coalitions, and reprisals of political life." Nuns frequently complained to religious authorities about the tyranny of their abbesses, and violent encounters were not unknown. The convents were also the scenes of a busy social life; the nuns received their visitors unveiled, despite the rule for-

bidding them to uncover their faces in the presence of outsiders, and they rarely observed the rule requiring separation by wooden bars. "These nuns excelled in exquisite confectionary arts," writes Paz, "and in the no less exquisite arts of martyring themselves and their sisters." Paz wonders that Sor Juana, a lucid intellect familiar with seventeenth-century European rationalist thought, kept her reason in that atmosphere of flagellations and mysticism. In her autobiographical letter to the bishop of Puebla, she confessed that convent life imposed obligations "most repugnant to my temperament" and referred to the "conventual bustle" that disturbed "the restful quiet of my books." Somehow, she managed to keep a distance between her intellect and that atmosphere, so foreign to her nature, but occasionally her self-control snapped under strain. Paz tells the story of a mother superior who complained to the archbishop of Sor Juana's haughtiness and accused her of having rudely said, "Quiet, Mother, you are a silly woman." The archbishop, a friend of Sor Juana, wrote on the margin of the complaint, "Prove the contrary, and I shall pass judgment."

Despite these drawbacks, the convent represented a heaven-sent opportunity for a young woman like Sor Juana, who was of a modest family background and who had no particular religious vocation. Her intellectual brilliance made it difficult for her to find a suitable marriage partner, and, in any case, she lacked the dowry to attract such a man. The convent, though, offered Sor Juana an escape from the traps of sexual exploitation and a way to cultivate her immense talents. A recent study of Hispanic women in colonial Peru by Luís Martín describes the Peruvian nunnery as "a fortress of women, a true island of women, where ... women could protect themselves from the corroding and dehumanizing forces of Don Juanism." A caveat, however, is in order: The subjects of Martín's book are mostly upper-class Hispanic women who often scorned and sometimes abused the slaves and servants who surrounded them.

Much more scholarship focuses on the lives of indigenous women in colonial Spanish America. Evidence suggests that, despite the damaging impact of Spanish patriarchal social relations, native women were far from passive victims. They enjoyed economic importance as producers and traders of goods, owned property in their own right, litigated, countered male abuse with a variety of strategies ranging from mobilization of kin to witchcraft, and played leading roles in the organization of resistance to Spanish measures that threatened their communities. In his study of 142 native rebellions in colonial Mexico, William Taylor notes the highly visible role of women. "In at least one-fourth of the cases," he writes, "women were visibly more aggressive, insulting, and rebellious."

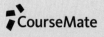 Go to the CourseMate website at **www.cengagebrain.com** for primary sources, additional study tools, and review materials—including audio and video clips—for this chapter.

Colonial Brazil

6

FOCUS QUESTIONS

- What were the main features of the Portuguese colonial system, and how did it compare to that of the Spanish?
- How did transatlantic markets, foreign competition, and Portuguese policy toward indigenous peoples affect the economic and social organization of the *fazenda*?
- What was the role of black slavery in the economic and social life of colonial Brazil?
- What were the relationships among the *fazendeiros* (great landowners) and high colonial officials, church dignitaries, and wealthy merchants?

BRAZIL'S EXISTENCE was unknown in Europe when the Treaty of Tordesillas (1494) between Spain and Portugal fixed the dividing line between their overseas possessions 370 leagues west of the Cape Verde Islands, assigning a large stretch of the coastline of South America to the Portuguese zone of exploration and settlement. In 1500, Pedro Alvares Cabral sailed with a large fleet to follow up Vasco da Gama's great voyage to India. He was, according to one explanation, driven by a storm farther west than he had intended and therefore made landfall on the Brazilian coast on April 22. Some historians speculate that he purposely changed course to investigate reports of land to the west or to verify a previous discovery. Whatever the reason for his westward course, Cabral promptly claimed the land for his country and sent a ship to report his discovery to the king.

The Beginning of Colonial Brazil

Portugal's limited resources, already committed to the exploitation of the wealth of Africa and the Far East, made it impossible to undertake a full-scale colonization of Brazil. However, Portugal did not entirely neglect its new possession. Royal expeditions established the presence of a valuable dyewood, called brazilwood, that grew abundantly on the coast between the present states of Pernambuco and São Paulo. Merchant capitalists soon obtained concessions to engage in the brazilwood trade and established a scattering of trading posts, where Europeans exchanged trinkets and other goods with natives for brazil logs and other exotic commodities. A small trickle of settlers began— some castaways, others *degredados* (criminals exiled from Portugal to distant parts of the empire). These exiles were often well received by the local natives and lived to sire a large number of mixed-race people who gave valuable assistance to Portuguese colonization. Meanwhile, French merchant ships, also drawn by the lure of brazilwood, began to appear on the Brazilian coast. Alarmed by the presence of these interlopers, King João III in 1530 sent an expedition under Martim Affonso de Sousa to drive away the intruders and to establish permanent settlements in Brazil. In 1532, the Portuguese founded their first town in Brazil, named São Vicente, near the present port of Santos.

THE CAPTAINCY SYSTEM

The limited resources of the Portuguese crown, combined with its heavy commitments in the

1494	Treaty of Tordesillas established the boundary between Portuguese and Spanish overseas territories
1500	Pedro Cabral landed on the coast of Brazil and claimed it for the Portuguese empire
1530–1700	Rise and fall of the Sugar Cycle in Brazil
1534–1536	King João III established the captaincy system, which allocated governing authority over fifteen separate captaincies to individual proprietors
1550–1640	Dramatic expansion of transatlantic trade in enslaved Africans in Brazil
1603	Creation of the Quilombo dos Palmares, perhaps the largest and most well known community of Africans who had escaped enslavement
1630–1654	Dutch West India Company seizes and occupies richest sugar-growing lands of the Brazilian coast
1653	Father Antônio Vieira denounces indigenous slavery
1695	Domingo Jorge Velho leads Portuguese assault on Palmares and defeats its last warrior king, Zumbi
1695–1760	Rise and decline of the Gold Cycle in Brazil
1703	Portuguese sign Methuen Treaty, which permitted English merchants to participate in Portuguese colonial trade and rendered Portugal dependent on England
1710–1711	War of the Mascates, which pitted Brazilian-born sugar planters against Portuguese-born merchants, foreshadowing the later struggle for independence
1720	Creation of independent captaincies of "São Paulo" and "Minas Gerais" (General Mines) to assert royal authority in the gold fields and ensure collection of the royal fifth
1750–1777	Marquis de Pombal inaugurates reforms designed to increase production, consolidate royal control over Brazilian colony, and end indigenous slavery even as it expanded the enslavement of Africans
1788–1789	Tiradentes Revolt is organized by José da Silva Xavier, a plebeian "tooth-puller" by trade, resists Portuguese colonial power

spice-rich East, forced the king to assign to private individuals the major responsibility for the colonization of Brazil. This responsibility took the form of the captaincy system, already used by Portugal in Madeira, the Azores, and the Cape Verde Islands. The crown divided the Brazilian coastline into fifteen parallel strips extending inland to the uncertain line of Tordesillas and granted them as hereditary captaincies to a dozen individuals, each of whom agreed to colonize, develop, and defend his captaincy or captaincies at his own expense. The captaincy system represented a curious fusion of feudal and commercial elements. The grantee or donatory was not only a vassal who owed allegiance to his lord the king, but also a businessman who hoped to derive large profits from his own estates and from taxes obtained from the colonists to whom he had given land. This fusion of feudal and commercial elements characterized the entire Portuguese colonial enterprise in Brazil from the beginning.

Few of the captaincies proved successful from either the economic or the political point of view because few donatories possessed the combination of investment capital and administrative ability required to attract settlers and defend their captaincies against indigenous attacks and foreign intruders. One of the most successful was Duarte Coelho, a veteran of the India enterprise who received the captaincy of Pernambuco. His heavy investment in the colony paid off so well that, by 1575, his son was the richest man in Brazil, collecting large amounts in *quitrents* (rents paid in lieu of feudal services) from the fifty sugar mills of the province and himself exporting more than fifty shiploads of sugar a year.

By the mid-sixteenth century, sugar had replaced brazilwood as the foundation of the Brazilian economy. Favored by its soil and climate, the northeast (the provinces of Pernambuco and Bahia) became the seat of a sugar-cane civilization characterized by three features: the *fazenda* (large estate), monoculture, and slave labor. A class of large landholders soon arose. Their extensive plantations and wealth marked them off from their less affluent neighbors. Only the largest planters could afford to erect the *engenhos* (mills) needed to process the sugar before export. Small farmers had to bring their sugar to the millowner for grinding, paying

Colonial Brazil

one-fourth to one-third of the harvest for the privilege. Because Europe's apparently insatiable demand for sugar yielded quick and large profits, planters had no incentive to diversify crops, and food agriculture was largely limited to small farms.

Although the basic techniques of sugar making remained relatively unchanged from the late sixteenth to the late eighteenth centuries, the reputation of the Brazilian sugar industry for being traditional and less developed appears unjustified. In the seventeenth century, the Brazilian system became a model that other powers sought to copy. Not until the mid-eighteenth century, when declining demand and prices for Brazilian sugar produced a crisis and Brazil's Caribbean rivals developed some new techniques, did this reputation for backwardness arise, and even then, according to historian Stuart Schwartz, "the charge was undeserved."

PORTUGAL'S INDIGENOUS POLICY

The Portuguese first sought to solve their labor shortage by raiding local villages, returning with trains of captives, and selling them to planters or other employers of labor. These aggressions were the primary cause of the chronic warfare between indigenous peoples and the Portuguese. However, this labor was unsatisfactory from an economic point of view because the natives lacked any tradition of organized work of the kind required by plantation agriculture, were especially susceptible to Old World diseases to which they had no acquired immunity, and offered many forms of resistance, ranging from attempts at escape to suicide. (In this last respect, of course, their response did not differ from that of the enslaved Africans who gradually replaced them.)

Soldiers of mixed racial background, like this mulatto soldier, played a large role in expeditions into the Brazilian interior in search of gold, indigenous slaves, and runaway black slaves.

As a result, after 1550, planters turned increasingly to the use of black slave labor imported from Africa. However, Dutch pirates and other foreign foes often cut off, or sharply reduced, the supply of black slaves, and Brazilian slave hunters continued to find a market for their wares throughout the colonial period. The most celebrated slave hunters were the **bandeirantes** (from the word *bandeira*, meaning "banner" or "military company") from the upland settlement of São Paulo. Unable to compete in sugar production with the more favorably situated plantation areas of the northeast, these men, who were themselves mestiço in most cases, made slave raiding in the interior their principal occupation. The eternal hope of finding gold or silver in the mysterious interior gave added incentive to their expeditions. As natives near the coast dwindled in numbers or fled before the invaders, the bandeirantes pushed even deeper south and west, expanding the frontiers of Brazil in the process.

Indigenous peoples in Brazil did not accept the loss of land and liberty without a struggle, but the fatal tendency of tribes to war against each other, a situation the Portuguese utilized to their advantage, handicapped their resistance. Forced to retreat into the interior by the superior arms and organization of the Portuguese, the natives often returned to make destructive forays on isolated Portuguese communities. As late as the first part of the nineteenth century, this unremitting warfare made stretches of the Brazilian shore uninhabitable.

However, the unequal struggle at last ended here, as in the Spanish colonies, in the total defeat of the natives. Overwork, loss of the will to live, and the ravages of European diseases caused heavy loss of life among the enslaved indigenous people. Punitive expeditions against those who resisted enslavement or gave some other pretext for sanctions also caused depopulation. The Jesuit father Antônio Vieira, whose denunciations of Portuguese cruelty recall the accusations of Las Casas about the Spanish, claimed that Portuguese mistreatment of natives had caused the loss of more than 2 million lives in Amazonia in forty years. A distinguished English historian, Charles R. Boxer, considers this claim exaggerated but concedes that the Portuguese "often exterminated whole tribes in a singularly barbarous way."

Almost the only voices raised in protest against the enslavement and mistreatment of native peoples were those of the Jesuit missionaries. The first fathers, led by Manoel da Nóbrega, came in 1549 with the captain general Tomé de Sousa. Four years later, another celebrated missionary, José de Anchieta, arrived in Brazil. Far to the south, on the plains of Piratininga, Nóbrega and Anchieta established a *colegio* (school) for Portuguese, mixed-race, and native children that became a model institution of its kind. Around this settlement gradually arose the town of São Paulo, which English historian Robert Southey identified as an important point of departure into the interior for "adventurers in search of gold and missionaries in search of souls."

The Jesuits followed a program for the settlement of their native converts in *aldeias* (villages), where they lived under the care of the priests, completely segregated from the harmful influence of Portuguese colonists. This program provoked many clashes with the slave hunters and the planters, who had different ends in view. In an angry protest to the *Mesa da Consciência*, a royal council entrusted with responsibility for the religious affairs of the colony, the planters sought to turn the tables on the Jesuits. The council claimed that residents in the Jesuit villages were "true slaves, who labored as such not only in the colegios but on the so-called Indian lands, which in the end became the estates and sugar mills of the Jesuit fathers."

The clash of interests between the planters and slave hunters and the Jesuit missionaries reached a climax about the middle of the seventeenth century, an era of great activity on the part of the bandeirantes of São Paulo. In various parts of Brazil, the landowners rose in revolt, expelled the Jesuits, and defied royal edicts proclaiming the freedom of native peoples. In 1653, Antônio Vieira, a priest of extraordinary oratorical and literary powers, arrived in Brazil with full authority from the king to settle these questions as he saw fit. During Lent, Vieira preached a famous sermon to the people of Maranhão in which he denounced indigenous slavery in terms comparable to those used by Father Montesinos on Santo Domingo in 1511. The force of Vieira's tremendous blast was weakened by his suggestion that slavery should be continued under certain conditions and by the well-known fact that the Jesuit order had enslaved both indigenous and black peoples. Yet there can be no doubt that the condition of natives in the Jesuit mission villages was superior to that of the slaves in the Portuguese towns and plantations. A stronger argument against Jesuit practices was the fact that the system of segregation, however benevolent in intent, represented an arbitrary and mechanical imposition of alien cultural patterns on the native population and hindered rather than facilitated true social integration.

The crown, generally sympathetic to the Jesuit position but under strong pressure from the planter class, pursued for two centuries a policy of compromise that satisfied neither Jesuits nor planters. A decisive turn came during the reform ministry of the marquis de Pombal (1750–1777), who expelled the Jesuits from Portugal and Brazil and secularized their missions. His legislation, forbidding enslavement, accepted the Jesuit thesis of indigenous rights; he also accepted the need for preparing the natives for civilized life and even the principle of concentrating them in communities under the care of administrators responsible for their education and welfare. However, his policy did not segregate them from the Portuguese community; it made them available for use as paid workers by the colonists and actually encouraged contact and mingling between the two races, including interracial marriage. Meanwhile, the growth of the African slave trade, also encouraged by Pombal, diminished the demand for native labor. Whether Pombal's reform legislation significantly improved the material condition of indigenous peoples is doubtful, but it contributed to their absorption into the colonial population and ultimately into the Brazilian nation. The decisive factor in this case was race mixture, which increased because of the passing of the Jesuit temporal power.

THE FRENCH AND DUTCH CHALLENGES

The dyewood, the sugar, and the tobacco of Brazil early attracted the attention of foreign powers. The

French were the first to challenge Portuguese control of the colony. With the aid of indigenous allies, they made sporadic efforts to entrench themselves on the coast and in 1555 founded Rio de Janeiro as the capital of what they called Antarctic France. One cultural by-product of French contact with natives was the creation of a French image of them as "noble savages," immortalized by the sixteenth-century French philosopher Montaigne in his essay "On Cannibals." But the French offensive in Brazil was weakened by Catholic-Huguenot strife at home, and in 1567 the Portuguese commander Mem de São ousted the French and occupied the settlement of Rio de Janeiro.

A more serious threat to Portuguese sovereignty over Brazil was posed by the Dutch, whose West India Company seized and occupied for a quarter of a century (1630–1654) the richest sugar-growing portions of the Brazilian coast. Under the administration of Prince Maurice of Nassau (1637–1644), Dutch Brazil, with its capital at Recife, became the site of brilliant scientific and artistic activity. The Portuguese struggle against the Dutch became an incipient struggle for independence, uniting elements of all races from various parts of Brazil. These motley forces won victories over the Dutch at the first and second battles of Guararapes (1648–1649). Weakened by tenacious Brazilian resistance and a simultaneous war with England, the Dutch withdrew from Pernambuco in 1654. Nonetheless, they took with them the lessons they had learned in the production of sugar and tobacco and reestablished themselves in the West Indies. Soon the plantations and refineries of Barbados and other Caribbean islands gave serious competition to Brazilian sugar in the world market, with a resulting fall of prices. By the last decade of the seventeenth century, the Brazilian sugar industry had entered a long period of stagnation.

THE MINERAL CYCLE, THE CATTLE INDUSTRY, AND THE COMMERCIAL SYSTEM

In this time of gloom, news of the discovery of gold in the southwestern region, later known as Minas Gerais, reached the coast in 1695. This discovery opened a new economic cycle, led to the first effective settlement of the interior, and initiated a major shift in Brazil's center of economic and political gravity from north to south. Large numbers of colonists from Bahia, Pernambuco, and Rio de Janeiro, accompanied by their slaves and servants, swarmed into the mining area. Their exodus from the older regions caused an acute shortage of field hands that continued until the gold boom had run its course by the middle of the eighteenth century. The crown tried to stem the exodus by legislation and by policing the trails that led to the mining area, but its efforts were in vain. For two decades (1700–1720), it had no success in asserting royal authority and collecting the royal fifth in the gold fields. Violence between rival groups, especially pioneers from São Paulo and European-born newcomers, reached the scale of civil war in 1708. The mutual weakening of the two sides because of these struggles finally enabled the crown to restore order.

In 1710, the crown established a new captaincy of "São Paulo and the Mines of Gold" and, in 1720, divided it into "São Paulo" and "Minas Gerais." A decade later, wild excitement accompanied the discovery that certain stones found in the area, hitherto thought to be crystals, were in reality diamonds; many adventurers, along with their slaves, turned from gold to diamond washing. The great increase in the supply of diamonds to Europe upset the market, causing a serious decline in price. As a result, the Portuguese government instituted a regime of drastic control over the **Diamantina** (Diamond District) to limit mining and prevent smuggling and thus maintain prices; this regime effectively isolated the district from the outside world.

Like sugar production, the mineral cycle occasioned rapid and superficial exploitation of the new sources of wealth, followed by an equally swift decline. Mining revenue peaked about 1760, and thereafter both the river gold washings of Minas Gerais and the Diamond District suffered a progressive exhaustion of deposits. By 1809, the English traveler John Mawe described the gold-mining center of Villa Rica as a town that "scarcely retains a shadow of its former splendor."

Yet the mineral cycle left a permanent mark on the Brazilian landscape in the form of new centers of settlement in the southwest in Minas Gerais and in the future provinces of Goias and Matto Grosso, Brazil's Far West, which pioneers penetrated in their search for gold. If the mining camps became deserted, the new towns survived, although with diminished vitality. The decline of the mining industry also spurred efforts to promote the agricultural and pastoral wealth of the region. The crown formally recognized the shift in the center of economic and political gravity southward from Pernambuco and Bahia to Minas Gerais and Rio de Janeiro, when it moved the seat of the viceregal capital to Rio de Janeiro.

As the provinces of Minas Gerais and Goias sank into decay, the northeast experienced a partial revival based on increasing European demand for sugar, cotton, and other semitropical products. Between 1750 and 1800, Brazilian cotton production made significant progress but then declined just as rapidly because of competition from the more efficient cotton growers of the United States. The beginnings of the coffee industry—the future giant of the Brazilian economy—also date from the late colonial period.

Cattle raising made its contribution to the advance of the Brazilian frontier and the growing importance of the south. The intensive agriculture of the coast and the concentration of population in coastal cities like Bahia and Pernambuco created a demand for fresh meat that gave an initial stimulus to cattle raising. Because the expansion of plantation agriculture in the coastal zone did not leave enough land for grazing, the cattle industry inevitably had to move inland.

By the second half of the seventeenth century, the penetration of the distant São Francisco Valley from Bahia and Pernambuco was well under way. Powerful cattlemen, with their herds of cattle, their *vaqueiros* (cowboys), and their slaves, entered the *sertão* (backcountry), drove out the indigenous peoples, and established fortified ranches and villages for their retainers. The crown legitimized such occupation before or after the fact by officially granting a huge tract of land, a virtual feudal domain, to the cattle baron in question, whose word became law on his estate. The landowner's cattle provided meat for the coastal cities and mining camps, draft animals for the plantations, and hides for export to Europe.

The cattle industry later expanded into the extreme southern region of Rio Grande do Sul, which the government colonized in the interests of defense against Spanish expansionist designs. In this case, too, the crown made vast land grants. The counterpart of the vaqueiro in the south was the *gaucho*. Like the vaqueiro, the gaucho was an expert horseman, but he reflected the blend of cultures in the Río de la Plata. His speech was a mixture of Portuguese, Spanish, and indigenous dialects; his dress was the loose, baggy trousers typical of the Argentine cowboy; and his chief implement, the **bolas** (balls of stone attached to a rawhide rope), was the chief weapon that the pampas natives used to entangle and bring down animals.

Portugal, like Spain (with which it loosely united, 1580–1640), pursued a mercantilist commercial policy, although not as consistently or rigorously. During this period, the crown firmly restricted Brazil's commerce to Portuguese nationals and ships. The Dutch, principal carriers of Brazilian sugar and tobacco to European markets, responded with extensive smuggling and a direct attack on the richest sugar-growing area of Brazil.

Following the successful Portuguese revolt against Spain, it signed the Methuen treaty (1703) with England, Portugal's ally. This treaty permitted British merchants to trade between Portuguese and Brazilian ports. However, English ships frequently neglected the formality of touching at Lisbon and plied a direct contraband trade with the colony. Because the Portuguese industry was incapable of supplying the colonists with the required quantity and quality of manufactured goods, a large proportion of the outward-bound cargoes consisted of foreign textiles and other products, of which England provided the lion's share. Thus, Portugal, master of Brazil, itself became a colony of Dutch and English merchants with offices in Lisbon.

In the eighteenth century, during the reign of Dom José I (1750–1777), his prime minister, the marquis de Pombal, an able representative of the ideology of enlightened despotism, launched an administrative and economic reform of the Portuguese empire that bears comparison with the Bourbon reforms in Spain and Spanish America that were taking place at the same time. Pombal's design was to nationalize Portuguese-Brazilian trade by creating a Portuguese merchant class with enough capital to compete with British merchants and a national industry whose production could dislodge English goods from the Brazilian market. The program required an active state intervention in the imperial economy. Therefore, he created a Board of Trade, which subsidized merchant-financiers with lucrative concessions in Portugal and Brazil. He formed companies and granted them monopolies over trade with particular regions of Brazil. Finally, he expected to develop the economies of those regions by implementing a policy of import substitution through state assistance to old and new industries. Despite mistakes, failures, and a partial retreat from Pombal's program after he left office in 1777, the Pombaline reform achieved at least partial success in its effort to reconquer Brazilian markets for Portugal. Between 1796 and 1802, 30 percent of all the goods shipped to Brazil consisted of Portuguese manufactures, especially cotton cloth. Nonetheless, according to historian James Lang, the flight of the Portuguese royal family from Lisbon to Brazil in 1808 as a result of Napoleon's invasion of Portugal, followed two years later by the signing of a treaty with England that gave the British all the trade privileges they requested, effectively "dismantled the protective edifice so painfully put together since 1750." Britain once again enjoyed a virtual monopoly of trade with Brazil.

Government and Church

The donatory system of government first established in Brazil by the Portuguese crown soon proved unsatisfactory. A glaring contradiction existed between the vast powers granted to the donatories and the authority of the monarch; moreover, few donatories were able to cope with the tasks of defense and colonization for which the crown had made them responsible. The result was a governmental reform. In 1549, the king sent Tomé de Sousa out as governor general to head a central colonial administration for Brazil. Bahia, situated about midway between the flourishing settlements of Pernambuco and São Vicente, became his capital. Gradually, he revoked the hereditary rights and privileges of the donatories and replaced them with governors appointed by the king. As the colony expanded, new captaincies developed. In 1763, as noted, the governor of Rio de Janeiro replaced his colleague at Bahia as head of the colonial administration, with the title of viceroy. In practice, however, his authority over the other governors was negligible.

THE ADMINISTRATORS AND THEIR DEFICIENCIES

The government of Portuguese Brazil broadly resembled that of the Spanish colonies in its spirit, structure, and vices. One notable difference, however, was the much smaller scale of the Portuguese administration. The differing economies of the two empires explain this divergence. The Spanish Indies had a relatively diversified economy that served local and regional, as well as overseas, markets and a large native population that was an important source of labor and royal tribute. Combined with a Spanish population that numbered 300,000 in 1600 (when only 30,000 Portuguese lived in Brazil), these conditions created an economic base for the rise of hundreds of towns and the need for a numerous officialdom charged with the regulation of labor, the collection of tribute, and many other fiscal and administrative duties. In Portuguese America, on the other hand, several factors rendered the establishment of an elaborate bureaucracy unnecessary. They included the overwhelming importance of exports, especially of sugar, which the crown taxed when it arrived in Lisbon; the economic and social dominance of the plantation, which undermined development of urban life; and the minor role of the native population as a source of labor and royal revenue.

During the union of Portugal and Spain, the colonial policies of the two countries aligned in the creation of the *Conselho de India*, whose functions resembled those of the Spanish Council of the Indies. In 1736, the functions of the conselho shifted to a newly created ministry of *Marinha e Ultramar* (Marine and Overseas). Under the king, this body framed laws for Brazil, appointed governors, and supervised their conduct. The governor, captain general, or viceroy combined in himself military, administrative, and even some judicial duties. His power tended to be absolute, but certain factors tempered it. These included the constant intervention of the home government, which bound him with precise, strict, and detailed instructions; the counterweights of other authorities, especially the *relações* (high courts), which were both administrative and judicial bodies; and the existence of special administrative organs, such as the intendancies created in the gold and diamond districts, which were completely independent of the governor. Thus, in Brazil, as in the Spanish colonies, a system of checks and balances operated through overlapping functions and the oversight of some officials by others with similar or competing authority. This system reflected above all the home government's distrust for its agents. Other factors that tended to diminish the authority of the governor were the vastness of the country, the scattered population, the lack of social stability, and the existence of enormous landholdings that undermined challenges to the feudal power of the great planters and cattle barons.

The most important institution of local government was the **Senado da Câmara** (municipal council). The influence of this body varied with the size of the city. Whether elected by a restricted property-owning electorate or chosen by the crown, its membership represented the ruling class of merchants, planters, and professional men. Elections often were marked by struggles for control by rival factions, planters and creoles on one side, merchants and peninsulars on the other. The authority of the câmara extended over its entire *comarca* (district), which often was very large. Nonetheless, the frequent intervention of the *ouvidor* (royal judge), who usually combined his judicial functions with the administrative duties of corregidor, limited its

power. Generally speaking, the greater the size and wealth of the city, and the farther it was from the viceregal capital, the greater its powers.

Both the crown and the municipal councils levied numerous taxes, whose collection they usually farmed out to private individuals. In return for making a fixed payment to the treasury, these men collected the taxes for the crown and could keep the surplus once they had met the quota. The system, of course, encouraged fraud and extortion of every kind. Another crippling burden on the population was tithes, which came to 10 percent of the total product, originally payable in kind but later only in cash. Tithes, writes the Brazilian historian Caio Prado Júnior, "ran neck and neck with conscription as one of the great scourges inflicted on the population by the colonial administration."

The besetting vices of Spanish colonial administration—inefficiency, bureaucratic attitudes, slowness, and corruption—were equally prominent in the Portuguese colonial system. Justice was not only costly but also incredibly slow and complicated. Cases brought before lower courts ascended the ladder of the higher tribunals: ouvidor, relação, and up to the crown Board of Appeals, taking as long as ten to fifteen years for resolution.

Over vast areas of the colony, however, administration and courts were virtually nonexistent. Away from the few large towns, local government often meant the rule of great landowners, who joined to their personal influence the authority of office, for it was from their ranks that the royal governors invariably appointed the **capitães mores** (district militia officers). Armed with unlimited power to enlist, command, arrest, and punish, the capitão mor became a popular symbol of despotism and oppression. Sometimes these men used the local militia as feudal levies for war against a rival family; duels or pitched battles between retainers of rival clans often settled boundary disputes and questions of honor.

Corruption pervaded the administrative apparatus from top to bottom. The miserably paid officials prostituted their trusts in innumerable ways: Embezzlement, graft, and bribery were well-nigh universal. Some improvement, at least on the higher levels of administration, took place under the auspices of the extremely able and energetic marquis de Pombal. The same tendency toward centralization that characterized Bourbon colonial policy appeared in Portuguese policy in this period. Pombal abolished the remaining hereditary captaincies, restricted the special privileges of the municipalities, and increased the power of the viceroy. In a mercantilist spirit, Pombaline reforms sought to promote the economic advance of Brazil with a view toward promoting the reconstruction of Portugal, whose condition was truly forlorn.

Typical of these enlightened viceroys was the marquis de Lavradio (1769–1779), whose achievements included the transfer of coffee from Pará into São Paulo, in whose fertile red soil it was to flourish mightily. Lavradio's letter of instructions to his successor suggests the small impact that Pombaline reform had on Brazil's administration. In it, he gloomily observed that

> as the salaries of these magistrates [the judges] are small … they seek to multiply their emoluments by litigation and discord, which they foment, and not only keep the people unquiet, but put them to heavy expenses, and divert them from their occupations, with the end of promoting their own vile interest and that of their subalterns, who are the principal concocters of these disorders.

During the twelve years he had governed in Brazil, wrote the viceroy, he had never found one useful establishment instituted by any of these magistrates.

THE CHURCH AND THE STATE

In Brazil, as in the Spanish colonies, church and state were intimately united. By comparison with the Spanish monarchs, however, the Portuguese kings seemed almost niggardly in their dealings with the church. However, their control over its affairs, exercised through the *padroado* (the ecclesiastical patronage granted by the pope to the Portuguese king in his realm and overseas possessions) was absolute. The king exercised his power through

a special board, the *Mesa da Consciência e Ordens* (Board of Conscience and Orders). Rome, however, long maintained a strong indirect influence through the agency of the Jesuits, who were influential in the Portuguese court until 1759 when it expelled them from Portugal and Brazil.

With some honorable exceptions, notably that of the entire Jesuit order, the tone of clerical morality and conduct in Brazil was deplorably low. The clergy faced much criticism for their extortionate fees and the negligence they displayed in the performance of their spiritual duties. Occasionally, priests combined those duties with more mundane activities. Many were planters; others carried on a variety of businesses. One high-ranking crown official summed up his impressions of the clergy in the statement, "All they want is money, and they care not a jot for their good name."

Yet the church and the clergy made their own contributions to the life of colonial Brazil. The clergy provided such educational and humanitarian establishments as existed in the colony. From its ranks—which were open to talent and even admitted individuals of mixed race despite the formal requirement of a special dispensation—came most of the few distinguished names in Brazilian colonial science, learning, and literature. Among them, Jesuit writers again occupied a prominent place, but colonial Brazil's lack of a university or printing press reflected its cultural poverty.

Masters and Slaves

Race mixture played a decisive role in the formation of the Brazilian people. The scarcity of Portuguese women in the colony, the absence of puritanical attitudes, and the despotic power of the great planters over their enslaved indigenous and black women gave impetus to miscegenation. Of the three possible race combinations—white-black, white-native, black-native—the first was the most common. The immense majority of these unions were outside wedlock. In 1755, the marquis de Pombal, pursuing the goals of population growth and strengthening Brazil's borders, issued an order encouraging marriages between Portuguese men and native women and proclaiming the descendants of such unions eligible to positions of honor and dignity. He did not extend this favor to other interracial unions, however.

COLOR, CLASS, AND SLAVERY

In principle, color lines were strictly drawn. A "pure" white wife or husband, for example, was indispensable to a member of the upper class. But the enormous number of mixed unions outside wedlock and the resulting large progeny, some of whom, at least, were regarded with affection by Portuguese fathers and were provided with some education and property, inevitably led to the blurring of color lines and the fairly frequent phenomenon of "passing." The tendency was to classify individuals racially, if their color was not too dark, on the basis of social and economic position rather than on their physical appearance. The English traveler Henry Koster alludes to this "polite fiction" in his anecdote concerning a certain great personage, a capitão mor, whom Koster suspected of being a mulatto. In response to his question, his servant replied, "He was, but is not now." Asked to explain, the servant continued, "Can a capitão mor be a mulatto man?"

Slavery played as important a role in the social organization of Brazil as race mixture did in its ethnic makeup. The social consequences of the system were entirely negative. Slavery brutalized enslaved Africans, corrupted both master and slave, fostered harmful attitudes with respect to the dignity of labor, and distorted the economic development of Brazil. The tendency to identify labor with slavery sharply limited the number of socially acceptable occupations in which Portuguese or free mixed-race peoples could engage. This gave rise to a populous class of vagrants, beggars, "poor whites," and other degraded or disorderly elements who would not or could not compete with the enslaved in agriculture and industry. Inevitably, given the almost total absence of incentive to work on the part of the slave, the level of efficiency and productivity of his or her labor was very low.

Much older historical writing fostered the idea that Brazilian slavery was mild by comparison with slavery in other colonies. In part, this tradition

owed its popularity to the writings of the Brazilian sociologist Gilberto Freyre, who emphasized the patriarchal relations existing between masters and slaves in the sugar plantation society of the northeast. But the slaves described by Freyre were usually house slaves who occupied a privileged position. Their situation was quite different from that of the great majority of slaves, who worked on the sugar and tobacco plantations of Bahia and Pernambuco. During harvest time and when the mills were grinding the cane, says Charles Boxer, the slaves sometimes worked around the clock and often at least from dawn to dusk. In the off-season, the hours were not so long, but "discipline was maintained with a severity that often degenerated into sadistic cruelty where the infliction of corporal punishment was concerned." A royal dispatch of 1700 denounced the barbarity with which owners of both sexes treated their slaves and singled out for special condemnation the practice of women owners who forced their female slaves to engage in prostitution.

The harsh labor discipline on the plantation reflected calculations of cost and profit. "Slave owners," says Stuart Schwartz,

> estimated that a slave could produce on the average about three-quarters of a ton of sugar a year. At the prices of the period, this meant in effect that a slave would produce in two or three years an amount of sugar equal to the slave's original purchase price and the cost of maintenance. Thus if the slave lived only five or six years, the investment of the planter would be doubled, and a new and vigorous replacement could be bought.

This reasoning provided little incentive to improve work conditions or foster a higher birthrate among slaves because slaveholders would have to support children for twelve or fourteen years before they became productive. The basic theory of slave management, concludes Schwartz, was to "[w]ork them hard, make a profit, buy another."

Obviously, the treatment of slaves varied considerably with the temperament of the individual

A scene of Brazilian slavery. New arrivals from Africa wait in a slave dealer's establishment while the seated proprietor negotiates the sale of a child to a prospective customer.

slave owner. Although the crown provided slaves with legal means of redress, little evidence exists that these were effective in relieving their plight. The church, represented on the plantation by a chaplain paid and housed by the landowner, probably exerted little influence on the problem. A low rate of reproduction among slaves and frequent suicides spoke volumes about their condition. Many slaves ran away and formed *quilombos* (settlements of fugitive slaves in the bush). The most famous of these was the so-called republic of Palmares, founded in 1603 in the interior of the northeastern captaincy of Alagoas. A self-sufficient African kingdom with several thousand inhabitants who lived in ten villages spread over a ninety-mile territory, Palmares was exceptional among quilombos in its size, complex organization, and ability to survive repeated expeditions sent against

it by colonial authorities. Not until 1694 did a Paulista army destroy it after a two-year siege. Nonetheless, the quilombos continued to alarm planters and authorities, and, as late as 1760, complaints about the threat posed by quilombos around Bahia were common.

Manumission was another way that slaves achieved freedom. Slave owners, in their wills or at a slave's baptism, frequently freed favored slaves or children (sometimes their own) whom they reared in the **Casa Grande** (Big House). Sometimes slaves bought their own freedom by combining the resources of family and friends. The grant of freedom might be conditional on assurance of further service of one kind or another. Thus, in a variety of ways, combining economic, cultural, and religious motives, a class of freedmen and their descendants arose and, by the eighteenth century, had achieved a certain importance in the economic and social life of colonial Brazil.

Slavery played a decisive role in the economic life of colonial Brazil and placed its stamp on all social relations. In addition to masters and slaves, however, a large free peasant population of varied racial makeup lived on estates and in villages and hamlets scattered throughout the Brazilian countryside. Some were small landowners, often possessing a few slaves of their own, who brought their sugar cane for processing or sale to the **senhor de engenho** (sugar-mill owner). Their economic inferiority made their independence precarious, and their land and slaves tended to pass into the hands of the great planters in a process of concentration of landownership and growing social stratification. The majority, however, were **lavradores**, **moradores**, or **foreiros** (tenant farmers or sharecroppers) who owed labor and allegiance to a great landowner in return for the privilege of farming a parcel of land. Other free peasants were squatters who, in the seventeenth and eighteenth centuries, pushed out of the coastal zone to settle in the backcountry, where they were regarded as intruders by the cattle barons and other great landowners who laid claim to those lands.

Other free commoners were the artisans, including many black or mulatto freedmen, who served the needs of the urban population. An important group of salaried workers—overseers, mechanics, coopers, and the like—supplied the special skills required by the sugar industry.

LARGE ESTATES AND COLONIAL TOWNS

The nucleus of Brazilian social as well as economic organization was the large estate, or fazenda, which usually rested on a base of black slavery. The large estate centered about the Casa Grande and constituted a patriarchal community that included the owner and his family, his chaplain and overseers, his slaves, his **obrigados** (sharecroppers), and his **agregados** (retainers), free men of low social status who received the landowner's protection and assistance in return for a variety of services.

In this self-contained world, an intricate web of relations arose between the master and his slaves and white or mixed-race subordinates. No doubt, prolonged contact sometimes mellowed and humanized these relationships and added to mere commercial relationships a variety of emotional ties. The protective role of the master found expression in the relationship of **compadrio** (godfathership), in which the master became sponsor or godfather of a baptized child or a bridal pair whose marriage he witnessed. The system implied relations of mutual aid and a paternalistic interest in the welfare of the landowner's people. But it by no means excluded intense exploitation of those people or the display of the most ferocious cruelty if they should cross the landowner or dispute his absolute power.

In the sugar-growing northeast, the great planters became a distinct aristocratic class, possessed of family traditions and pride in their name and blood. In the cattle-raising regions of the sertão and the south, the small number of slaves, the self-reliant character of the vaqueiro or gaucho, and the greater freedom of movement of workers gave society a more democratic tone. Everywhere, however, says the Brazilian historian Caio Prado Júnior, "the existence of pronounced social distinctions and the absolute and patriarchal domination of the owner and master were elements invariably associated with all the colony's large landed estates."

In contrast to the decisive importance of the fazenda, most colonial towns were mere appendages of the countryside, dominated politically and socially by the rural magnates. Even in the few large cities like Bahia and Rio de Janeiro, the dominant social group was composed of *fazendeiros* (great landowners) and sugar-mill owners. These men often left the supervision of their estates to majordomos and overseers, preferring the pleasures and bustle of the cities to the dreary routines of the countryside. Other social groups lived in the city and these groups disputed or shared power with the great landowners: high officials of the colonial administration; dignitaries of the church; wealthy professional men, especially lawyers; and the large merchants, almost exclusively peninsulars, who monopolized the export-import trade and financed the industry of the planters.

The social position of the merchant was not high, because of the medieval prejudice against commerce brought over from Portugal (a prejudice that did not prevent the highest officials from engaging in trade, albeit discreetly), but nothing barred the merchants from membership on the municipal councils. The conflict between native-born landowners and European-born merchants, aggravated by nationalistic resentment against upstart immigrants, sometimes broke out into armed struggle. For example, the petty War of the Mascates (1710–1711) pitted the sugar planters who dominated Olinda, the provincial capital of Pernambuco, against the merchants who controlled its neighboring seaport of Recife.

This struggle between *mazombos* (Brazilian-born whites) and *reinóis* (peninsulars) foreshadowed the later rise of a broader Brazilian nationalism and the first projects of Brazilian independence. In the late eighteenth century, Minas Gerais, the most urbanized Brazilian region, had the most diversified economy. It became a seat of much unrest because of official efforts to reinforce the area's dependency on Portuguese exporters, collect large amounts of delinquent taxes, and impose a new head tax. A group of dissidents, most of whom were highly placed members of the colonial elite, hatched a conspiracy to revolt and to establish a republic on the North American model in 1788–1789. The only leading conspirator who was not a member of the aristocracy was José da Silva Xavier, a military officer of low rank who practiced the part-time profession of "tooth-puller," from which the Tiradentes Rebellion drew its name. An enthusiast for the American Revolution, Silva Xavier apparently possessed copies of the Declaration of Independence and U.S. state constitutions. When the colonial officials discovered the conspiracy, they condemned all the principal conspirators to death but commuted the sentences to exile for all but the plebeian Silva Xavier. His barbarous execution, which he faced with great courage, made him a martyr as well as a precursor of Brazilian independence.

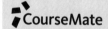 Go to the CourseMate website at **www.cengagebrain.com** for primary sources, additional study tools, and review materials—including audio and video clips—for this chapter.

The Bourbon Reforms and Spanish America

7

FOCUS QUESTIONS

- What were the major Bourbon economic and political reforms, and how did they affect the colonial economy and social relations?
- How did creole nationalism draw on the European Enlightenment and the "classical antiquity" of ancient American indigenous societies?
- How did Bourbon reforms affect indigenous communities, enslaved Africans, and mixed-race peoples?
- Why did the Bourbon Era produce the largest scale popular revolts in colonial history?
- How is the phrase "growth without development" relevant to the colonial economy of the Bourbon Era?

THE DEATH OF the sickly Charles II in November 1700 marked the end of an era in Spanish history and the beginning of a new and better day, although the signs under which the new day began were far from hopeful. On his deathbed, the unhappy Charles, more kingly in his dying than he had ever been before, fought desperately to prevent the triumph of an intrigue for the partition of the Spanish dominions among three claimants of that inheritance: the prince of Bavaria, the archduke Charles of Austria, and Louis XIV's grandson, Philip of Anjou. In one of his last acts, Charles signed a will naming the French Philip, who became Philip V, successor to all his dominions.

English fears at the prospect of a union of France and Spain under a single ruler precipitated the War of the Spanish Succession (1702–1713). The war ended with the Treaty of Utrecht (1713), which granted Gibraltar and Minorca to Great Britain, established major trade concessions in the Spanish Indies, and forbade any union of French and Spanish thrones under Philip. Another peace treaty, concluded the following year, gave the Spanish Netherlands and Spain's Italian possessions to Austria.

Reform and Recovery

Spain's humiliating losses deepened the prevailing sense of pessimism and defeatism, but there were compensations. The shock of defeat in the succession war drove home the need for sweeping reform of Spanish institutions. Moreover, the loss of the Netherlands and the Italian possessions left Spain with a more manageable, more truly Spanish, empire composed of the kingdoms of Castile and Aragón and the Indies.

THE BOURBON REFORMS

The return of peace permitted the new dynasty to turn its attention to implementing a program of reform inspired by the French model. The reform and ensuing revival of Spain are associated with three princes of the House of Bourbon: Philip V (1700–1746) and his two sons, Ferdinand VI

1713	Treaty of Utrecht ends the War of Spanish Succession, recognizes Bourbon dynasty in Spain, forebids any union of French and Spanish thrones, and grants British major trade concessions in the Spanish Indies, including a monopoly over the African slave trade
1700–1746	Philip V introduces Bourbon reforms to restore Spanish imperial power and to increase royal authority in the colonies
1730–1781	128 rebellions break out throughout the Spanish American colonies
1739	Creation of viceroyalty of New Granada
1759–1788	Charles III introduces administrative, economic, and religious reforms to increase royal revenues and imperial control
1756–1763	Seven Years' War leads to Spanish defeat and temporary loss of Havana to English
1765	Quito insurrection protests new taxes and changes in the *aguardiente* (rum) monopoly
1766–1775	Real del Monte silver miners' strikes
1776	Creation of viceroyalty of the Río de la Plata to reduce contraband trade and strengthen Spanish empire against Portuguese and English incursions
1778	Decree of free trade within the Spanish empire
1780–1781	Tupac Amaru II revolt seeks to abolish the mita, the repartimiento, the alcabala, and other taxes
1781–1782	Comunero Revolt in New Granada seeks reduction of indigenous and mestizo tribute, return of usurped land, abolition of new tax on tobacco, and preference for creoles over Europeans in colonial government
1782–1790	Establishment of intendency system to increase efficient government administration and royal revenues
1788–1808	Charles IV levies taxes on Spanish colonial trade to finance French Bourbon resistance to revolution and alienates criollos
1804	Spain enacts *Consolidación de Vales Reales* that increased royal revenues by forcing church institutions in the colonies to call in outstanding loans
1808	Napoleon occupies Spain, exiles Ferdinand VII, and appoints his brother Joseph Bonaparte King of Spain

(1746–1759) and Charles III (1759–1788). Under the aegis of "enlightened despotism," the Bourbon kings attempted nothing less than a total overhaul of existing political and economic structures—a total renovation of the national life. Only such sweeping reform could close the gap that separated Spain from the foremost European powers and arm the country with the weapons—a powerful industry, a prosperous agriculture, a strong middle class— it needed to prevent its defeat by England and England's allies in the struggle for empire that dominated the eighteenth century.

The movement for reform, although carried out within the framework of royal absolutism and Catholic orthodoxy, inevitably provoked the hostility of reactionary elements within the church and the nobility. As a result, the Bourbons, although supported by such liberal grandees as the count of Floridablanca and the count of Aranda, recruited many of their principal ministers and officials from the ranks of the lesser nobility and the small middle class. These men were strongly influenced by the rationalist spirit of the French Encyclopedists,[1] although they rejected French **anticlericalism** and **deism**. They were characteristic of the Spanish Enlightenment in their rigid orthodoxy in religion and politics combined with the enthusiastic pursuit of useful knowledge, criticism of defects in the church and clergy, and belief in the power of informed reason to improve society by reorganizing it along more rational lines.

The work of national reconstruction began under Philip V but reached its climax under Charles III. This great reformer–king attempted to revive Spanish industry by removing the stigma attached to manual labor, establishing state-owned textile factories, inviting foreign technical experts into Spain, and encouraging technical education. He aided agriculture by curbing the privileges of the *Mesta* (stockbreeders' corporation) and by settling colonies of Spanish and foreign peasants in abandoned regions of the peninsula. He continued and expanded the efforts of his predecessors to

---

1. These were writers of the famous *Encyclopédie* (1751–1780), who identified with the Enlightenment and advocated deism and a rationalist world outlook.

encourage shipbuilding and foster trade and communication by the building of roads and canals. Clerical influence declined because of the expulsion of the Jesuits in 1767 and decrees restricting the authority of the Inquisition. Under the cleansing influence of able and honest ministers, a new spirit of austerity and service began to appear among public officials.

However, the changes that took place in Spanish economic and social life under the Bourbons were not extensive. The crown, linked by a thousand bonds to the feudal nobility and church, never touched the foundation of the old order—the land monopoly of the nobility—with its corollaries of mass poverty and archaic agricultural methods. These weaknesses, along with its lack of capital for industrial development and the debility of its middle class, made Spain, despite its marked advances in population and production, a second- or third-class power compared with Great Britain, France, or Holland.

The outbreak of the French Revolution, which followed by a few months the death of Charles III in December 1788, brought the reform era effectively to a halt. Frightened by the overthrow of the French monarchy and the execution of his royal relative, Charles IV and his ministers banished or imprisoned leading reformers and forbade the importation of French rationalist and revolutionary literature. Yet they could not entirely turn back the clock, either in Spain or in the colonies. Under the corrupt government of Charles IV, for example, the expedition of Francisco Xavier Balmis sailed from Spain (1803) to carry the procedure of vaccination to the Spanish dominions in America and Asia, an act that probably saved innumerable lives.

In the field of colonial reform, the Bourbons moved slowly and cautiously, as was natural in view of the powerful vested interests identified with the old social order. The Bourbons never considered giving a greater measure of self-government to the colonists or of permitting them to trade more freely with the non-Spanish world. On the contrary, the Bourbons centralized colonial administration still further, with a view toward making it more efficient. In addition, their commercial reforms aimed to diminish smuggling and strengthen the exclusive commercial ties between Spain and its colonies, to "reconquer" the colonies economically for Spain.

REVIVAL OF COLONIAL COMMERCE AND BREAKDOWN OF TRADING MONOPOLY

The first Bourbon, Philip V, concentrated his efforts on an attempt to reduce smuggling and to revive the fleet system, which had fallen into decay in the late seventeenth century. With the Treaty of Utrecht, the English merchant class had scored an impressive victory in the shape of the asiento. The English South Sea Company received the exclusive right to supply enslaved Africans to Spanish America, with the additional right of sending a shipload of merchandise to Portobelo every year. Spanish authorities also knew that the slaveships carried contraband merchandise, as did the provision ships that annually engaged in the Portobelo trade. Buenos Aires, where the South Sea Company maintained a trading post, was another funnel through which English traders poured large quantities of contraband goods that penetrated as far as Peru.

The Spanish government sought to check smuggling in the Caribbean by commissioning *guardacostas* (private warships), which prowled the main lanes of trade in search of ships loaded with contraband. It also tried to end the monopoly of the Cádiz *consulado* (merchant guild), whose members alone could load Spanish merchant vessels. The first breach in the wall of this monopoly came in the 1720s, with the organization of the Caracas Company, which the Bourbon crown founded with the aid of capitalists in the Biscay region. In return for the privilege of trade with Venezuela, this company undertook to police the coast against smugglers and develop the resources of the region. Despite the company's claims of success in achieving these objectives, it failed to stop a lively contraband trade with the nearby Dutch colony of Curaçao or to overcome the bitter hostility of Venezuelan planters and merchants, who accused the company of paying too little for cocoa, taking too little tobacco and other products, and charging excessive prices for Spanish goods.

Biscayan and Catalan capital organized similar companies for trade with Havana, Hispaniola, and other places that the old system of colonial trade had left undeveloped. These enterprises, however, were financial failures, partly because of inadequate capital and partly because of poor management. These breaches of the Cádiz monopoly brought no benefits to creole merchants, most of whom the crown continued to exclude from the legal trade between Spain and its colonies.

The first Bourbons made few changes in the administrative structure of colonial government, contenting themselves with efforts to improve the quality of administration through more careful selection of officeholders. One major reorganization was the separation of the northern Andean region (present-day Ecuador, Colombia, and Venezuela) from the viceroyalty of Peru. In 1739, it became a viceroyalty, named New Granada, with its capital at Santa Fe (modern Bogotá). This change had strategic significance, reflecting a desire to provide better protection for the Caribbean coast, especially the fortress of Cartagena. It also reflected the rapid growth of population in the central highlands of Colombia. Within the new viceroyalty, Venezuela became a captaincy general virtually independent of Santa Fe, with its capital at Caracas.

The movement for colonial reform, like the program of domestic reform, reached a climax in the reign of Charles III. José Campillo, a remarkable Spanish economist and minister of finance and war under Ferdinand VI, had foreshadowed this reform in his writings. Shortly before his death in 1743, Campillo wrote a memorial on colonial affairs that advocated the abolition of the Cádiz monopoly, a reduction of duties on goods bound for America, and the organization of a frequent mail service to America. It also encouraged expansion of trade between the colonies and the development of colonial agriculture and other economic activities that did not compete with Spanish manufacturers.

In 1765, a royal commission incorporated most of these recommendations in a report to Charles III. The shock of Spain's defeat in the Seven Years' War, which cost it the loss of Florida and almost the loss of Cuba, provided the impetus for a program of imperial reorganization and reform.

In this period, the crown gradually eliminated the trading monopoly of Cádiz. In 1765, commerce with the West Indies opened to seven other ports besides Cádiz and Seville; this reform, coming at a time when Cuban sugar production began to expand, gave a sharp stimulus to the island's economy. The Bourbons gradually expanded this privilege to other regions until the famous decree of free trade in 1778 permitted commerce between all qualified Spanish ports and all the American provinces except New Spain and Venezuela. In 1789, the crown lifted restrictions on trade with them.[2] Simple ad valorem duties of 6 or 7 percent also replaced the burdensome duties levied on this trade. Bourbon economic reforms progressively lifted restrictions on intercolonial trade, but this usually involved non-European products that did not compete with Spanish goods. A major beneficiary of this change was the Río de la Plata area, which in 1776 began to trade freely with the rest of the Indies. Meanwhile, the Casa de Contratación, a symbol of the old order, steadily declined in importance until it closed its doors in 1789. A similar fate overtook the venerable Council of the Indies. As a consultative body, it lasted on into the nineteenth century, but a colonial minister appointed by the king assumed most of its duties.

The "free-trade" policy stimulated a spectacular increase in the value of Spain's commerce with Spanish America, an increase said to have amounted to about 700 percent between 1778 and 1788. The entrance of new trading centers and merchant groups into the Indies trade, the reduction of duties, and the removal of irksome restrictions had the ef-

---

2. These reforms did not seriously weaken the dominant role of the Cádiz monopolists and their American agents in colonial trade. As late as 1790, more than 85 percent of the trade moved through Cádiz, thanks to its superior facilities for shipping, insurance, warehousing, and communication.

fect of increasing the volume of business, reducing prices, and perhaps diminishing contraband (although one cannot speak with certainty here, for the easing of restrictions inevitably facilitated the activity of smugglers).

Nevertheless, the Bourbon commercial reform had limited achievements, and it ultimately failed to reconquer colonial markets for Spain because, despite their best efforts, the Bourbons failed to overcome Spanish industrial weakness. Moreover, Spain failed to keep its sea-lanes to America open in time of war with England, when foreign traders again swarmed into Spanish American ports. Indeed, during the war years from 1797 to 1799 and again from 1805 to 1809, the Spanish government openly confessed its inability to supply the colonies with needed goods by lifting the ban against foreign vessels of neutral origin (which meant United States ships, above all). This permission to trade with neutrals gave rise to spirited commerce between the United States and the Caribbean area and the Río de la Plata.

INCREASED ECONOMIC ACTIVITY

Perhaps the most significant result of the Bourbon commercial reform was the stimulus it gave to economic activity in Spanish America. It is uncertain how much this increased economic activity is owed to the beneficial effects of the Bourbon reform or to the general economic upsurge in western Europe in the eighteenth century. What is certain is that the latter part of the century saw a rising level of agricultural, pastoral, and mining production in Spanish America. Stimulated by the Bourbon reform and the growing European demand for sugar, tobacco, hides, and other staples, production of these products rose sharply in this period. A marked trend developed toward regional specialization and monoculture in the production of cash crops. After 1770, coffee, grown in Venezuela and Cuba, joined cacao and sugar as a major export crop of the

Caribbean area. The gradual increase in population also stimulated the production of food crops for local markets, notably wheat, which the European population preferred over maize. Tithe collections offer an index of agricultural growth: In the decade from 1779 to 1789, tithe collections in the principal agricultural areas were 40 percent greater than in the previous decade.

However, agricultural prosperity was largely limited to areas that produced export crops or had easy access to domestic markets. David Brading paints a gloomy picture of the financial condition of the Mexican haciendas in the eighteenth century. Except in the Valley of Mexico, the Bajío,[3] and the Guadalajara region, markets were too small to yield satisfactory returns. Great distances, poor roads, and high freight costs prevented haciendas from developing their productive capacity beyond the requirements of the local market. Private estates were even worse off than church haciendas because they had to pay tithes and sales taxes and bore the double burden of absentee landowners and resident administrators. Great landed families, who possessed numerous estates in different regions, producing varied products for multiple markets, were more fortunate; their profits averaged from 6 to 9 percent of capital value in the late eighteenth century. Thanks to cheap labor, however, even a low productivity yielded large revenues, which enabled hacendados to maintain a lavish, seigneurial style of life. Many haciendas were heavily indebted to ecclesiastical institutions, the principal bankers of the time.

The increase in agricultural production resulted from more extensive use of land and labor than from the use of improved implements or techniques. The inefficient *latifundio* (great estate), which used poorly paid peón labor, and the slave plantation accounted for the bulk of commercial agricultural production. The Prussian traveler Alexander von Humboldt, commenting on the semifeudal land tenure system of Mexico, observed that

---

3. This refers to a relatively urbanized area with a diversified economy (agriculture, mining, manufacturing) lying within the modern Mexican states of Guanajuato and Querétaro.

the property of New Spain, like that of Old Spain, is in a great measure in the hands of a few powerful families, who have gradually absorbed the smaller estates. In America, as well as in Europe, large commons are condemned to the pasturage of cattle and to perpetual sterility.

The increasing concentration of landownership in Mexico and the central Andes in the second half of the eighteenth century reflected the desire of hacendados to eliminate the competition of small producers in restricted markets and to maintain prices at a high level. To help achieve this end, great landowners hoarded their harvests in their granaries and sent grain to market at that time of the year when it was scarcest and prices were at their highest. Given the low productivity of colonial agriculture, however, such natural disasters as drought, premature frosts, or excessive rains easily upset the precarious balance between food supplies and population, producing frightful famines like that of 1785–1787 in central Mexico. Thousands died of hunger or diseases induced by that famine.

What sugar, cacao, and coffee were for the Caribbean area, hides were for the Río de la Plata. The rising European demand for leather for footwear and industrial purposes and the permission given in 1735 for direct trade with Spain in register ships sparked an economic upsurge in the Plata area. The unregulated hunting of wild cattle on the open pampa soon gave way to the herding of cattle on established *estancias* (cattle ranches). By the end of the century, these ranches were often huge, measuring 15 to 20 square leagues and having as many as eighty or a hundred thousand head of cattle. By 1790, Buenos Aires exported nearly a million and a half hides annually. The meat of the animal, hitherto almost worthless except for the small quantity that locals consumed immediately, now gained in value because of the demand for salt beef, processed in large-scale *saladeros* (salting plants). Markets for salt beef expanded above all in the Caribbean area, especially Cuba, where it chiefly fed the slave population. The growth of

cattle raising in La Plata, however, stimulated the concentration of land in ever fewer hands and took place at the expense of agriculture, which remained in a depressed state.

The eighteenth century also saw a marked revival of silver mining in the Spanish colonies. Peru and Mexico shared in this advance, but the Mexican mines forged far ahead of their Peruvian rivals in the Bourbon Era. The mine owners included creoles and peninsulars, but the Spanish merchants who financed the mining operations received most of the profits. As in the case of agriculture, the increase in silver production was not primarily due to improved technique; rather, it resulted from the opening of many new as well as old mines and the growth of the labor force. The crown, however, especially under Charles III, contributed materially to the revival by offering new incentives to entrepreneurs and by its efforts to overcome the backwardness of the mining industry. The incentives included reductions in taxes and in the cost of mercury, a government monopoly.

In New Spain, the crown promoted the establishment of a mining guild (1777), whose activities included the operation of a bank to finance development. Under this guild's auspices was founded the first school of mines in America (1792). Staffed by able professors and provided with modern equipment, it offered excellent theoretical and practical instruction and represented an important source of Enlightenment thought in Mexico. Foreign and Spanish experts, accompanied by teams of technicians, came to Mexico and Peru to show the mine owners the advantages of new machinery and techniques. However, these praiseworthy efforts faced many obstacles, including the traditionalism of the mine owners, the lack of capital to finance changes, and mismanagement. Yet the production of silver steadily increased. Supplemented by the gold of Brazil, it helped spark the Industrial Revolution in northern Europe and stimulated commercial activity on a worldwide scale. In addition, American silver helped the Bourbons meet the enormous expenses of their chronic wars.

In 1774, José Antonio Areche, the reformist *fiscal* (attorney) to Viceroy Antonio María Bucareli y Ursua of Spain, prepared a report on the state of the Mexican economy. He described it as a backward economic system, marked by practices and ideas that offered insuperable obstacles to modernization. People increasingly deserted the countryside for the city, filling the cities with the unemployed and unemployable. A major cause of this flight was an inefficient agriculture whose low productivity and unprofitability were the result of primitive tilling methods, heavily indebted estates, and poor working conditions. Areche complained of landowners who paid wages in goods rather than in cash, treated their workers badly, and preferred to concentrate on production of a few basic commodities rather than experiment with new products and seek new markets. Retail trade lagged because of the practice of paying workers in goods rather than cash and because too few coins were in circulation. Areche also criticized merchants who preferred to engage in the forced sale of goods to indigenous villages (repartimiento de mercancías), failing to see that these communities were potential vast markets for a wide variety of consumer goods. But Areche failed to see that Spain's use of Mexico as an "extraction machine," in the words of John Coatsworth, that funneled off a substantial part of the colony's silver output (some 500 to 600 million pesos in the last half-century of Spanish rule) contributed to Mexico's lack of capital formation and structural economic backwardness.

Areche's report makes it clear that increased economic activity in the Bourbon Era was not accompanied by significant qualitative changes in the colonial economy; the phrase "growth without development," often applied to Latin America's economic performance in modern times, applies equally to the colonial economy in the Bourbon Era.

Colonial manufacturing, after a long and fairly consistent growth, began to decline in the last part of the eighteenth century, principally because of the influx of cheap foreign wares with which the domestic products could not compete. The textile and wine industries of western Argentina fell into decay as they lost their markets in Buenos Aires and Montevideo to lower priced foreign wines and cloth.

The textile producers of the province of Quito in Ecuador complained of injury from the same cause. In the Mexican manufacturing center of Puebla, production of chinaware slumped catastrophically between 1793 and 1802. Puebla and Querétaro, however, continued to be important centers of textile manufacturing.

Although Spain adopted mercantilist legislation designed to restrict colonial manufacturing—especially of fine textiles—this legislation was only a small deterrent to the growth of large-scale manufacturing. More important obstacles included a lack of investment capital, the characteristic preference of Spaniards for land and mining as fields of investment, and a semiservile system of labor that was equally harmful to the workers and to productivity. Humboldt, who visited the woolen workshops of Querétaro in 1803, was disagreeably impressed

> not only with the great imperfection of the technical process in the preparation for dyeing, but in a particular manner also with the unhealthiness of the situation, and the bad treatment to which the workers are exposed. Free men, Indians, and people of color are confounded with the criminals distributed by justice among the manufactories, in order to be compelled to work. All appear half naked, covered with rags, meager, and deformed. Every workshop resembles a dark prison. The doors, which are double, remain constantly shut, and the workmen are not permitted to quit the house. Those who are married are only allowed to see their families on Sunday. All are unmercifully flogged, if they commit the smallest trespass on the order established in the manufactory.

One of the few large-scale lines of industry was the manufacture of cigars and cigarettes. In the same town of Querétaro, Humboldt visited a tobacco factory that employed three thousand workers, including nineteen hundred women.

Women, especially indigenous women like this Otavalo worker in Ecuador, often worked in unsanitary conditions in textile obrajes, where they spun wool into thread and used rudimentary looms to weave it into cloth.

LABOR SYSTEMS IN THE EIGHTEENTH CENTURY

Humboldt's comments testify to the persistence of servitude and coercion as essential elements of the labor system from the beginning to the end of the colonial period. Despite the Bourbons' theoretical dislike of forced labor, they sought to tighten legal enforcement of debt peonage in the Indies. Concerned with more efficient tribute collection, José de Gálvez, the reforming minister of Charles III, tried to attach the natives more firmly to their pueblos and haciendas. In 1769, he introduced in New Spain the system of clearance certificates, documents that certified that peons had no outstanding debts and could seek employment with

other landowners. The absence of these papers restricted the mobility of peons. Moreover, the Mining Ordinances of New Spain authorized expansion of debt peonage in that industry, and it also spread to the gold and silver mines of Chile, where the crown employed a system of clearance certificates like that used in Mexico. A study by James D. Riley notes a trend in Bourbon policy to make debts "considerably less coercive" in Mexico after 1785, but he also notes that there was little official reluctance to pursue debtors and force them to pay up or work. On Jesuit farms in eighteenth-century Quito (Ecuador), says Nicholas Cushner, "the debt was a mechanism for maintaining a stable work force" whose wages were pitifully low. "It was an Indian analogue of black slavery," adds Cushner.

In practice, as noted, the importance of debt peonage and the severity of its enforcement depended on the availability of labor. In New Spain, by the late eighteenth century, the growth of the labor force through population increase and the elimination of small producers had sharply reduced the importance of debt as a means of securing and holding laborers. Eric Van Young, for example, has documented a reduction of the per capita indebtedness of resident peons in the Guadalajara area, suggesting their decreased bargaining power in dealing with employers. The new situation enabled hacendados to retain or discharge workers in line with changing levels of production. Thus in late-eighteenth-century Mexico, landowners simply dismissed workers when crop failures occurred to save on their rations. These changes accompanied a tendency for real wages and rural living standards to decline.

In the Andean area, the mita—in provinces subject to it—continued to play an important role in the provision of mining and agricultural labor almost to the end of the colonial period. In other provinces, agricultural labor was theoretically free, but heavy tribute demands and the operations of the repartimiento de mercancías created a need for cash that compelled many natives to seek employment on Spanish haciendas. These yanaconas included a large number of so-called ***forasteros*** (outsiders) who had fled their native

© Craig Lovell/CORBIS

pueblos to escape the dreaded mita service and tribute burdens. In addition to working the hacendado's land, these laborers or sharecroppers and their families had to render personal service in the master's household. Theoretically free, their dependent status must have sharply limited their mobility.

Early Labor Struggles

Our knowledge of labor struggles in colonial Spanish America is fragmentary, in part because historians took little interest in the subject until recently. The first labor conflicts of a relatively modern type seem to have taken place in late-eighteenth-century Mexico, the colony with the most developed and diversified economy. Strikes sometimes took place in artisan shops; in 1784, for example, the workers in the bakery of Basilio Badamler went on strike to protest "horrible working conditions." More commonly, they occurred in industries that had large concentrations of workers or a division of labor that promoted workers' cooperation and solidarity. One large-scale industry was the manufacture of cigars and cigarettes by the royal tobacco monopoly, whose founding accompanied a ruthless suppression (1773–1776) of artisan production of these goods. The immense factory operated by the monopoly in Mexico City employed about seven thousand workers of both sexes. The workers, who included natives, mestizos, and some Spaniards, received cash payments, and the annual payroll in the 1780s and 1790s came to about 750,000 pesos. The militancy that these workers displayed in strikes and protests worried the authorities. In 1788, the consulado of Mexico City declared that this large assembly of workers presented a threat to public order, citing a march on the viceroy's palace caused by a "small increase" in the length of the workday. The workers, heedless of the guards, swarmed into the palace and occupied the patios, stairs, and corridors. The viceroy, having heard their complaint, "prudently gave them a note ordering the factory's administrator to rescind that change, and so with God's help that tumult ended, the multitude left, bearing that

note as if in triumph, and the viceroy decided to overlook that turbulent action, so likely to cause sedition." In 1794, the workers again marched on the viceregal palace to protest a change in the contractual arrangement that permitted them to take part of their work home to prepare for the next day's tasks.

A more dramatic labor struggle broke out in the 1780s in the Mexican silver mining industry. The scene of the conflict was the mines of Real del Monte in northern Mexico. Here, as in all other Mexican silver mines, the majority of the work force was free, but mine owners conscripted a minority of the workers from the surrounding indigenous villages through a repartimiento, or labor draft. Press gangs also picked up men charged with "idleness" or "vagrancy" to relieve the chronic shortage of labor. It was the grievances of the free skilled workers, however, that caused a series of confrontations and ultimately a work stoppage with an arrogant, unyielding employer. The extreme division of labor in the silver mining industry—to get the ore out of the vein below and load it on mules above required some thirty different specialized tasks—tended to develop a sense of shared interests and cooperation among the workers.

Work in the mines was dangerous, daily exposing the miners to loss of life and limb through accidents and even more to debilitating or fatal diseases. According to Francisco de Gamboa, the leading Mexican mining expert of the time, the miners worked "in terror of ladders giving way, rocks sliding, heavy loads breaking their backs, dripping icy waters, diseases, and the damp, hot, suffocating heat." Humboldt, who visited Mexico in the last years of the colony, claimed that Mexican miners seldom lived past the age of thirty-five. Nevertheless, the pay was good by colonial standards: Workers who went below received 4 reales ($0.50) for each twelve-hour shift (1 real would buy a pound of wool or 5 pounds of beef or veal), more than double the pay of agricultural workers. The partido, the skilled worker's right to a certain share of his day's haul of silver ore over an assigned quota, further supplemented this customary pay.

Attempts by mine owner Romero de Terreros to lower wage rates of **peones** (ore carriers) from 4 to 3 reales, increase quotas, and gradually eliminate partidos provoked a series of crises culminating in the strike. Although his activism later earned a sympathetic parish priest expulsion from the pueblo, he advised the workers on legal ways to achieve their objectives and sought to mediate their dispute with the employer. Eventually, the state intervened, aware of the critical importance of silver production to the royal treasury and of the workers' strong bargaining position because of the chronic labor shortage. The crown sent Francisco de Gamboa, the leading expert on mining and mining law, to arbitrate the conflict. His arbitration satisfied virtually all the workers' demands: He fired abusive bosses, revoked pay cuts, and confirmed in writing the right to partidos.[4]

Doris Ladd has written a brilliant, sensitive reconstruction of these events. She interprets the conflict at Real del Monte as a class struggle before the existence of a working class—reflecting an emerging class consciousness—and describes the workers' ideas as "radical" and "revolutionary." She cites the strikers' insistence on social and economic justice, expressed in the words of their lawyer: "It is a precept in all systems of divine, natural, and secular law that there should be a just proportion between labor and profit." However, this appeal for justice had a limited scope and significance. It applied to a group of free, relatively privileged, skilled workers but did not call into question the forced labor of natives dragged by press gangs from their homes to the mines. Thanks to a set of favorable conditions, the strikers won a victory, meaning a return to the situation that had prevailed before the dispute broke out. Still, the victory left the conscripted indigenous workers in the same intolerable conditions as before. One wonders whether ideas that accepted such servitude as normal were truly "radical" or "revolutionary."

POLITICAL REFORMS

Under Charles III, the work of territorial reorganization of the sprawling empire continued. The viceroyalty of Peru, already diminished by the creation of New Granada, became still less influential with the creation in 1776 of the viceroyalty of the Río de la Plata, with its capital at Buenos Aires. This act reflected official Spanish concern over the large volume of contraband in the estuary. It also reflected fear of a possible foreign attack on the area by the British, who recently had entrenched themselves in the nearby Malvinas, or Falkland, Islands, or by the Portuguese who, advancing southward from Brazil, had established the settlement of Sacramento on the banks of the estuary, a base from which they threatened shipping and the town of Montevideo. To put an end to this danger, the Spanish government mounted a major military expedition designed to establish full control of both banks of the river. The commander Pedro de Cevallos came out with the temporary title of viceroy of Buenos Aires. In 1778, the viceroyalty became permanent with the appointment of the viceroy Juan José de Vértiz y Salcedo, whose rule of over a decade saw a remarkable growth in the prosperity of the area. This prosperity owed much to the decree of "free trade" of 1778, which authorized direct trade between Buenos Aires and Spain and permitted intercolonial trade. In 1783, the establishment of a royal audiencia at Buenos Aires completed the liberation of the Río de la Plata provinces from the distant rule of Lima. The inclusion of Upper Peru in the new viceroyalty, with the resulting redirection of the flow of Potosí silver from Lima to Buenos Aires, signified a stunning victory for the landowners and merchants of Buenos Aires over their mercantile rivals in Lima.

The trend toward decentralization in the administration of Spanish America, combined with a greater stress on supervision and control from Madrid, reflected the struggle against foreign military

---

4. But the workers' victory at the Real del Monte was not the usual outcome of labor conflicts in the mining areas of New Spain in this period. In the late Bourbon Era, Mexican mine owners displayed a more aggressive attitude toward their workers. Supported by military and paramilitary forces, they often successfully reduced wages and eliminated or reduced the partidos that they permitted workers to keep.

NEW
FRANCE

Disputed by
England, Russia,
and Spain

*ATLANTIC
OCEAN*

Effective frontier
of Spanish settlement

ENGLISH COLONIES

FLORIDA
Ceded to England,
1763–1783

**VICEROYALTY OF
NEW SPAIN**

Guadalajara

Mexico City★

Guatemala•

HAITI
(SAINT DOMINGUE)
Ceded to France, 1697

Santo
Domingo

JAMAICA
Conquered by
England, 1655

Caracas•

*PACIFIC
OCEAN*

**VICEROYALTY OF
NEW GRANADA**

Bogotá★

GUIANA

Separated by
Viceroyalty of Peru,
1717, 1739

Quito•

**VICEROYALTY
OF PERU**

Lima★
Cuzco•

Chuquisaca•
(La Plata; Sucre)

**VICEROYALTY
OF BRAZIL**

Pernambuco•

Bahia•

São Paulo• ★ **Rio de Janeiro**
(Capital, 1763)

**VICEROYALTY
OF LA PLATA**

Santiago•

Separated by
Viceroyalty
of Peru, 1776

AUDIENCIA OF CHILE
Retained by
Viceroyalty of Peru,
1776

Buenos Aires★

Claimed but
not settled
by Spain

Viceroyalty of Brazil

Viceroyalty of Peru and
Audencia of Chile

Viceroyalty of La Plata

Viceroyalty of New Granada

Viceroyalty of New Spain

★ Viceregal capital

• Audiencia seat

0   500   1000 Km.

0   500   1000 Mi.

© Cengage Learning

Viceroyalties in Latin America in 1780

and commercial penetration. It also revealed an enlightened awareness of the problems of communication and government posed by the great distances between the various provinces, an awareness spurred by advances in cartography and knowledge of the geography of the continent in general. Two indications of this tendency were the greater autonomy enjoyed by the captaincies general in the eighteenth century and the increase in their number. Thus, the crown raised Venezuela and Chile to the status of a captaincy general. The increased autonomy enjoyed by the captains general enabled an enlightened ruler like Ambrosio O'Higgins in Chile to attempt major economic reforms, stimulate mining and manufacturing, introduce new crops, and in general try to promote not only the interests of the Spanish crown but also the welfare of the Chilean people.

The creation of new viceroyalties and captaincies general went hand in hand with another major political reform: the transfer to the colonies between 1782 and 1790 of the intendant system, which France already had introduced to Spain. This reform aimed to secure greater administrative efficiency in the hope of increasing royal revenues from the colonies. The intendants, provincial governors who ruled from the capitals of their provinces, sought to relieve the overburdened viceroys of many of their duties, especially in financial matters. Among their other duties, the intendants aimed to further the economic development of their districts by promoting the cultivation of new crops, the improvement of mining, the building of roads and bridges, and the establishment of consulados and economic societies. Under their prodding, the lethargic cabildos or town councils were in some cases stirred to greater activity. The Ordinance of Intendants also abolished the offices of corregidor and alcalde mayor, notorious vehicles for the oppression of the natives. In their place, intendants nominated and viceroys confirmed men called **subdelegados** (deputy intendants) to govern indigenous towns.

Many of the intendants at the height of the reform era were capable and cultivated men who not only achieved the objectives of increased economic activity and revenue collection but also promoted education and cultural progress generally. However, the same was not true of the majority of their subordinates, the subdelegados, who, like their predecessors, soon became notorious for their oppressive practices. A common complaint was that they continued to compel the natives to trade with them, although the Ordinance of Intendants had forbidden the repartimiento. The great popular revolts of the 1780s were fueled in large part by the failure of the indigenous and mixed-race populations to share in the fruits of the eighteenth-century economic advance, whose principal beneficiaries were Spanish and creole landowners, mine owners, and merchants.

STRENGTHENING THE DEFENSES

A major objective of the Bourbon commercial and political reforms was increased revenue required to strengthen the empire's sea and land defenses. Before the eighteenth century, imperial defense primarily depended on naval power: convoy escorts and cruiser squadrons. Before the middle of the eighteenth century, standing armed forces in the colonies were negligible, and authorities relied on local forces raised for particular emergencies. The disasters of the Seven Years' War and the loss of Havana and Manila (1762) to the English, in particular, resulted in a decision to correct the shortcomings in the defense system of the colonies. The Bourbons strengthened fortifications of important American ports and created colonial armies. These included regular units stationed permanently in the colonies or rotated between peninsular and overseas service. Volunteers or drafted recruits filled the ranks of the colonial militia.

To make military service attractive to the creole upper class, which provided the officer corps of the new force, the crown granted extensive privileges and exemptions to creole youths who accepted commissions. To the lure of prestige and honors, the grant of the **fuero militar** (military perquisite) added protection from civil legal jurisdiction and liability, except for certain specified offenses. The special legal and social position thus accorded to the colonial officer class helped form a tradition that survived into the present in Latin America. The armed forces became a special caste with its own set of interests, not subject to the civil power, and it typically acted as the arbiter of political life, usually in the interests of conservative ruling classes. However, the Bourbons used competing groups like the church and the civil bureaucracy to check the power of the colonial military.

Although the expansion of the colonial military establishment under the Bourbons offered some opportunities and advantages to upper-class creole youth, it did nothing to allay the longstanding resentment creoles felt about their virtual exclusion from the higher offices of state and church and from large-scale commerce. Bourbon policy on this creole problem went through two phases. In the first half of the eighteenth century, wealthy creoles sometimes could purchase high official posts, and for a time, they dominated the prestigious audiencias of Mexico City and Lima. In the second half of the century, however, an anti-creole reaction took place. José de Gálvez, Charles III's colonial minister, was the very embodiment of the spirit of enlightened despotism that characterized his reign. Gálvez distrusted creole capacity and integrity and removed high-ranking creoles from positions in the imperial administration. The new upper bureaucracy, including the intendants who took over much of the authority of viceroys and governors, was mostly Spanish born.

Other Bourbon policies injured creole vested interests or wounded their sensibilities and traditions. In 1804, the Spanish crown enacted an emergency revenue measure—the *Consolidación de Vales Reales*—that ordered church institutions in the colonies to call in all their outstanding capital, the liens and mortgages whose interest supported the charitable and pious works of the church. It required the church to loan this money to the crown, which promised to pay annual interest to the church to fund its ecclesiastical activities. Although the primary motive of the Consolidation was to relieve the crown's urgent financial needs, it had the secondary reformist aim of freeing the colonial economy from the burden of mortmain and thus promoted a greater circulation of property.

The measure, however, struck hard at two bulwarks of the colonial order: the church and the propertied elite. The numerous hacendados, merchants, and mine owners who had borrowed large sums from church institutions now had to repay those sums in full or face loss of property or bankruptcy. Many elite families had also assigned part of the value of their estates to the church to found a chaplaincy, paying annual interest to provide the stipend of the chaplain, often a family member. Although the church had not loaned this capital, officials in charge of the Consolidation demanded that the families involved immediately turn over the value of these endowments, in cash. The Consolidation decree also threatened many small and medium landowners and other middle-class borrowers from the church.

The measure caused a storm of protest, and its impact gradually softened when officials in charge proved willing to negotiate the amounts and other terms of payment. So strong was the opposition of debtors, both creoles and peninsulars, to the decree that the crown made little effort to implement it outside of New Spain, which provided more than two-thirds of the 15 million pesos collected before it ended in 1808 following Napoleon's invasion of Spain. The Consolidation left a heritage of bitterness, especially among individuals like Father Miguel Hidalgo, future torchbearer of the Mexican War for Independence, whose hacienda the crown had embargoed for several years for failure to pay his debts to the Consolidation.

Thus, the reformist spirit of the Bourbon kings progressively alienated creoles from the Spanish crown. Their alienation intensified an incipient creole nationalism that, denied direct political outlets, found its chief expression in culture and religion.

Colonial Culture and the Enlightenment

At least until the eighteenth century, a neomedieval climate of opinion, enforced by the authority of church and state, sharply restricted the play of the colonial intellect and imagination. Colonial culture thus suffered from all the infirmities of its parent but inevitably lacked the breadth and vitality of Spanish literature and art, the product of a much older and more mature civilization. Despite these and other difficulties, such as the limited market for books, colonial culture left a remarkably large and valuable heritage.

Colonial art drew its principal inspiration from Spanish sources, but, especially in the sixteenth century, indigenous influence was sometimes visible in design and ornamentation. Quito in Ecuador and Mexico City were among the chief centers of artistic activity. The crown established the first school of fine arts in the New World in Mexico City in 1779. As might be expected, religious motifs dominated painting and sculpture. In architecture, the colonies followed Spanish examples, with the severe classical style of the sixteenth century giving way in the seventeenth to the highly ornamented baroque and in the eighteenth to a style that was even more ornate.

The intellectual atmosphere of the Spanish colonies was not conducive to scientific inquiry or achievement. As late as 1773, Bourbon officials charged the Colombian botanist Mutis with heresy for giving lectures in Bogotá on the Copernican system. The prosecutor of the Inquisition asserted that Mutis was "perhaps the only man in Latin America to uphold Copernicus." In the last decades of the eighteenth century, however, the growing volume of economic and intellectual contacts with Europe and the patronage and protection of enlightened governors created more favorable conditions for scientific activity. Science made its greatest strides in the wealthy province of New Spain, where the expansion of the mining industry stimulated interest in geology, chemistry, mathematics, and metallurgy. A school of mines, a botanical garden, and an academy of fine arts arose in Mexico City. The Mexican scientific renaissance produced a galaxy of brilliant figures that included Antonio de León y Gama, Antonio de Alzate, and Joaquín Velázquez Cárdenas y León. These men combined Enlightenment enthusiasm for rationalism, empiricism, and progress with a strict Catholic

orthodoxy; Alzate, for example, vehemently denounced the "infidelity" and skepticism of Europe's philosophes.

Spain itself, now under the rule of the enlightened Bourbon kings, contributed to the intellectual renovation of the colonies. The early eighteenth-century friar Benito Feijóo, whose numerous essays waged war on folly and superstition of every kind, exerted a major liberalizing influence in both Spain and its colonies. Feijóo helped to naturalize the Enlightenment in the Spanish-speaking world by his lucid exposition of the ideas of Bacon, Newton, and Descartes. Spanish and foreign scientific expeditions to Spanish America, authorized and sometimes financed by the crown, also stimulated the growth of scientific thought and introduced the colonists to such distinguished representatives of European science as the Frenchman Charles Marie de La Condamine and the German Alexander von Humboldt.

Among the clergy, the Jesuits were most skillful and resourceful in the effort to reconcile church dogma with the ideas of the Enlightenment, in bridging the old and the new. In Mexico, Jesuit writers like Andrés de Guevara, Pedro José Marquez, and Francisco Javier Clavigero praised and taught the doctrines of Bacon, Descartes, and Newton. These Jesuits exalted physics above metaphysics and the experimental method over abstract reasoning and speculation, but they all combined these beliefs with undeviating loyalty to the teachings of the church. Thus, the expulsion of the Jesuits from Spanish America removed from the scene the ablest, most subtle defenders of the traditional Catholic worldview. In their Italian exile—for it was in Italy that most of the Jesuit exiles settled—some of them occupied their leisure time writing books about the history and geography of their American homelands. The most important of these works was the *History of Ancient Mexico* (1780–1781) by Francisco Clavigero, the best work of its kind written to date and an excellent illustration of the characteristic Jesuit blend of Catholic orthodoxy with the critical, rationalist approach of the Enlightenment.

Despite their frequent and sincere professions of loyalty to the crown, the writings of colonial intellectuals revealed an awareness of social and political abuses, a discontent with economic backwardness, and a dawning sense of nationality that contained potential dangers for the Spanish regime. Colonial newspapers and journals played a significant part in the development of a critical and reformist spirit among the educated creoles of Spanish America. Subjected to an oppressive censorship by church and state and beset by chronic financial difficulties, they generally had short and precarious lives.

The circulation and influence of forbidden books among educated colonials steadily increased in the closing decades of the eighteenth century and the first years of the nineteenth. Nevertheless, contrary to some historians, the Inquisition was no toothless tiger in the eighteenth century and radical ideas did not circulate with impunity. Although its influence weakened under the Bourbons, especially Charles III, because of the growth of French influence, the Inquisition never relaxed its censorship. It continued to be vigilant, and, with every turn of the diplomatic wheel that drew Spain and France apart, the inquisitorial screws tightened. Thus, the outbreak of the French Revolution brought a wave of repression against advocates of radical ideas in Mexico, culminating in a major auto-da-fé in Mexico City that handed out long prison sentences and other severe penalties. However, the writings of the fathers of Spanish American independence illustrated how powerless these repressions were to check the movement of new thought. Their works revealed a thorough knowledge of the ideas of Locke, Montesquieu, Raynal, and other important figures of the Enlightenment.

Creole Nationalism

The incipient creole nationalism, however, built on other foundations than the ideas of the European Enlightenment, which were alien and suspect to the masses. Increasingly identifying themselves with their respective provinces as their *patrias* (fatherlands), eighteenth-century creole intellectuals

assembled an imposing body of data designed to refute the attacks of eminent European writers like Comte Georges de Buffon and Cornelius de Pauw, who proclaimed the inherent inferiority of the New World and its inhabitants.

In the largest sense, the creole patria was all American. As early as 1696, the Mexican Franciscan Agustín de Vetancurt claimed that the New World was superior to the Old in natural beauty and resources. New Spain and Peru, he wrote in florid prose, were two breasts from which the whole world drew sustenance, drinking blood changed into the milk of gold and silver. In a change of imagery, he compared America to a beautiful woman adorned with pearls, emeralds, sapphires, chrysolites, and topazes, drawn from the jewel boxes of her rich mines.

In the prologue to his *History of Ancient Mexico*, Clavigero stated that his aim was "to restore the truth to its splendor, truth obscured by an incredible multitude of writers on America." The epic, heroic character that Clavigero gave to the history of ancient Mexico reflected the creole search for origins, for a classical antiquity other than the European, to which the peninsulars could lay better claim. The annals of the Toltecs and the Aztecs, he insisted, offered as many examples of valor, patriotism, wisdom, and virtue as the histories of Greece and Rome. Mexican antiquity displayed such models of just and benevolent rule as the wise Chichimec king Xolotl and philosopher-kings such as Nezahualcoyotl and Nezahualpilli. In this way, Clavigero provided the nascent Mexican nationality with a suitably dignified and heroic past. The Chilean Jesuit Juan Ignacio Molina developed similar themes in his *History of Chile* (1782).

The creole effort to develop a collective self-consciousness also found expression in religious thought and symbolism. In his *Quetzalcóatl and Guadalupe: The Formation of Mexican National Consciousness* (1976), Jacques Lafaye shows how creole intellectuals exploited two powerful myths in the attempt to achieve Mexican spiritual autonomy and even superiority in relation to Spain. One was the myth that the Virgin Mary appeared in 1531 on the hill of Tepeyac, near Mexico City, to an indígena from Cuauhtitlan named Juan Diego and through him commanded the bishop of Mexico to build a church there. The proof demanded by the bishop came in the form of winter roses from Tepeyac, enfolded in Juan Diego's cloak, which contained a miraculously painted image of the Virgin. From the seventeenth century, common people throughout Mexico venerated the **indita** (the brown-faced Virgin of Guadalupe) rather than the Virgin of Los Remedios, who had allegedly aided Cortés. Under her banner, in fact, Miguel Hidalgo in 1810 was to lead the indigenous and mestizo masses in a great revolt against Spanish rule.

The other great myth was that of Quetzalcóatl, the Toltec redeemer-king and god. Successive colonial writers had suggested that Quetzalcóatl was none other than the Christian apostle St. Thomas. On December 12, 1794, the creole Dominican Servando Teresa de Mier arose in his pulpit in the town of Guadalupe to proclaim that Quetzalcóatl was in fact St. Thomas, who long centuries before had come with four disciples to preach the Gospel in the New World. In this the apostle had succeeded, and at the time of the Conquest, Christianity—somewhat altered, to be sure—had reigned in Mexico. If Mier was right, America owed nothing to Spain, not even Christianity. Spanish officials, quickly recognizing the revolutionary implications of Mier's sermon, arrested him and exiled him to Spain.

The episode illustrates the devious channels through which creole nationalism moved to achieve its ends. One of those ends was creole hegemony over the indigenous and mixed-race masses, based on their awareness of their common patria and their collective adherence to such national cults as that of the Virgin of Guadalupe in Mexico. In the 1780s, however, the accumulated wrath of those people broke out in a series of explosions that threatened the very existence of the colonial social and political order. In this crisis, the creole upper class showed that its aristocratic patria did not really include indígenas, mestizos, and blacks among its children and that its rhetorical sympathy for the dead of Moctezuma's and Atahualpa's time did not extend to their descendants.

The myth of the Virgin of Guadalupe, appropriated by creole nationalists to advance their nineteenth-century struggle for independence and cultural hegemony, later served lower-class indigenous and mestizo peasants in their fight for social justice.

Colonial Society in Transition, 1750–1810: An Overview

An estimate by the late historian Charles Gibson put the population of Spanish America toward the end of the colonial period at about 17 million people. Gibson supposed that of this total some 7.5 million were indígenas; 5.5 million were castas; about 3.2 million were Europeans; and perhaps 750,000 were blacks. Those figures point to a continuing steady revival of the native population from the low point of its decline in the early seventeenth century, a more rapid increase of the European population, and an even faster increase of the castas.

In the late colonial period, the racial categories used to describe and rank the groups that made up the colonial population in terms of their "honor" or lack of "honor" became increasingly ambiguous. One reason for this ambiguity was the growing mobility of the colonial population, resulting in a more rapid pace of Hispanicization and racial mixture. People now generally disregarded the laws forbidding indígenas to reside in Spanish towns and requiring them and mestizos to live in native towns. Large numbers of indígenas, seeking escape from heavy tribute and repartimiento burdens, migrated to the Spanish cities and mining camps, where they learned to speak Spanish, wore European clothes, and adopted other Spanish ways. Those who lived in villages remote from the main areas of Spanish economic activity were less likely to adopt Spanish traditions and therefore remained more "indigenous." For a variety of reasons connected with the area's history, geography, and economic patterns, the native communities in the viceroyalty of Peru seem to have resisted acculturation more tenaciously than those of New Spain. Nonetheless, the process of political and social change gradually transformed the Peruvian ayllu as well. Its kinship basis declined in time because of the influx of forasteros, peasant squatters fleeing from distant provinces subject to the mining mita. It also endured attacks by late-eighteenth-century Bourbon policy, which defined it by its geographic location, periodically redistributed its lands on the basis of its population, and sold any "excess" land in auctions for the benefit of the royal exchequer.

In the late eighteenth century, indigenous people who left their native pueblos and assimilated into the Spanish population in dress and language and who achieved even a modest level of prosperity increasingly became Spaniards—that is, creoles—in law. The same was true of Hispanicized mestizos

and—less frequently, perhaps—of blacks and mulattos. Traits such as occupation, dress, speech, and self-perception, rather than skin color, increasingly came to define an individual's race.

The economic advance of the late Bourbon Era, marked by the rapid growth of commercial agriculture, mining, and domestic and foreign trade, created opportunities for some fortunate lower-class individuals and contributed to the declining significance of racial labels. A growing number of wealthy mestizo and mulatto families sought to rise in the social scale by marrying their sons and daughters to children of the Spanish elite. Charles III's policy on interracial marriage reflected the dilemmas of this reformer-king, who wished to promote the rise of a progressive middle class but feared to undermine the foundations of the old aristocratic order. Charles, who removed the stigma attached to artisan labor by decreeing that it was no bar to nobility, also issued decrees that empowered colonial parents to refuse consent to interracial marriages of their children that threatened the family's "honor." As interpreted by high colonial courts, however, these decrees as a rule only sanctioned such parental refusal when the parties to a proposed marriage were unequal in wealth, meaning that a wealthy mulatto was a suitable marriage partner for a member of the Spanish elite. The last Bourbon kings also promoted social mobility by permitting **pardos** (free mulattos), despised for their slave origin, to buy legal whiteness through the purchase of **cédulas de gracias al sacar** (royal dispensations) that freed them from the status of "infamous."

However, these concessions to a small number of wealthy mixed-race people did not reflect a crumbling of the caste system and the racist ideology on which it drew. Racial prejudice and stereotypes continued to dominate the colonial mentality. For example, mulattos and mestizos eagerly sought to achieve whiteness by purchasing dispensations just mentioned, and elite groups like the cabildo of Caracas protested that the more liberal Bourbon racial policy promoted "the amalgamation of whites and pardos." Finally, some parents were prepared to litigate against their children to prevent their marriage to dark-skinned individuals.

The partial penetration of elite society, even on its highest levels, by individuals with some traces of indigenous or African blood did not alter the rigidity of the class structure, the sharp class distinctions, or the vast gulf that separated the rich from the poor. Humboldt spoke of "that monstrous inequality of rights and wealth" that characterized late colonial Mexico. Nonetheless, the late colonial period saw some change in the economic base of the elite and some shifts in the relative weight of its various sectors. If the seventeenth century was the golden age of the large landowners, then the eighteenth century, especially its last decades, saw their ascendancy challenged by the growing wealth and political and social influence of the export-import merchant class, most of whose members were of Spanish immigrant origin. The merchants provided the capital needed by the mining industry and absorbed much of its profits. They also financed the purchase of the posts of corregidors, officials who monopolized trade with indigenous communities in collusion with the merchants. To provide a hedge against commercial losses—not just to secure the prestige identified with landownership—wealthy merchants acquired estates and established hacienda complexes that produced a variety of crops to supply the nearby major markets. They further diversified by acquiring flour mills or obrajes and by establishing themselves as major retailers, not only in the cities but also in the countryside. The wealthiest married into rich and powerful creole extended families, forming an Establishment whose offspring had preference in appointments to important and prestigious positions in the colonial government and church.

The second half of the eighteenth century saw a new wave of immigration from the peninsula. The presence of these newcomers, often of humble origins, who competed with the American-born Spaniards for limited employment opportunities, sharpened the traditional creole resentment of gachupines or chapetones (tenderfoots). Although, according to Humboldt, "the lowest, least educated and uncultivated European believes himself superior to the white born in the New World," most of the new arrivals failed to find the high-status and well-paid employments they had expected. The 1753 and 1811 census reports for Mexico City listed some Spaniards working as unskilled laborers and house servants and still others as unemployed. The *Diario de México* often carried advertisements by jobless Spanish immigrants who were willing to accept any kind of low-level supervisory post. Two observant Spanish officials, Jorge Juan and Antonio de Ulloa, who visited the city of Cartagena in New Granada about 1750, found that the creoles and Europeans there disdained any trade below that of commerce.

> But it being impossible for all to succeed, great numbers not being able to secure sufficient credit, they become poor and miserable from their aversion to the trades they follow in Europe, and instead of the riches which they flattered themselves with possessing in the Indies, they experience the most complicated wretchedness.

The Revolt of the Masses

A traditional view portrayed indigenous peoples as the more or less passive objects of Spanish rule or of an acculturation process. In recent decades, careful study of their response to Spanish rule has revealed that they were not mere "passive victims of Spanish colonization." On the contrary, evidence abounds that they were activists who from the first resisted Spanish rule with a variety of strategies and thereby modified the colonial environment and shaped their own lives and futures. These strategies included revolts, flight, riots, sabotage, and sometimes even using their masters' legal codes for purposes of defense and offense.

Flight, under conditions of intense Spanish competition for indigenous labor, effectively evaded Spanish pressures. For example, natives routinely abandoned pueblos that were subject to the mita so that they could work as yanaconas on farms, ranches, and other enterprises in exempted areas. Historian Jeffrey Cole rightly points out that this "was their most effective means of opposing the mita, the demands of their curacas and corregidores, and other obligations." Indigenous peoples also skillfully used Spanish legal codes for purposes of "defense, redress, and even offense." Historian Steve Stern's study of the Peruvian province of Huamanga shows that they lightened the burdens of the mita by "engaging in aggressive, persistent, often shrewd use of Spanish juridical institutions to lower legal quotas, delay delivery of specific corvées and tributes, disrupt production, and the like." In Mexico, countless *tumultos* (riots) occurred in the eighteenth century. Indígenas let Spanish authority know that it could not take them for granted and must heed their complaints.

The recent historiographic stress on native peoples as agents who in some degree shaped their own lives and futures by using Spanish juridical institutions and disrupting production is salutary but can be misleading. Such efforts were by no means always successful, and sometimes they resulted in severe reprisals. Historian Martin Minchom's study of eighteenth-century Quito (in modern Ecuador) reports that, when indígenas complained of a powerful Spanish nobleman's encroachment on their communal lands, local officials responded to their "temerity" in bringing him before the law-courts by burning down seventy-one indigenous houses in the area. Another case study by Mexican historian Hildeberto Martínez of indigenous efforts to halt alienation of their lands in two former native domains in sixteenth- and seventeenth-century Mexico (in the modern state of Puebla) suggests that their resort to lawsuits and other peaceful tactics proved completely futile. Spanish methods of spoliation included outright violence, fraudulent manipulation of sales and rental agreements, theft of title documents, and the unleashing of livestock on lands they coveted, in addition to more subtle maneuvers. Between 1521 and 1644, these methods resulted in the loss of more than 137,000 hectares of land by the two native communities.

Revolt was the most dramatic form of resistance to Spanish rule by oppressed groups. Numerous indigenous and black slave revolts punctuated the colonial period of Spanish American history. Before the Spanish had firmly established their rule, indígenas rose against their new masters in

many regions. In Mexico, the Mixton war raged from 1540 to 1542. The Maya of Yucatán staged a great uprising in 1546. A descendant of the Inca kings, Manco II, led a nationwide revolt in 1536 against the Spanish conquerors of Peru. In Chile, the indomitable Araucanians began a struggle for independence that continued into the late nineteenth century. In the jungles and mountains of the West Indies, Central America, and northern South America, groups of runaway black slaves established communities that successfully resisted Spanish efforts to destroy them. The revolutionary wave subsided in the seventeenth century but peaked again in the eighteenth when Bourbon reforms imposed new burdens on the common people.

The Bourbon reforms helped enrich colonial landowners, merchants, and mine owners, beautified their cities, and broadened the intellectual horizons of upper-class youths, but the multitude did not share in these benefits. On the contrary, Bourbon efforts to increase the royal revenues by the creation of governmental monopolies and privileged companies and the imposition of new taxes actually made more acute the misery of the lower classes. This circumstance helps explain the popular character of the revolts of 1780–1781 as distinct from the creole wars of independence of the next generation. With rare exceptions, the privileged creole group either supported the Spaniards against the native uprisings or joined the revolutionary movements under pressure, only to desert them later.

Most eighteenth-century revolts had a predominantly native peasant character. A significant exception was the Quito insurrection of 1765; in his study of this revolt, Anthony McFarlane calls it "the longest, largest, and most formidable urban insurrection of eighteenth-century Spanish America." Against a backdrop of economic depression caused by the decline of Quito's textile industry as a result of competition from Spanish and foreign contraband imports, sections of the elite joined artisans and shopkeepers in protest against threatened new taxes and changes in the aguardiente (rum) monopoly that endangered vested interests. Despite the large size of the ensuing riots and the strong hostility displayed toward Spanish merchants, the insurrection never challenged Spanish sovereignty. Mexico City had a series of riots in the eighteenth century, sparked by efforts of Bourbon administrators to suppress begging, regulate the use of liquor, and change working conditions in the tobacco factory. Silvia Arróm finds it significant that in Mexico City, as in Quito, the urban poor successfully resisted Bourbon efforts to regulate their lives: "Thus, the popular classes contested the state for control of their daily lives, and they often won."

THE REVOLT IN PERU

In the eighteenth century, Spanish pressures and demands on Peru's indígenas increased considerably. A major mechanism for the exploitation of natives was the previously mentioned repartimiento de mercancías, among the most hateful of the exactions to which the Spanish subjected indigenous people. A recent study finds that it figured as a cause in the great majority of revolts in Peru in the eighteenth century. The system functioned as follows: A Lima merchant advanced the sum of money needed by a corregidor to buy his post from the crown. The merchant also outfitted the corregidor with the stock of goods that he would "distribute"—that is, force indigenous residents of his district to buy, sometimes for six or eight times their fair market price. In the Cuzco region, typical repartimiento goods were mules and textiles, but sometimes these goods included items for which the natives had no possible use. Spanish colonial law forced them to pay for their purchases within an allotted time or go to prison; many had to leave their villages to work in mines, obrajes, and haciendas to obtain the needed cash. The system thus served to erode the traditional peasant economy and promoted two objectives of the state, the merchants, and other ruling-class groups: the expansion of the internal market for goods and the enlargement of the labor market.

In the same period, the burdens imposed by the mining mita increased. Determined to return the output of Potosí silver to its former high levels,

the crown and the mine owners made innovations that greatly intensified the exploitation of native labor. They doubled the ore quotas that they required *mitayos* (drafted workers) to produce between 1740 and 1790 from about fifteen loads per day to thirty, forcing the mitayos to work longer for the same wages and compelling their wives and children to assist them in meeting the quotas. They also reduced the wages of both mitayos and *mingas* (free workers). These innovations produced the desired revival of Potosí, with a doubling of silver production, but these gains came at a heavy price in native health and living standards.

Coupled with increases in alcabalas (sales taxes), the continuing abuses of the repartimiento de mercancías and the mita caused intense discontent. A critical point was reached when visitador José de Areche, sent out by Charles III in 1777 to reform conditions in the colony, tightened up the collection of tribute and sales taxes and broadened the tributary category to include all mestizos. This change increased the contribution of indígenas by 1 million pesos annually. These measures not only caused great hardships to the commoners, but also created greater difficulties for the native curacas, or chiefs, who were responsible for meeting tribute quotas. Areche himself foretold the storm to come when he wrote, "The lack of righteous judges, the mita of the Indians, and provincial commerce have made a corpse of this America. Corregidores are interested only in themselves.... How near everything is to ruin if these terrible abuses are not corrected, for they have been going on a long time."

The discontent of the masses with their intolerable conditions inspired messianic dreams and expectations of a speedy return of the Inca and the Inca empire. The popular imagination transformed this Inca empire into an ideal state, free from hunger and injustice, and free from the presence of oppressive colonial officials and exploitative mines, haciendas, and obrajes. This utopian vision of a restored Inca empire played a part in causing the great revolt of 1780–1781 and determining its direction.

That revolt had its forerunners; between 1730 and 1780, 128 rebellions, large and small, took place in the Andean area. From 1742 to 1755, a native leader called Juan Santos, "the invincible," waged partisan warfare against the Spaniards from his base in the eastern slopes of the Andes. The memory of his exploits was still alive when the revolt of José Gabriel Condorcanqui began. Accounts of Inca splendor in Garcilaso de la Vega's *Royal Commentaries* also strongly influenced this well-educated, wealthy mestizo descendant of Inca kings. Condorcanqui made repeated, fruitless efforts to obtain relief for his people through legal channels. In November 1780, he raised the standard of revolt by ambushing the hated corregidor Antonio de Arriaga near the town of Tinta and putting him to death after a summary trial. At this time, he also took the name of the last head of the neo-Inca state and became Tupac Amaru II. His actions followed an uprising led by the Catari brothers in the territory of present-day Bolivia. By the first months of 1781, the southern highlands of the viceroyalty of Peru were aflame with revolt. Although the various revolutionary movements lacked a unified direction, the rebel leaders generally recognized Tupac Amaru as their chief and continued to invoke his name even after his death.

In the first stage of the revolt, Tupac Amaru did not make his objectives entirely clear. In some public statements, he proclaimed his loyalty to the Spanish king and church, limiting his demands to the abolition of the mita, the repartimiento, the alcabala, and other taxes; the suppression of the corregidors; and the appointment of indigenous governors for the provinces. However, the well-educated Tupac Amaru, with years of experience in dealing with Spanish officialdom, never seriously believed that he could obtain sweeping reforms from the crown by negotiation, especially after his execution of the corregidor Arriaga. Much evidence suggests that his protestations of loyalty were a ruse designed to delay the inevitable royal reaction. For example, he disseminated certain documents in which he styled himself king of Peru and urged a war of "fire and blood" against peninsular Spaniards (excepting only the clergy). He also established a government to rule the territory under his control. No doubt, his professions of loyalty to Spain represented a mask by which he

Mireille Vautier

A descendant of the last great Inca, José Gabriel Condorcanqui assumed the name Tupac Amaru II, and in 1780 he and his wife, Micaela Bastidas, led a broad-based rebellion against the corruption of the corregidores. The revolt became a precursor of the independence wars that spread across the continent a few decades later.

utilized the still strong belief of many in the mythical benevolence of the Spanish king, attracted creole supporters of reform to his cause, and perhaps softened his punishment in case of defeat.

For Tupac Amaru, who had received his education in a Spanish colegio and had thoroughly absorbed the values of Spanish culture, the objective of the revolt was the establishment of an independent Peruvian state that would be essentially European in its political and social organization. His program called for complete independence from Spain, expulsion of peninsular Spaniards, and the abolition of the offices of viceroy, audiencia, and corregidor. The Inca empire would be restored, with himself as king and assisted by a nobility formed from other descendants of the Cuzco noble clans. Caste distinctions would disappear, and creoles, on whose support Tupac Amaru heavily counted, would live in harmony with native peoples, blacks, and mestizos. The Catholic Church would remain the state church, supported by tithes. Tupac Amaru's economic program called for suppression of the mita, the repartimiento de mercancías, customhouses, and sales taxes, and for the elimination of great estates and servitude, but it permitted small and medium-size landholdings and encouraged trade. Tupac Amaru's plan, in short, called for an anticolonial, national revolution that would create a unified people and a modern state of European type to promote economic development.

However, the native peasantry who responded to his call for revolt had a different conception of its meaning and goal. In an atmosphere of messianic excitement, they came to view it as a *pachacuti*, a great cataclysm or "overthrow" that would bring a total inversion of the existing social order and a return to an idealized Inca empire where the humble *runa* or peasant would not be last but first. In their desire to avenge the cruelties of the Conquest and two and a half centuries of brutal exploitation, they sacked haciendas and killed their owners without troubling to ascertain whether they were creoles or Europeans; a Spaniard was one who had a white skin and wore European dress. As the revolt spread, the old pagan religion emerged from the underground where it had hidden and flourished for centuries. Two priests always accompanied Tupac Amaru, who sought to maintain good relations with the Catholic Church, and he hoped for support of Bishop Moscoso of Cuzco. But his peasant followers sacked the vestments and ornaments of churches and attacked and killed priests, hanging a number of friars during the siege of Cuzco. In December 1780, Tupac Amaru entered one village and summoned its inhabitants, who greeted him with the words "You are our God and we ask that there be no priests to pester us." He replied that he could not allow this, for it

would mean that no one would attend them "in the moment of death."

These opposed conceptions of the meaning and objectives of the revolt held by Tupac Amaru and his peasant followers spelled defeat for Tupac Amaru's strategy of forming a common proindependence front of all social and racial groups except the peninsular Spaniards. The spontaneous, uncontrollable violence of the peasant rebels ended what little chance existed of attracting the support of the creoles, reformist clergy like Bishop Moscoso, and many indigenous nobles. At least twenty of these caciques, jealous of Tupac Amaru or fearful of losing their privileged status, led their subjects into the Spanish camp. A prominent loyalist figure was Diego Choquehanca, head of the wealthiest and most powerful kuraka family in Peru. The Spanish crown had declared his sixteenth-century ancestor of the same name a hidalgo and granted him the title of marquis de Salinas; by 1780, the Choquehancas owned eleven estancias (estates) in the province of Azangaro. "Not surprisingly," says Nils Jacobsen, "the Choquehanca family remained firmly loyal during the Tupac Amaru crisis."

Although the principal base of the revolt was the ayllus (free peasant communities), it also attracted a number of mestizos and a few creoles, mostly of middle-class status (artisans, shopkeepers, clerks, urban wage earners), some of whom formed part of the rebel command. Starting in the corregimiento of Tinta, near the southeastern rim of the strategic Cuzco valley system, the rebellion exploded into the Lake Titicaca basin, the scene of the longest and most intensive fighting. Encouraged by his initial victories, Tupac Amaru moved south with a rebel army in the thousands and in a short time took control of the whole altiplano south of Puno. Nonetheless, he failed to take advantage of those initial successes. Tactical errors that contributed to his defeat included the failure to attack Cuzco early, as his wife Micaela had strongly urged. A heroine of the revolt and Tupac's principal adviser, she had wanted to capitalize on the political and psychological significance of the ancient Inca capital before the arrival of Spanish reinforcements. In addition, communications among the rebel forces were poor, and the royalist armies possessed vastly superior arms and organization. The Spaniards also mobilized large numbers of yanaconas, who helped break the siege of Cuzco and suppress the revolt. Despite some initial successes, the rebel leader soon suffered a complete rout. The Spanish forces captured Tupac Amaru, members of his family, and his leading captains and promptly executed them, some with ferocious cruelty. In the territory of present-day Bolivia, the insurrection continued two years longer, reaching its high point in two prolonged sieges of La Paz (between March and October of 1781).

The last Inca revolt moved the crown to enact a series of reforms that included the replacement of the hated corregidores by the system of intendants and subdelegados and the establishment of an audiencia or high court in Cuzco, another of Tupac Amaru's goals before the revolt. However, these and other reforms proved to be changes more in form than in substance. The miserably paid subdelegados, many of whom were former corregidores, continued the exploitative practices of their predecessors less regularly and on a smaller scale, including the repartimiento de mercancías, which the Ordinance of Intendants had forbidden. Meanwhile the death or flight of some Hispanic landowners, clergy, and loyal kurakas because of the revolt had led to the occupation of their estates by peasant squatters. "In the last decades before independence," writes Nils Jacobsen, "a sense of uncertainty permeated social and property relations in the altiplano. To say that the peasants lost the Tupac Amaru Rebellion is only half true."

The Insurrection in New Granada, 1781

The revolt of the Comuneros in New Granada, like that in Peru, had its origin in intolerable economic conditions. Unlike the Peruvian upheaval, however, it was more clearly limited in its aims to the redress of grievances. Increases in the alcabala and a whole series of new taxes, including one on tobacco and a poll tax, provoked an uprising in Socorro, an important agricultural and manufacturing center in the north. The disturbances soon spread to other communities. The reformist spirit of the revolt appeared in the insurgent slogan *Viva el rey y muera el mal gobierno!* (Long live the king, down with the evil government!).

In view of its organization and its effort to form a common front of all colonial groups with grievances against Spanish authority (excepting the black slaves), the revolt of the Comuneros marked an advance over the rather chaotic course of events to the south. A *común* (central committee), elected in the town of Socorro by thousands of peasants and artisans from adjacent towns, directed the insurrection. Each of the towns in revolt also had its común and a captain chosen by popular election.

Under the command of hesitant or unwilling creole leaders, a multitude of indigenous and mestizo peasants and artisans marched on the capital of Bogotá, capturing or putting to flight the small forces sent from the capital. Playing for time until reinforcements arrived from the coast, the royal audiencia dispatched a commission headed by the archbishop to negotiate with the Comuneros. The demands that rebel delegates presented to the Spanish commissioners attested to the popular character of the movement and the unity of oppressed groups that they represented. These included reduction of indigenous and mestizo tribute and sales taxes, return of usurped land, abolition of the new tax on tobacco, and preference for creoles over Europeans in the filling of official posts.

In a special religious service sanctified by the archbishop, both parties signed an agreement on June 4, 1781, that satisfied virtually all the demands of the rebels. Secretly, however, the Spanish commissioners signed another document that declared the agreement void because it was obtained by force. The jubilant insurgents scattered and returned to their homes. Only José Antonio Galán, a young mestizo peasant leader, maintained his small force intact and sought to keep the revolt alive.

Having achieved their objective of disbanding the rebel army, the Spanish officials prepared to crush the insurrection completely. The viceroy Manuel Antonio Flores openly repudiated the agreement with the Comuneros. Following a pastoral visit to the disaffected region by the archbishop, who combined seductive promises of reform with threats of eternal damnation for confirmed rebels, Spanish troops brought up from the coast moved into the region and took large numbers of prisoners. The creole leaders of the revolt hastened to atone for their political sins by collaborating with the royalists. A renegade leader seized Galán, who had vainly urged a new march on Bogotá, and handed him over to the Spaniards, who put him to death by hanging on January 30, 1782. The revolt of the Comuneros had ended.

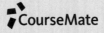 Go to the CourseMate website at www.cengagebrain.com for primary sources, additional study tools, and review materials—including audio and video clips—for this chapter.

8

The Independence of Latin America

FOCUS QUESTIONS

- What were the causes of the Latin American wars of independence?
- How and why were the Latin American and North American struggles for independence different?
- How was the struggle for home rule different from the struggle over who would rule at home?
- What were the four main centers of the struggle for independence, and how did they compare?
- What were the main political, economic, and social consequences of the wars for independence?

T HE BOURBON REFORMS, combined with the upsurge of the European economy in the eighteenth century, brought material prosperity and less tangible benefits to many upper-class creoles of Spanish America. Enlightened viceroys and intendants introduced improvements and refinements that made life in colonial cities more healthful and attractive. Education reforms, the influx of new books and ideas, and increased opportunities to travel and study in Europe widened the intellectual horizons of creole youth.

These gains, however, did not strengthen creole feelings of loyalty to the mother country. Instead, they enlarged their aspirations and sharpened their sense of grievance. The growing wealth of some sections of the creole elite made more galling its virtual exclusion from important posts in administration and the church. Meanwhile, the swelling production of creole haciendas, plantations, and ranches pressed against the trade barriers maintained by Spanish mercantilism. The intendant of Caracas, José Abalos, warned that, "if His Majesty does not grant them [the creoles] the freedom of trade which they desire, then he cannot count on their loyalty."

At the same time, Bourbon policy denied American manufacturers the protection they needed against crippling European competition.

Background of the Wars of Independence

CREOLES AND PENINSULAR SPANIARDS

The conflict of interest between Spain and its colonies appeared most sharply in the cleavage between the creoles and the peninsular Spaniards. The arrival of more Spaniards continually deepened these disagreements. In the late eighteenth century, a typical immigrant was a poor but hardworking and thrifty Basque or Navarrese who became an apprentice to a peninsular merchant, often a relative. In the course of time, as his merits won recognition, the immigrant might receive a daughter of the house in marriage and eventually succeed to the ownership of the business. One of the merchant's own creole sons might inherit a landed estate; other creole sons might enter the church or the law, both overcrowded professions.

1789–1800	French Revolution challenges monarchy and aristocratic rule
1791–1803	Toussaint L'Ouverture leads Haitian Revolution to abolish slavery and establish political independence
1800–1815	Rise of Napoleon and spread of French Revolution throughout Europe
1807	Napoleon invades Portugal and, with British support, Braganza dynasty flees to colonial Brazil
1808	Napoleon invades Spain and appoints Joseph Bonaparte to replace Ferdinand VII; Primo de Verdad, Viceroy José de Iturrigaray, and Mexico City Cabildo declare independence in the name of exiled King Ferdinand
1810	Indigenous popular revolution, led by Miguel Hidalgo and later José María Morelos, opposes both Bonapartist imperial rule and independent conservative Mexican creole government
1812	Spanish and English forces end Napoleonic occupation and establish liberal Constitution of 1812 that provides for a limited monarchy, promises freedom of speech and assembly, and abolishes the Inquisition
1816	Congress of Tucumán meets to declare independence of the United Provinces of La Plata and names José de San Martín to lead the Army of the Andes
1817	San Martín crosses the Andes to defeat royalists at the Battle of Chacabuco and liberate Chile
1819	Bolívar defeats royalists at Battle of Boyacá to liberate New Granada and convenes Congress of Angostura
1820	Liberal revolution in Spain, led by Rafael Riego, deposes Spanish monarchy and restores the liberal constitution of 1812
1821	Bolívar and José Antonio Páez defeat Spanish at Carabobo and convene Congress of Cúcuta that integrates Venezuela into Gran Colombia; Mexico declares independence and forms a constitutional monarchy under Augustín Iturbide
1822	Bolívar and San Martín meet at Guayaquil, where San Martín abandons Peru and the movement for independence; Iturbide becomes Agustín I, Emperor of Mexico; Dom Pedro refuses to return to Portugal and issues "Cry of Ipiranga" that declares Brazil independent

Thus, although there was some elite creole presence in both foreign and domestic trade, peninsular Spaniards continued to dominate the lucrative export-import trade and provincial trade. Spanish-born merchants, organized in powerful consulados, or merchant guilds, also played a key role in financing mining and the repartimiento business carried on among the natives by Spanish officials. Naturally, some upper-class creoles, excluded from mercantile activity and responsible posts in the government and church, developed the aristocratic manners and idle, spendthrift ways with which the peninsulars reproached them. Many other creoles of the middling sort, vegetating in ill-paid indigenous curacies and minor government jobs, bitterly resented the institutionalized discrimination that barred their way to advancement.

As a result, although some wealthy and powerful creoles maintained excellent relations with their peninsular counterparts, fusing their economic interests through marriage and forming a single colonial Establishment, creoles and peninsulars tended to become mutually hostile castes. The peninsulars sometimes justified their privileged position by charging the creoles with innate indolence and incapacity, qualities that some Spanish writers attributed to the noxious effects of the American climate and soil; the creoles retorted by describing the Europeans as mean and grasping parvenus. So intense was the hatred among many members of these groups that a Spanish bishop in New Spain protested against the feeling of some young creoles that "if they could empty their veins of the Spanish part of their blood, they would gladly do so." This inevitably fostered the growth of creole nationalism; Humboldt, who traveled in Spanish America in the twilight years of the colony, reports a common saying: "I am not a Spaniard, I am an American."

The entrance of Enlightenment ideas into Latin America certainly contributed to the growth of creole discontent, but the relative weight of various influences is uncertain. Bourbon Spain itself contributed to the creole awakening by the many-sided effort of reforming officials to improve the quality of colonial life. Typical of this group was the intendant Juan Antonio Riaño, who introduced to the Mexican city of Guanajuato, the capital of his province, a taste for the French language and literature. According to the nineteenth-century Mexican historian and conservative political leader, Lucas Alamán, Riaño was also responsible "for the development of interest in drawing and music, and for the cultivation of mathematics, physics, and chemistry in the school that had been formerly maintained by the Jesuits."

Many educated creoles read the forbidden writings of Raynal, Montesquieu, Voltaire, Rousseau, and other radical philosophes, but another, innocuous-seeming agency for the spread of Enlightenment ideas in Latin America consisted of scientific texts, based on the theories of Descartes, Leibnitz, and Newton, which circulated freely in the colonies. By 1800, the creole elite had become familiar with the most advanced thought of contemporary Europe.

The American Revolution contributed to the growth of "dangerous ideas" in the colonies. Spain was well aware of the ideological as well as the political threat the United States posed to its empire. Spain had reluctantly joined its ally France in war against England during the American Revolution, but it kept the rebels at arm's length, refused to recognize American independence, and in the peace negotiations tried unsuccessfully to coop up the United States within the Allegheny Mountains. After 1783, a growing number of U.S. ships touched legally or illegally at Spanish American ports. Together with "Yankee notions," these vessels sometimes introduced such subversive documents as the writings of Thomas Paine and Thomas Jefferson.

The French Revolution probably exerted an even greater influence on the creole mind. The Argentine revolutionary Manuel Belgrano recalled:

> Since I was in Spain in 1789, and the French Revolution was then causing a change in ideas, especially among the men of letters with whom I associated, the ideals of liberty, equality, security, and property took a firm hold on me, and I saw only tyrants in those who would restrain a man, wherever he might be, from enjoying the rights with which God and Nature had endowed him.

Another cultivated creole, the Colombian Antonio Nariño, incurred Spanish wrath in 1794 by translating and printing on his own press the French Declaration of the Rights of Man of 1789. Sentenced to prison in Africa for ten years, Nariño lived to become leader and patriarch of the independence movement in Colombia and to witness its triumph.

However, the French Revolution soon took a radical turn, and the creole aristocracy became disenchanted with it as a model. Scattered conspiracies in some Spanish colonies and Brazil owed their inspiration to the French example, but they were invariably the work of a few radicals, drawing their support almost exclusively from lower-class elements. The most important result directly attributable to the French Revolution was the slave revolt in the French part of Haiti under talented black and mulatto leaders: Toussaint L'Ouverture, Jean Jacques Dessalines, Henri Christophe, and Alexandre Pétion. In 1804, Toussaint's lieutenant, General Dessalines, proclaimed the independence of the new state of Haiti. Black revolutionaries had established the first liberated territory in Latin America, ending colonialism and slavery simultaneously. Nevertheless, this achievement dampened, rather than aroused, support for independence among the creole elite of other colonies. Thus, fear that secession from Spain might touch off a slave revolt helped keep the planter class of neighboring Cuba loyal to Spain during and after the Latin American wars of independence.

Despite the existence of small conspiratorial groups, organized in secret societies with correspondents in Europe as well as America, the movement for independence might have long remained puny and ineffectual. As late as 1806, when the precursor of revolution, Francisco de Miranda, landed on the coast of his native Venezuela with a force of some two hundred foreign volunteers, his call for revolution evoked no response, and he had to make a hasty retreat. Creole timidity and political inexperience and the apathy of the people might have long postponed the coming of independence if external developments had not hastened its arrival. The revolution that Miranda and other

This sculpture of an enslaved Haitian, with machete in hand and using a conch shell to call his comrades to rebel against the odious institution of slavery, commemorates the struggle that produced Haiti's independence and struck fear into the hearts of creole aristocrats throughout the Americas.

forerunners could not set in motion came as a result of decisions by European powers with very different ends in view.

THE CAUSES OF REVOLUTION

Among the causes of the revolutionary crisis that matured from 1808 to 1810, the decline of Spain under the inept Charles IV was certainly significant. The European wars unleashed by the French Revolution glaringly revealed the failure of the Bourbon reforms to correct the structural defects in Spanish economic and social life. In 1793, Spain joined a coalition of England and other states in war against the French republic. The struggle went badly for Spain, and, in 1795, the royal favorite and chief minister, Manuel de Godoy, signed the Peace of Basel. The next year, Spain became France's ally. English sea power promptly drove Spanish shipping from the Atlantic, virtually cutting off communication between Spain and its colonies. Hard necessity compelled Spain to permit neutral ships, sailing from Spanish for foreign ports, to trade with its overseas subjects. United States merchants and shipowners were the principal beneficiaries of this departure from the old, restrictive system.

Godoy's disastrous policy of war with England had other results. An English naval officer, Sir Home Popham, undertook on his own initiative to attack Buenos Aires. His fleet sailed from the Cape of Good Hope for La Plata in April 1806 with a regiment of soldiers on board. In its wake followed a great number of English merchant ships eager to pour a mass of goods through a breach in the Spanish colonial system. A swift victory followed the landing of the British troops. The English soldiers entered Buenos Aires, meeting only token resistance. Hoping to obtain the support of the population, the English commander issued a proclamation that guaranteed the right of private property, free trade, and freedom of religion. But creoles and peninsulars joined to expel their unwanted liberators. A volunteer army, secretly organized, attacked and routed the occupation troops, capturing the English general and twelve hundred of his men. To an English officer who tempted him with ideas of independence under a British protectorate, the creole Manuel Belgrano replied, "Either our old master or none at all."

The British government, meanwhile, had sent strong reinforcements to La Plata. This second invasion force met a murderous hail of fire as it tried to advance through the narrow streets of Buenos Aires and soon retreated with heavy losses. Impressed by the tenacity of the defense, the British commander gave up the struggle and agreed to evacuate Buenos Aires and the previously captured town of Montevideo. Spearheaded by the legion of *patricios* (creoles), this defeat of a veteran British army by a people's militia was a large step down the road toward Argentine independence. The creoles of Buenos Aires, having tasted power, would not willingly relinquish it again.

In Europe, Spain's distresses now reached a climax. Napoleon, at the helm of France, gradually reduced Spain to a helpless satellite. In 1807, angered by Portugal's refusal to cooperate with his Continental System by closing its ports to English shipping, Napoleon obtained from Charles IV permission to invade Portugal through Spain. French troops swept across the peninsula; as they approached Lisbon, the Portuguese royal family and court escaped to Brazil in a fleet under British convoy. A hundred thousand French troops continued to occupy Spanish towns. Popular resentment at their presence, and at the pro-French policies of the royal favorite Godoy, broke out in stormy riots that compelled Charles IV to abdicate in favor of his son Ferdinand. Napoleon now intervened and offered his services as a mediator in the dispute

between father and son. Foolishly, the trusting pair accepted Napoleon's invitation to confer with him in the French city of Bayonne. There, Napoleon forced both to abdicate in favor of his brother Joseph, his candidate for the Spanish throne. Napoleon then summoned a congress of Spanish grandees, who meekly approved his dictate.

The Spanish people had yet to say their word. On May 2, 1808, an insurrection against French occupation troops began in Madrid and spread like wildfire throughout the country. The insurgents established local governing juntas in the regions under their control. Later, a central junta assumed direction of the resistance movement in the name of the captive Ferdinand VII. This junta promptly made peace with England. When the Spanish armies fought the superbly trained French troops in conventional battles in the field, they usually suffered defeat, but guerrilla warfare pinned down large French forces and made Napoleon's control of conquered territory extremely precarious.

By early 1810, however, French victory seemed inevitable, for French armies had overrun Andalusia and were threatening Cádiz, the last city in Spanish hands. The central junta now dissolved itself and appointed a regency to rule Spain; this body in turn yielded its power to a national Cortes, or parliament, which met in Cádiz from 1810 to 1814 under the protection of English naval guns. Because most of the delegates came from Cádiz, whose liberal, cosmopolitan atmosphere was hardly typical of Spain, their views were much more liberal than those of the Spanish people as a whole. The constitution the Cortes approved in 1812 provided for a limited monarchy, promised freedom of speech and assembly, and abolished the Inquisition. However, the Cortes made few concessions to Spain's American colonies. It invited Spanish American delegates to join its deliberations but made clear that the system of peninsular domination and commercial monopoly would remain essentially intact.

In Spanish America, creole leaders, anticipating the imminent collapse of Spain, considered how they might turn this dramatic rush of events to their own advantage. Those events had transformed the idea of self-rule or total independence, until lately a remote prospect, into a realistic goal. Confident that the armies of the invincible Napoleon would crush all opposition, some creole leaders prepared to take power into their hands with the pretext of loyalty to the "beloved Ferdinand." They could justify their action by the example of the Spanish regional juntas formed to govern in the name of the captive king. The confusion caused among Spanish officials by the coming of rival emissaries who proclaimed both Ferdinand and Joseph Bonaparte the legitimate king of Spain also played into creole hands.

In the spring of 1810, with the fall of Cádiz apparently imminent, the creole leaders moved into action. Charging viceroys and other royal officials with doubtful loyalty to Ferdinand, they organized popular demonstrations in Caracas, Buenos Aires, Santiago, and Bogotá that compelled those authorities to surrender control to local juntas dominated by creoles. However, creole hopes of a peaceful transition to independence were doomed to failure. Their claims of loyalty did not deceive the groups truly loyal to Spain, and fighting broke out between patriots and royalists.

The Liberation of South America

The Latin American struggle for independence suggests comparison with the American Revolution. Some obvious parallels existed between the two upheavals. Both sought to throw off the rule of a mother country whose mercantilist system hindered the further development of a rapidly growing colonial economy. Well-educated elites led both, and they drew their slogans or ideas from the ideological arsenal of the Enlightenment. Both were civil wars in which large elements of the population sided with the mother country. Both owed their final success in part to foreign assistance (although the North American rebels received far more help from their French ally than Latin America received from outside sources).

The differences between the two revolutions are no less impressive, however. Unlike the American Revolution, the Latin American struggle for independence did not have a unified direction or strategy, due to vast distances that separated them, other geographic obstacles to unity, and the economic and cultural isolation of the various Latin American regions from each other. Moreover, the Latin American movement for independence lacked the strong popular base provided by the more democratic and fluid society of the English colonies. The creole elite, itself part of an exploitative white minority, feared the oppressed natives, blacks, and half-castes, and as a rule sought to keep their intervention in the struggle to a minimum. This lack of unity of regions and classes helps explain why Latin America had to struggle so long against a power like Spain, weak and beset by many internal and external problems.

The struggle for independence had four main centers. Spanish South America had two principal theaters of military operations, one in the north and one in the south. One stream of liberation flowed southward from Venezuela; another ran northward from Argentina. In Peru, the last Spanish bastion on the continent, these two currents joined. Brazil achieved its own swift and relatively peaceful separation from Portugal. Finally, Mexico had to travel a difficult, circuitous road before gaining its independence.

SIMÓN BOLÍVAR, THE LIBERATOR

Simón Bolívar is the symbol and hero of the liberation struggle in northern South America. Born in Caracas, Venezuela, in 1783, he came from an aristocratic creole family rich in land, slaves, and mines. His reading of the rationalist, materialist classics of the Enlightenment greatly influenced his intellectual formation. Travel in various European countries between 1803 and 1807 further widened his intellectual horizons. He returned to Caracas and soon became involved in conspiratorial activity directed at the overthrow of the Spanish regime.

In April 1810, the creole party in Caracas organized a demonstration that forced the abdication of the captain general. A creole-dominated junta that pledged to defend the rights of the captive Ferdinand took power, but its assurances of loyalty deceived neither local Spaniards nor the Regency Council in Cádiz. A considerable number of wealthy creoles of the planter class also opposed independence, and when it triumphed, many emigrated to Cuba or Puerto Rico. The patriots also disagreed over what policy to follow; some, like Bolívar, favored an immediate declaration of independence, whereas others preferred to postpone the issue.

Perhaps to get Bolívar out of the way, the junta sent him to England to solicit British aid. He had no success in this mission but convinced the veteran revolutionary Francisco de Miranda to return to Venezuela and take command of the patriot army. In 1811, a Venezuelan congress proclaimed the country's independence and framed a republican constitution that abolished *fueros* (special privileges) and native tribute but retained black slavery, made Catholicism the state religion, and limited the rights of full citizenship to property owners. This last provision excluded the free *pardo* (mulatto) population.

A portrait of the liberator, Simón Bolívar, by José Gil de Castro. His appearance conforms closely to descriptions of Bolívar in contemporary accounts.

The Granger Collection

Fighting had already broken out between patriots and royalists. In addition to peninsulars, the troops sent from Puerto Rico by the Regency Council, and a section of the creole aristocracy, the royalist cause had the support of some free blacks and mulattos, angered by the republic's denial of full citizenship to them. In many areas, the black slaves took advantage of the chaotic situation to rise in revolt, impartially killing creole and peninsular Spanish hacendados. Nonetheless, the majority of the population remained neutral, fleeing from their villages at the approach of royal or republican conscription officers; if conscripted, they often deserted when they could or changed sides if prospects seemed better.

On the patriot side, differences arose between the commander in chief, Miranda, and his young officers, especially Bolívar, who were contemptuous of Miranda's military conservatism and indecisiveness. Amid these disputes came the earthquake of March 26, 1812, which caused great loss of life and property in Caracas and other patriot territories but spared the regions under Spanish control. The royalist clergy proclaimed this disaster a divine retribution against the rebels. A series of military defeats completed the discomfiture of the revolutionary cause.

With his forces disintegrating, Miranda attempted to negotiate a treaty with the royalist commander and then tried to flee the country, taking with him part of the republic's treasury. He may have intended to continue working for independence, but the circumstances made it appear as if he wished to save his own skin. Bolívar and some of his comrades, regarding Miranda's act as a form of treachery, seized him before he could embark and turned him over to the Spaniards. He died in a Spanish prison four years later. Bolívar, saved from the Spanish reaction by the influence of a friend of his family, received a safe conduct to leave the country.

Bolívar departed for New Granada (present-day Colombia), which was still partially under patriot control. Here, as in Venezuela, creole leaders squabbled over forms of government. Two months after his arrival, Bolívar issued a Manifesto to the

Citizens of New Granada in which he called for unity, condemned the federalist system as impractical under war conditions, and urged the liberation of Venezuela as necessary for Colombian security. Given command of a small detachment of troops to clear the Magdalena River of enemy troops, he employed a strategy that featured swift movement, aggressive tactics, and the advancement of soldiers for merit without regard to social background or color.

A victory at Cúcuta gained Bolívar the rank of general in the Colombian army and approval of his plan for the liberation of Venezuela. In a forced march of three months, he led five hundred men through Venezuela's Andean region toward Caracas. In Venezuela the Spaniards had unleashed a campaign of terror against all patriots. At Trujillo, midway in his advance on Caracas, Bolívar proclaimed a counterterror, a war to the death against all Spaniards. As Bolívar approached the capital, the Spanish forces withdrew. He entered Caracas in triumph and received from the city council the title of liberator; soon afterward, the grateful congress of the restored republic voted to grant him dictatorial powers.

Bolívar's success was short-lived, for developments abroad and at home worked against him. The fall of Napoleon in 1814 brought Ferdinand VII to the Spanish throne, released Spanish troops for use in Spanish America, and gave an important lift to the royal cause. Meanwhile, the republic's policies alienated large sectors of the lower classes. The creole aristocrats stubbornly refused to grant freedom to their slaves. As a result, the slaves continued their struggle, independent of Spaniards and creoles, and republican forces often redeployed for punitive expeditions into areas of slave revolt.

The *llaneros* (cowboys) of the Venezuelan *llanos* (plains) also turned against the republic because of agrarian edicts that attempted to end the hunting or rounding up of cattle in the llanos without written permission from the owner of the land in question. These edicts also sought to transform the llaneros into semiservile peons by forcing them to carry an identity card and belong to a ranch. These attacks on their customary rights and freedom

angered the llaneros. Under the leadership of the formidable José Tomás Boves, a mass of cowboys, armed with the dreaded lance, invaded the highlands and swept down on Caracas, crushing all resistance. In July 1814, Bolívar hastily abandoned the city and retreated toward Colombia with the remains of his army. Although Boves died in battle in late 1814, he had destroyed the Venezuelan "second republic."

Bolívar reached Cartagena in September to find that Colombia was on the verge of chaos. Despite the imminent threat of a Spanish invasion, the provinces quarreled with each other and defied the authority of the weak central government. Having determined that the situation was hopeless, Bolívar left in May 1815 for the British island of Jamaica. Meanwhile, a strong Spanish army under General Pablo Morillo had landed in Venezuela, completed the Reconquest of the colony, and then sailed to lay siege to Cartagena. Cut off by land and sea, the city surrendered in December, and the rest of Colombia was pacified within a few months. Of all the provinces of Spanish America, only Argentina remained in revolt. If Ferdinand had conceded a grant of legal equality between whites and the mixed-race people who supported his cause, the Spanish empire in America might have survived much longer. But the reactionary Ferdinand made no concessions.

Bolívar still had an unshakable faith in the inevitable triumph of independence. From Jamaica, he sent a famous letter in which he affirmed that faith and offered a remarkable analysis of the situation and prospects of Spanish America. He scoffed at the ability of Spain—that "aged serpent"—to maintain Spanish America forever in subjection. Bolívar also looked into the political future of the continent. Monarchy, he argued, was foreign to the genius of Latin America, whose people could only accept a republican regime. A single government for the region was impracticable, divided as it was by "climatic differences, geographic diversity, conflicting interests, and dissimilar characteristics." Bolívar boldly forecast the destiny of the different regions, taking account of their economic and social structures. Chile, for example, seemed to him to have a democratic future, whereas Peru was fated to suffer dictatorship because it contained "two factors that clash with every just and liberal principle: gold and slaves."

From Jamaica, Bolívar went to Haiti, where he received a sympathetic hearing and the offer of some material support from the mulatto president Alexandre Pétion, who asked in return for the freedom of the slaves in the territory that Bolívar should liberate. In March 1816, Bolívar and a small band of followers landed on the island of Margarita off the Venezuelan coast. Two attempts to gain a foothold on the mainland failed, and soon Bolívar was back in the West Indies. Reflecting on his failures, he concluded that the effort to invade the well-fortified western coast of Venezuela was a mistake and decided to establish a base in the Orinoco River valley, far from the centers of Spanish power. Roving patriot bands still operated in this region, and Bolívar hoped to win the allegiance of disillusioned llaneros, who increasingly abandoned their Spanish allies. In September 1816, Bolívar sailed from Haiti for the Orinoco River delta, which he ascended until he reached the small town of Angostura (modern Ciudad Bolívar), which he made his headquarters.

The tide of war now began to flow in his favor. The patriot guerrilla bands accepted his leadership. Even more important, he gained the support of the principal llanero chieftain, José Antonio Páez. European developments also favored Bolívar. The end of the Napoleonic wars idled a large number of British soldiers; many of these veterans came to Venezuela, forming a British Legion that distinguished itself in battle by its valor. English merchants made loans that enabled Bolívar to secure men and arms for the coming campaign. The mulish attitude of Ferdinand VII also helped. He refused to consider making any concessions to the colonists, which caused the English government to lose patience and regard with more friendly eyes the prospect of Spanish American independence.

On the eve of the decisive campaign of 1819, Bolívar summoned to Angostura a makeshift congress that vested him with dictatorial powers. To this congress, he presented a project for a constitution for

Venezuela, in which he urged the abolition of slavery and the distribution of land to revolutionary soldiers. Nonetheless, the proposed constitution also had some nondemocratic features. They included a president with virtually royal powers, a hereditary senate, and restriction on suffrage and office-holding to the propertied and educated elite. The congress disregarded Bolívar's reform proposals but elected him president of the republic and adopted a constitution that embodied many of his ideas.

The rebels, however, still had to win the war. Bolívar's bold strategy for the liberation of Venezuela and Colombia envisaged striking a heavy blow at Spanish forces from a completely unexpected direction. While llanero cavalry under Páez distracted and pinned down the main body of Spanish troops in northern Venezuela with swift raids, Bolívar advanced with an army of some twenty-five hundred men along the winding Orinoco and Arauco rivers, across the plains, and then up the towering Colombian Andes until he reached the plateau where lay Bogotá, capital of New Granada. On the field of Boyacá, the patriot army surprised and defeated the royalists in a short, sharp battle that netted sixteen hundred prisoners and considerable supplies. Bogotá lay defenseless, and Bolívar entered the capital to the cheers of its people, who had suffered greatly under Spanish rule.

Leaving his aide, Francisco Santander, to organize a government, Bolívar hurried off to Angostura to prepare the liberation of Venezuela. Then thrilling news arrived from Spain: On January 1, 1820, a regiment awaiting embarkation for South America had mutinied, starting a revolt that forced Ferdinand to restore the liberal constitution of 1812 and give up his plans to reconquer the colonies. This news caused joy among the patriots and gloom and desertions among the Venezuelan royalists. In July 1821, the troops of Bolívar and Páez crushed the last important Spanish force in Venezuela at Carabobo. Except for some coastal towns and forts still held by beleaguered royalists, Venezuela was free.

Bolívar had already turned his attention southward. The independence of Spanish America remained precarious as long as the Spaniards held the immense mountain bastion of the central Andes. While Bolívar prepared a major offensive from Bogotá against Quito, he sent his able young lieutenant, Antonio José Sucre, by sea from Colombia's Pacific coast to seize the port of Guayaquil. Before Sucre even arrived, the creole party in Guayaquil revolted, proclaimed independence, and placed the port under Bolívar's protection. With his forces swelled by reinforcements sent by the Argentine general José de San Martín, Sucre advanced into the Ecuadoran highlands and defeated a Spanish army on the slopes of Mount Pichincha, near Quito. Bolívar, meanwhile, advancing southward from Bogotá along the Cauca River valley, encountered stiff royalist resistance, but this crumbled on news of Sucre's victory at Pichincha. The provinces that comprised the former viceroyalty of New Granada—the future republics of Venezuela, Colombia, Ecuador, and Panama—were now free from Spanish control. They temporarily united into a large state named Colombia or Gran Colombia, established, at Bolívar's initiative, by the union of New Granada and Venezuela in 1821.

THE SOUTHERN LIBERATION MOVEMENT AND SAN MARTÍN

The time had come for the movement of liberation led by Bolívar to merge with that flowing northward from Argentina. Ever since the defeat of the British invasions of 1806–1807, the creole party, although nominally loyal to Spain, had effectively controlled Buenos Aires. The hero of the invasions and the temporary viceroy, Santiago Liniers, cooperated fully with the creole leaders. A new viceroy, sent by the Seville junta to replace Liniers, joined with the viceroy at Lima to crush abortive creole revolts in Upper Peru (Bolivia). However, in Buenos Aires he walked softly, for he recognized the superior power of the creoles. Under their pressure, he issued a decree permitting free trade with allied and neutral nations, a measure bitterly opposed by representatives of the Cádiz monopoly. But this concession could not save the Spanish regime. Revolution was in the air, and the creole leaders waited

only, in the words of one of their number, "for the figs to be ripe."

In May 1810, when word came that French troops had entered Seville and threatened Cádiz, the secret patriot society organized a demonstration that forced the viceroy to summon an open town meeting to decide the future government of the colony. This first Argentine congress voted to depose the viceroy and establish a junta to govern in the name of Ferdinand. The junta promptly attempted to consolidate its control of the vast viceroyalty and subdued the interior provinces after sharp fighting. However, Montevideo, the capital of modern Uruguay, which lay across the Río de la Plata on the eastern shore, remained in Spanish hands until 1814, when it fell to an Argentine siege. The junta met even more tenacious resistance from the gauchos of the Uruguayan pampa. Led by José Gervasio Artigas, they demanded Uruguayan autonomy in a loose federal connection with Buenos Aires. The *porteños* (inhabitants of Buenos Aires) would have nothing to do with Artigas's gaucho democracy, and a new struggle began. It ended when Artigas, caught between the fire of Buenos Aires and that of Portuguese forces claiming Uruguay for Brazil, had to flee to Paraguay. Uruguay did not achieve independence until 1828.

The creole aristocracy in another portion of the old viceroyalty of La Plata, Paraguay, also suspected the designs of the Buenos Aires junta and defeated a porteño force sent to liberate Asunción. This done, the creole party in Asunción rose up, deposed Spanish officials, and proclaimed the independence of Paraguay. A key figure in this uprising was the remarkable Dr. José Rodríguez de Francia, soon to become his country's first president and dictator.

Efforts by the Buenos Aires junta to liberate the mountainous northern province of Upper Peru also failed. Two thrusts by a patriot army into this area were defeated, and the invaders rolled back. The steep terrain, long lines of communication, and the apathy of Bolivian indigenous peoples contributed to these defeats.

The Buenos Aires government also had serious internal problems. A dispute broke out between liberal supporters of the fiery Mariano Moreno, secretary of the junta and champion of social reform, and a conservative faction led by the great landowner Cornelio Saavedra. This dispute foreshadowed the liberal-conservative cleavage that dominated the first decades of Argentine history after independence. In 1813, a national assembly gave the country the name of the United Provinces of La Plata and enacted such reforms as the abolition of mita, encomienda, titles of nobility, and the Inquisition, but it delayed a declaration of independence until 1816.

Also in 1816, the military genius of José de San Martín broke the long-standing military stalemate. San Martín, born in what is now northeastern Argentina, was a colonel in the Spanish army with twenty years of service behind him when revolution broke out in Buenos Aires. He promptly sailed for La Plata to offer his sword to the patriot junta. He soon earned a promotion to command the army of Upper Peru, which was recuperating in Tucumán after a sound defeat at royalist hands. Perceiving that a frontal attack on the Spanish position in Upper Peru was doomed to failure, San Martín offered a plan for total victory that gained the support of the director of the United Provinces, Juan Martín de Pueyrredón. San Martín proposed a march over the Andes to liberate Chile, where a Spanish reaction had toppled the revolutionary regime established by Bernardo O'Higgins and other patriot leaders in 1810. This done, the united forces of La Plata and Chile would descend on Peru from the sea.

To mask his plans from Spanish eyes and gain time for a large organizational effort, San Martín obtained an appointment as governor of the province of Cuyo, whose capital, Mendoza, lay at the eastern end of a strategic pass leading across the Andes to Chile. He spent two years recruiting, training, and equipping his Army of the Andes. Like Bolívar, he used the promise of freedom to secure black and mulatto volunteers, and later declared they were his best soldiers. Chilean refugees fleeing the Spanish reaction in their country also joined his forces.

San Martín, methodical and thorough, demanded of the Buenos Aires government arms, munitions, food, and equipment of every kind. In January 1817, the army began its march over the frozen Andean passes, which equaled in difficulty Bolívar's scaling of the Colombian sierra. Twenty-one days later, the army issued onto Chilean soil. A decisive defeat of the Spanish army at Chacabuco in February opened the gates of Santiago to San Martín. He won another victory at Maipú (1818), in a battle that ended the threat to Chile's independence. Rejecting Chilean invitations to become supreme ruler of the republic, a post assumed by O'Higgins, San Martín began to prepare the attack by sea on Lima, fifteen hundred miles away.

The execution of his plan required the creation of a navy. He secured a number of ships in England and the United States and engaged a competent though eccentric naval officer, Thomas, Lord Cochrane, to organize the patriot navy. In August 1820, the expedition sailed for Peru in a fleet made up of seven ships of war and eighteen transports. San Martín landed his army about a hundred miles south of Lima but delayed moving on the Peruvian capital. He hoped to obtain its surrender by economic blockade, propaganda, and direct negotiation with the Spanish officials. The desire of the Lima aristocracy, creole and peninsular, to avoid an armed struggle that might unleash an indigenous and slave revolt worked in favor of San Martín's strategy. In June 1821, the Spanish army evacuated Lima and retreated toward the Andes. San Martín entered the capital and in a festive atmosphere proclaimed the independence of Peru.

His victory was far from complete, however. He had to deal with counterrevolutionary plots and the resistance of Lima's corrupt elite to his program of social reform, which included ending indigenous tribute and granting freedom to the children of slaves. San Martín's assumption of supreme military and civil power in August 1821 added to the factional opposition. Meanwhile, a large Spanish army maneuvered in front of Lima, challenging San Martín to a battle he dared not join with his much smaller force. Disheartened by the atmosphere of intrigue and hostility that surrounded him, San Martín became convinced that only monarchy could bring stability to Spanish

America, and he sent a secret mission to Europe to search for a prince for the throne of Peru.

Such was the background of San Martín's departure for Guayaquil, where he met in conference with Bolívar on July 26 and 27, 1822. The agenda of the meeting included several points. One concerned the future of Guayaquil. San Martín claimed the port city for Peru; Bolívar, however, had already annexed it to Gran Colombia, confronting San Martín with a fait accompli. Another topic was the political future of all Spanish America. San Martín favored monarchy as the solution for the emergent chaos of the new states; Bolívar believed in a government system that was republican in form and oligarchical in content. Nevertheless, the critical question before the two men was how to complete the liberation of the continent by defeating the Spanish forces in Peru.

San Martín's abrupt retirement from public life after the conference, the reluctance of the two liberators to share what they discussed, and the meager authentic documentary record of the proceedings have surrounded the meeting with an atmosphere of mystery and produced two opposed and partisan interpretations. According to Argentine historians, San Martín came to Guayaquil in search of military aid, which Bolívar rebuffed because he was unwilling to share with a rival the glory of bringing the struggle for independence to an end. San Martín then magnanimously decided to leave Peru and allowed Bolívar to complete the work he had begun. Venezuelan historians, on the other hand, argue that San Martín came to Guayaquil primarily to recover Guayaquil for Peru. The historians deny that San Martín asked Bolívar for more troops and insist that he left Peru for personal reasons that had nothing to do with the conference.

Both interpretations tend to diminish the stature and sense of realism of the two liberators. San Martín was no martyr, nor was Bolívar an ambitious schemer who sacrificed San Martín to his passion for power and glory. San Martín surely understood that Bolívar alone combined the military, political, and psychological assets needed to liquidate the factional hornets' nest in Peru and gain final victory over the powerful Spanish army in the sierra. Given

the situation in Lima, San Martín's presence could only hinder the performance of those tasks. In this light, Bolívar's decision to assume sole direction of the war and San Martín's determination to withdraw reflected a realistic appraisal of the Peruvian problem and the solution it required.

San Martín returned to Lima to find that in his absence his enemies had rallied and struck at him by driving his reforming chief minister, Bernardo Monteagudo, out of the country. San Martín made no effort to reassert his power. In September 1822, before the first Peruvian congress, he announced his resignation as protector and his impending departure. He returned to Buenos Aires by way of Chile, where the government of his friend O'Higgins was on the verge of collapse. In Buenos Aires, the people seemed to have forgotten his existence. Accompanied by his daughter, he sailed for Europe at the end of 1823. He died in France in 1850 in virtual obscurity. His transfiguration into an Argentine national hero began a quarter-century later.

San Martín's departure left Lima and the territory under its control in serious danger of reconquest by the strong Spanish army in the sierra. Bolívar made no move to rescue the squabbling factions in Lima from their predicament; he allowed the situation to deteriorate until May 1823, when the Peruvian congress called on him for help. Then he sent Sucre with only a few thousand men, for he wanted to bring the Lima politicians to their knees. The scare produced by a brief reoccupation of the capital by the Spanish army prepared the creole leaders to accept Bolívar's absolute rule.

Bolívar arrived in Peru in September 1823. He required almost a year to achieve political stability and to meld into a united force the army he brought with him and the different national units under his command. After a month of difficult ascent of the sierra, in an altitude so high that Bolívar and most of his men suffered from mountain sickness, cavalry elements of the patriot and royalist armies clashed near the lake of Junín, and the Spaniards suffered defeat (August 6, 1824). The royalist commander, José de Canterac, retreated toward Cuzco. Leaving Sucre in command, Bolívar returned to Lima to gather reinforcements. To Sucre fell the glory of defeating the Spanish army in the last major engagement of the war, at Ayacucho (December 9, 1824). Only scattered resistance at some points in the highlands and on the coast remained. The racially and ethnically diverse movement for Spanish American independence had achieved its goal of continental liberation.

THE ACHIEVEMENT OF BRAZILIAN INDEPENDENCE

In contrast to the political anarchy, economic dislocation, and military destruction in Spanish America, Brazil's drive toward independence proceeded as a relatively bloodless transition between 1808 and 1822. The idea of Brazilian independence first arose in the late eighteenth century as a Brazilian reaction to the Portuguese policy of tightening political and economic control over the colony in the interests of the mother country. The first significant conspiracy against Portuguese rule appeared in 1788–1789 in Minas Gerais, where rigid governmental control over the production and prices of gold and diamonds, as well as heavy taxes, caused much discontent, and where there existed a group of intellectuals educated in Europe and familiar with the ideas of the Enlightenment. However, this conspiracy never went beyond the stage of discussion, and the Portuguese crown easily discovered and crushed it. Other conspiracies in Rio de Janeiro (1794), Bahia (1798), and Pernambuco (1801), as well as a brief revolt in Pernambuco (1817), reflected the influence of republican ideas over sections of the elite and even the lower strata of urban society. All proved abortive or soon suffered ignominious defeat. The stagnation of Brazilian life and, as in Cuba, the fear of slave owners that resistance to the crown might spark slave insurrections effectively inhibited the spirit of revolt. Were it not for an accident of European history, the independence of Brazil might not have occurred.

The French invasion of Portugal (1807), followed by the flight of the Portuguese court to Rio de Janeiro, brought large benefits to Brazil. Indeed, the transfer of the court in effect signified achievement of Brazilian independence. The Portuguese prince regent João opened Brazil's ports to the trade of friendly nations, permitted the rise of local industries, and founded a Bank of Brazil. In 1815, he elevated Brazil to the legal status of a kingdom co-equal with Portugal. In one sense, however, Brazil's new status substituted one form of dependence for another. Freed from Portuguese control, Brazil came under the economic domination of England, which obtained major tariff concessions and other privileges by the Strangford Treaty of 1810. One result was an influx of cheap machine-made goods that swamped the handicrafts industry of the country.

Brazilian elites took satisfaction in Brazil's new role and the growth of educational, cultural, and economic opportunities for their class. Nevertheless, this feeling combined with resentment at the thousands of Portuguese courtiers and hangers-on who came with the court and who competed with Brazilians for jobs and favors. Portuguese merchants in Brazil, for their part, were bitter over the passing of the Lisbon monopoly. Thus, the change in the status of Brazil sharpened the conflict between *mazombos* (Portuguese elites born in Brazil) and *reinóis* (elites born in Portugal and loyal to the Portuguese crown).

The event that precipitated the break with the mother country was the revolution of 1820 in Portugal. The Portuguese revolutionists framed a liberal constitution for the kingdom, but they were conservative or reactionary in relation to Brazil. They demanded the immediate return of Dom João to Lisbon, an end to the system of dual monarchy that he had devised, and the restoration of the Portuguese commercial monopoly. Timid and vacillating, Dom João did not know which way to turn. Under the pressure of his courtiers, who hungered to return to Portugal and their lost estates, he finally approved the new constitution and sailed for Portugal. He left behind him, however, his son and heir, Dom Pedro, as regent of Brazil, and in a private letter advised him, in the event the Brazilians should demand independence, to assume leadership of the movement and set the crown of Brazil on his head. Pedro received the same advice from José Bonifácio de Andrada, a Brazilian scientist whose stay in Portugal had completely disillusioned him about the Portuguese capacity for colonial reform.

Soon it became clear that the Portuguese Côrtes intended to set the clock back by abrogating all the liberties and concessions won by Brazil since 1808. One of its decrees insisted on the immediate return of Dom Pedro from Brazil to complete his political education. The pace of events moved more rapidly in 1822. On January 9, Dom Pedro, urged on by José Bonifácio de Andrada and other Brazilian advisers who perceived a golden opportunity to make an orderly transition to independence without the intervention of the masses, refused an order from the Côrtes to return to Portugal and issued his famous *fico* ("I remain"). On September 7, regarded by all Brazilians as Independence Day, he issued the even more celebrated Cry of Ipiranga: "Independence or Death!" In December 1822, having overcome slight resistance by Portuguese troops, Dom Pedro was formally proclaimed constitutional emperor of Brazil.

Mexico's Road to Independence

In New Spain, as in other colonies, the crisis of the Bourbon monarchy in 1808–1810 encouraged some creole leaders to strike a blow for self-rule or total independence under "the mask of Ferdinand." In Mexico, however, the movement for independence took an unexpected turn, revealing stark differences between those who struggled merely for home rule against Spain and those who fought to rule at home. Here the masses, instead of remaining aloof, joined the struggle and for a time managed to convert it from a private quarrel between two elites into an incipient social revolution.

In July 1808, news of Napoleon's capture of Charles IV and Ferdinand VII and his invasion of Spain reached Mexico City and provoked intense debates and maneuvers among Mexican elites to take advantage of these dramatic events. Faced with the prospect of an imminent collapse of Spain, creoles and peninsulars alike prepared to seize power and ensure that their group would control New Spain, whatever the outcome of the Spanish crisis. The creoles moved first. The Mexico City cabildo, a creole stronghold, called on the viceroy to summon an assembly of representatives from the creole-dominated cabildos. This assembly, composed of members of various elite groups, would govern Mexico until Ferdinand VII, whose forced abdication was null and void, regained his throne. The viceroy, José de Iturrigaray, supported such a call, noting that Spain was in "a state of anarchy."

The conservative landed elite who sponsored the movement for a colonial assembly desired free trade and autonomy or home rule within the Spanish empire, not independence. They had no intention of taking up arms in a struggle that might bring a dangerous intervention of the exploited classes and thus endanger their own personal and economic survival. The reforms that the chief creole ideologist, Fray Melchor de Talamantes, recommended to the proposed assembly suggested the limits of creole elite ambitions: abolition of the Inquisition and the ecclesiastical fuero (the clergy's privilege of exemption from civil courts); free trade; and measures to promote the reform of mining, agriculture, and industry.

The creole movement for home rule and free trade, however, posed a threat to the peninsular merchants, whose prosperity depended on the continuance of the existing closed commercial system with Seville as its center. On the night of September 15, 1808, the merchants struck back. The wealthy peninsular merchant Gabriel de Yermo led the consulado's militia in a preemptive coup, ousting Viceroy Iturrigaray and arresting leading creole supporters of autonomy. A series of transient, peninsular-dominated regimes then held power until a new viceroy, Francisco Javier de Venegas, arrived from Spain in September 1810.

The leaders of the creole aristocracy, mindful of its large property interests, did not respond to the peninsular counteroffensive. The leadership of the movement for creole control of Mexico's destiny now passed to a group consisting predominantly of "marginal elites"—upper-class individuals of relatively modest economic and social standing—in the Bajío, a geographic region roughly corresponding to the intendency of Querétaro.

The special economic and social conditions of this region help explain its decisive role in the first stage of the Mexican struggle for independence. It was the most modern of Mexican regions in its agrarian and industrial structure. Few indigenous communities were traditional; the bulk of its population consisted of partially Europeanized urban workers, miners, and peons or various types of tenants. Large, commercial, irrigated estates dominated agriculture and produced wheat or other products for the upper classes; meanwhile, impoverished tenants chiefly grew maize, the diet of the masses, on marginal lands. An important textile industry had experienced a shift from large obrajes using slaves and other coerced labor to a putting-out system. Here, merchant-financiers provided artisan families with cotton and wool, which they turned into cloth on their own looms, "forcing growing numbers of artisan families to exploit themselves by working long hours for little compensation." Mining was the most profitable and capital-intensive industry of the region; in some good years, the largest mine at Guanajuato, the Valenciana, netted its owners more than 1 million pesos in profits.

The quasi-capitalist structure of the Bajío's economy, based largely on free wage labor, promoted a growth of workers' class consciousness and militancy. The mineworkers at Guanajuato, for example, resisted attempts to end their partidos (shares of the ores they mined over a given quota) by methods that included a production slowdown; the employers responded by calling in the militia to force resumption of full production. The Bajío's labor force experienced a decline of wage and living standards and employment opportunities in the last decades of the eighteenth century. These losses were a result of conditions over which they had no control: rapid population growth that enabled landowners to drive down wages or replace permanent workers by seasonal laborers; competition for domestic textiles from cheap, industrially produced imports; and the rising cost of aging mines. These factors caused deep insecurity and resentment. Then in 1808 and 1809, drought and famine again struck the Bajío, further aggravating the existing tensions and grievances. As during the earlier drought and famine in 1785, the great landowners

profited from the misery of the poor by holding their reserves of grain off the market until prices reached their peak. It was against this background of profound social unrest and a grave subsistence crisis that the struggle for Mexican independence began. The Bajío was its storm center, and the Bajío's peasantry and working class formed its spearhead.

In 1810, a creole plot for revolt was taking shape in the important political and industrial center of Querétaro. Only two of the conspirators belonged to the highest circle of the creole regional elite, and efforts to draw other prominent creoles into the scheme failed. The majority were "marginal elites"—struggling landowners, a grocer, an estate administrator, a parish priest. From the first, the conspirators planned to mobilize the indigenous and mixed-race proletariat, probably because they doubted their ability to win over the majority of their own class. Although the motive of most plotters was the desire to raise troops, a genuine sympathy with the natives seemed to inspire Miguel Hidalgo y Costilla, a priest in the town of Dolores and one-time rector of the colegio of San Nicolás at Valladolid. The scholarly Hidalgo had already called the attention of Spanish authorities to himself by his freethinking ideas; he also had a reputation for his interest in science and his efforts to develop new industries in his parish.

Informed that Spanish officials had received word of their plot, the conspirators held an urgent council and decided to launch their revolt even though arrangements were incomplete. On Sunday, September 16, 1810, Hidalgo called on the people of his parish who had assembled for Mass to rise against their Spanish rulers. Here, as elsewhere in Spanish America, the "mask of Ferdinand" came into play; Hidalgo claimed to be leading an insurrection in support of a beloved king treacherously captured and deposed by godless Frenchmen. In less than two weeks, the insurgent leaders had assembled thousands of rebels and had begun a march on the industrial and mining center of Guanajuato. On the march, Hidalgo secured a banner bearing the image of the Virgin of Guadalupe and proclaimed her the patron of his movement, thus appealing to the religious devotion of his followers. All along the route, the established elites held back from joining the revolt. They watched with dismay as the rebels looted stores and seized the crops provided by the bountiful harvest of 1810, after two years of drought and famine. The rebels captured Guanajuato on September 28 with the aid of several thousand mineworkers, who joined in storming the massive municipal granary in which Spanish officials, militia, and local elites attempted to hold out. The killing of hundreds of Spaniards in the granary and the city soon followed. The massacre and sack of Guanajuato was a turning point in the rebellion, for it brought into the open the conflict between the basic objective of Hidalgo

José Clemente Orozco, one of Mexico's famous muralists, produced this defiant image of the Mexican liberator, Miguel Hidalgo, with flaming torch in hand, leading the Mexican crusade against political oppression and social injustice.

The Granger Collection

and his allies—creole domination of an autonomous or independent Mexico—and the thirst for revenge and social justice of their lower-class followers. Learning of the events at Guanajuato, the great majority of the creole elite recoiled in horror before the elemental violence of a movement that Hidalgo failed to control.

After his first victories, Hidalgo issued decrees that abolished slavery and tribute, the yearly head tax paid by indígenas and mulattos. Three months later, from his headquarters at Guadalajara, in his first and only reference to the land problem, he ordered the return of indigenous communal lands near the city, which Spaniards had rented; his wish was that "only the Indians in their respective pueblos should enjoy the use of those lands." Moderate though they were, these reforms gave the Mexican struggle a popular character that had been absent from the movement for independence in South America, but it further alienated many creoles who may have desired autonomy or independence, but not social revolution. On the other hand, these reforms did not go far enough to redress the fundamental grievances of Hidalgo's peasant and working-class followers in regions like the Bajío and Jalisco: landlessness, starvation wages, high rents, lack of tenant security, and the monopoly of grain by profiteering landowners. In the absence of a clearly defined program of structural social and economic reform, Hidalgo's followers vented their rage at an intolerable situation by killing Spaniards and plundering the properties of creoles and peninsulars alike.

Hidalgo proved unable to weld his rebel horde into a disciplined army or to capitalize on his early victories. Having defeated a royalist army near Mexico City, he camped outside the city for three days and then, after the Spanish forces rejected his demand for its surrender, inexplicably withdrew from the almost defenseless capital without attacking. Perhaps he feared a repetition of the atrocities that followed earlier victories, or perhaps he believed that he could not hold the great city without the support of the local population. Either way, according to historian Eric Van Young, the decision doomed Hidalgo's movement to defeat. However, the peasantry of the central highlands, who still possessed communal lands that satisfied their minimal needs and supplemented their meager crops by wage labor on large haciendas, also did not rally to Hidalgo's cause. With his army melting away through desertions, Hidalgo retreated toward the Bajío. Driven out of Guanajuato by royalist forces, Hidalgo and other rebel leaders fled northward, hoping to establish new bases for their movement in Coahuila and Texas. Less than one year after his revolt had begun, Hidalgo was captured as he fled toward the U.S. border, condemned as a heretic and subversive by an inquisitorial court, and executed by a firing squad.

The defeat and death of Hidalgo did not end the insurrection he had begun. The fires of revolt continued to smolder over vast areas of Mexico. New leaders arose who learned from the failure of Hidalgo's tactics. Many, abandoning the effort to defeat the royalist forces with their superior arms and training in conventional warfare, developed a flexible and mobile guerrilla style of fighting. The Spaniards themselves had effectively employed guerrilla warfare—a war of swift movement by small units that strike and flee—in their struggle against Napoleon, taking advantage of familiar terrain and the support of rural populations to foil pursuit and repression. The new Mexican rebel strategy was not to win a quick victory but to exhaust the enemy and undermine his social and economic base by pillaging the stores and haciendas of his elite allies, disrupting trade, and creating war weariness and hostility toward an increasingly arbitrary colonial regime.

Following Hidalgo's death, a mixed-race priest, José María Morelos, assumed supreme command of the revolutionary movement. Morelos had ministered to poor congregations in the hot, humid Pacific lowlands of Michoacán before offering his services to Hidalgo, who asked him to organize insurrection in that area. Economic and social conditions in the coastal lowlands region bore some resemblance to those of the Bajío; its principal industries, sugar, cotton, and indigo, were in decline as a result of competition from regions closer to highland markets and from imported cloth. As a result, the position of estate tenants and laborers had become increasingly dependent and insecure. The material conditions of indigenous villagers had also deteriorated because of the renting of community lands by village leaders to outsiders, a practice that left many families without the minimal land needed for subsistence.

The discontent generated by these conditions provided Morelos and his insurgent movement with a mass base in the coastal lowlands. Morelos was sensitive to the problems and needs of the area's rural folk. Like Hidalgo, he ordered an end to slavery and tribute. He also ended the rental of indigenous community lands and abolished the **cajas de comunidad** (community treasuries), whose funds were often misused by village notables or drained off by royal officials; henceforth, the villagers were to keep the proceeds of their labor. Morelos also extended Hidalgo's program of social reform by prohibiting all forced labor and forbidding the use of all racial terms except *gachupines*, applied to the hated peninsular Spaniards. There seems little doubt that in principle Morelos favored a radical land reform. In a "plan" found among his papers, he proposed the division of all haciendas greater than two leagues into smaller plots, denounced a situation in which "a single individual owns vast extents of uncultivated land and enslaves thousands of people who must work the land as *gañanes* [peons] or slaves," and proclaimed the social benefits of the small landholding. Nonetheless, Morelos's links with the creole landowning elite restrained his freedom of action. Some of his lieutenants were landowners whose property he had promised to respect.

A brilliant guerrilla leader who substituted strict discipline, training, and centralized direction for the loose methods of Hidalgo, Morelos, having established a firm base in the Pacific lowlands, advanced toward the strategic central highlands and the capital. His thrust into the rich sugar-producing area (modern Morelos) just south of Mexico City failed to gain sufficient support from the local indigenous communities, which retained substantial landholdings, and this forced him to retreat southward into the rugged mountainous region of Oaxaca. His military efforts also suffered because of differences with fractious civilian allies and a fateful decision to establish a representative government at a time when his military situation was turning precarious. In the fall of 1813, a congress he had convened at Chilpancingo declared Mexico's independence, enacted Morelos's social reforms, and vested him with supreme military and executive power. However, in the months that followed, the tide of war turned against the insurgent cause, in part because of Morelos' tactical mistakes that involved abandonment of fluid guerrilla warfare in favor of fixed-position warfare, illustrated by his prolonged siege of the fortress of Acapulco. In late 1813, Morelos suffered several defeats at the hands of royalist forces directed by the able and aggressive viceroy Felix Calleja.

The defeat of Napoleon and the return of the ferociously reactionary Ferdinand VII to the throne of Spain in 1814 released thousands of soldiers who redeployed overseas to suppress the Spanish American revolts. The congress of Chilpancingo, put to flight, became a wandering body whose squabbling and need for protection diverted Morelos's attention from the all-important military problem. Hoping to revitalize the rebel cause and gain creole elite support by offering an alternative to Ferdinand's brutal despotism, the congress met at Apatzingan and drafted a liberal constitution (October 1814) that provided for a republican frame of government and included an article that proclaimed the equality of citizens before the law and freedom of speech and the press. In the course of the year 1815, unrelenting royalist pressure forced the congress to flee from place to place. In November, fighting a rearguard action that enabled the congress to escape, Morelos was captured by a royalist force and brought to the capital. An Inquisition court found him guilty of heresy and treason, like Hidalgo, and later ordered his execution by a firing squad on December 22, 1815.

The great guerrilla leader had died, but the revolutionary movement, although fragmented, continued. Indeed, the struggle between numerous insurgent bands and the Spanish counterinsurgency reached new heights of virulence between 1815 and 1820. Avoiding the mistakes of Hidalgo and

even Morelos, the rebel leaders shunned pitched battles and made no effort to capture large population centers. Instead, they conducted a fluid warfare in which small units sacked and destroyed loyalist haciendas, disrupted or levied tolls on trade, severed communications, and controlled large stretches of the countryside. They fled when counterinsurgent forces pursued and reappeared when the overextended Spanish troops had departed. The destructive effects of a hopeless war on the economy, the heavy taxes imposed on all inhabitants by regional commanders and local juntas for the support of that war, and the harsh treatment meted out not only to insurgents but also to high-ranking creoles who favored compromise and autonomy alienated even the most loyal elements of the creole elite.

These elements, as well as many conservative Spaniards, sought a way out of the impasse that would avoid radical social change under a republican regime of the kind Morelos had proposed. A way out seemed to appear in 1820, when a liberal revolt in Spain forced Ferdinand VII to accept the constitution of 1812. Mexican deputies elected to the Spanish Cortes, or parliament, proposed a solution that would have retained ties with Spain but granted New Spain and the other American "kingdoms" autonomy within the empire. The Spanish majority in the Cortes rejected the proposal and sealed the doom of the empire.

The radical reforms that the Cortes adopted in 1820, including the abolition of the ecclesiastical and military fueros, antagonized conservative landlords, clergy, army officers, and merchants, whether creole or peninsular. Fearing the loss of privileges, they schemed to separate Mexico from the mother country and to establish independence under conservative auspices. Their instrument was the creole officer Agustín de Iturbide, who had waged implacable war against the insurgents. Iturbide offered peace and reconciliation to the principal rebel leader, Vicente Guerrero. His plan combined independence, monarchy, the supremacy of the Roman Catholic Church, and the civil equality of creoles and peninsulars. Guerrero was a sincere liberal and republican, Iturbide an unprincipled opportunist who dreamed of placing a crown on his own head. For the moment, however, Iturbide's program offered advantages to both sides, and Guerrero reluctantly accepted it. The united forces of Iturbide and Guerrero swiftly overcame scattered loyalist resistance. On September 28, 1821, Iturbide proclaimed Mexican independence, and eight months later, an elected congress summoned by Iturbide confirmed him as Agustín I, emperor of Mexico.

Despite its tinsel splendor, Iturbide's empire had no popular base. Within a few months, Agustín I had to abdicate, with a warning never to return. Hoping for a comeback, Iturbide returned from England in 1824 and landed on the coast with a small party. Troops of the new republican regime promptly captured and shot him.

The liberation of Mexico brought the struggle for Latin American independence to a successful conclusion, but the story of that struggle would not be complete without mention of the contribution made by Latin American women to its outcome. A courageous Mexican heroine, Doña Josefa Ortiz de Domínguez, wife of the creole corregidor of Querétaro, warned Miguel Hidalgo and other conspirators of their impending arrest by Spanish authorities and thereby saved the revolution from destruction before it had even begun. The lands freed under Simón Bolívar's leadership remember his bright and saucy mistress, Manuela Saenz, who left her prosy British husband to join the Liberator and saved him from death at the hands of assassins. "That she shared his thoughts, consoled him, and encouraged him to fight for his beliefs cannot be denied," writes Harold Bierck. "In many respects she was, as many called her, *La Libertadora.*"

In every part of Latin America, women, often drawn from the middle and lower classes, took part in the armed struggle. Bolívar praised the "Amazons" of Gran Colombia; among them was the heroic Policarpa Salvarrieta, who was only twenty-three when the Spaniards executed her for aiding the revolution. In Brazil, María Quiteira de Jesus, born on a small cattle- and cotton-raising ranch in the province of Bahia, disguised herself as a young man to join the revolutionary army. Her valor won her a decoration

AP Photo/Jose Caruci

The illegitimate daughter of a Spanish aristocrat, Manuela Saenz was expelled from a Catholic convent and later became a fierce proponent of political independence and women's rights. During the struggle for independence, she met and fell in love with Simón Bolívar, whose life she saved in 1828.

in 1823 from Dom Pedro, the first ruler of independent Brazil. In the struggle for the independence of Haiti, says Francesca Miller, women were "omnipresent," and some commanded troops.

In the aftermath of the struggle for independence, some women drew the logical consequences of their participation in that cause: If women fought and died for independence, why did they not have the right to vote and stand for office? This was the message of a petition submitted in 1824 to the government of the Mexican state of Zacatecas: "Women also wish to have the title of citizen … to see themselves counted in the census as 'la ciudadana H … la ciudadana N.'" But another century and a half would pass before all Latin American women realized that wish.

Latin American Independence: A Reckoning

After more than a decade of war, accompanied by immense loss of life and property, most of Latin America had won its political independence. The revolutions achieved a number of social changes. Independence brought the death of the Inquisition, the end of legal discrimination based on race, and the abolition of titles of nobility in most lands. It also gave an impetus to the abolition of slavery, to the founding of public schools, and to similar reforms. All these changes, however, were marginal; independence left intact the existing economic and social structures. This was natural, for the creole elite that headed the movement had no intention of transforming the existing order. They sought to replace the peninsulars in the seats of power and open their ports to the commerce of the world but desired no change of labor and land systems. Indeed, their interests as producers of raw materials and foodstuffs for sale in the markets of Europe and North America required the maintenance of the system of great estates worked by a semiservile native **proletariat**. No agrarian reform accompanied independence. The haciendas abandoned by or confiscated from loyalists usually fell into the hands of the creole aristocracy. Some land also passed into the possession of mestizo or mulatto officers, who often assimilated into the creole elite and as a rule promptly forgot the groups from which they had come.

Instead of broadening the base of landownership in Latin America, the revolutions actually helped narrow it. The liberal, individualist ideology of the revolutionary governments undermined indigenous communal land tenure in some cases by requiring the division of community lands among its members. This process facilitated creole landlords' usurpation of these communal lands and hastened the transformation of the native peasantry into a class of peons or serfs on Spanish haciendas (see Chapters 9–11). Because no structural economic change took place, aristocratic values continued to dominate Latin American society, despite an elaborate façade of republican constitutions and law codes.

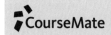

Go to the CourseMate website at **www.cengagebrain.com** for primary sources, additional study tools, and review materials—including audio and video clips—for this chapter.

PART TWO

1823	Rise of liberal republics in independent Spanish America
1829–1852	Establishment of Juan Manuel de Rosas's conservative rule in Argentina
1830	Creation of conservative rule in Chile under influence of Diego Portales
1835–1837	Revolution of Ragamuffins in Brazil and popular protests against aristocratic rule and slavery
1838	Destruction of liberal United Provinces of Central America and consolidation of conservative rule under Rafael Carrera
1839–1852	Spread of slave revolts throughout Venezuela, prompting legal abolition of slavery in 1854
1844	Spread of slave rebellions across Cuba, some led by enslaved Afro-Cuban women
1846–1848	U.S. invasion of Mexico, Treaty of Guadalupe Hidalgo, and surrender of half of Mexico's territory
1854–1862	War of the Reform, pitting Mexican Liberals led by Benito Juárez against the Conservatives
1860s	Expansion of abolitionist movement and agitation against the emperor in Brazil
1862–1868	French intervention and occupation of Mexico under Emperor Ferdinand Maximilian
1864	War of Triple Alliance and destruction of two decades of Paraguayan development initiated by Dr. José Gáspar de Francia
1868–1878	Ten Years' War, seeking abolition of slavery and political independence for Cuba and Puerto Rico
1870–1900	Expansion of foreign investment and rise of Liberal *caudillos* like Antonio Guzmán Blanco in Venezuela (1870–1899), Porfirio Díaz in Mexico (1876–1910), Rafael Núñez in Colombia (1879–1888), and Julio Roca in Argentina (1880–1904)
1871	Passage of Rio Branco law in Brazil, manumitting newborn slave children but requiring them to remain with their masters until age twenty-one
1880	Abolition of slavery in Cuba and establishment of *patronato*, an eight-year apprenticeship for liberated slaves
1889	Overthrow of Dom Pedro II and establishment of Brazilian Republic

186

Latin America in the Nineteenth Century

Coffee Plantation, 1935, by Candido Portinari

INDEPENDENCE LEFT MUCH of the colonial social structure intact. This fact was very apparent to liberal leaders of the Postindependence Era. "The war against Spain," declared the Colombian liberal Ramón Mercado in 1853, "was not a revolution.... Independence only scratched the surface of the social problem, without changing its essential nature." After winning their independence, the new Latin American states began a long, uphill struggle to achieve economic and political stability. They faced immense obstacles, for independence did not bring economic and social changes that could spur rapid progress—for example, no redistribution of land and income in favor of the lower classes took place. The large estate, which generally relied on primitive methods and slave or peon labor, continued to dominate economic life. Far from diminishing, the influence of the landed aristocracy actually increased because of the leading military role it had played in the wars of independence and the passing of Spanish authority. We should not, however, minimize the extent and importance of the changes that did take place. Independence may not have produced a major social upheaval, but it did produce a minor one. It opened wide fissures within the elite, dividing aristocratic supporters of the old social order from others who wanted a more democratic, bourgeois order. Their struggle is an integral aspect of the first half-century after the end of Spanish and Portuguese rule. Independence also enabled such formerly submerged groups as artisans and gauchos to enter the political arena, although in subordinate roles, and even allowed a few to climb into the ranks of the elite. The opening of Latin American ports to foreign goods also established a relatively free market in ideas, at least in the capitals and other cities. With almost no time lag, such new European doctrines as utopian socialism, romanticism, and positivism entered Latin America to propose solutions to the continent's problems. These new doctrinal winds, blowing through what had lately been dusty colonial corridors, contributed to the area's intellectual renovation and promoted further social change.

Verbally, at least, the new republican constitutions established the equality of all before the law, destroying the legal foundations of colonial caste society. Because little change in property relations took place, however, the racial, ethnic, and social class lines of division remained essentially the same. Wealth, power, and prestige continued to be concentrated in the hands of a ruling class that reproduced colonial racial structures and identified itself with whiteness; in some countries, such as Venezuela, however, it included individuals of darker skin who had managed to climb the social ladder through their prowess in war or politics.

Of all the groups composing the old society of castes, the status of indígenas changed least of all. Mexican historian Carlos María Bustamante was one of the few creole leaders who recognized that independence had not freed them from their yoke. "They still drag the same chains," he wrote, "although they are flattered with the name of freemen." Even native tribute and forced labor, abolished during or after the wars of independence, soon reappeared in many countries under other names. Still worse, indigenous communal landholding, social organization, and culture, which Spanish law and policy had to some extent protected in colonial times, came under increasing attack. Liberals especially believed that these communal traditions constituted as much of an obstacle to progress as the Spanish system of castes and special privileges did.

Until about 1870, however, large, compact indigenous populations continued to live under the traditional communal landholding system in Mexico, Central America, and the Andean region. Then, the rapid growth of the export economy, the coming of the railroads, and the resulting rise in land values and demand for labor caused "white" and mestizo landowners and landowner-dominated governments to launch a massive assault on native lands. The expropriation of these lands was accompanied by a growth of peonage and tenantry. Employers used a variety of devices, ranging from debt servitude to outright coercion, to attach laborers to their estates. In some areas, an indigenous serfdom arose that closely resembled the classic European model. In the Andean region, for example, Aymara tenants, in addition to working their masters' land, had to render personal service in their households, sometimes at the hacienda, sometimes in the city. Their masters also had the right to give or sell them to friends during the term of domestic service. This and other forms of serfdom survived well into the twentieth century.

The master class, aided by the clergy and local magistrates, sought to reinforce the economic subjugation of indigenous peoples with psychological domination. There evolved a pattern of relations and role-playing that assigned to the *patrones* the role of benevolent figures who assured their peons or tenants of a livelihood and protected them in all emergencies in return for their absolute obedience. In countries with large indigenous populations, the relations between masters and peons often included an elaborate ritual that required natives to request permission to speak to *patrones*, to appear before them with head uncovered and bowed, and to seek their approval for all major personal decisions, including marriage.

Nonetheless, not all indigenous peoples accepted these relationships and attitudes of submission and servility, which were more characteristic of resident peons. In the Andean area, Mexico, and elsewhere during the second half of the nineteenth century, the surviving native landowning communities fought stubbornly to prevent the absorption of their lands by advancing haciendas and to halt the process by which they became landless laborers. They fought with all the means at their disposal, including armed revolts as a last resort. Landowners and government officials called the revolts that occurred in Mexico in the 1860s and 1870s "communist" and sought to crush them with superior military force.

The greater freedom of movement that came with independence, the progressive disappearance of autonomous indigenous communities, and the growth of the hacienda, in which natives mingled with mestizos, strengthened a trend toward acculturation that had begun in the late colonial period. This acculturation reflected a growth of bilingualism: Indigenous peoples increasingly used

Spanish in dealing with criollos, reserving their native languages for use among themselves. To the limited extent that public schools entered their regions, they contributed to the adoption of Spanish as a second language or sometimes led to total abandonment of their native tongues. Mexican historian Eduardo Ruiz recalled that as a child he spoke only Tarascan but had forgotten it during his twelve years of study at the colegio: "I did not want to remember, I must confess, because I was ashamed of being thought to be an Indian." Some acculturation also occurred in dress, with frequent abandonment of regional fashions in favor of a quasi-European style, sometimes enforced by legislation and fines. Over much of Mexico, for example, the white trousers and shirt of coarse cotton cloth and the broad-brimmed hat became almost a native uniform.

Yet pressures toward indigenous acculturation or assimilation failed to achieve integration into criollo society that well-meaning Liberals had hoped to secure through education and employment in the modern world of industry and trade. At the end of the nineteenth century, the processes of acculturation had not significantly reduced the size of the indigenous sector in the five countries with the largest native populations: Mexico, Guatemala, Ecuador, Peru, and Bolivia. The various reasons for this included the economic stagnation and political troubles of the early postindependence decades, which tended to reinforce the isolation and cultural separateness of their communities. When the Latin American economies revived because of the expansion of the export sector, indigenous peoples suffered most because this revival served mainly to accentuate their poverty and backwardness. Their economic marginality; their almost total exclusion from the political process; the intense exploitation to which white and mestizo landowners, priests, and officials subjected them; and the barriers of distrust and hatred that separated them from the white world prevented any thorough-going acculturation, much less integration.

Indigenous communities made such concessions to the pressures for assimilation as were necessary but preserved their traditional housing, diet, social organization, and religion, which combined indigenous and Christian features. In some regions, the pre-Conquest cults and rituals, including occasional human sacrifice, survived. The existence in a number of countries of large native populations, intensely exploited and branded as inferior by the ruling social Darwinist ideology, constituted a major obstacle to the formation of a national consciousness in those lands. With good reason, pioneer Mexican anthropologist Manuel Gamio wrote in 1916 that Mexico, rather than a unified nation in the European sense, was really a collection of numerous small nations, differing in speech, economy, social organization, and psychology.

The wars for independence, by throwing "careers open to talent," enabled a few natives and a larger number of mestizos of humble origins to rise high on the military, political, and social scales. The liberal caudillos, Vicente Guerrero and Juan Alvarez in Mexico, and such talented leaders as Juan José Flores of Ecuador, Andrés Santa Cruz of Bolivia, and Ramón Castilla of Peru illustrate the ascent of mixed-race people.

The rise of these mestizo or mulatto leaders inspired fears in some members of the creole elite, beginning with Bolívar, who gloomily predicted a race war that would also be a struggle between haves and have-nots. Bolívar revealed his obsessive race prejudice in his description of the valiant and generous Mexican patriot Vicente Guerrero as the "vile abortion of a savage Indian and a fierce African." These fears proved groundless; although some mixed-race leaders, like Guerrero and Alvarez, remained to one degree or another loyal to the humble masses from which they had sprung, the majority soon declared their allegiance to the creole aristocracy and firmly defended its interests.

Conversely, creole politicians of the Postcolonial Era had to take account of the new political weight of the mixed-race middle and lower classes, especially the artisan groups. Despite promises to satisfy the aspirations of the masses, white elites exploited them politically and failed to fulfill their pledges. This happened in Bogotá, where Colombian liberals courted the artisans in their struggle against Conservatives, and in Buenos Aires, where Juan Manuel Rosas demagogically identified himself with provincial mixed-race gauchos and urban artisans against the aristocratic liberal *unitarios*, who favored a centralized national government that monopolized customs revenues collected in the port city.

After mid-century, the growing influence of European racist ideologies, especially Spencerian biological determinism, led to a heightened sensitivity to color. From Mexico to Chile, members of the so-called white elite and even the middle class claimed to be superior to natives and mestizos. Dark skin increasingly became an obstacle to social advancement. Typical of the rampant pseudoscientific racism by the turn of the century was the remark of the Argentine Carlos Bunge, son of a German immigrant, that mestizos and mulattos were "impure, atavistically anti-Christian; they are like the two heads of a fabulous hydra that surrounds, constricts, and strangles with its giant spiral a beautiful, pale virgin, Spanish America."

As a rule, neither Liberals nor Conservatives were free from the pervasive racism of the time. Carried away by his enthusiasm for what he called "civilization," the Argentine liberal Domingo Sarmiento identified it with the European bourgeois order and white supremacy. "It may appear unjust to exterminate savages, destroy nascent civilizations, and conquer peoples who occupy land that is rightly theirs, but thanks to this injustice," he proclaimed, "America, instead of being abandoned to savages who are incapable of progress, is today occupied by the Caucasian race, the most perfect, intelligent, beautiful, and progressive of all the races that inhabit the earth." A handful of Latin American intellectuals dissented from such a view. One was the Chilean Francisco Bilbao, who condemned "the great hypocrisy of covering up every crime and outrage with the word *civilization*" and pointedly referred to Sarmiento's war against native peoples and gauchos. Another was the Cuban José Martí, who denounced "the pretext that 'civilization,' the name commonly given to the present state of Europe, has the natural right to seize the land of 'barbarians,' the name that those who hunger for other people's land give to everyone who is not European or of European descent."

Even before the wars of independence, black slavery had declined in various parts of Latin America. This occurred in part because of economic developments that made slavery unprofitable and favored manumission or commutation of slavery to tenantry. An even more significant reason, perhaps, was the frequent flight of slaves to remote jungles and mountains, where they formed self-governing communities. For example, in 1800, officials estimated that Venezuela held some eighty-seven thousand slaves, but some twenty-four thousand had escaped to freedom in the inaccessible hinterland. Of course, arguably the most powerful force shaping the movement to abolish slavery was enslaved Africans and their descendants who, following the lead of Toussaint L'Ouverture and his comrades in Haiti, took up arms to secure their collective freedom from Latin American slavery.

The wars of independence gave a major stimulus to emancipation. Patriot commanders like Bolívar and San Martín and royalist officers frequently offered slaves freedom in return for military service, and black slaves sometimes formed a majority of the fighting forces on both sides. About a third of San Martín's army in the campaign of the Andes was black. Moreover, the confusion and disorder produced by the fighting often led to a collapse of plantation discipline, easing the flight of slaves and making their recovery difficult if not impossible.

After independence, slavery further declined, partly because of its patent incompatibility with the libertarian ideals proclaimed by the new states, but the hostile attitude of Great Britain, which had abolished the slave trade in all its possessions in 1807, also brought pressure for similar action by all countries still trading in slaves. British pressure on Brazil further contributed to the crisis of Brazilian slavery and its ultimate demise.

Emancipation came most easily and quickly in countries where slaves were a negligible element in the labor force; thus, Chile, Mexico, and the Federation of Central America (1823–1839) abolished slavery between 1823 and 1829. In other countries, the slave owners fought a tenacious rear-guard action. For example, Venezuela adopted a gradual manumission law in 1821 but did not finally abolish slavery until 1854. Ramón Castilla abolished slavery in Peru in 1855. After a long and violent struggle to subdue rebellious slaves, the Spanish Cortes finally decreed the end of slavery in Puerto Rico in 1873 and in Cuba in 1880, but the Cuban institution continued in a disguised form (the ***patronato***, a period of apprenticeship) until 1886, when it finally ended.

The record of Latin American slavery in the nineteenth century does not support the thesis of some historians that cultural and religious factors made Hispanic slavery inherently milder than the North American variety. In its two main centers of Cuba and Brazil, under conditions of mounting demand for Brazilian coffee and Cuban sugar and a critical labor shortage, ample evidence exists of systematic brutality with the use of the lash to make the enslaved work longer and harder. The enslaved responded with a resistance that varied from slow-downs to flight to open rebellion—a resistance that contributed to the final demise of the institution.

Patriarchal family organization, highly ceremonial conduct, and leisurely life-style continued to characterize the landed aristocracy and Latin American elites after independence. The kinship network extended beyond the large patriarchal family because of ***compadrazgo*** (the Spanish cultural institution that established a relationship of patronage and protection on the part of an upper-class godparent toward a lower-status godchild and his or her parents). The lower-class family members in turn formed part of the godparent's following and devoted themselves to the godparent's interests.

As in colonial times, great landowners generally resided most of the time in the cities, leaving their estates in the charge of administrators (who often scrutinized account books and were equally concerned with considerations of profit and loss). From the same upper class came a small minority of would-be entrepreneurs who challenged the traditional agrarian bias of their society. In the words of historian Richard Graham, they were "caught up by the idea of capitalism, by the belief in industrialization, and by a faith in work and practicality." Typical of this group was the Brazilian Viscount Mauá, who created a banking and industrial empire between 1850 and 1875 against the opposition of traditionalists. Mauá's empire collapsed, however, partly because the objective conditions for capitalist development in Brazil had not fully matured and partly because of official apathy and even disfavor. The day of the entrepreneur had not yet come; the economic history of Latin America in the nineteenth century is strewn with the wrecks of abortive industrial projects. These fiascos also represented defeats for the capitalist mentality and values.

After mid-century, with the gradual rise of a neocolonial order based on the integration of the Latin American economy into the international capitalist system, the ruling class, although retaining certain precapitalist traits, became more receptive to bourgeois values and ideals. An Argentine writer of the 1880s noted that "the latifundist no longer has that semibarbarous, semifeudal air; he has become a scientific administrator, who alternates between his home on the estate, his Buenos Aires mansion, and his house in Paris." In fact, few *estancieros* or hacendados became "scientific administrators." They preferred to leave the task of managing their estates to others, but the writer accurately identified this gradual Europeanization of elites under way throughout the continent.

The process began right after independence but greatly accelerated after mid-century. Within a decade after independence, marked changes in manners and consumption patterns had occurred. "Fashions alter," wrote Fanny Calderón de la Barca, Scottish-born wife of the Spanish minister to Mexico, who described Mexican upper-class society in the age of Santa Anna in a series of sprightly letters. According to Calderón de la Barca, "The graceful mantilla gradually gives place to the ungraceful bonnet. The old painted coach, moving slowly like a caravan, with Guido's Aurora painted on its gaudy panels, is dismissed for the London-built carriage."

The old yielded much more slowly and grudgingly to the new in drowsy colonial cities like Quito, capital of Ecuador, but yield it did, at least in externals. The U.S. minister to Ecuador in the 1860s, Friedrich Hassaurek, who was harshly critical of Quitonian society and manners, noted that, "in spite of the difficulty of transportation, there are about one hundred and twenty pianos in Quito, very indifferently tuned." Another U.S. visitor to Quito in this period, Professor James Orton, observed that "the upper class follow *la mode de Paris*, gentlemen adding the classic cloak of Old Spain." He added sourly that "this modern toga fits an Ecuadorian admirably, preventing the arms from doing anything, and covers a multitude of sins, especially pride and poverty."

Under the republic, as in colonial times, dress was an important index of social status. Orton reported that "no gentleman will be seen walking in the streets of Quito under a poncho. Hence citizens are divided into men with ponchos and gentlemen with cloaks." Dress even served to distinguish followers of different political factions or parties. In Buenos Aires under Rosas, the artisans who formed part of the dictator's mass base were called *gente de chaqueta* (wearers of jackets), as opposed to the aristocratic Unitarian Liberals, who wore dress coats. In the gaucho army of Justo José de Urquiza, Rosas's conqueror, the only Argentine officer dressed as a European was Sarmiento, a strange sight in his frock coat and *kepi* (a French military cap) among the gauchos with their lances and ponchos. For Sarmiento, writes John Lynch, "it was a matter of principle, a protest against barbarism, against Rosas and the caudillos.... 'As long as we do not change the dress of the Argentine soldier,' said Sarmiento, 'we are bound to have caudillos.'"

By the close of the century, European styles of dress had triumphed in such great cities as Mexico City and Buenos Aires and among all except native peoples. Attitudes toward clothes continued to reflect aristocratic values, especially scorn for manual labor. In Buenos Aires, for example, at the turn of the century, a worker's blouse would bar the entrance of its wearer to a bank or the halls of Congress. As a result, according to James Scobie, "everyone sought to hide the link with manual labor," and even workingmen preferred to wear the traditional coat and tie.

After 1880, European immigrants swarmed into Argentina, Uruguay, and Brazil and, in lesser numbers, into such countries as Chile and Mexico. Combined with growing urbanization and continued expansion of the export sector, this helped accelerate the rate of social change. These developments helped

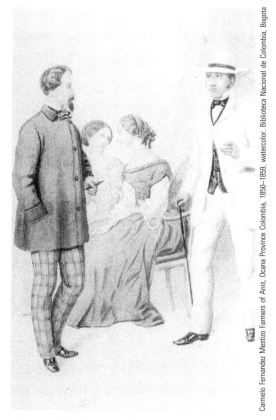

Carmelo Fernandez Mestizo Farmers of Anis, Ocana Province Colombia, 1850–1859, watercolor. Biblioteca Nacional de Colombia, Bogota

These fine sketches of Colombian mestizo farmers and upper-class figures effectively make the point that, in nineteenth-century Latin America, clothes still made the man.

create a small, modern industrial working class and swelled the ranks of blue-collar and middle-class white-collar workers.

However, aside from that minority of the working class that adopted socialist, anarchist, or syndicalist doctrines, the immigrants posed no threat to the existing social structure or the prevailing aristocratic ideology; instead, many surrendered to that ideology. The foreigners who entered the upper class as a rule already belonged to the educated or managerial class. Movement from the middle class of immigrant origin to the upper class was extremely difficult and rare, and for the lower-class immigrant it was almost impossible. A few immigrants made their fortunes by commerce or speculation. Their children or grandchildren took care to camouflage the origins of their wealth and to make it respectable by investing it in land. These nouveaux riches regarded natives and workers with the same contempt as their aristocratic associates.

Independence did not better the status of women. Indeed, their civil status probably worsened because of new bourgeois-style law codes that strengthened husbands' control over their wives' property. More than ever, men relegated women to the four walls of their houses and household duties. Church and parents taught women to be submissive and sweetly clinging, and to have no wills of their own. Typical of the patriarchal attitudes that prevailed with regard to relations between the sexes was the advice that Colombian Mariano Ospina Rodríguez gave in an 1864 letter to his daughter María on the eve of her marriage to José Mariano Roma y Batres. "Your happiness," he wrote, "depends … on the sincere and constant practice of these modest virtues: humility, patience, resignation, abnegation, and … the proper conduct of the domestic relations that depend on those same Christian virtues." Mariano Ospina went on to caution his daughter,

> One of your first cares must be to study your husband's inclinations, habits, and tastes, so that you never contradict them. Never seek to impose your will or make him give up his habits or tastes, no matter how insignificant they may seem; on the contrary, act in such a manner that he may continue them without disturbance…. Frequently you will find that you have different tastes and habits; never hesitate for a moment to sacrifice your own tastes and habits in favor of his.

The double standard of sexual conduct prevailed; women were taught to deny their sexuality and believe that procreation was the sole purpose of sexual intercourse. However, women's actual conduct did not necessarily conform to the law and ideology. Silvia Arróm has shown, for example, that these restrictions did not deter women in early nineteenth-century Mexico from engaging in extramarital affairs.

Few Latin American women of the elite class, however, strayed so far beyond the bounds of propriety as did Flora Tristán (1803–1844), pioneer feminist and socialist. Daughter of an aristocratic Peruvian landowner and a French mother, she spent most of her life in France, but Peruvian feminists and socialists regard her as one of their own. A woman of striking beauty, she separated early from her husband and became active in French feminist and socialist circles. In 1835, she published a novel, *Méphis*, which proposed the transformation of society on socialist and feminist principles, and in 1840, she published *Promenades in London*, a description of the monstrous contrasts between wealth and poverty in the English metropolis. In her last book, *The Workers' Union* (1844), she called on "the working men and women of the world" to unite, anticipating by four years Marx's appeal in *The Communist Manifesto*. Tristán clearly identified the gendered layers of exploitation. "The most oppressed male can oppress another human being who is his own wife," she wrote. "Woman is the proletariat of the proletariat." She also presaged theoretical formulations of twentieth-century feminists, arguing that "the liberation of women is the necessary condition for the liberation of men."

The democratic, liberal movements of the first half-century after independence stimulated some developments in favor of women. In Argentina, Sarmiento wrote that "the level of civilization of a people can be judged by the social position of its women"; his educational program envisaged a major role for women as primary-school teachers. In Mexico, the triumph of the Reforma led to promulgation of a new school law that called for the establishment of secondary schools for girls and normal schools for the training of women primary-school teachers. In both countries after 1870, small feminist movements, largely composed of schoolteachers, arose and formed societies, edited journals, and worked for the cultural, economic, and social improvement of women.

Even in a backward slave society like Brazil, a women's rights press was created, pioneered by Joana Paula Manso de Noronha, who stated in the introductory editorial to *O Jornal das Senhoras* (1852) her intention to work for "social betterment and the moral emancipation of women." In the last decades of the century, with the development of industry, women in increasing numbers entered factories and sweatshops, where they often were paid half of what male workers earned, becoming a source of superprofits for capitalist employers. By 1887, according to the census of Buenos Aires, 39 percent of the paid workforce of that city was composed of women.

The church, which in some countries had suffered discredit because of the royalist posture of many clergy during the wars of independence, experienced a further decline in influence because of increasing contacts with the outside world and a new and relatively tolerant climate of opinion. In country after country, Liberals pressed with varying success for restrictions on the church's monopoly over education, marriage, burials, and the like. Because the church invariably aligned itself with the conservative opposition, liberal victories brought reprisals in the form of heavy attacks on its accumulated wealth and privileges.

The colonial principle of monolithic religious unity dissolved because of the need to allow freedom of worship to the prestigious and powerful British merchants. In fact, the reactionary Rosas, who disliked foreigners and brought the Jesuits back to Argentina, himself donated the land on which the Anglicans built their first church in Buenos Aires. Despite the efforts of some fanatical clergy to incite the populace against foreign heretics, a system of peaceful coexistence between Catholics and dissenters gradually evolved, based on reciprocal goodwill and tact.

The Inquisition, whose excesses had made it odious even to the faithful, disappeared during the wars of independence. In many countries, however, the civil authorities assumed its right to censor or ban subversive or heretical writings. Occasionally, governments exercised this right. In the 1820s, clerical and conservative opposition forced the liberal vice president of Gran Colombia, Francisco de Paula Santander, to authorize the dropping of a textbook by the materialist Jeremy Bentham from law school courses. In Buenos Aires, Rosas publicly burned subversive books and other materials. According to Tulio Halperin-Donghi, however, a reading of the press advertisements of Buenos Aires booksellers suggests that this repression was singularly ineffective. In Santiago in the 1840s, the public hangman burned Francisco Bilbao's fiery polemic against Spain and Catholicism. According to Sarmiento, however, the violent, strident tone of Bilbao's book, not its content, caused this reaction; Bilbao, he added, had been justly punished for his clumsiness.

After mid-century, with the enthronement of positivism, which glorified science and rejected theology as an approach to truth, efforts to suppress heretical or anticlerical writings diminished or ended completely in many countries. In general, during the last half of the nineteenth century, there existed in Latin America a relatively free market in ideas—free, that is, as long as these ideas were couched in theoretical terms or referred primarily to other parts of the world and did not threaten an incumbent regime. Governments often were quick to suppress and confiscate newspapers and pamphlets whose contents they considered dangerous to their security, but they remained indifferent to the circulation of books containing the most audacious social theories. By way of example, the Díaz dictatorship in Mexico struck at opposition journalists and newspapers but permitted the free sale and distribution of the writings of Marx and anarchist theoretician Peter Kropotkin.

Because of the ascendancy of positivism, the church suffered a further decline in influence and power. Conservative victories over liberalism sometimes produced a strong proclerical reaction, typified by Gabriel García Moreno, who ruled Ecuador from 1860 to 1875 and carried his fanaticism to the point of dedicating the republic to the Sacred Heart of Jesus. Rafael Núñez, dictator of Colombia from 1880 to 1894, drafted a concordat with the Vatican that restored to the church most of the rights it had enjoyed in colonial times. Nonetheless, such victories failed to arrest the general decline of the church's social and intellectual influence among the literate classes. Anticlericalism became an integral part of the ideology of most Latin American intellectuals and a large proportion of other upper-class and middle-class males, including many who were faithful churchgoers and observed the outward forms and rituals of the church. However, church influence continued to be strong among women of all classes, indigenous peoples, and the submerged groups generally.

After independence, economic life initially stagnated, for the anticipated large-scale influx of foreign capital did not materialize and the European demand for Latin American staples remained far below expectations. Free trade brought increased commercial activity to the coasts, but it also caused the near destruction of some local craft industries that could not compete with cheap, factory-made European imports. The sluggish pace of economic activity and the relative absence of interregional trade and true national markets encouraged local self-sufficiency, isolation, political instability, and even chaos.

Because of these factors, the period from about 1820 to about 1870 was for many Latin American countries an age of violence, alternating dictatorship and revolution in a collective postcolonial struggle to construct distinctive national identities. Its symbol was the caudillo (strongman), whose power always depended on force, no matter what kind of constitution the country had. Usually the caudillo ruled with the aid of a coalition of lesser caudillos, each supreme in his region. Whatever their methods, the caudillos generally displayed some regard for republican ideology and institutions. Political parties, bearing such labels as "Conservative" and "Liberal," "Unitarian" and "Federalist," were active in most of the new states. Conservatism drew most of its support from the great landowners and their urban allies. Liberalism typically attracted provincial landowners, professional men, and other groups that had enjoyed little power in the past and were dissatisfied with the existing order. As a rule, Conservatives sought to retain many of the social arrangements of the Colonial Era and favored a highly centralized government. Liberals, often inspired by the example of the United States, usually advocated a federal form of government, guarantees of individual rights, lay control of education, and an end to special privileges for the clergy and military. Neither party displayed much interest in the problems of the native peasantry and other lower-class groups.

Beginning around 1870, the accelerating tempo of the Industrial Revolution in Europe stimulated more rapid change in the Latin American economy and politics. European capital flowed into the area and created the facilities needed to expand and modernize production and trade. The pace and degree of economic progress of the various countries were uneven and depended largely on their geographic position and natural resources.

Extreme one-sidedness was a feature of the new economic order. One or two products became the basis of each country's prosperity, making these commodities highly vulnerable to fluctuations in world demand and price. Meanwhile, other sectors of the economy remained stagnant or even declined through diversion of labor and land to other industries.

The late-nineteenth-century expansion had two other characteristics: In the main, it took place within the framework of the hacienda system of land tenure and labor, and it accompanied a steady growth of foreign control over the natural and human-made resources of the region. Thus, by 1900 a new structure of dependency, or colonialism, had arisen, called neocolonialism, with Great Britain and later the United States replacing Spain and Portugal as the dominant powers in the area.

The new economic order demanded peace and continuity in government, and after 1870 political conditions in Latin America grew more stable. Old party lines dissolved as Conservatives adopted the positivist dogma of science and progress, whereas Liberals abandoned their concern with constitutional methods and civil liberties in favor of an interest in material prosperity. A new type of liberal caudillo—Porfirio Díaz in Mexico, Rafael Núñez in Colombia, Antonio Guzmán Blanco in Venezuela—symbolized the politics of acquisition. The cycle of dictatorship and revolution continued in many lands, but the revolutions became less frequent and less devastating.

These major trends in the political and economic history of Latin America in the period extending from about 1820 to 1900 accompanied other changes in the Latin American way of life and culture. In Part Two, we present short histories of Argentina, Brazil, Chile, Cuba, Gran Colombia, Mexico, Peru, and the United Provinces of Central America in the nineteenth century. These histories all contain themes and problems common to Latin America in that period, but each displays variations that reflect its distinctive struggle to define the newly emerging postcolonial nation.

9

Decolonization and the Search for National Identities, 1821–1870

FOCUS QUESTIONS

- How did the wars of independence affect the landed aristocracy, the military, and foreign dependence?
- What were the economic and social roots of *caudillismo?*
- What were the principal differences between Liberals and Conservatives in early nineteenth-century Latin America?
- How did the liberal ideas of the Mexican Reforma change?
- How was Paraguay's early nineteenth-century development different from Argentina's?
- How did foreign interventions and class, racial, and ethnic conflicts shape the development of early nineteenth-century national identities in the United Provinces of Central America?

INDEPENDENCE DID NOT bring Latin America the ordered freedom and prosperity for which the liberators had hoped. In most of these newly emerging states, decades of civil strife followed the passing of Spanish and Portuguese colonial rule. Bolívar reflected the disillusionment of many patriot leaders when he wrote in 1829, "There is no good faith in America, nor among the nations of America. Treaties are scraps of paper; constitutions, printed matter; elections, battles; freedom, anarchy; and life, a torment." The contrast between Latin American stagnation and disorder and the meteoric advance of the former English colonies—the United States—intensified the pessimism and self-doubt of some Latin American leaders and intellectuals.

The Fruits of Independence

Frustration of the great hopes with which the struggle for liberation began was inevitable, for independence did not produce the economic and social changes that could shatter the colonial mold. Aside from the passing of the Spanish and Portuguese trade monopolies, the colonial economic and social structures remained intact. The hacienda, fazenda, or estancia, employing archaic techniques and a labor force of peons or slaves, continued to dominate agriculture; no significant class of small farmers arose to challenge the economic and political might of the great landowners. Indeed, the independence wars strengthened the power of the landed aristocracy by removing the agencies of Spanish rule—viceroys, audiencias, intendants—and by weakening among the landowners the ingrained habits of obedience to a central authority. In contrast, all other colonial elites—the merchant class, weakened by the expulsion or emigration of many loyalist merchants; the mine owners, ruined by wartime destruction or confiscation of their properties; and the church hierarchy, often in

1814–1840	Paraguayan dictator Dr. Francia establishes state-owned farms called *estancias de la patria* and promotes balanced agricultural and industrial development
1815–1817	José Artigas declares independence of Banda Oriental (Uruguay) and calls for redistribution of royalist lands to landless people
1818–1823	Bernardo O'Higgins establishes liberal rule in Chile
1821–1823	Rise and fall of Agustín Iturbide's conservative empire in Mexico
1821–1827	Rise and fall of Bernardino Rivadavia's liberal state in the United Provinces of La Plata (Argentina)
1823–1842	Emergence of the United Provinces of Central America under the liberal leadership of Francisco Morazán
1830–1837	Era of conservative rule under Diego Portales in Chile
1831–1852	Juan Manuel de Rosas establishes conservative rule in the United Provinces of La Plata
1834–1854	Antonio de Santa Anna inaugurates conservative rule in Mexico
1839–1847	Caste War of Yucatán combines resistance to conservative rule with demands for indigenous autonomy and defense of ancestral lands
1842–1865	Rafael Carrera defeats Morazán, dissolves United Provinces of Central America, and brings conservative rule to Guatemala
1846–1848	North American Invasion (Mexican War) ends with Treaty of Guadalupe Hidalgo that surrenders one-half of Mexican territories to United States
1854–1862	Juan Álvarez announces Plan de Ayutla, inaugurating War of the Reform, a decade of civil war and liberal rule
1862–1868	French intervention and restoration of Mexican empire under the rule of Maximilian and Carlota; establishment of Argentine Republic under leadership of liberal Bartolomé Mitre
1865–1870	War of the Triple Alliance destroys Paraguayan development
1868–1876	Expulsion of French occupation and creation of Mexico's Restored Republic under liberals Benito Juárez and Sebastián Lerdo de Tejada

disgrace for having sided with Spain—emerged from the conflict with diminished weight.

To their other sources of influence, members of the landed aristocracy added the prestige of a military elite crowned with the laurels of victory, for many revolutionary officers had arisen from its ranks. The militarization of the new states because of years of destructive warfare and postwar instability ensured a large political role for this officer group. Standing armies that often consumed more than half of the national budgets arose. Not content with the role of guardians of order and national security, military officers became the arbiter of political disputes, usually deciding in favor of the conservative landowning interests and their allies among the urban elites.

ECONOMIC STAGNATION

Independence leaders had expected that a vast expansion of foreign trade would follow the passing of Spanish commercial monopoly and aid economic recovery. In fact, some countries, favored by their natural resources or geographic position, soon recovered from the revolutionary crisis and scored modest to large economic advances; these included Brazil (coffee and sugar), Argentina (hides), and Chile (metals and hides). Others, such as Mexico, Bolivia, and Peru, whose mining economies had suffered shattering blows, failed to recover colonial levels of production.

Several factors accounted for the economic stagnation that plagued many of the new states in the first half of the nineteenth century. Independence did not usher in a redistribution of land and income that might have stimulated a growth of internal markets and productive forces. The anticipated large-scale influx of foreign capital also did not materialize—partly because political disorder discouraged foreign investment and partly because Europe and the United States, then financing their own industrial revolutions, had little capital to export. Exports of Latin American staples remained below expectations, for Europe still viewed Latin America primarily as an outlet for manufactured goods, especially English textiles. The resulting flood of cheap, factory-made European products damaged local craft industries and drained the new states of their stocks of gold and silver, creating a chronic balance-of-trade problem. The British conquest of the Latin American markets further weakened the local merchant class, which was unable to compete with its English rivals. By mid-century, the wealthiest and most prestigious merchant houses, from Mexico City to Buenos Aires and Valparaíso, bore English names. Iberian merchants, however, continued to dominate the urban and provincial retail trade in many areas.

Taken together, these developments retarded the development of native capitalism and capitalist relations and reinforced the dominant role of the hacienda in the economic and political life of the new states. Aggravated by the lack of roads and by natural obstacles to communication (such as jungles and mountains), the deepening stagnation in their respective interiors intensified tendencies toward regionalism. This also enhanced local rule by *caudillos* (powerful political bosses) great and small, who usually were large landowners.[1] The sluggish tempo of economic activity encouraged these caudillos to employ their private followings of peons and retainers as pawns in the game of politics and revolution on a national scale. Indeed, in some countries, politics and revolution became a form of economic activity that compensated for the lack of other opportunities. Having gained control of the all-important customhouse (which collected duties on imports and exports) and other official sources of revenue, the victors often rewarded themselves and their followers with government jobs, contracts, grants of public land, and other favors. This reliance by members of the elite on political and military activity as a career and on the customhouse as a source of government revenue had two negative results. One was the rise of bloated military and bureaucratic establishments that diverted resources from economic development, and the other was

a stress on foreign trade that intensified the trend toward dependency.

POLITICS: THE CONSERVATIVE AND LIBERAL PROGRAMS

The political systems of the new states made large formal concessions to the liberal ideology of the nineteenth century. With the exception of Brazil, all the new states adopted the republican form of government (Mexico had two brief intervals of imperial rule) and paid their respects to the formulas of parliamentary and representative government. Their constitutions provided for presidents, congresses, and courts; often they contained elaborate safeguards of individual rights.

These façades of modernity, however, poorly concealed the dictatorial or oligarchical reality behind them. Typically, the chief executive was a caudillo whose power rested on force, no matter what the constitutional form; usually, he ruled with the support of a coalition of lesser caudillos, each more or less supreme in his own domain. The supposed independence of the judicial and legislative branches was a fiction. As a rule, elections were exercises in futility. Because the party in power generally counted the votes, the opposition had no alternative but revolt.

Literacy and property qualifications disfranchised most natives and mixed-race peoples, and if they had the right to vote, the *patrón* (master) often herded them to the polls to vote for him or for his candidates. The lack of the secret ballot (voting was usually open, with colored ballots) made coercion of voters easy. Whether Liberal or Conservative, all sections of the ruling class agreed on keeping the peasantry, gauchos, and other "lower orders" on the margins of political life, on preventing their emergence as groups with collective philosophies and goals. The very privileges that the new creole constitutions and law codes granted indigenous

---

1. The term *caudillo* commonly applies to politico-military leaders who held power on the national and regional level in Latin America before more or less stable parliamentary government became the norm in the area beginning about 1870. Military ability and charisma were qualities often associated with caudillos, who, although assuming many guises, did not all possess the same traits.

peoples—equality before the law, the "right" to divide and dispose of their communal lands—weakened their solidarity and their ability to resist the creole world's competitive individualism. But especially gifted, ambitious, and fortunate members of these marginal groups were sometimes co-opted into the creole elite and provided some of its most distinguished leaders; two examples are the Zapotec Benito Juárez in Mexico and the mestizo president Andrés Santa Cruz in Bolivia.

At first glance, the political history of Latin America in the first half-century after independence, with its dreary alternation of dictatorship and revolt, seems pointless and trivial. Nonetheless, the political struggles of this period were more than disputes over spoils between sections of a small upper class. Genuine social and ideological cleavages helped produce those struggles and the bitterness with which they were fought. Such labels as "Conservative" and "Liberal," "Unitarian" and "Federalist," assigned by the various parties to themselves or each other, were more than masks in a pageant, although opportunism contributed to the ease with which some leaders assumed and discarded these labels.

Conservatism generally reflected the interests of the traditional holders of power and privilege, men who had a stake in maintaining the existing order. Hence, the great landowners, the upper clergy, the higher ranks of the military and the civil bureaucracy, and monopolistic merchant groups tended to be Conservatives. Liberalism, in contrast, appealed to those groups who in colonial times had little or no access to the main structures of economic and political power and were naturally eager to alter the existing order. Thus, liberalism drew much support from provincial landowners, lawyers and other professionals (the groups most receptive to new ideas), shopkeepers, and artisans; it also appealed to ambitious, aspiring indígenas and mixed-race people. Nonetheless, regional conflicts and clan or family loyalties often cut across the lines of social and occupational cleavage, complicating the political picture.

Liberals wanted to break up the hierarchical social structure inherited from the colonial period. They had a vision of their countries remade into dynamic middle-class states on the model of the United States or England. Inspired by the success of the United States, they usually favored a federal form of government, guarantees of individual rights, lay control of education, and an end to a special legal status for the clergy and military. In their modernizing zeal, Liberals sometimes called for the abolition of entails (which restricted the right to inherit property to a particular descendant or descendants of the owner), dissolution of convents, confiscation of church wealth, and abolition of slavery. The **federalism** of the Liberals had a special appeal for secondary regions of the new states, which were eager to develop their resources and free themselves from domination by capitals and wealthy primary regions.

Conservatives typically upheld a strong centralized government, the religious and education monopoly of the Roman Catholic Church, and the special privileges of the clergy and military. They distrusted such radical novelties as freedom of speech and the press and religious toleration. Conservatives, in short, sought to salvage as much of the colonial social order as was compatible with the new republican system. Indeed, some conservative leaders ultimately despaired of that system and dreamed of implanting monarchy in their countries.

Neither Conservatives nor Liberals displayed much interest in the problems of the indigenous, black, and mixed-race masses that formed the majority of the population in most Latin American countries. Liberals, impatient with the supposed backwardness of indigenous peoples, regarded their communalism as an impediment to the development of a capitalist spirit of enterprise and initiated legislation providing for the division of communal lands—a policy that favored land grabbing at the expense of indigenous villages. Despite their theoretical preference for small landholdings and a rural middle class, Liberals recoiled from any program of radical land reform. Conservatives correctly regarded the great estate as the very foundation of their power. As traditionalists, however, the Conservatives sometimes claimed to continue the Spanish paternalist policy toward indigenous communities and often enjoyed their support.

This summary of the conservative and liberal programs for Latin America in the first half-century after independence inevitably overlooks variations from the theoretical liberal and conservative norms, variations that reflected the specific conditions and problems of the different states. A brief examination of the history of Mexico, Argentina, Chile, and the United Provinces of Central America reveals not only certain common themes but also a rich diversity of political experience.

Mexico

The struggle for Mexican independence, ironically begun by the radical priests Hidalgo and Morelos, ended with Agustín de Iturbide, who headed a coalition of creole and peninsular Conservatives. These men were terrified at the prospect of an imperial government that sought in 1820 to reestablish the liberal Spanish constitution of 1812. Independence, achieved under such conservative auspices, meant that Mexico's economic and social patterns underwent little change. To be sure, the popular insurgency begun by Hidalgo had at least a short-term impact on the social, economic, and political patterns of Mexican development. John Tutino, for example, has shown that in the Bajío the insurgency destroyed commercial hacienda production, which generated profit by storing maize until prices peaked with scarcity. It also forced a shift to tenant ranchero production, which maximized maize production, bringing "real and enduring benefits to both rural producers and urban consumers of maize across the Bajío during the first half-century of national life." Similarly, Florencia Mallon and Peter Guardino stress the revolutionary participation of popular urban and rural groups in Mexican nineteenth-century political struggles, revealing their long-term impact on Mexican state formation and peasant consciousness.

Nonetheless, the great hacienda continued to dominate the countryside in many areas. Although indigenous villages managed to retain substantial community lands until after mid-century and even improved their economic and political position somewhat with the passing of Spanish centralized authority, the trend toward usurpation of indigenous lands grew stronger because of the lapse of Spanish protective legislation. Peons and tenants on the haciendas often suffered from debt servitude, miserable wages, oppressive rents, and excessive religious fees. At the constitutional convention of 1856–1857, the liberal Ponciano Arriaga declared:

> With some honorable exceptions, the rich landowners of Mexico … resemble the feudal lords of the Middle Ages. On his seigneurial lands, with more or less formalities, the landowner makes and executes laws, administers justice and exercises civil power, imposes taxes and fines, has his own jails and irons, metes out punishments and tortures, monopolizes commerce, and forbids the conduct without his permission of any business but that of the estate.

An anonymous contemporary writer similarly reflected the disillusion of the lower classes with the fruits of independence: "Independence is only a name. Previously they ruled us from Spain, now from here. It is always the same priest on a different mule. But as for work, food, and clothing, there is no difference."

THE MEXICAN ECONOMY

The ravages of war had left mineshafts flooded, haciendas deserted, and the economy stagnant. The end of the Spanish commercial monopoly, however, brought a large increase in the volume of foreign trade; the number of ships entering Mexican ports jumped from 148 in 1823 to 639 in 1826. However, exports did not keep pace with imports, leaving a trade deficit that had to be covered by exporting precious metals. The drain of gold and silver aggravated the problems of the new government, which had inherited a bankrupt treasury and had to support a swollen bureaucracy and an officer class ready to revolt against any government that suggested a cut in their numbers or pay. The exodus of Spanish merchants and their capital added to the economic problems of the new state. Complicating those problems was the disorder that was a legacy of the war; according to Fanny Calderón de la Barca, bands of robbers made travel on the roads so unsafe that "whether coming or going from Puebla or Veracruz, the Mexico City traveler expected to be robbed."

Foreign loans appeared to be the only way out of the crisis. In 1824–1825, English bankers loaned Mexico 32 million pesos, guaranteed by Mexican customs revenues. Of this amount, the Mexicans received only a little more than 11 million pesos, as the bankers went bankrupt before they paid all the money due to Mexico from the loan. By 1843, unpaid interest and principal had raised the nation's foreign debt to more than 54 million pesos. This growing foreign debt created crushing interest burdens, threatened Mexico's independence, and endangered its territorial integrity, for behind foreign capitalists stood governments ready to intervene militarily in case of default.

Foreign investments, however, mainly from Britain, made possible a partial recovery of the decisive mining sector. Old mines, abandoned and flooded during the wars, reopened, but the available capital proved inadequate, the technical problems of reconstruction were greater than anticipated, and production remained relatively low.

An ambitious effort to revive and modernize Mexican industry also got under way, spurred on by the founding in 1830 of the *Banco de Avío*, which provided government assistance to industry. Manufacturing, paced by textiles, made some limited progress in the three decades after independence. Leading industrial centers included Mexico City, Puebla, Guadalajara, Durango, and Veracruz. But shortages of capital, lack of a consistent policy of protection for domestic industry, and a socioeconomic structure that sharply limited the internal market hampered the growth of Mexican factory capitalism. By 1843, the Banco de Avío had to close its doors for lack of funds. The Mexican economy, therefore, continued to rely heavily on mining and agriculture. Mexico's principal exports were precious metals, especially silver, and such agricultural products as tobacco, coffee, vanilla, cochineal, and henequen (a plant fiber used in rope and twine). Imports consisted primarily of manufactured goods that Mexican industry could not supply.

POLITICS: LIBERALS VERSUS CONSERVATIVES

A Liberal–Conservative cleavage dominated Mexican political life in the half-century after independence. That conflict was latent from the moment that the "liberator" Iturbide, the former scourge of insurgents, rode into Mexico City on September 27, 1821, flanked on either side by two insurgent generals, Vicente Guerrero and Guadalupe Victoria, firm republicans and Liberals. The fall of Iturbide in 1823 cleared the way for the establishment of a republic. But it soon became apparent that the republicans were divided into Liberals and Conservatives, Federalists and Centralists.

The constitution of 1824 represented a compromise between liberal and conservative interests. It appeased regional economic interests, which were fearful of a too-powerful central government, by creating nineteen states that possessed taxing power; their legislatures, each casting one vote, chose the president and vice president for four-year terms. The national legislature was bicameral, with an upper house (Senate) and a lower house (Chamber of Deputies). By ensuring the creation of local civil bureaucracies, the federalist structure also satisfied the demand of the provincial middle classes for greater access to political activity and office. However, the constitution also had a conservative tinge: Although the church lost its monopoly on education, it declared Catholicism the official religion and specifically confirmed the fueros of the church and the army.

A hero of the war of independence, the liberal general Guadalupe Victoria won the first presidential election under the new constitution. Anxious to preserve unity, Victoria brought the conservative Lucas Alamán into his cabinet, but this era of good feeling was short-lived; by 1825, Liberals forced Alamán out of the government. The Liberal–Conservative cleavage now assumed the form of a rivalry that reflected the Anglo-American competition for economic and political influence in Mexico. Founded by the American minister Joel Roberts Poinsett, the York Rite Masonic lodge favored Liberals and Federalists, who regarded the United States as a model for their own reform

Latin America, 1830

program. Its rival, the Scottish Rite lodge, sponsored by the British chargé d'affaires Henry Ward, appealed to the Conservative Party, which represented the old landed and mining aristocracy, the clerical and military hierarchy, monopolistic merchants, and some manufacturers. Its intellectual spokesman and organizer was Lucas Alamán, statesman, champion of industry, and author of a brilliant history of Mexico from the Conservative point of view.

The Liberal Party represented a creole and mestizo middle class—provincial landowners, professional men, artisans, the lower ranks of the clergy and military—determined to end special privileges and the concentration of political and economic power in the upper class. A priest-economist, José María Luís Mora, presented the liberal position with great force and lucidity. However, the Liberal Party was divided: The *moderados* (the moderate wing) wanted to proceed slowly and sometimes joined the Conservatives, whereas the *puros* (literally, the people) advocated sweeping antifeudal, anticlerical reforms.

During the first decade after independence, none of these factions consolidated its control over the nation, but the year 1833 was a high-water mark of liberal achievement. Aided by Mora, his minister of education, the puro President Valentín Gómez Farías pushed through Congress a series of radical reforms. These included abolition of the special privileges and immunities of the army and church (meaning that officers and priests would now be subject to the jurisdiction of civil courts), abolition of tithes, secularization of the clerical University of Mexico, creation of a department of public instruction, reduction of the army, and creation of a civilian militia. These measures accompanied a program of internal improvements designed to increase the prosperity of the interior by linking it to the capital and the coasts. In their use of the central government to promote education and national economic development, the Liberals showed that they were not doctrinaire adherents of **laissez-faire**.

This liberal program inevitably provoked clerical and conservative resistance. Army officers began to organize revolts; priests proclaimed from their pulpits that the great cholera epidemic of 1833 was a sign of divine displeasure with the works of the impious Liberals. Meanwhile, Gen. Antonio López de Santa Anna, a classic caudillo who earlier had supported liberal movements, now placed himself at the head of the conservative rebellion, occupied the capital, and sent Gómez Farías and Mora into exile. Assuming the presidency, he summoned a hand-picked, reactionary congress that repealed the reform laws of 1833 and suspended the constitution of 1824. The new conservative constitution of 1836 reduced the states to departments completely dominated by the central government, ensured upper-class control of politics through high property and income qualifications for holding office, and restored the fueros of the church and army.

Santa Anna and the Conservatives ruled Mexico for the greater part of two decades, 1834 to 1854. Politically and economically, the conservative rule subordinated the interests of the regions and the country as a whole to a wealthy, densely populated central core linking Mexico City, Puebla, and Veracruz. The Tariff Act of 1837 reflected its centralist trend. It restored the alcabala, or sales tax system, inland customhouses, and the government tobacco monopoly, ensuring the continuous flow of revenues to Mexico City.

Thereafter, conservative neglect and abuse of outlying or border areas like northern Mexico and Yucatán contributed to the loss of Texas in 1836 and almost led to the loss of Yucatán. Santa Anna's destruction of provincial autonomy enabled American colonists in Texas, led by Sam Houston, to pose as patriotic Federalists in a revolt against Santa Anna's tyranny. In Yucatán, the Caste or Social War of 1839 combined elements of a regional war against conservative centralism and an indigenous war against feudal landlords. For almost a decade, Yucatán remained outside Mexico.

After the United States annexed Texas in 1845, the North American Invasion or Mexican War (1846–1848) marked another conservative disaster. Its immediate cause was a dispute between Mexico and the United States over the boundary of Texas, but the decisive factor was the Polk administration's determination to acquire California and New Mexico. The war ended in catastrophic Mexican defeat, largely because Conservatives, dreading the mobilization of peasant armies in a prolonged guerrilla war against the U.S. invasion, concluded a hasty surrender. "The Mexican government," says Mexican historian Leticia Reina, "preferred coming to terms with the United States rather than endanger the interests of the ruling class." By the treaty of Guadalupe Hidalgo (1848), Mexico gave up half the country, ceding Texas, California, and New Mexico to the United States; in return, Mexico received $15 million and the cancellation of certain claims against it.

Naturally, puro leaders, including Benito Juárez, Melchor Ocampo, and Ponciano Arriaga, urged continued resistance. "Give the people arms," said Ocampo, "and they will defend themselves." In some regions of the country, peasant revolts broke out that combined demands for division of large haciendas among the peasantry and other reforms with calls for a continued resistance to the invaders. Congressional opposition mobilized against ratification of the treaty and urged continuing the war. In his "Observations on the Treaty of Guadalupe Hidalgo," the liberal Manuel Rejón predicted that the treaty would mean the inevitable economic conquest of Mexico by the United States. He foresaw that the new boundary, bringing American commerce closer to the Mexican heartland, would lead to the Americanization of Mexico; he argued that "we will never be able to compete in our own markets with the American imports.... The treaty is our sentence of death." Finally, in view of the intense American racism, he questioned whether the new U.S. government in the ceded territories would protect Mexican citizens in their civil and property rights as the treaty promised.

Rejón's fears concerning the treatment of Mexican citizens in the newly annexed territories were soon justified. The gold rush in California caused a wave of attacks by Anglo-American miners against native Californians. In his reminiscences, Antonio Coronel, from Los Angeles, described "stabbings, extortions, and lynchings as commonplace American reactions to native Californios, whom they regarded as interlopers." Even worse was the fate of indigenous Californians, whom the constitution of 1824 considered full Mexican citizens. Denied the protection specified in the treaty of Guadalupe Hidalgo, they "became the victims of murder, slavery, land theft, and starvation." In two decades, the indigenous population of the state declined by more than one hundred thousand. "Genocide," writes Richard Griswold del Castillo, "is not too strong a word to use in describing what happened to the California Indians during that period." In New Mexico, which became a territory rather than a state, Hispanic inhabitants did not gain citizenship status until New Mexico achieved statehood in 1912, and it continued to deny its native peoples the vote until 1953.

A major grievance of many Mexican Americans was (and remains) violation of their land rights, the protection of which the treaty of Guadalupe Hidalgo promised. Claiming that the great majority of Mexican land grants in the ceded territory were "imperfect," American courts ruled that the U.S. government had inherited the right to complete the process of land confirmation. In California and New Mexico, this process, creating for Mexican American landowners an immense expense of litigation and legal fees, aggravated by usurious interest rates and falling cattle prices, resulted in the loss of their land by most rancheros. Even the few who survived the confirmation process came under great pressure from squatters, mostly wealthy and influential Anglo-Americans, to surrender their land. In New Mexico, writes historian Richard Griswold del Castillo, a fraternity of predatory lawyers and politicians, the so-called Santa Fe Ring, "used the long legal battles over land grants to acquire empires extending over millions of acres." Here, the struggle of Mexican Americans to regain the lost lands of their ancestors, on the basis of the claim that the United States violated the articles of the treaty of Guadalupe Hidalgo that guaranteed the citizenship and property rights of Mexicans, continues into the twenty-first century.

LA REFORMA, CIVIL WAR, AND THE FRENCH INTERVENTION

The disasters suffered by Mexico under conservative rule had created widespread revulsion against conservative policies and stimulated a revival of puro liberalism. In 1846, during the war, liberal administrations came to power in the states of Oaxaca and Michoacán. In Michoacán the new governor was Melchor Ocampo, a scholar and scientist whom Rousseau and French utopian socialist thought profoundly influenced. In Oaxaca, Benito Juárez, a Zapotec lawyer, became governor and earned a reputation for honesty, efficiency, and democratic simplicity.

Ocampo and Juárez were two leaders of a renovated liberalism that ushered in the movement called *La Reforma*. Like the older liberalism of the 1830s, the Reforma sought to destroy feudal vestiges and implant capitalism in Mexico. Its ideology, however, was more spirited than the aristocratic, intellectual liberalism of Mora. Puros like Ponciano Arriaga and Ignacio Ramírez transcended liberal ideology with their attacks on the latifundio, the defense of labor and women's rights, and other advanced ideas. Meanwhile, Santa Anna returned to power in 1853 and, accompanied by a terrorist campaign against all dissenters, proclaimed himself "His Most Supreme Highness." This spurred a gathering of opposition forces, including many disgruntled moderados and Conservatives. In early 1854, the old liberal caudillo, Juan Alvarez, and the moderado general Ignacio Comonfort issued a call for revolt: the Plan of Ayutla, which demanded the end of the dictatorship and the election of a convention to draft a new constitution. Within a year, Santa Anna, seeing the handwriting on the wall, went into exile for the last time, and a puro-dominated provisional government took office. Alvarez became provisional president and named Benito Juárez as minister of justice and Miguel Lerdo de Tejada as treasury minister.

One of Juárez's first official acts was to issue a decree, the *Ley Juárez*, proclaiming the state's right to limit clerical and military fueros to matters of internal discipline. The *Ley Lerdo* (Lerdo Law) of 1856, drafted by Lerdo de Tejada, also struck a heavy blow at the material base of the church's power: its landed wealth. The law barred the church from holding land not used for religious purposes and compelled the sale of all such property

to tenants. It also auctioned unrented real estate to the highest bidder, with payment of a large sales tax to the government.

The law aimed to create a rural middle class, but because it made no provision for division of the church estates, the bulk of the land passed into the hands of great landowners, merchants, and capitalists, both Mexican and foreign. Worse, the law barred indigenous villages from owning land and ordered the sale of such land in the same manner as church property, excepting only land and buildings designed exclusively for the public use of the inhabitants and for *ejidos* (communal pastures). As a result, land-grabbers descended on the native villages, "denounced" their land to the local courts, and proceeded to buy it at auction for paltry sums. The law provided that the native owners should have the first opportunity to buy property, but few could pay the minimum purchase price. When they responded with protests and revolts, Lerdo explained in a circular that the intent of his law was to ensure that community lands should be divided among the natives, not sold to others. But he insisted that "the continued existence of the Indian communities ought not to be tolerated …, and this is exactly one of the goals of the law."

Lerdo was also adamant that those who rented indigenous lands had the right to buy them if they chose to do so. Consequently, during the summer and fall of 1856, many *pueblos* (towns) lost crop and pasturelands from which they had derived revenues vitally needed to defray the cost of their religious ceremonies and other communal expenses. Indigenous resistance and the Liberals' need to attract popular support in their struggle with the conservative counterrevolution and French interventionists in the decade 1857–1867 slowed enforcement of the Lerdo Law as it applied to native villages. However, the long-range tendency of liberal agrarian policy compelled division of communal lands, facilitating their acquisition by hacendados and even small and mid-size farmers. This strengthened the latifundio and increased the size of the rural middle class.

Meanwhile, a constitutional convention dominated by moderate Liberals drafted the constitution of 1857, which proclaimed freedom of speech, press, and assembly; limited fueros; forbade ecclesiastical and civil corporations to own land; and proclaimed the sanctity of private property. It restored the federalist structure of 1824, but it replaced the bicameral national legislature with a single house and eliminated the office of vice president. A few voices denounced the land monopoly, peonage, and immense inequalities of wealth. "We proclaim ideas and forget realities," complained the radical delegate Ponciano Arriaga. "How can a hungry, naked, miserable people practice popular government? How can we condemn slavery in words, while the lot of most of our fellow citizens is more grievous than that of the black slaves of Cuba or the United States?" Despite his caustic attack on the land monopoly, Arriaga offered a relatively moderate solution: The state should seize and auction off large uncultivated estates. The conservative opposition promptly branded Arriaga's project "communist"; the moderate majority in the convention passed over it in silence.

Because the new constitution incorporated the Lerdo Law and the Juárez Law, the church now openly entered the political struggle by excommunicating all public officials who took the required oath of loyalty. Counterrevolution had been gathering its forces for months, and the Three Years' War soon erupted in 1857. As the struggle progressed, both sides found themselves in serious financial difficulties. The Conservatives, however, had the advantage of generous support from the church. In July 1859, Juárez struck back at the clergy with reform laws that nationalized without compensation all ecclesiastical property except church buildings; the laws also suppressed all monasteries, established freedom of religion, and separated church and state.

By the middle of 1860, although conservative bands in the provinces continued to make devastating raids, the tide of war had turned in favor of the Liberals. The war was effectively over, but diehard reactionaries now looked for help abroad. The conservative governments of England, France, and Spain had no love for the Mexican Liberals and Juárez. Moreover, both sides had ample pretexts

for intervention, for they both had seized or destroyed foreign property without compensation, and foreign bondholders were clamoring for payments from an empty Mexican treasury. The three European powers demanded compensation for damages to their nationals and payment of just debts. Noting the dubious nature of some of the claims, Juárez vainly pleaded poverty, but the three powers nonetheless invaded and occupied Veracruz in 1862. France wanted more than payment of debts, however. A group of Mexican conservative exiles had convinced Napoleon III that the Mexican people would welcome a French army of liberation and the establishment of a monarchy. Napoleon had visions of a French-protected Mexican empire that would yield him great political and economic advantages. It remained only to find a suitable unemployed prince like Archduke Ferdinand Maximilian of Hapsburg, brother of Austrian emperor Franz Josef.

To prepare the ground for the arrival of the new ruler of Mexico, the French army advanced from Veracruz into the interior toward Puebla, where, instead of a festive welcome as liberators, the invaders met determined resistance from a poorly armed Mexican garrison and suffered heavy losses. Mexicans still celebrate the date—Cinco de Mayo de 1862—as a national holiday to commemorate the struggle against imperialism. Nonetheless, the French soon secured control of some major cities, but republican guerrilla detachments controlled most of the national territory.

Meanwhile, a delegation of conservative exiles called on Maximilian to offer him a Mexican crown, which he and his wife Carlota gratefully accepted in 1864. The conservative conspirators had counted on Maximilian to help them recover their lost wealth and privileges, but the emperor, mindful of realities, would not consent to their demands; the purchase of church lands by native and foreign landlords and capitalists had created new interests that Maximilian refused to antagonize. Confident of conservative support, Maximilian even wooed moderate Liberals.

But the hopes of both conservatives and misguided Liberals were built on quicksand. The victories of Maximilian's generals could not destroy the fluid and elusive liberal resistance, firmly grounded in popular hatred for the invaders and aided by Mexico's rugged terrain. In 1865, with its triumph over the Confederacy, the Union government demanded that the French evacuate Mexico, a region regarded by Secretary of State William Seward as a U.S. zone of economic and political influence. Facing serious domestic and diplomatic problems at home, Napoleon decided to cut his losses and liquidate the Mexican adventure. Abandoned by his Mexican and French allies, Maximilian and his leading generals, Miguel Miramón and

Tomás Mejía, were captured, found guilty of treason, and executed by a *Juarista* firing squad.

POSTWAR TRANSFORMATION OF *LA REFORMA*

Juárez, symbol of Mexican resistance to a foreign usurper, assumed the presidency in August 1867. His government inherited a devastated country. Agriculture and industry were in ruins; as late as 1873, the value of Mexican exports was below the level of 1810. To reduce the state's financial burdens and end the danger of military control, Juárez dismissed two-thirds of the army, an act that produced discontent

Mexico's José Clemente Orozco celebrated Mexican national resistance to French colonialism and the heroic leadership of Benito Juárez in this painting entitled *The Triumph of Juarez*. It depicts ordinary Mexican citizens rising to assist outgunned and overmatched Mexican regular army soldiers in a great victory over the French Legion at the Battle of Puebla on May 5, 1862.

and uprisings that his generals managed to suppress. He also devoted the state's limited resources to the development of a public school system, especially on the elementary level; by 1874, eight thousand schools with some three hundred fifty thousand pupils were in operation.

Juárez's agrarian policy continued the liberal program that aimed to implant capitalism in the countryside, at the expense of indigenous communities, not the haciendas. Indeed, the period of the Restored Republic (1868–1876) saw the federal government's intensified effort to implement the Lerdo Law by compelling dissolution and partition of indigenous communal lands, opening the way for a new wave of fraud and seizures by neighboring hacendados and other land-grabbers. The result was a series of nationwide peasant revolts, the most serious occurring in the state of Hidalgo (1869–1870). Denouncing the rebels as communists, the hacendados, aided by state and federal authorities, restored order by the traditional violent methods. A few Liberals like Ignacio Ramírez raised their voices in protest, but they were ignored. Ramírez condemned the usurpation and fraud practiced by the hacendados with the complicity of corrupt judges and officials and called for suspension of the law.

Reelected president in 1871, Juárez put down a revolt by a hero of the wars of the Reforma, Gen. Porfirio Díaz, who charged Juárez with attempting to become a dictator. Juárez died the next year of a heart attack and Sebastián Lerdo de Tejada, chief justice of the Supreme Court, succeeded him as acting president. He governed until 1876 when Díaz, aided by a group of Texas capitalists with strong links to New York banks, successfully overthrew him.

Díaz seized power in the name of the ideals of the Reforma, but thereafter, he embraced a new, profoundly antirevolutionary ideology of positivism, which ranked order and progress above freedom. This ideological change reflected the material transformation of the Mexican **bourgeoisie** from a revolutionary class into a ruling class that was more predatory and acquisitive than the old creole aristocracy. The remnants of that aristocracy speedily adapted to the ways of the new ruling class and merged with it. The interests of the old and the new rich required political stability, a docile labor force, internal improvements, and a political and economic climate that was favorable to foreign investments. This was the mission of Porfirio Díaz's government—what Porfirista intellectual Francisco Cosmes called an "honorable tyranny."

Argentina

In 1816, delegates to the congress of Tucumán proclaimed the independence of the United Provinces of the Río de la Plata. "Disunited," however, would have better described the political condition of the La Plata area, for the creole seizure of power in Buenos Aires in 1810 brought in its wake a dissolution of the vast viceroyalty of the Río de la Plata.

THE LIBERATION OF PARAGUAY, URUGUAY, AND UPPER PERU

Paraguay was the first to repel the Buenos Aires junta's efforts to liberate it, and, under the dictatorial rule of the creole lawyer José Gaspar Rodríguez de Francia, it declared its own independence. Thereafter, Francia effectively sealed it off from its neighbors to avoid submission and payment of tribute to Buenos Aires, which controlled Paraguay's river outlets to the sea. Francia did permit a limited licensed trade with the outside world by way of Brazil, chiefly to satisfy military needs.

Francia's state-controlled economy brought certain benefits: The planned diversification of agriculture, which reduced the production of such export crops as yerba maté, tobacco, and sugar, ensured a plentiful supply of foodstuffs and the well-being of the indigenous and mestizo masses. An interesting feature of Francia's system was the establishment of *estancias de la patria* (state farms or ranches) that successfully specialized in the raising of livestock and ended Paraguay's dependence on livestock imports from the Argentine province of Entre Ríos. Those who suffered most under Francia's dictatorship were Spaniards, many of whom he expelled or penalized in various ways, and creole aristocrats, who were kept under perpetual surveillance and subjected to severe repression.

The gaucho chieftain José Artigas also resisted the efforts of the Buenos Aires junta to dominate the area and led Uruguay, then known as the Banda Oriental, toward independence. In 1815, the junta abandoned these efforts, evacuated Montevideo, and turned it over to Artigas. No ordinary caudillo, Artigas defended Uruguayan nationality and sought to achieve social reform. In 1815, he issued a plan for distributing royalist lands to the landless, with preference shown to blacks, indigenous peoples, zambos, and poor whites. He did not, however, have the opportunity to implement this radical program. In 1817, a powerful Brazilian army invaded Uruguay and soon had a secure grip on the Banda Oriental. Occupied by foreign armies until 1828, Uruguay became independent only after Great Britain, unwilling to see it fall under the control of either Brazil or Argentina, intervened to negotiate its liberation.

Upper Peru, the mountainous northern corner of the old viceroyalty of La Plata, also escaped the grasp of Buenos Aires after 1810. Three expeditions into the high country won initial victories and then retreated under pressure from Spanish counteroffensives. Logistical problems, the apathy of the native population, and the hostility of the creole aristocracy, which remained loyal to Spain until it became clear that the royalist cause was doomed, contributed to the patriot defeats. Not until 1825 did Gen. Antonio José de Sucre, Bolívar's lieutenant, finally liberate Peru. Renamed Bolivia in honor of the liberator, it began its independent life the next year under a complicated, totally impractical constitution drafted by Bolívar.

THE STRUGGLE FOR PROGRESS AND NATIONAL UNITY

Even among the provinces that had joined at Tucumán to form the United Provinces of La Plata, discord grew and threatened the dissolution of the new state. The efforts of the wealthy port and province of Buenos Aires to impose its hegemony over the interior met with tenacious resistance. The end of the Spanish trade monopoly brought large gains to Buenos Aires and lesser gains to the littoral provinces of Santa Fe, Entre Ríos, and Corrientes; their exports of meat and hides increased, and the value of their lands rose. However, the wine and textile industries of the interior, which the colonial monopoly had protected, suffered from the competition of cheaper and superior European wares imported through the port of Buenos Aires.

The interests of the interior provinces required a measure of autonomy, or even independence, to protect their primitive industries, but Buenos Aires preferred a single free-trade zone under a government dominated by the port city. This was one cause of the conflict between Argentine *federales* (Federalists) and **unitarios** (Unitarians). By 1820, the federalist solution had triumphed: The United Provinces had in effect dissolved into a number of independent republics, with the interior provinces ruled by caudillos, each representing the local ruling class and having a gaucho army behind him.

A new start toward unity came in 1821 when Bernardino Rivadavia, an ardent liberal who acknowledged the strong influence of English philosopher Jeremy Bentham, launched an ambitious program of education, social, and economic reform. He promoted primary education, founded the University of Buenos Aires, abolished the ecclesiastical fuero and the tithe, and suppressed some monasteries. Rivadavia envisioned a balanced development of industry and agriculture, with a large role assigned to British investment and colonization. The obstacles to industrialization proved too great, however, and little came of efforts in this direction. The greatest progress occurred in cattle raising, which expanded rapidly southward into territory formerly claimed by native peoples. To control the large floating population of gauchos, Rivadavia enacted vagrancy laws requiring them to have passports for travel and to have written permission from the *estanciero* to leave his ranch.

In 1822, hoping to raise revenue and increase production, Rivadavia introduced the system of **emphyteusis**, a program that distributed public lands to leaseholders at fixed rentals. Some writers have seen in this system an effort at agrarian reform, but the size of grants was not limited, and the measure actually contributed to the growth of latifundios. The lure of large profits in livestock raising

GENERAL ROSAS.

Although he cultivated the populist image of a *gaucho*, Juan Manuel Rosas was a wealthy *estanciero* and military *caudillo*, whose policies inevitably defended the interests of Argentina's landed aristocracy.

induced many native and foreign merchants, politicians, and members of the military to join the rush for land. The net result was the creation not of a small-farmer class but of a new and more powerful estanciero class that was the enemy of Rivadavia's progressive ideals.

Rivadavia's planning went beyond the province of Buenos Aires; he had a vision of a unified Argentina under a strong central government that would promote the rounded economic development of the whole national territory. In 1825, a constituent congress met in Buenos Aires at Rivadavia's call to draft a constitution for the United Provinces of the Río de la Plata. Rivadavia, who was elected president of the new state, made a dramatic proposal to federalize the city and port of Buenos Aires. The former capital of the province would henceforth belong to the whole nation, with the revenues of its customhouse used to advance the general welfare.

Rivadavia's proposal reflected his nationalism and the need to mobilize national resources for a war with Brazil (1825–1828) over Uruguay. Congress approved Rivadavia's project, but the federalist caudillos of the interior, fearing that the rise of a strong national government would mean the end of their power, refused to ratify the constitution and even withdrew their delegates from the congress. In Buenos Aires, a similar stand was taken by the powerful estancieros, who had no intention of surrendering the privileges of their province and regarded Rivadavia's program of social and economic reform as a costly folly. Defeated on the issue of the constitution, Rivadavia resigned the presidency in 1827 and went into exile. The liberal program for achieving national unity had failed.

After an interval of factional struggles, the federalism espoused by the landed oligarchy of Buenos Aires triumphed in the person of Juan Manuel Rosas, who became governor of the province in 1829. In 1831, he forged a federal pact under which Buenos Aires assumed representation for the other provinces in foreign affairs but left them free to run their own affairs in all other respects. Federalism, as defined by Rosas, meant that Buenos Aires retained the revenues of its customhouse for its exclusive use and controlled trade on the Río de la Plata system for the benefit of its merchants. A network of personal alliances between Rosas and provincial caudillos, backed by the use of force against recalcitrant leaders, ensured for him a large measure of control over the interior.

Rosas's long reign saw a reversal of Rivadavia's policies. For Rosas and the ruling class of estancieros, virtually the only economic concern was the export of hides and salted meat and the import of foreign goods. The dictator also showed some favor to wheat farming and artisan industry, which he protected by the Tariff Act of 1835, but the competition for land, pressure from the cattle industry, and the primitive character of artisan manufacturing combined to prevent both from taking much advantage of the act. Rosas himself was a great estanciero and owner of a *saladero* (salting plant) for the curing of meat and hides. He vigorously pressed the conquest of indigenous territory, bringing much new land under the control of the province of Buenos Aires; his government then sold it at low prices to estancieros, quickly abandoning Rivadavia's policy of state ownership of land.

Although he professed to favor the gauchos, Rosas enforced the vagrancy laws against them even more rigorously, seeking to convert so-called idlers into ranch hands or soldiers for his army. Contrary to some historians who argue that Rosas represented the rural masses against the urban aristocracy, Rosas clearly acknowledged his fear of the masses and his tactical support of gauchos and urban blacks to control them. "As you know," he wrote in a letter, "the dispossessed are always inclined to rise against the rich and the powerful. So … I thought it very important to gain a decisive influence over this class in order to control and direct it." Rosas's "populism," his cultivation of gaucho manners and dress, did nothing to improve the condition of the poor majority. Under Rosas, discipline on the estancias relied on punishments inherited from the colonial past that included torture, the lash, the stocks, and staking delinquent peons out "like hides in the sun." His government, observes John Lynch, was a seigneurial regime based on an informal alliance of estancieros and militia commanders, often the same people.

By degrees, Rosas cowed or destroyed the press and all other potential dissidents. To enforce the dictator's will, a secret organization known as the *Mazorca* (ear of corn—a reference to the close unity of its members) arose. In collaboration with the police, this terrorist organization assaulted and sometimes murdered Rosas's opponents. The masthead of the official journal and all official papers carried the slogan "Death to the savage, filthy unitarians!" Even horses had to display the red ribbon that was the federalist symbol. Those opponents who did not knuckle under to escape death fled by the thousands to Montevideo, Chile, Brazil, or other places of refuge.

Under Rosas, the merchants of the city and the estancieros of the province of Buenos Aires enjoyed a measure of prosperity, but it bore no proportion to the possibilities of economic growth. Technical backwardness marked all aspects of livestock raising and agriculture, and port facilities were totally inadequate.

Meanwhile, the littoral provinces, which had experienced some advance of livestock raising and agriculture, became increasingly aware that Rosas's brand of federalism was harmful to their interests and that free navigation of the river system of La Plata was necessary to ensure their prosperity. In 1852, the anti-Rosas forces formed a coalition that united liberal émigrés with the caudillo Justo José de Urquiza of Entre Ríos, who together defeated Rosas's army and sent him fleeing to an English exile.

Victory over Rosas did not end the dispute between Buenos Aires and the other provinces or between federalism and unitarianism. Only the slower process of economic change would forge the desired unity. A rift soon arose between the liberal exiles, who assumed leadership in Buenos Aires, and the caudillo Urquiza of Entre Ríos, who still sported the red ribbon of federalism. A sincere convert to the gospel of modernity and progress, he had proposed a loose union of the provinces, with all of them sharing the revenues of the Buenos Aires customhouse. However, the leaders of Buenos Aires feared the loss of their economic and political predominance to Urquiza, whom they wrongly considered a caudillo of the Rosas type.

After Urquiza had attempted unsuccessfully to make Buenos Aires accept unification by armed force, the two sides agreed to a peaceful separation. As a result, delegates from Buenos Aires were absent from the constitutional convention that met at Santa Fe in Entre Ríos in 1852.

The constitution of 1853 reflected the influence of the ideas of the journalist Juan Bautista Alberdi on the delegates. His forcefully written pamphlet, *Bases and Points of Departure for the Political Organization of the Argentine Republic*, offered the United States as a model for Argentina. The new constitution strongly resembled that of the United States in certain respects. The former United Provinces became a federal republic, presided over by a president with significant power who served a six-year term without the possibility of immediate reelection. It vested legislative functions in a bicameral legislature, a senate and a house of representatives. It proclaimed Catholicism the official religion of the nation, but assured freedom of worship for non-Catholics. The states could elect governors and legislatures and frame their own constitutions, but the federal government had the right of intervention— including armed intervention—to ensure respect for the provisions of the constitution. General Urquiza became the first elected president of the Argentine Republic.

The liberal leaders of Buenos Aires, joined by the conservative estancieros who had been Rosas's firmest supporters, refused to accept the constitution of 1853, for they feared the creation of any state they did not control. As a result, two Argentinas arose: the Argentine Confederation, headed by Urquiza, and the province of Buenos Aires. For five years, the two states maintained their separate existences. In Paraná, capital of the confederation, Urquiza struggled to repress gaucho revolts, stimulate economic development, and foster education and immigration. Modest advances occurred, but the tempo of growth lagged far behind that of the wealthy city and province of Buenos Aires, which prospered on the base of a steadily increasing trade with Europe in hides, tallow, salted beef, and wool.

Hoping to increase the confederation's scanty revenues, Urquiza began a tariff war with Buenos Aires, levying surcharges on any goods that landed at the Paraná River port of Rosario if duties had been paid on them at Buenos Aires. Buenos Aires responded with sanctions against ships sailing to Rosario and threatened to close commerce on the Paraná altogether. In 1859, war between the two Argentine states broke out, and the forces of Bartolomé Mitre, governor of Buenos Aires, emerged victorious.

The military and economic superiority of Buenos Aires, the need of the other provinces to use its port, and awareness on all sides of the urgent need to achieve national unity dictated a compromise. At an 1862 congress representing all the provinces, it finally was agreed that the city should be the provisional capital of both the Argentine Republic and the province and that the Buenos Aires custom-house should be nationalized, with the proviso that for a period of five years the revenues of the province would not fall below the 1859 level. Bartolomé Mitre—distinguished historian, poet, soldier, and statesman—was elected the first president of a united Argentina.

Mitre promoted economic progress and consolidated national unity. He nationalized the customhouse, as he had promised, and made plans for the federalization of the capital. The construction of railways and telegraph lines that forged closer links between Buenos Aires and the interior had begun, and European immigrants arrived in growing numbers. His government made some progress in the establishment of a public school system, but great problems remained, the most difficult of which was the long, exhausting Paraguayan War (1865–1870).

THE PARAGUAYAN WAR

On the death of the dictator Francia in 1840, power in Paraguay passed to a triumvirate, in which Carlos Antonio López soon emerged as the dominant figure. In essence, López continued Francia's dictatorial system but gave it a thin disguise of constitutional, representative government. Because he had inherited a stable, prosperous state, López could afford to rule in a less repressive fashion than his predecessor did. More flexible than Francia, too, with a better understanding of the outside world, López made a successful effort to end Paraguay's diplomatic and commercial isolation. After the fall of Rosas, a stubborn enemy of Paraguayan independence, López obtained Argentine recognition of his country's independence and opened the Paraná to Paraguayan trade. López also established diplomatic relations with a series of countries, including England, France, and the United States.

The end of the policy of isolation accompanied a major expansion of the Paraguayan economy. Although agriculture (especially the production of such export crops as tobacco and yerba maté) continued to be the principal economic activity, López assigned great importance to the development of industry. One of his proudest achievements in this field was the construction of an iron foundry, the most modern enterprise of its type in Latin America. Transportation improved with the building of roads and canals, the creation of a fleet of merchant ships, and the construction of a short railroad line.

Continuing Francia's policy, López enlarged the role of the state sector in the national economy. In 1848, he transferred to state ownership forestlands that produced yerba maté and other commercial wood products and much arable land. The lucrative export trade in yerba maté and some other products became a government monopoly, and the number of state-owned ranches rose to sixty-four. López promoted education as well as economic growth; by the time of his death, Paraguay had 435 elementary schools, with some twenty-five thousand pupils, and a larger proportion of literate inhabitants than any other Latin American country.

At the same time, López took advantage of his position to concentrate ownership of land and various commercial enterprises in his own hands and those of his children, relatives, and associates; thus, a bourgeoisie arose that profited by its close connection with the state. Few large private estates, however, existed; small or mid-size farms cultivated by owners or tenants, sometimes with the help of a few hired laborers, dominated the private agricultural sector. In contrast with the situation in other Latin American countries, peonage and debt servitude were rare, and the regime gradually abolished slavery with an 1842 manumission law. The relative absence of peonage and other feudal survivals contributed to a rapid growth of Paraguayan capitalism and the well-being of its predominantly indigenous and mestizo population. When López died in 1862, Paraguay was one of the most progressive and prosperous states in South America.

His son, Francisco Solano, succeeded him as dictator. The younger López inherited a tradition of border disputes with Brazil that erupted into open war when Brazil sent an army into Uruguay in 1864 to ensure the victory of a pro-Brazilian faction in that country's civil strife. López could not be indifferent to this action, which threatened the delicate balance of power in the basin of La Plata. López also feared that Brazilian control of

Uruguay would end unrestricted Paraguayan access to the port of Montevideo, which would make Paraguayan trade dependent entirely on the goodwill of Buenos Aires.

When the Brazilian government disregarded his protests, López declared war, and Brazil quickly concluded a Triple Alliance with Argentina and Uruguay; a separate secret treaty between Brazil and Argentina provided for the partition of more than half of Paraguay's territory between them. Paraguay thus faced a coalition that included the two largest states in South America, with an immense superiority in manpower and other resources.

Yet the war dragged on for five years, for at its outset Paraguay possessed an army of some seventy thousand well-armed and disciplined soldiers that outnumbered the combined forces of its foes. By 1870, however, the Triple Alliance had depleted Paraguay's economic strength and defeated its military forces. Perhaps as much as 20 percent of Paraguay's prewar population of some three hundred thousand perished because of military action, famine, disease, and a devastating Brazilian occupation. The peace treaty assigned much Paraguayan territory to the victors and burdened Paraguay with extremely heavy reparations. Brazil, the occupying power, installed a puppet regime that radically reconstructed the Paraguayan economy and state.

The essence of the new policy was to liquidate the progressive changes made under the Francia and López regimes. The new regime sold most state-owned lands to land speculators and foreign businesses at bargain prices, with no restriction on the size of holdings. It expelled tenants who could not present the necessary documents, even though they and their forebears had cultivated the land for decades. By the early 1890s, the state-owned lands were almost gone. Foreign penetration of the economy through loans, concessions, and land purchases soon deprived Paraguay of its economic as well as its political independence.

PROGRESS AND DEVELOPMENT UNDER SARMIENTO

The Paraguayan War also changed Argentina, which obtained its share of Paraguayan reparations

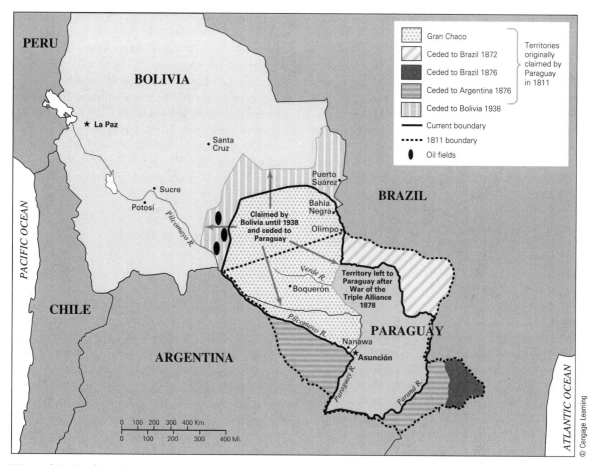

War and National Development in Paraguay and Bolivia, 1864–1938

and territorial concessions (Formosa, Chaco, and Misiones). Politically, it ushered in a transfer of power to Domingo Faustino Sarmiento (1868–1874), a gifted essayist, sociologist, and diplomat, who worked for Argentine unity and economic and social progress.

Even more important, however, a flood of technological change began to sweep over Argentina. Railways penetrated the interior, extending the stock-raising and farming area. The gradual introduction of barbed-wire fencing and alfalfa ranges made possible a dramatic improvement in the quality of livestock. In 1876, the arrival of an experimental shipload of chilled carcasses from France prepared the way for the triumph of frozen over

salted meat. This led to a vast expansion of European demand for Argentine beef and greater need for labor to exploit the rapidly expanding pasturelands and farmlands. As a result, Sarmiento's administration promoted immigration, and some three hundred thousand immigrants poured into the country. Sarmiento, believing it necessary to educate the citizens of a democratic republic, expanded the public school system and introduced to Argentina teacher-training institutions of the kind his friend Horace Mann had founded in the United States. But Sarmiento's policies had a dark side as well. Regarding native peoples and gauchos as obstacles to the advance of "civilization," he waged a war of extermination against indigenous communities and used vagrancy laws, press gangs, and other repressive measures to control the gauchos.

When Sarmiento left office, Argentina presented the appearance of a rapidly developing, prosperous state, but clouds soon invaded the generally bright Argentine sky. The growth of exports and the rise in land values did not benefit the majority of European immigrants or the forlorn gauchos, aliens in a land over which they once had freely roamed. Immigrants rarely acquired homesteads, and those who wished to farm usually found the price of land out of reach; as a result, many preferred to remain in Buenos Aires or other cities of the littoral, where they began to form an urban middle class largely devoted to trade. Meanwhile, foreign economic influence grew because of increasing dependence on foreign capital—chiefly British—to finance the construction of railways, telegraph lines, gasworks, and other needed facilities. Colonial patterns of land tenure and trade soon reemerged with the growing concentration of landownership, the tightening British control of markets and national economic infrastructure, and increasing dependence on a foreign metropolis, with London replacing Seville as the commercial center. Nevertheless, Mitre, Sarmiento, and other builders of the new Argentina celebrated their successes in nation-building. They believed wrongly that this climate of prosperity was permanent, and they did not suspect the extent of the problems in the making, nor did they anticipate the nature of the problems future generations of Argentines would face.

Chile

The victories of José de San Martín's Army of the Andes over royalist forces at Chacabuco and Maipú in 1817 and 1818 gave Chile its definitive independence. From 1818 until 1823, Bernardo O'Higgins, a hero of the struggle for Chilean liberation and a true son of the Enlightenment, ruled the country with the title of supreme director. O'Higgins energetically pushed a program of reform designed to weaken the landed aristocracy and the church and promote rapid development of the Chilean econ-

omy along capitalist lines. His abolition of titles of nobility and entails angered the great landowners of the fertile Central Valley between the Andes and the Pacific; his expulsion of the royalist bishop of Santiago and his restrictions on the number of religious processions and the veneration of images infuriated the church. Dissident Liberals who resented his sometimes heavy-handed rule joined the opposition to O'Higgins. In 1823, O'Higgins resigned and went into exile in Lima. There followed seven turbulent years, with presidents and constitutions rising and falling.

PORTALES AND ECONOMIC GROWTH

In Chile, as in other Latin American countries, the political and armed struggle gradually assumed the form of a conflict between Conservatives, who usually were Centralists, and Liberals, who generally were Federalists. The Conservative–Centralists were the party of the great landowners of the Central Valley and the wealthy merchants of Santiago; the Liberal–Federalists spoke for the landowners, merchants, and artisans of the northern and southern provinces, who were resentful of political and economic domination by the wealthy central area. By 1830, the Conservatives emerged victorious under the leadership of Joaquín Prieto and his cabinet minister Diego Portales.

Until 1837, Portales, who never held an elective office, indelibly stamped his ideas on Chilean politics and society. A business executive of aristocratic origins and owner of a successful import house, he faithfully served the interests of an oligarchy of great landlords and merchants that dominated the Chilean scene for decades. Although Portales expressed atheist views in private, he supported the authority of the church as an instrument for keeping the lower classes in order. He understood the importance of trade, industry, and mining and promoted their interests by removing remaining obstacles to internal trade. He introduced income and property taxes to increase the state's revenues and trimmed government spending by dismissing unnecessary employees. High tariffs on agricultural imports protected Chilean agriculture.

His government improved port facilities, strengthened the Chilean merchant marine, and, in 1835, supported construction of a steamship line to connect Chilean ports. Under the fostering care of the conservative regime and in response to a growing European demand for Chilean silver, copper, and hides, the national economy made steady progress in the 1830s.

Measures designed to stimulate economic growth complemented others that fortified the social and political power of the oligarchy. Portales restored the privileges the church had lost under liberal rule and normalized the troubled relations between Chile and the papacy.

In 1833, a conservative-dominated assembly adopted a constitution that further consolidated the power of the oligarchy. It made elections indirect, with the suffrage limited to men of twenty-five years or over who could satisfy literacy and property qualifications. It required still higher property qualifications for the lower and upper houses. The constitution restored entails, ensuring the perpetuation of the latifundio, declared Catholicism the state religion, and gave the church control over marriage. The president enjoyed an absolute veto over congressional legislation, appointed all high officials, and could proclaim a state of siege. The process of amending the constitution was so difficult as to be virtually impossible. Because the president controlled the electoral machinery, the outcome of elections was a foregone conclusion.

ECONOMIC EXPANSION UNDER BULNES

In 1841, Gen. Manuel Bulnes succeeded Prieto to the presidency and won reelection to a second five-year term in 1846. Victorious at home and abroad, the conservative leadership decided it could relax the strict discipline of the Portales period. Chile's economic life began a renewed advance. Commerce, mining, and agriculture prospered as never before. The Crimean War and the gold rushes to California and Australia of the 1850s created large, new markets for Chilean wheat, stimulating a considerable expansion of the cultivated area. In 1840, a North American, William Wheelright, established

a steamship line to operate on the Chilean coast, using coal from newly developed hard coal mines. Wheelright also founded a company that in 1852 completed Chile's first railroad line, providing an outlet to the sea for the production of the mining district of Copiapó. The major Santiago-Valparaíso line, begun in 1852, was not completed until 1863. Foreign capital—especially British—began to penetrate the Chilean economy; Britain dominated foreign trade and had a large interest in mining and railroads, but Chilean capitalists constituted an important, vigorous group and displayed much initiative in the formation of joint stock companies and banks.

The great landowners were the principal beneficiaries of this economic upsurge; their lands appreciated in value without any effort on their part. Some great landowners invested their money in railroads, mining, and trade. However, the essential conservatism of the landed aristocracy and the urge to preserve a semifeudal control over its peons discouraged the transformation of the great landowners into capitalist farmers. A pattern of small landholdings arose in southern Chile, to which German as well as Chilean colonists came in increasing numbers in the 1840s and 1850s. The rich Central Valley, still dominated by the latifundio, reflected inefficient techniques and reliance on the labor of *inquilinos* (tenants who also had to work the master's fields). Thus, alongside an emerging capitalist sector composed of mining, trade, banking, intensive agriculture, and some industry, a semifeudal sector flourished; it drew on the latifundio, peonage, and an aristocracy that hindered the development of Chilean capitalism.

Although Chile appeared more progressive than most other Latin American states, militants like José Victorino Lastarria—historian, sociologist, and a deputy of the Liberal Party—were dissatisfied with the new Conservatives' modest concessions to modernity. They wanted to accelerate the rate of change and demanded both a radical revision of the constitution of 1833 and an end to oligarchical rule.

To the left of Lastarria stood the firebrand Francisco Bilbao, author of a scorching attack on the church and Hispanic heritage, "The Nature of

Artists Rights Society (ARS), New York/SOMAAP, Mexico City

This David Siqueiros mural, *Death to the Invader*, depicts the fused bodies of Chile's indigenous warriors Lautaro, Galvarino, and Caupolicán, joined with Francisco Bilbao, the mid-nineteenth-century crusader for freedom and social justice. In the background, Bernardo O'Higgins and José Manuel Balmaceda join in the fight against foreign invasion.

Chilean Society" (1844). Later, he spent several years in France, where utopian socialist and radical republican thought profoundly influenced him. He returned to Chile in 1850 to found, with Santiago Arcos, the Society of Equality, uniting radical intellectuals and artisans, which advocated these advanced ideas. The society carried on an intensive antigovernmental campaign and within a few months had a membership of four thousand.

MONTT'S MODERATE REFORMS

The Society of Equality emerged on the eve of the 1850 election, for which President Bulnes had des-

ignated Manuel Montt his heir. Despite Montt's progressive educational policies and patronage of the arts and letters, Liberals identified him with the repressive system of Portales and the constitution of 1833. Liberals like Lastarria and radical democrats like Bilbao proclaimed the impending election a fraud and demanded constitutional reforms. The government responded by proclaiming a state of siege and suppressing the Society of Equality. Regarding these acts as a prelude to an attempt to liquidate the opposition, groups of Liberals in Santiago and La Serena rose in revolts that the government quickly crushed. Lastarria was exiled, and Bilbao and Arcos fled to Argentina. Montt became president and immediately crushed another liberal revolt but thereafter took steps to resolve future crises by granting amnesty to the insurgents and abolishing both entails and tithes.

The abolition of entails, which aimed to encourage the breakup of landed estates among the children of the great landowners, affected a dwindling number of great aristocratic clans. Its effects were less drastic than the anguished cries of the affected parties suggested, for other latifundists almost invariably acquired the divided estates, and the condition of the inquilinos who worked the land remained the same. The elimination of the tithe and Montt's refusal to allow the return of the Jesuits greatly angered the reactionary clergy. Responding to their attacks, Montt promulgated a new civil code in 1857 that placed education under state control, gave the state jurisdiction over the clergy, and granted non-Catholics the right of civil marriage.

The abolition of entails and tithes represented a compromise between Liberals and Conservatives, between the new bourgeoisie and the great landowners. In the process, the bourgeoisie gained little, and the landowners lost almost nothing; the chief loser was the church. Although Montt's reforms alienated the most reactionary elements of the Conservative Party, they gained him the support of moderate Liberals, who joined with moderate Conservatives to form a new coalition, the National Party. Its motto was the typically positivist slogan "Freedom in Order."

In the last years of his second term, President Montt faced severe economic and political problems. The 1857 depression caused a sharp fall in the price of copper and reduced Australian and Californian demand for Chilean wheat. The economic decline fed the fires of political discontent, and another large-scale revolt erupted in January 1859. The rebels included radical intellectuals, northern mining capitalists and their workers, artisans, and small farmers, all groups with grievances against the dominant Central Valley alliance of great merchants and landowners. Their demands included a democratic republic, state support for mining and industry, the splitting up of the great estates, and

abolition of the semifeudal *inquilinaje* system of peonage as incompatible with democratic principles. Before it ended, the revolt had taken five thousand lives. Thereafter, Montt imprisoned some of the revolt's bourgeois leaders, deported others, and still others fled into exile, but a large number of miners, artisans, and peasants were executed. Maurice Zeitlin regards it as a crucial turning point in Chilean history: "Defeat of the revolutionary bourgeoisie amounted to virtual suppression of an alternative and independent path of capitalist development for Chile—a realm of objective historical possibilities unfulfilled because of the failure of the bourgeois revolution."

By 1861, the depression had lifted and another boom began, creating new fortunes and bringing large shifts of regional influence. A growing stream of settlers, including many Germans, flowed into southern Chile, founding cities and transforming woodlands into farms.

Nonetheless, Chile's true center of economic gravity became the desert north, rich in copper, nitrates, and guano; the last two, in particular, were objects of Europe's insatiable demand for fertilizers. The major nitrate deposits, however, lay in the Bolivian province of Antofagasta and the Peruvian province of Tarapacá. Chilean capital, supplemented by English and German capital, began to pour into these regions and soon dominated the Peruvian and Bolivian nitrate industries. In the north, an aggressive mining capitalist class demanded a place in the sun for itself and its region. A rich mine owner, Pedro León Gallo, abandoned the Liberals to form a new middle-class party called Radical, which fought more militantly than the Liberals for limited constitutional changes, religious toleration, and an end to repressive policies.

LIBERAL CONTROL

The transition of Chile's political life to liberal control, begun under Montt, culminated in 1871 with the election of the first liberal president, Federico Errázuriz Zañartú. Between 1873 and 1875, a coalition of Liberals and radicals pushed through the congress a series of constitutional reforms: reduction of senatorial terms from nine to six years; direct election of senators; and freedom of speech, press, and assembly. These victories for enlightenment also represented a victory of new capitalist groups over the old merchant-landowner oligarchy that traced its beginnings back to colonial times. By 1880, of the fifty-nine Chilean personal fortunes of more than 1 million pesos, only twenty-four were of colonial origin, and only twenty had made their fortunes in agriculture; the rest belonged to coal, nitrate, copper, and silver interests or to merchants whose wealth had been formed only in the nineteenth century. Arnold Bauer has observed that the more interesting point is "not that only twenty made their fortune in agriculture, but that the remaining thirty-nine—designated as miners, bankers, and capitalists—subsequently invested their earnings in rural estates. This would be comparable to Andrew Carnegie sinking his steel income into Scarlett O'Hara's plantation." Bauer's comment points to the "powerful social model" that the Chilean agrarian oligarchy continued to exert. For the rest, the victories of the new bourgeoisie brought no relief to the Chilean masses, the migrant laborers and tenant farmers on the haciendas, and the young working class in Chile's mines and factories.

During the first half-century after independence in Chile, collective fear of subaltern social sectors caused liberal and conservative elites to overcome their considerable differences and create a national political identity that stressed oligarchic unity and collaboration with foreign capitalists. Meanwhile, the great majority of Chilean peasants, propertyless wage workers, and indigenous communities, all of whom were largely excluded from this definition of citizenship, mobilized around issues of democracy, equality, and anticolonialism to promote their rival vision of a more inclusive nation-state. Ironically, José Manuel Balmaceda, himself born to a wealthy aristocratic family, soon became a national voice for this growing reform movement.

United Provinces of Central America

On the eve of independence, the five republics—Guatemala, El Salvador, Honduras, Nicaragua, and Costa Rica[2]—were provinces of the captaincy general of Guatemala, with its capital at Guatemala City. Under the captain general and his audiencia, a small group of wealthy creole merchants, organized in a powerful consulado, had dominated the economic, social, and political life of the colony. Spain's hold over its American colonies had weakened after 1800, however, because of its involvement in European wars, the resulting disruption of trade, and growing political turmoil at home. Central America drifted toward independence. When Mexico proclaimed its independence in 1821, Central America followed suit. City after city declared its independence, not only from Spain but from Guatemala and rival cities and towns, as well. The captaincy general dissolved into a multitude of autonomous cabildo (municipal) governments. The transition to independence grew more complicated because of Agustín de Iturbide's efforts to incorporate Central America into his Mexican empire, efforts supported by Central American Conservatives and opposed by many Liberals. In 1822, a majority of cabildos supported union with Mexico, but Iturbide's overthrow the next year permanently ended the Mexican connection.

INDEPENDENCE AND THE FAILURE OF UNION, 1810–1865

Despite provincial rivalries and resentment against Guatemalan domination, a tradition of Central American unity remained, which liberals sought to strengthen. In 1823, a constituent assembly met and created the federal republic of Central America out of the five former provinces: Guatemala, Honduras, Nicaragua, Costa Rica, and El Salvador. The constitution provided for a federal government with free and independent state governments and

---

2. Although, for descriptive convenience, Belize and Panama usually are included in Central America, the former was a British colony and the latter a province of Colombia. Therefore, neither had historical links to the region.

had a strong liberal tinge: It abolished slavery and the special privileges of the clergy and established the principles of laissez-faire, free trade, and free contract of labor. The next year, a Salvadoran liberal, Manuel José Arce, won the election as the first president of the republic. Meanwhile, the states were forming their own governments. On the state as on the federal level, Conservatives and Liberals struggled for power: Conservatism—the ideology of the old monopolistic merchant clique, many great landowners, and the church—had its base in Guatemala; liberalism was the dominant doctrine among many large and small landowners of the other states and the small middle class of artisans, professionals, and intellectuals. Behind the façade of elections and universal male suffrage, great landowning and mercantile families held power throughout the area, and they often mobilized their private armies of retainers and tenants in a struggle for control of regions and states.

The superficial unity of Central America soon dissolved as it became clear that the states were neither willing nor able to finance both their own governments and the federal government in Guatemala City. Efforts by Arce's federal government to assert its prerogatives by the establishment of a strong army and the collection of taxes led him to abandon liberalism, which ignited a destructive civil war between 1826 and 1829. The struggle ended with the defeat of the national government and its conservative leadership by liberal forces headed by Francisco Morazán and the reorganization of the union on a basis of liberal hegemony.

Morazán, elected president of the federal republic and commander of its armed forces, both based in San Salvador, defended it against conservative plots and attacks. At the same time, a former Conservative turned Liberal, Mariano Gálvez, the governor of Guatemala, launched a program for the economic and social reconstruction of his state. The program included establishment of civil marriage and divorce, secular schools on all levels, anticlerical measures that allowed nuns to leave their orders, and fewer church holidays. It also granted large land concessions to British companies that were to colonize the land with foreign immigrants

and develop basic economic infrastructure. It even provided an agrarian reform that allowed squatters to buy land for half its value and permitted natives to settle on vacant land. Gálvez also sought to reform Guatemala's judicial system by providing for trial by jury and *habeas corpus* and by vesting power to appoint all judges in the governor of the state. This last feature alienated powerful landed interests who often served as *jefes políticos* (local officials who combined judicial and administrative functions and claimed a share of tax collections as compensation).

The loss of the support of local landed interests combined with the ravages of a cholera epidemic that spread over Central America in 1837 to bring down the Gálvez regime and its ambitious reform program. Stirred up by local clergy who proclaimed the epidemic to be divine retribution for the heresies of civil marriage and divorce, the native and mixed-race masses rose in revolt against Gálvez's radical innovations in law and taxation, attacks on their landholdings by creole landowners, and sanitary measures instituted to prevent the spread of disease. Led by the mestizo Rafael Carrera, the principal revolt in February 1838 mobilized an army of indígenas and castas who cried, "Long live religion, and death to all foreigners!"

Carrera took Guatemala City, defeated Morazán in 1842, and ended the federal republic. He then established a conservative regime in Guatemala, which he controlled until his death in 1865. In 1854, dispensing with the formality of elections, he had Congress name him president for life. Thereafter, he implemented a reactionary program that revived the authority of the church, returned church and indigenous communal properties to their original owners, brought back native forced labor, and even changed the title of local officials from jefe político to the old colonial title of corregidor. What had begun as a lower-class protest against modernization and the spoliation of communal lands, however, soon changed into a conservative government controlled by a merchant oligarchy that provided the taxes Carrera needed to pay his army and foreign loans. Conservative ministers drawn from the elite surrounded the dictator. Alongside the traditional labor arrangements, free labor and a money economy existed, along with landless natives and mestizos working, sometimes under debt peonage, on the plantations.

Similar trends prevailed throughout Central America in the age of Carrera, although labor was freer in most of the area than it was in Guatemala. By the 1850s, an increasing world demand for coffee stimulated expansion of the crop, which had been grown on a large scale in Costa Rica since the 1830s, and spurred attacks on indigenous communal lands. Coffee in Costa Rica and El Salvador, along with indigo, made for relative political stability in those countries. In the more backward republics of Nicaragua and Honduras, where cattle barons warred with each other, little centralized authority existed.

The discovery of gold in California gave a new importance to Central America as a transoceanic transit route and sharpened the rivalry of the United States and Great Britain in the area. The threat to the sovereignty and territorial integrity of the Central American republics grew acute because of the folly of Nicaraguan Liberals, who in 1855 invited William Walker, an adventurer from the United States, to help them overthrow a conservative regime. Having brought the Liberals to power, Walker, supported by a band of some three hundred compatriots, staged a coup, proclaimed himself president, legalized slavery, and made English the official language. By mid-1856, in a rare display of unity, Nicaraguan Liberals and Conservatives, joined by all the other Central American republics, had combined in the National War against the Yankee intruders, but the Central American army that opposed Walker was essentially a conservative army. Defeated in 1857, Walker returned to the United States. He nevertheless made two more attempts to conquer Central America, the last ending with his death before a Honduran firing squad in 1860.

The National War revived the moribund movement for Central American unity. The liberal Salvadoran president Gerardo Barrios was a leading advocate of federation. His efforts to realize Morazán's dream provoked Carrera, who was determined to maintain conservative domination over Central America and to send troops into El Salvador and its ally Honduras. The war ended with Barrios's defeat and exile; every Central American republic now had conservative regimes. In 1865, Barrios attempted to make a comeback, but his enemies captured and executed him. Carrera died in the same year. With his death, the violence-filled formative period of Central American history ended.

Clearly, the wars of independence failed to effect major changes in colonial economic and social structures in Mexico, Argentina, Chile, and Central America. In the difficult process of decolonization, these young republics faced extraordinary obstacles, including regionalism, economic stagnation, and political instability, that challenged the capacity of each to create a distinctive national identity. The republican political systems adopted by these new states functioned in practice very differently from the political theory that informed them. A Conservative–Liberal cleavage, with its roots in the conflicting interests and ideals of various elite groups, dominated political, economic, and cultural life. Although these same elite conflicts also characterized the experience of decolonization and the postcolonial reconstruction of national identities in Brazil, Cuba, Peru, and Gran Colombia, popular opposition to slavery and the demand for freedom decisively shaped the process in those countries.

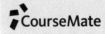

CourseMate Go to the CourseMate website at **www.cengagebrain.com** for primary sources, additional study tools, and review materials—including audio and video clips—for this chapter.

Race, Nation, and the Meaning of Freedom, 1821–1888

10

FOCUS QUESTIONS

- How did movements to abolish slavery variously affect the development of national identities in Brazil, Peru, Cuba, and Gran Colombia?
- What were the causes of the crisis of Brazilian slavery after mid-century?
- Why did the creole elite in Peru oppose the movement of national liberation led by San Martín and Bolívar?
- How did conflicts over race and slavery within the rebel community affect the nineteenth-century evolution of Cuban nationalism?
- How did the struggle over emancipation affect the rivalry between Liberals and Conservatives in Venezuela and Colombia?

W ITH THE ACHIEVEMENT OF INDEPEN-DENCE, the new nations then under construction immediately faced questions that their successful struggle for home rule had not answered. Who would rule at home, how, and through what institutions of the state? Who was a citizen, and what did it mean to be free? How would the state limit individual freedom and regulate relations among diverse social classes, racial and ethnic groups, and foreign interests? In the process of resolving these questions and building the postcolonial institutions that expressed the national interest, the colonial legacy of slavery and **race** played an influential role. Enslaved Africans and their descendants in the Americas actively participated in this postcolonial struggle to fashion unified nation-states out of societies that historically were divided by region, class, race, ethnicity, and gender. A popular desire for freedom from the slaveholder easily translated into calls for freedom from **patriarchy**, foreign control, and aristocratic class rule. This struggle, along with elite conflicts between Liberals and Conservatives, shaped the meaning of citizenship and the contours of new nationalities emerging in Brazil, Cuba, Peru, and Gran

Colombia. Although their motives often varied greatly, black slaves, free people of color, peasants, urban workers, merchants, radical intellectuals, and others joined together to demand the abolition of slavery, but they faced the equally determined resistance of slaveholders. In this conflict, race informed the negotiations that structured institutional relations between citizen and state, defining these new nations in the nineteenth century and beyond.

Initially, historians like Frank Tannenbaum argued that, contrary to the experience of emancipation in the United States, creole independence leaders like Simón Bolívar enthusiastically supported abolitionism, which consequently "was achieved in every case without violence, without bloodshed, and without civil war." Since then, historians have examined postcolonial elite decision making and concluded that political and military expediency, rather than moral enthusiasm, largely drove abolitionism in Latin America. According to this view, republican elites mostly embraced the idea of abolitionism to recruit black soldiers, counter royalist recruitment strategies, or curry favor with foreigners like Haiti's Alexandre Petion,

1812	Aponte slave rebellion in Cuba
1821	Congress of Cúcuta in Gran Colombia preserves slavery but decrees "free wombs" and encourages voluntary manumission
1823–1889	Independent empire of Brazil preserves the essential institutions of its colonial past
1823–1826	In Peru, Bolívar restores slavery, which San Martín had abolished
1829	José Antonio Páez dissolves Gran Colombia and preserves slavery in independent republic of Venezuela
1835–1845	Local Brazilian uprisings like the *cabanagem* and Sabinada revolts, Balaiada Rebellion, and Revolution of the Ragamuffins demand independence, republican government, racial equality, and abolition of slavery
1844	Cuban creole elite and Spanish colonial officials suppress Escalera slave conspiracy
1851	Brazil ends slave trade; slave revolt in Peru's Chicama Valley mobilizes abolitionist movement; José Hilario López abolishes slavery in Colombia
1854	Ramón Castilla abolishes slavery and indigenous tribute in Peru; Venezuela abolishes slavery
1858–1863	Federal War in Venezuela mobilizes poor majority against wealthy propertied elite
1868–1878	Ten Years' War, initially led by Cuban creoles like Carlos Manuel de Céspedes, mobilizes Afro-Cubans like Antonio Maceo to demand freedom from Spain, slavery, and social injustice
1871	Brazil passes Rio Branco law, freeing newborn slave children and encouraging voluntary manumission
1878	Pact of Zanjón ends Ten Years' War without winning Cuban independence or ending slavery and racial discrimination
1886	Cuba formally abolishes slavery
1888	Brazil abolishes slavery

who provided food and munitions in exchange for Bolívar's 1816 pledge to liberate all slaves. Although this offered a more critical and nuanced interpretation than Tannenbaum, it still focused on elite ideas and actions, thereby effectively silencing the voices of enslaved Africans and their descendants.

More recently, however, a new generation of historians, increasingly interested in recovering this lost voice, have asked new questions and examined new archival collections. Although they agree that elites mostly lacked the moral conviction that slavery was wrong (or failed independently to act on it), they stress the active role of enslaved and free people of color in opposing slavery and forcing reluctant elites to abolish it. Their study of Afro-Latino culture, religion, and family life reveals that the enslaved and free people of color pursued both legal and extralegal strategies in their relentless search for freedom. Court records, for example, show that slaves, grounding their arguments in appeals to republican laws, routinely petitioned the government for their liberty. Still more frequently, however, slaves employed the strategy of what W. E. B. Du Bois famously called "the general strike": they defied legal constraints, refused to work, escaped to join **maroon** communities called *palenques* or quilombos, engaged in social banditry, and, less frequently, openly rebelled against the institution of slavery. Taken together, this history of popular resistance decisively shaped both the institutions of government and citizen participation in the newly developing nations.

In general, a new consensus on the origins and implications of emancipation has emerged. First, it is clear that independence did not immediately produce the abolition of slavery. Second, creole independence leaders vigorously debated the morality of slavery and ultimately sought compromise that effectively prolonged its existence for decades. This most commonly involved passage of "Free Womb" laws that freed the children of enslaved women, required slave owners to support them (and control their labor) until adulthood, and thereafter paid the slaveholders compensation for their liberation. Third, slave owners accepted abolition only after the enslaved and free people of color rebelled, often violently, and threatened the long-term security of private property rights in the new republics. Elite fears of social revolution from below fueled reform programs that gradually abolished slavery, but they simultaneously established income and literacy requirements that limited free people's political participation. Finally, decades of civil strife and political mobilization of cross-class, multiracial coalitions ultimately prepared the way for emancipation, but the experience effectively silenced the struggle for racial justice, as citizen activists abandoned the divisive idea of race in favor of the unifying language of nation. As a result, emancipation generally compensated slave owners for their losses, and the newly emerging nations preferred not to speak about the enduring racial inequalities that remained for future generations of black and mixed-race peoples.

Naturally, the specific historical experiences of these nations varied, depending on local traditions, availability of land, proximity to transatlantic markets, reliance on slave labor, the size of the population of free people of color, and the influence of foreign nations. A careful study of this complex history therefore requires an examination of particular events in Peru, Gran Colombia, Cuba, and Brazil, where slave populations were largest and the iniquitous institution endured the longest.

Brazil

Brazil took its first major step toward independence in 1808, when the Portuguese crown and court, fleeing before a French invasion of Portugal, arrived in Rio de Janeiro to make it the new capital of the Portuguese empire. Formal national independence came in 1822 when Dom Pedro, who ruled Brazil as regent for his father, João VI, rejected a demand that he return to Portugal and issued the famous Cry of Ipiranga: "Independence or Death!"

DOM PEDRO, EMPEROR

Dom Pedro acted with the advice and support of the Brazilian aristocracy, which was determined to

preserve the autonomy Brazil had enjoyed since 1808. It was equally determined to make a transition to independence without the violence that marked the Spanish American movement of liberation elsewhere. The Brazilian aristocracy had its wish; Brazil made a transition to independence with comparatively little disruption and bloodshed. But this meant that independent Brazil retained its colonial social structure: monarchy, slavery, large landed estates, monoculture, an inefficient agricultural system, a highly stratified society, and a free population that was 90 percent illiterate.

Dom Pedro had promised to give his subjects a constitution, but the constituent assembly he summoned in 1823 drafted a document that placed excessive limits on his power. In response, he dissolved the assembly and assigned a handpicked commission the task of making a new constitution, which he promulgated by imperial proclamation. This constitution, under which Brazil was governed until the fall of the monarchy in 1889, concentrated great power in the hands of the monarch. In addition to a Council of State, it provided for a two-chamber parliament: a lifetime Senate, the members of which the emperor chose, and a Chamber of Deputies who were elected only by voters who met certain property and income requirements that effectively disenfranchised the great majority. The emperor had the right to appoint and dismiss ministers and summon or dissolve parliament at will. He also appointed the provincial governors or presidents.

Resentment over Dom Pedro's high-handed dissolution of the constituent assembly and the highly centralist character of the constitution of 1824 was particularly strong in Pernambuco, a center of republican and federalist ferment. Here in 1824, a group of rebels, led by the merchant Manoel de Carvalho, proclaimed the creation of a Confederation of the Equator that would unite the six northern provinces under a republican government. A few leaders voiced antislavery sentiments, but they did nothing to abolish slavery, partly because they feared that this would mobilize the enslaved and free people of color to produce a revolutionary outcome modeled on the Haitian experience. This fear deprived the movement of the potential support of a large slave population, and, within a year, imperial troops had smashed the revolt.

Dom Pedro had won a victory, but resentment of his autocratic tendencies continued to smolder, and his popularity steadily waned. Once again, the issue of slavery loomed large. The emperor's foreign policies contributed to this growing discontent. In 1826, in return for recognition of Brazilian independence and a trade agreement, Dom Pedro signed a treaty with Great Britain that obligated Brazil to end the slave traffic by 1830. Despite this ban and the British Navy's efforts to seize the slave ships, the trade continued with the full knowledge and approval of the Brazilian government. Nonetheless, British policing practices caused the price of slaves to rise sharply. The prospering coffee growers of Rio de Janeiro, São Paulo, and Minas Gerais could afford to pay high prices for slaves, but the cotton and sugar growers of the depressed north could not compete with them for workers and blamed Dom Pedro for their difficulties.

News of the July Revolution of 1830 in France, a revolution that toppled an unpopular, autocratic king, produced rejoicing and violent demonstrations in Brazilian cities. *Exaltados* (radical Liberals) placed themselves at the head of the revolt and called for the abolition of the monarchy and the establishment of a federal republic. In the countryside, enslaved and free people of color seized the opportunity to demand the abolition of slavery, which had long functioned as the bedrock of a fragile elite provincial unity. In the face of the growing crisis, Dom Pedro abdicated in favor of his five-year-old son Pedro and, two weeks later, he sailed for Portugal, never to return. These developments, eliminating the dominant influence of Portuguese merchants and Portuguese-born courtiers under Emperor Pedro I, completed the transition to full Brazilian independence.

REGENCY, REVOLT, AND A BOY EMPEROR

The revolution had been the work of radical Liberals, who viewed Dom Pedro's downfall as the first step toward the establishment of a federal republic, but the moderates enjoyed its fruits. In effect, the radicals had played the game of the monarchist Liberals, who had guided the movement of secession from Portugal and later lost influence at court because of Dom Pedro's embrace of conservative *fazendeiros*. Dom Pedro's departure was a victory for these moderates, who hastened to restore their ascendancy over the central government and prevent the revolution from getting out of hand.

As a first step, parliament appointed a three-man regency composed of moderate Liberals to govern for the child emperor until he reached the age of eighteen. Another measure created a national guard, recruited from the propertied classes, to repress urban mobs and slave revolts. Simultaneously, the new government began work on a project of constitutional reform designed to appease the strong federalist sentiment. After a three-year debate, parliament approved the Additional Act of 1834, which gave the provinces elective legislative assemblies with broad powers, including control over local budgets and taxes. This provision ensured that the great landowners had a large measure of control over their regions and abolished the Council of State, long identified with Dom Pedro's reactionary rule. The regency did not abandon centralism, however, for the national government continued to appoint provincial governors with a partial veto over the acts of the provincial assemblies.

Almost immediately, the regency government struggled against a rash of revolts, mostly in the northern provinces, where the economy suffered from a loss of markets for their staple crops, sugar and cotton. None occurred in the central southern zone (the provinces of Rio de Janeiro, São Paulo, and Minas Gerais), whose coffee economy prospered and whose planter aristocracy had secure control of the central government. These revolts had a variety of local causes. Some were elemental, popular revolts, such as the so-called *cabanagem* (from the word *cabana*, meaning "cabin") of Pará, which originated in the grievances of small tradesmen, farmers, and lower-class elements against the rich Portuguese merchants who monopolized local trade. Others, like the republican and separatist

Sabinada revolt in Bahia (1837–1838), reflected the frustrations of the planter aristocracy of this once-prosperous area over its loss of economic and political power, but it also mobilized the large majority of black and mixed-race people who had long advocated slavery's abolition. A slaveholders' petition complained about "insubordination" on plantations where "slaves walk around with arms and there is to be feared some sad incident, besides the bad example they give to the neighboring fazendas, especially when, because of the events of Bahia, the slaves in general are losing their deference which is so necessary." Another measure of the regency's fear of these abolitionist rebellions was its 1834 decree of the death penalty for insurgent slaves.

Most serious of all was the revolt that broke out in 1835 in the province of Rio Grande do Sul. Although it was dubbed the *Revolução Farroupilha* (Revolution of the Ragamuffins) in contemptuous reference to its supposed lower-class origins, cattle barons who more or less controlled the gauchos—the rank-and-file of the rebel armies—actually led the movement. An intense regionalism, resentment over taxes and unpopular governors imposed by the central government, and the strength of republican sentiment all induced the revolt that established the independent republic of Rio Grande in 1836. The presence of considerable numbers of Italian exiles such as Giuseppe Garibaldi—ardent republicans who opposed slavery—gave a special radical tinge to the revolt. For almost a decade, two states—one a republic and one an empire—existed on Brazilian territory.

The inability of imperial troops to quell the Rio Grande revolt further weakened the regency government, and, in 1838, the Balaiada rebellion raged across the northern provinces of Maranhão, Piauí, and Ceará. Initiated in Maranhão, the province with the greatest share of slaves (some 55 percent of the population), this revolt began as a lower-class protest against conscription and blossomed into an insurgency that appealed to black slaves, indigenous people, free people of color, and well-established maroon communities. One maroon leader, Cosme Bento das Chagas, recruited a slave army of two thousand and forced local plantation owners to free their slaves. According to historian Matthias Röhrig Assunção, another mixed-race leader, Raimundo Gomes, proclaimed "equal rights for all people of colour, *cabras* [dark mulattos], and **caboclos** [poor, usually landless, people of mixed indigenous and European descent]."

Doubtlessly, the revolt's increasingly radical, egalitarian program reflected the broad cross-class, multiracial nature of its rebel army, which government officials confirmed. For example, military commander Luis Alves de Lima described Gomes as a rebel leader who "claimed that he did not want to ally himself to the insurrected negroes, but now, without resources and always persecuted, tries to attract them." This growing subaltern alliance clearly threatened the monarchy, the plantation oligarchs, and the private property rights that secured them. To preserve their power and privilege, these elites used the issue of race to divide the rebels, promising amnesty to all free rebels in exchange for their agreement to "hunt down" runaway slaves. According to Lima, "in order to avoid further insurrections," his amnesty proposal aimed "to excite the hate between slaves and free rebels."

While the army tried to restore order on the battlefield, moderate Liberals, who favored concessions to federalism, sought political accommodation with a Conservative Party that preferred to strengthen the central government. On such essential issues as the monarchy, slavery, and the maintenance of the status quo in general, these Liberals and Conservatives saw eye to eye. They also agreed on the need to suppress the Rio Grande rebellion and other regional revolts in the north. The Rio Grande experiment in republican government and its offer of freedom to all slaves who joined the republic's armed forces posed an especially serious threat to monarchy and slavery. To strengthen the central government in its war against these subversive and separatist movements, Liberals and Conservatives decided to call the young Pedro to rule before his legal majority. In 1840 the two legislative chambers orchestrated a parliamentary coup d'état and proclaimed the fourteen-year-old Dom Pedro emperor. He empowered a conservative government that dismantled the federalist reforms in the

Slavery in Brazil by Jean-Baptiste Debret depicts the cruelty that characterized Brazilian slavery and produced the Balaiada Rebellion, named for the Afro-Brazilian basket weaver Manuel Francisco dos Anjos Ferreira, who led thousands of Afro-Brazilians in a movement to abolish slavery and establish an independent republic.

Additional Act of 1834, sharply curtailed the powers of provincial assemblies, and stripped locally elected judges of their judicial and police powers.

Thereafter, the government undertook to settle scores with the rebels of Rio Grande. Because of internal squabbles and the cessation of aid from friendly Uruguay after Argentina invaded it in February 1843, the situation of the republic became extremely difficult. Facing the prospect of military defeat, the republican leaders accepted an offer from Rio de Janeiro to negotiate a peace, and they signed a peace treaty in February 1845. It extended amnesty to all rebels but annulled all laws of the republican regime. The cattle barons won certain concessions, including the right to nominate

their candidate for provincial governor and retain their military titles.

The last large-scale revolt in the series that shook Brazil in the 1830s and 1840s was the uprising of 1848 in Pernambuco. Centered in the city of Recife, its causes included hostility toward the Portuguese merchants who monopolized local trade, the appointment of an unpopular governor by the conservative government, and hatred for the greatest landowners of the region, the powerful Cavalcanti family. The rebel program called for the removal from Recife of all Portuguese merchants, expansion of provincial autonomy, work for the unemployed, and division of the Cavalcanti lands. Even this radical program, however, contained no reference to the abolition of slavery. The movement collapsed after imperial troops captured Recife in 1849. Many captured leaders were condemned to prison for life, but all were amnestied in 1852.

Underlying these rebellions and armed conflicts of the 1830s and 1840s was economic stagnation caused by the weakness of foreign markets for Brazil's traditional exports. Coffee, already important in the 1830s but flourishing after 1850, expanded into the center-south, which strengthened the hand of the central government with increased revenues and laid the foundation for a new era of cooperation between regional elites and the national government. The new coffee prosperity, confirming the apparent viability and rationality of the neocolonial emphasis on export agriculture, also discouraged any thought of taking the more durable but difficult path of Brazilian autonomous development.

THE GAME OF POLITICS AND THE CRISIS OF SLAVERY

By 1850, Brazil seemed at peace. The emperor presided over a pseudo-parliamentary regime, exercising his power in the interests of a tiny ruling class. He paid his respects to parliamentary forms by alternately appointing conservative and liberal prime ministers at will; if the new ministry did not command a majority in parliament, he obtained one by holding rigged elections. Because the ruling class united on essential issues, the only issue at stake in party struggles was patronage, the spoils of office. An admirer of Dom Pedro, Joaquim Nabuco, described the operation of the system in his book *O abolicionismo*:

> The representative system, then, is a graft of parliamentary forms on a patriarchal government, and senators and deputies only take their roles seriously in this parody of democracy because of the personal advantage they derive therefrom. Suppress the subsidies, force them to stop using their positions for personal and family ends, and no one who had anything else to do would waste his time in such shadow boxing.

The surface stability of Brazilian political life in the decades after 1850 rested on the prosperity of the coffee-growing zone of Rio de Janeiro, São Paulo, and Minas Gerais, itself the product of growing demand and good prices for Brazilian coffee. But the sugar-growing northeast and its plantation society continued to decline because of exhausted soil, archaic techniques, and competition from foreign sugars.

The crisis of the northeast grew more acute because of English pressure on Brazil to enforce the Anglo-Brazilian treaty banning the importation of slaves into Brazil after November 7, 1831. Before 1850, slavetraders virtually ignored this treaty and enslaved more than fifty thousand people a year in Brazil during the 1840s. In 1849 and 1850, however, the British government pressured Brazil to pass the Queiroz anti-slave-trade law and instructed its warships to enter Brazilian territorial waters if necessary to destroy Brazilian slave ships. By the middle 1850s, the importation of slaves had virtually ended.

Abolition of the slave trade had major consequences. Because poor food, harsh working conditions, and other negative factors produced high mortality among the enslaved, natural reproduction could not maintain the slave population, which ensured the slave system's eventual demise. The end of the slave trade created a serious labor shortage, with large numbers of slaves moving from the north to the south because of the coffee planters' greater capacity to compete for slave labor. This movement aggravated the imbalance between the declining north and the prosperous south-central zone. By the 1860s, a growing number of Brazilians had become convinced that slavery brought serious discredit to Brazil and insisted on its abolition. The abolition of slavery in the United States after the Civil War, which left Brazil and the Spanish colonies of Cuba and Puerto Rico the only slaveholding areas in the Western Hemisphere, sharpened sensitivity to the problem. The Paraguayan War also promoted the cause of emancipation. In an effort to fill the gaps caused by heavy losses at the front, the emperor issued a decree granting freedom to government-owned slaves who agreed to join the army, and some private slave owners followed the official example.

Criticism of slavery increasingly morphed into criticism of the emperor, whom abolitionists censured for his cautious posture on slavery. Although the monarchy believed it might survive the abolition of slavery, it greatly feared the growing independent organizations of "blacks, mulattos, caboclos, etc." that accompanied abolitionism. In the words of a royal councilor, Pimenta Bueno,

> Political experience teaches us that the best rule is not to talk about this. If one allows the principle to exist, then it will develop, and there will be consequences. Distinctions or divisions based on caste are always bad; homogeneity, if not real at least supposed, is the desired goal of nationalities.

This idea epitomized Brazil's nineteenth-century struggles and ultimately led historians like Sidney Chalhoub to conclude that they bequeathed a legacy of political exclusion for peoples of African descent.

Alongside the antislavery movement, a nascent republican movement arose. In 1869, the Reform Club, a group of militant Liberals, issued a manifesto demanding restrictions on the powers of the emperor and the grant of freedom to the newborn children of enslaved mothers. The crisis of slavery was fast becoming a crisis of the Brazilian empire.

THE ANTISLAVERY MOVEMENT

From the close of the Paraguayan War (1870), the slavery question surged forward, becoming the dominant issue in Brazilian political life. Dom Pedro, personally opposed to slavery, was caught in a crossfire between slave owners who were determined to postpone the inevitable as long as possible and a growing number of liberal leaders, intellectuals, urban middle-class groups, and free people of color—not to mention the enslaved themselves—all of whom demanded emancipation. In 1870, Spain freed all newborn and aged slaves in Cuba and Puerto Rico, leaving Brazil the only nation in the Americas to retain slavery in its original colonial form. Fearing the perpetual social instability promised by the slaves' defiant resistance to slavery, a conservative ministry soon yielded to pressure

and pushed the Rio Branco Law through parliament in 1871. This measure freed all newborn children of enslaved women but obligated their masters to care for them until they reached the age of eight. At that time, owners could either release the children to the government in return for an indemnity or retain them as laborers until they reached the age of twenty-one. The law also freed all slaves belonging to the state or crown and created a fund to compensate slaveholders for the manumission of their slaves.

The Rio Branco Law was a tactical retreat designed to put off a final solution of the slavery problem. As late as 1884, when Brazil still had more than 1 million slaves, Brazil's Free Womb legislation had freed only 113.

Abolitionist leaders denounced the law as a sham and illusion, and advanced ever more vigorously the demand for total and immediate emancipation. From 1880 on, the antislavery movement developed great momentum. Concentrated in the cities, it drew strength from the process of economic, social, and intellectual modernization under way. To the new urban groups, slavery was an anachronism, glaringly incompatible with modernity.

Among the slave owners, divisions of opinion appeared. In the north, where slavery had become economically inefficient, a growing number of planters shifted to wage labor, drawing on the *sertanejos* (inhabitants of the interior), poor whites and mixed-race people, who lived on the fringes of the plantation economy. Another factor in the decline of the enslaved population in the northeast was the great drought of 1877–1879, which caused many of the region's wealthier folk to sell their slaves or abandon the area, taking their slaves with them. Where native and mixed-race workers vastly outnumbered a few black slaves, provinces like Amazonas and Ceará abolished slavery within their borders in 1884. By contrast, the coffee planters of Rio de Janeiro, São Paulo, and Minas Gerais, joined by northern planters who trafficked in slaves, selling them to the coffee zone, offered the most tenacious resistance to the advance of abolition.

The abolitionist movement produced leaders of remarkable intellectual and moral stature. One

Slaves drying coffee on a plantation in Terreiros, in the state of Rio de Janeiro, about 1882.

was Joaquim Nabuco, the son of a distinguished liberal diplomat of the empire, whose eloquent dissection and indictment of slavery, *O abolicionismo*, had a profound impact on its readers. Another was a mulatto journalist, José de Patrocinio, a master propagandist noted for his fiery, biting style. Another mulatto, André Rebouças, an engineer and teacher whose intellectual gifts won him the respect and friendship of the emperor, was a leading organizer of the movement. For Nabuco and his comrades-in-arms, the antislavery struggle was the major front in a larger struggle for the transformation of Brazilian society. Abolition, they hoped, would pave the way for the attainment of other such goals as land reform, public education, and political democracy.

Yielding to mounting pressure, parliament adopted another measure on September 28, 1885, which liberated all slaves when they reached the age

of sixty but required them to continue to serve their masters for three years and forbade them to leave their place of residence for five years. These conditions, added to the fact that few slaves lived beyond the age of sixty-five, implied little change in the status of the vast majority of slaves. The imperial government also promised to purchase the freedom of the remaining slaves in fourteen years—a promise that few took seriously in light of their experience with the Rio Branco Law. Convinced that the new law was just another tactical maneuver, the abolitionists spurned all compromise solutions and demanded immediate, unconditional emancipation. By the mid-1880s, the antislavery movement had assumed massive proportions and a more militant character. Large numbers of slaves voted for freedom with their feet; they received assistance from abolitionists who organized an underground railroad that helped them escape from São Paulo to

Ceará, where slavery had ended. Efforts to secure the return of fugitive slaves encountered growing resistance. Army officers, organized in a *Club Militar*, protested against the use of the army for the pursuit of fugitive slaves.

In February 1887, São Paulo liberated all slaves in the city with funds raised by popular subscription. Many slave owners, seeing the handwriting on the wall, liberated their slaves on the condition that they remain at work for a certain period. By the end of 1887, even the diehard coffee planters of São Paulo were ready to adjust to new conditions by offering to pay wages to their slaves and improve their working and living conditions; they also increased efforts to induce European immigrants to come to São Paulo. These efforts were highly successful; the flow of immigrants into São Paulo rose from sixty-six hundred in 1885 to more than thirty-two thousand in 1887 and to ninety thousand in 1888. As a result, coffee production reached record levels. With its labor problem solved, São Paulo was ready to abandon its resistance to abolition and even joined the abolitionist crusade.

On May 13, 1888, Brazil finally abolished slavery, but contrary to a traditional interpretation, this decision was not the climax of a gradual process of slavery's decline and slave owners' peaceful acceptance of the inevitable. The total slave population dropped sharply only after 1885, as a result of abolitionist agitation, mass flights of slaves, armed clashes, and other upheavals that appeared to threaten anarchy. In effect, abolition had come not through reform but by revolution.

The aftermath of abolition refuted the dire predictions of its foes. Freed from the burdens of slavery and aided by the continuance of very high coffee prices all over the world (until about 1896), Brazil made more economic progress in a few years than it had during the nearly seven decades of imperial rule. Fazendeiros replaced freedmen with immigrants on the coffee plantations; in the cities, black artisans lost their jobs to immigrants. For the former slaves, however, little had changed. The abolitionist demand for the grant of land to the freedmen was forgotten. Relationships between former masters and slaves in many places remained largely

unchanged; racist traditions and the economic and political power of the fazendeiros gave them almost absolute control over their former slaves. Denied land and education, freedmen faced a future in which the "whip of hunger" now compelled them to labor at the hardest, most poorly paid jobs. Moreover, political reforms that established high income and literacy requirements for citizen participation effectively disenfranchised the freedmen, but they also dramatically reduced voting among free people of color and poor whites. In a society in which, according to the 1872 census, only 16 percent of the people were literate, this legislation disfranchised 99 percent of eligible voters and set the stage for a century of covert, race-based discrimination.

Peru

The liberation of Peru from Spanish rule had come from without, for the creole aristocracy, whose wealth was derived from the forced labor of indigenous peoples and enslaved Africans in mines, workshops, and haciendas, rightly feared that revolution might set fire to this combustible social material. The liberators, General José de San Martín and Simón Bolívar, had attempted to reform the social and economic institutions of the newly created Peruvian state. Before he left to meet Bolívar in Guayaquil, San Martín had decreed a ban on slave importation, the automatic emancipation of all children born of slaves in Peru, the abolition of native tribute, and the end of all other forms of indigenous forced labor; he also proclaimed that all inhabitants of Peru, whether native or creole, were Peruvians.

Because these reforms did not conform to the interests of elite creoles, however, they never implemented them after San Martín left Lima to meet Bolívar in Guayaquil. When Bolívar assumed power in Peru in 1823, he enacted reforms that reflected the same liberal ideology. Wishing to create a class of independent small-holders, he decreed the dissolution of indigenous communities and ordered the division of communal lands into individual parcels; each family was to hold its plot as private property, with the surplus to become part of the public domain. While attacking communal property, Bolívar left alone feudal property, the great haciendas serviced by yanaconas or **colonos** (native sharecroppers or serfs), who were required to pay their landlords a rent that amounted to as much as 50 to 90 percent of the value of their crops.

The well-intentioned Bolivarian land reform played into the hands of hacendados, public officials, and merchants, who used it to build up vast estates at the expense of indigenous communal lands; the process began slowly but gathered momentum as the century advanced. Bolívar's efforts to abolish native tribute had no greater success. After he left Peru in 1826, Peru's creole government reinstituted the tribute for **serranos** (inhabitants of the sierra) under the name of the **contribución de indígenas** (a head tax levied on indigenous peoples), and, for good measure, it also reintroduced the contribución de castas for the mestizo population of the coast.

The new government's heavy dependence on such tribute as a source of revenue reflected the stagnant condition of the Peruvian economy. The revolution completed the ruin of the mining industry and coastal plantation agriculture, both of which had been declining since the close of the eighteenth century, and the scanty volume of exports could not pay for the much greater volume of imports of manufactured goods from Britain. As a result, the new state, already burdened with large wartime debts to English capitalists, developed a massive trade deficit with Great Britain, its largest trading partner. Wool exports increased after 1836, and, in 1840, a new economic era opened on the coast with the exploitation of guano; in its first stage, however, the guano cycle failed to provide the capital accumulation needed to revive coastal agriculture.

PERUVIAN POLITICS AND ECONOMY

Peru's backward, stagnant economy, the profound cleavage between the sierra and the coast, and the absence of a governing class (such as arose in Chile)

that could give reliable and intelligent leadership to the state produced chronic political turbulence and civil wars. This provided abundant opportunities for slaves to initiate their self-liberation. First, urban slavery increasingly emerged as an alternative to the declining productivity of coastal agriculture and highland mining. Rural slaveholders could secure profits by renting their slaves in Lima and other cities, where they performed a broad range of skilled jobs and earned money to pay their owners or purchase their freedom. Second, urban slavery afforded black slaves greater mobility and weakened the slaveholder's direct control. Urban slaves took advantage of this position to challenge their owners in court, claiming that their masters had abused them physically in violation of republican laws. One even claimed the right of manumission because his owner was English and Protestant, an argument designed to appeal to the prejudices of Catholic criollo magistrates in Lima. Third, urban slaves also participated in various conspiracies like the 1835 plot, led by Juan de Dios Algorta, who sought to "overthrow the government and assassinate the whites in Lima." Lastly, although relatively rare by comparison to Caribbean slave revolts, black slaves played leading roles in armed rebellions like the Chicama Revolt of 1851. In the context of what anthropologist James Scott calls "everyday forms of resistance" to slavery, this violent armed rebellion doomed the "peculiar institution" in Peru. Elite property owners could no longer tolerate the social instability that slavery seemed to produce, especially when its economic advantages had long since disappeared.

Under these conditions, military caudillos, sometimes men of plebeian origin who had risen in the ranks during the wars of independence, came to play a decisive role in the political life of the new state. Some were more than selfish careerists or instruments of aristocratic creole cliques. The ablest and most enlightened of the military caudillos was the mestizo general Ramón Castilla, who served as president of Peru from 1845 to 1851 and again from 1855 to 1862. Castilla presided over an advance of the Peruvian economy that relied on the rapid growth of guano exports. British capitalists dominated this export trade and obtained the right to sell guano to specified regions of the world in return for loans to the Peruvian government (secured by guano shipments). Exorbitant interest and commission rates swelled their profits. Castilla contemplated direct government exploitation of some guano deposits, establishment of state controls over price and production, and reinvestment of guano revenues in state development projects, but he never acted on any of these ideas. The guano boom, however, stimulated some growth of native Peruvian commerce and banking and created the nucleus of a national capitalist class. Guano prosperity also financed the beginnings of a modern infrastructure; thus, in 1851 the first railway line began to operate between Lima and its port of Callao.

The rise of guano revenues enabled Castilla to carry out a series of social reforms that also contributed to the process of nation-building. In 1854, he abolished slavery and indigenous tribute, relieving natives of a heavy fiscal burden and freeing enslaved Africans, who numbered some twenty thousand. Abolition was advantageous to the planter aristocracy, who received compensation of up to 40 percent of their slaves' value. With these indemnities, planters could buy seeds, plants, and Chinese coolies brought to Peru on a contract basis that made them virtual slaves. Meanwhile, the freed blacks often became sharecroppers who lived on the margins of the hacienda and supplied a convenient unpaid labor force and a source of rent. Stimulated by these developments, cotton, sugar cane, and grain production expanded on the coast. Highland economic life also quickened, though on a smaller scale, with the rise of extensive livestock breeding for the export of wool and leather through Arequipa and Lima.

The general upward movement of the Peruvian economy after 1850 benefited greatly from such favorable factors as the temporary dislocation of the cotton industry of the southern United States and large inflows of foreign capital. As a result, exports of cotton and sugar increased sharply. The coastal latifundia continued to expand at the expense of indigenous communities, sharecroppers, and tenants, all of whom were expelled from their lands. This process accompanied the modernization of coastal agriculture through the introduction of cotton gins, boilers, refinery equipment for sugar, and steam-driven tractors.

Although profits from the agricultural sector enabled the commercial and landed aristocracy of Lima to live in luxury, the Peruvian state sank even deeper into debt. The unrestrained exploitation of guano deposits, Peru's collateral for its foreign borrowings, depleted this nonrenewable resource at an ever-accelerating rate, and the bulk of the proceeds from these loans went to pay interest on old and new debts. In 1868, during the administration of the military caudillo José Balta, his minister of the treasury, Nicolás de Piérola, devised a plan to extricate Peru from its difficulties and provide funds for development. The project eliminated the numerous consignees to whom the state had sold guano rights and awarded a monopoly of guano sales in Europe to the French firm of Dreyfus and Company. In return, the Dreyfus firm agreed to service its foreign debt and to make Peru a loan that would tide over its immediate difficulties. The contract initiated a new flow of loans that helped create a boundless euphoria, an invincible optimism, about the country's future.

U.S. adventurer and entrepreneur Henry Meiggs, who had made a reputation as a railway builder in Chile, easily convinced Balta and Piérola that they should support the construction of a railway system to tap the mineral wealth of the sierra. As a result, much of the money obtained under the Dreyfus contract, and a large part of the proceeds of the dwindling guano reserves, poured into railway projects that could not show a profit in the foreseeable future.

PARDO AND THE CIVILIANIST PARTY

The good fortune of Dreyfus and Company displeased the native commercial and banking bourgeoisie that had arisen in Lima. A group of these men—headed by the millionaire business executive Manuel Pardo and including former guano consignees whom the Dreyfus contracts had eliminated—challenged the legality of the contract before the

Supreme Court. They argued that assignment of guano sales to their corporation of native consignees would be more beneficial to Peru's economic development. This native bourgeoisie suffered defeat, but in 1871 they organized the *Civilista*, or Civilianist Party (in reference to their opposition to military caudillos), which ran Pardo as its candidate for president. An amalgam of "an old aristocracy and a newly emerging capitalist class," the Civilianist Party opposed clerical and military influence in politics and advocated a large directing role for the state in economic development. Pardo won handily over two rivals and took office in 1872.

Pardo presided over a continuing agricultural boom, with exports reaching a peak in 1876. Foreign capital poured into the country. In those years, an Irish immigrant, W. R. Grace, began to establish an industrial empire that included textile mills, a shipping line, vast sugar estates, and Peru's first large-scale sugar-refining plants. Whereas private industry prospered, the government sank ever deeper into a quagmire of debts and deficits. The guano cycle was nearing its end, with revenues steadily declining because of falling prices, depletion of guano beds, and competition from an important new source of fertilizer: nitrates exploited by Anglo-Chilean capitalists in the southern Peruvian province of Tarapacá. In 1875, wishing to control the nitrate industry and make it a dependable source of government income, Pardo expropriated the foreign companies in Tarapacá and established a state monopoly over the production and sale of nitrates. This measure angered the Anglo-Chilean entrepreneurs, whose holdings Pardo had nationalized and indemnified with bonds of dubious value. Meanwhile, because of unsatisfactory market conditions in Europe, the nationalization measure failed to yield the anticipated economic benefits.

In 1876, Peru felt the full force of a worldwide economic storm. Within a few months, it had forced all the banks of Lima to close; by the following year, the government had to suspend payments on its foreign debt and issue worthless paper money. A military disaster, the War of the Pacific, followed the economic collapse. Despite heroic resistance, Peru suffered a crushing defeat at the hands of a Chilean state that enjoyed a more advanced economic organization, political stability, and the support of British capitalists. The war completed the work of economic ruin begun by the depression. The Chileans occupied and ravaged the economically advanced coastal area: They levied taxes on the hacendados; dismantled equipment from the haciendas and sent it to Chile; and sent troops into the sierra to exact payment from hacendados, towns, and villages. Their extortions infuriated the native peasantry. Led by Gen. Andrés Cáceres, they began to wage an effective guerrilla war of attrition against the Chilean occupiers. The 1883 Treaty of Ancón finally ended the war.

Cuba

Because of its distinctive colonial past, Cuba's nineteenth-century development differed markedly from that of most other Latin American countries. For three centuries after Christopher Columbus landed in 1492, the island served primarily as a strategic stopover for the Spanish treasure fleet. Largely isolated from expanding transatlantic markets and without precious metals or a large indigenous population to exploit, Cuba remained a neglected, sparsely populated outpost of the empire. The island's inhabitants engaged, for the most part, in small-scale farming for domestic consumption. Unlike the sugar-producing islands of the Caribbean, at the end of the seventeenth century, Cuba had few slaves (its population of African descendants numbered 40,000, only one-tenth that of Haiti), many of whom worked in nonagricultural occupations, often as skilled artisans.

ECONOMIC AND SOCIAL CHANGE: THE BITTER HARVEST OF KING SUGAR

The second half of the eighteenth century, however, had brought profound economic and social change as Cuba transformed into a classic case of **monoculture** (an area dependent on the production and export of a single crop for its economic livelihood). Spurred on by the short-lived British occupation of Havana in 1762 and further stimulated by the growing U.S. market produced by independence in 1783, the island experienced a commercial awakening. Most important, Cuba developed into a major sugar producer and slave importer in the aftermath of the Haitian Revolution of the 1790s, which ruined that island as a sugar producer (until then, it had been the world's leader). During the next half-century, sugar production in Cuba skyrocketed, and nearly six hundred thousand enslaved Africans arrived on its shores. From 1774 to 1861, the island's population leaped from 171,620 to 1,396,530, some 30 percent of whom were of African descent.

Initially, the transfer to sugar did not stimulate the creation of the latifundio because much of the land converted to sugar was the underused acreage of large cattle haciendas. Moreover, many farmers did not change over to sugar, preferring instead to produce coffee and tobacco, which then enjoyed high prices resulting from the abolition of the royal monopoly on these commodities. Furthermore, the sugar mills themselves stimulated demand for livestock (to turn the mills) and food crops for the slaves. During the first decades of the nineteenth century, the number of farm proprietors increased markedly, and the leaders of Cuban society came from their ranks for the next century.

By 1800, the economic boom that had followed the destruction of Haitian sugar production ended because other Caribbean islands expanded and initiated production in response to the same stimuli, thereby creating an enormous glut on the market. Just as the industry recovered from this setback, diplomatic maneuvering during the Napoleonic wars closed U.S. ports. Shortly thereafter, two new challenges to the Cuban economy arose: the introduction of beet sugar in Europe and the British campaign to end the slave trade. England forced Spain to end the trade in 1821. Further impediments resulted from the restrictions imposed by Spanish hegemony: high tariffs, scarce and expensive credit, and the disruptions brought on by the Spanish American wars of independence.

By 1820, the first of a series of technological innovations began to transform the character of the sugar industry in Cuba. Mill owners had to expand operations and invest heavily in steam-operated machinery to compete with beet sugar. The larger the mill, the more sugar it could process, the more fuel it consumed, and the more labor it needed. Smaller and less efficient mills were at a severe competitive disadvantage. Modern machinery allowed the mills to expand in size, but they could do so only gradually because of limited transportation facilities. Because railroads were enormously expensive, and in any case capital was insufficient on the island and in Spain for large projects of this type, they did not become important until much later. The mills also carried a huge overhead because they largely lay idle during the off-season, but mill owners still had to feed and shelter their slaves and livestock even when they did not generate new revenues. The problem of fuel for the mills also slowed their expansion. The forests close to the mills quickly disappeared, and transport of wood to the mills proved prohibitively costly.

In response to the need for *centrales* (bigger mills), large plantations also developed in Cuba. Sugar production traditionally had been set up in one of two ways: Resident or temporary labor cultivated the land, or farmers, known as colonos, worked parcels of land for a salary or a share of the crop. They planted and harvested the cane and brought it to the mill, which processed it in exchange for a share of the sugar. Now, to satisfy market demand, successful planters expanded the land under cultivation and deployed massive numbers of enslaved Africans to work more than sixteen hours per day, clearing land, planting and cutting cane, and transporting it to the mills. Not surprisingly, given this high level of exploitation, most slaves died within eight years. This trend toward concentration in the ownership of land and increased capitalization of sugar plantations was a direct result of market-induced changes in the sugar industry.

As a result, sugar production expanded in the first half of the century through an increase in the size of plantations, the number of mills, and enslaved Africans. In 1827, one thousand mills were in operation; two decades later, more than fourteen hundred; and by 1860, two thousand. During the first few decades of the nineteenth century, a reinvigorated African slave trade increased the enslaved population from 18,000 in 1788 to 125,000 in 1810; Spanish slave traders sold 161,000 Africans into slavery between 1811 and 1820, and thereafter some two hundred thousand newly enslaved Africans worked the Cuban sugar plantations.

The expansion of trade and the introduction of large-scale sugar production created a fantastic economic boom and delayed the development of a creole rebellion against Spanish rule that swept the rest of Spanish America. Cuba stayed loyal to Spain during the Spanish American wars of independence, for its creole leaders feared slave rebellions and saw no reason to tamper with their newfound prosperity. Meanwhile, discontent grew among enslaved and free blacks because of the rise of an increasingly harsh plantation system. In addition to everyday acts of resistance, such as work slowdowns, feigned illness, equipment sabotage, and abortion, enslaved African men and women periodically punctuated their daily protests against enslavement with major slave revolts like the Aponte Rebellion in 1812 and La Escalera in 1844. Very much influenced by the Haitian Revolution and other slave insurrections throughout the Caribbean world, these rebellions united enslaved Africans, Cuban-born black slaves, free blacks, and free people of color to seek the destruction of slavery and plantation agriculture.

By the last half of the nineteenth century, however, wealthy creoles became increasingly

© Bettmann/CORBIS

An Afro-Cuban woman called Black Carlota led a fearsome slave rebellion in 1843 that terrified Spanish officials and creole plantation owners, who relied on enslaved African labor to work the sugar plantations, as depicted in this 1830 image.

resentful of corrupt Spanish officialdom, which was determined to enforce continued obedience from Spain's last and richest colony in the New World. The colony grew increasingly dissatisfied with repressive Spanish rule and less dependent economically on the mother country. As Cuba turned increasingly toward the United States as a market for its products and a source of needed imports, schemes for the annexation of Cuba to the United States emerged both on the island and in some North American circles. In Cuba, conservative creole planters saw annexation as an insurance policy against the abolition of slavery; in the United States, some proslavery groups regarded annexation as a means of gaining a vast new area for the expansion of plantation slavery. Some even dreamed that carving Cuba into three or five states would give the South increased power in the U.S. national government, but the Civil War ended these projects.

During the 1860s, a developing national and class consciousness intensified and spread creole discontent. The creole elite rejected various reform proposals offered by an ineffectual Spanish government that internal dissension and economic difficulties had weakened. It became increasingly clear to the creoles that Spanish economic and political policies severely restricted Cuban development—a feeling sharpened by a serious economic downturn.

Meanwhile, Cuba's sugar economy had developed a sectional specialization. To the east, a sparse population, predominantly composed of free whites with a relatively small share of black slaves, worked on cattle ranches that produced meat for consumption on the slave-based sugar plantations that dominated western Cuba. Creole landowners in the east, less dependent on slave labor, feared slave rebellions less than they feared Spanish domination. As a result, on October 10, 1868, in the small town of Yara in Oriente Province, Carlos Manuel de Céspedes, a creole landowner, voluntarily freed those he had enslaved and launched Cuba's first movement for independence from Spanish colonialism. During the Ten Years' War that followed, race increasingly divided the rebel movement, as free black and mixed-race leaders like Antonio Maceo predominated. Their demands were simple and straightforward: They wanted independence, the abolition of slavery, and the establishment of a postcolonial racial equality.

Even as the Spanish sought to divide the rebels by manipulating creole planters' racial fears, the movement's increasingly black military leadership celebrated the idea of nation over race. In 1869, the rebel movement drafted a constitution that declared "all inhabitants of the Republic entirely free" and granted citizenship to all "soldiers of the Liberation Army," a majority of whom were Afro-Cuban. But some creole rebel leaders, fearing the radicalism of the Afro-Cuban demand for freedom from Spain and slave masters alike, sought to amend the Constitution to require Cuban citizens to lend their "services according to their aptitudes," a clear attempt to discriminate against Afro-Cubans. They also drafted the *Reglamento de Libertos* that "assigned" freedmen to "pro-Cuban owners" or "other masters." Naturally, this alienated Afro-Cuban rebels, who refused to compromise on the issues of abolition, independence, and racial equality. For them, *cubanidad* (Cuban national identity) transcended race; to be Cuban meant equality and freedom from oppression, whether from Spain, the creole slave master, or self-described white men.

THE TEN YEARS' WAR

The Ten Years' War, a long, bitter, devastating guerrilla struggle, ended ignominiously in 1878 when Cuban creole leaders accepted a peace that granted them some autonomy but withheld independence. The Pact of Zanjón ended hostilities, but some rebel leaders, like the black revolutionary Antonio Maceo, the "Bronze Titan," rejected the settlement because it recognized the freedom only of slaves who had fought in the rebel army; it did not achieve the main goals of the revolution: complete independence and the abolition of slavery. Consequently, Afro-Cubans refused to surrender arms, more slaves escaped to maroon communities, and those who remained enslaved refused to work or obey plantation masters. New Spanish colonial laws sought to suppress this post-Zanjón rebelliousness by restricting movements of the enslaved, punishing the enslaved for communication with outsiders, prohibiting the enslaved from possession of machetes, and regulating sales of the enslaved.

Notwithstanding these efforts, however, Afro-Cuban resistance ultimately resulted in a new conflict, the 1879 *Guerra Chiquita* (Little War), which distinguished itself by the absence of creole participation and the prominence both of black military and political leadership that demanded abolition and equal rights. Desperate to stabilize the island, preserve Spanish colonial authority, and prevent a second black republic in the Caribbean, the Spanish government sought the loyalty of free Afro-Cubans by abolishing slavery in 1880, with provision for an eight-year **patronato** (period of apprenticeship) for the liberated slaves. Ironically, the abolition of slavery removed the last major factor that made creole planters loyal to Spain. Thereafter, the prospect of independence, offering free, unlimited trade with the United States, became increasingly attractive.

The Ten Years' War and the Guerra Chiquita had a far-reaching impact on the development of Cuban society. First, the conflicts decimated the creole landowning class, hindering the formation of a traditional Latin American landed elite on the island. Second, they convinced future Cuban independence leaders—black and white—that success required the abolition of race and the substitution of national identity. To that end, Cuban nationalists like José Martí and the Afro-Cuban journalist Juan Gualberto Gómez produced war memoirs that de-racialized black insurgents in the Ten Years' War and instead celebrated them as "national heroes." According to historian Ada Ferrer, these counter-hegemonic discourses contradicted Spanish propaganda about a future "black republic" and depicted images of faithful blacks who were "grateful" for "white generosity."

Naturally, this image of passive black insurgents starkly contradicted the reality of black political activism between 1886 and 1895. Afro-Cubans, drawing on their political experiences during the previous decade, organized the *Directorio Central de las Sociedades de las Clases de Color*, a group whose principal objective was to promote racial equality on the island. They aimed to create free public schools, abolish segregated civil registers and "titles of courtesy," and secure equal access to public roads, transportation, and public accommodations.

Third, the shakeout of mills during the war, the financial crisis of 1885–1890, and the expansion of the island's railroad network combined to stimulate the spread of latifundios. As they grew, the mills required more sugar cane, which came from a wider geographic area than they previously had. At the same time, the introduction of cheap rails spurred railroad construction in Cuba (and all around the world). In their quest for more cane, owners of centrales began to lay their own track, and a competition among centrales for cane, a condition previously unknown because of transportation limitations, resulted.

The owners of centrales confronted the necessity of guaranteeing enough cane at the lowest possible prices for the *zafra* (harvest). They could do this either by reducing the independence of the colonos or by acquiring their own cane land. The first method transformed the once-free farmers into satellites of the giant mills. The second led to the proliferation of latifundia. Small and midsize growers fell by the wayside, replaced by tenants or day laborers. The colonos managed to hold their own until independence, after which time the massive influx of foreign capital into the sugar mills overwhelmed them. With their dwindling financial resources, they were doomed.

Entrepreneurs from the United States filled the vacuum created by the ruin of the creole aristocracy and the bankruptcy of Spanish interests by the war. Thousands of North Americans accompanied their investment dollars to the island to run the sugar mills and merchant houses. The McKinley Tariff Act of 1890, which abolished import duties on raw sugar and molasses, greatly increased American trade with and economic influence in Cuba; by 1896, U.S. interests had invested $50 million in Cuba and controlled the sugar industry. The United States purchased 87 percent of Cuba's exports. The growth of U.S. investment in Cuba also brought about an increasing concentration of sugar production, a trend signaled by the entry of the "Sugar Trust" (the American Sugar Refining Company of Henry Q. Havemeyer) into the island in 1888.

Although the Ten Years' War had transformed Cuba into a haven for North Americans, it had done nothing to eliminate racial segregation and discrimination, even after emancipation. Elite Spanish and creole white supremacists dominated late-nineteenth-century Cuba and routinely blamed Afro-Cubans for all manner of Cuban social ills, denied them access to education and adequate health care, engaged in employment discrimination, and created obstacles to full citizenship. Interracial marriage, prohibited by law until 1881, remained socially stigmatized thereafter.

This racial apartheid created two Cubas—one steeped in Spanish cultural traditions and ritual practices like Catholicism and Freemasonry, and the other centered in African *santería* (a syncretic popular religion) and *ñáñigos* (secret mutual aid societies). According to historian Aline Helg, Afro-Cubans, frustrated by limits imposed on their ability to rise in Spanish society, increasingly relied on their African heritage to protect themselves and to organize social protest movements that demanded their "rightful share."

Gran Colombia

The early history of Venezuela and Colombia is indistinguishable from the life's work of the liberator Simón Bolívar. Venezuela was his homeland, and Colombia (then called New Granada) and Venezuela were the theaters of his first decisive victories in the war for Latin American independence. Bolívar sought to unite Venezuela and New Granada into a single large and powerful state and looked toward the creation of a vast federation of all the Spanish American republics, extending from Mexico to Cape Horn. In 1819, the Congress of Angostura (in Venezuela) approved the formation of the state of Colombia (later called Gran Colombia, or Greater Colombia) that would combine Venezuela, New

Granada, and Ecuador (then still in Spanish hands). In 1821, at Cúcuta on the Venezuelan-Colombian border, the revolutionary congress formalized the union and outlined a liberal reform program. It included the gradual abolition of slavery, the abolition of native tribute, the division of indigenous communal lands into private parcels (a "reform" that opened the door to land-grabbing), the suppression of smaller male convents and the seizure of their property for the support of public secondary education, and a general expansion of education. It also adopted a centralized constitution that guaranteed citizenship rights to all people, irrespective of gender or race.

Drafted according to Bolívar's wishes, the constitution created a nation-state that reflected his indictment of Spain's colonial domination. For him, Spain had functioned as a tyrannical father who enslaved his children for his own profit and thereby refused to allow them to develop into mature adults. As a result, he argued that the new republic, controlled by its enlightened "Founding Fathers," was obligated to prepare its rebellious children for the responsibilities of self-government before they could secure full and equal citizenship rights. Committed to the contradictory ideas of liberty, equality, property, and security, Bolívar's generation of wealthy propertied creoles aimed to create a patriarchal nation that would protect property and order against the chaotic protests of women, poor whites, and peoples of African descent, all of whom yearned for freedom and equality.

Arguably, the most pressing issue that faced the young republic was slavery. Naturally, enslaved Africans and their descendants variously had accommodated and resisted slavery since its introduction in the early colonial period. This included slave revolts; escape to *cumbes* (remote, autonomous village communities) or palenques; and other everyday acts of resistance. During the independence wars, Bolívar and his comrades had encouraged slave emancipation by recruiting them to service in the liberation army. Free blacks and pardos (mixed-race people) flocked to military service. However, in the aftermath of independence, women, slaves, free blacks, and pardos all seized on republican laws

Mural by Ian Pierce/Courtesy of Encontrarte

Slave rebellions marked Gran Colombia's transition from colony to republic and shaped the nature of nineteenth-century debates over citizenship in Colombia and Venezuela. One rebellion, led by José Leonardo Chirino, a free zambo, occurred in 1795 and was immortalized by the Chilean artist Ian Pierce, whose mural at the Colegio Andrés Bello in Caracas commemorates the event.

and the rhetoric of national liberation to petition the government for their emancipation. In response to this general clamor for equal citizenship rights, creole leaders aimed to fashion laws and political institutions that would protect private property and patriarchy.

The movement to abolish slavery offers a powerful example of this negotiation among creole elites and between them and subalterns. In 1820, pursuant to military exigencies and congressional proclamations that "no man can be the property of another," Bolívar had ordered Francisco de Paula Santander, a leading general under his command, to recruit an army of some five thousand slaves in the provinces of Antioquía and Chocó by promising emancipation. This naturally excited great enthusiasm

among the enslaved population, but it alienated mine owners and other proprietors who depended on slave labor. To reconcile these conflicting interests, Santander limited his recruitment to three thousand and directed all remaining slaves to return to their masters.

A similar compromise at the Congress of Cúcuta effectively prolonged the institution of slavery. It passed a law that called for the gradual abolition of slavery through a complicated process of manumission. Thereafter, all children born of enslaved mothers would be free, but they were required to work for their mother's master until age eighteen. The law also created a series of local **juntas de manumisión** (committees composed of local notables), who were responsible for collecting tax monies necessary to pay slaveholders compensation for their loss. The juntas, notoriously inefficient and largely representing the interests of slave owners, failed to liberate many slaves.

Nonetheless, slaves continued to pressure Bolívar and his creole nation by organizing revolts that swept across the republic between 1824 and 1827. Fearing the nation's imminent collapse, Bolívar issued an 1828 decree that effectively centralized control over the juntas and assessed financial penalties against local junta members who failed to act. This contributed to a growing chorus of criticism from elites and local military caudillos like José Antonio Páez, the pardo leader, who denounced Bolívar's "dictatorial" actions and called for the dissolution of Gran Colombia in 1829. In addition to the conflict over slavery, Gran Colombia's survival was doomed by its geographic, economic, and social realities. Immense distances separated its component parts, and a mountainous terrain made communication difficult; it took about a month for a letter to reach Bogotá from Caracas. These conditions also hindered the development of economic ties among Venezuela, New Granada, and Ecuador; Caracas and other Venezuelan coastal cities communicated more easily with Europe than overland via the Andes with Bogotá. Finally, the Venezuelan elite of cacao planters, merchants, and military leaders or caudillos had little sympathy for Bolívar's idea of fusing several independent Spanish American republics into one and even less for his vision of a confederation that would unite all the Spanish American states.

PÁEZ, THE CONSERVATIVE–LIBERAL SPLIT, AND THE FEDERAL WAR IN VENEZUELA, 1830–1863

On May 6, 1830, a congress assembled in Valencia to provide the independent state of Venezuela with a constitution, the third in the country's short history. The document limited suffrage to males who were twenty-one, were literate, and had a high income. These requirements excluded most of the population, numbering under 900,000, from participation in political life. Of these, some 60 percent were descended from Africans. Another 15 percent

were natives, and a quarter identified as white. A tiny minority of these, about ten thousand, composed the ruling class of wealthy merchants, great landowners, high officeholders, and military officers, who usually also owned large landed estates. The members of this class, often linked through family networks, dominated politics.

Military hero, longtime champion of Venezuelan independence, and former ranch hand José Antonio Páez was elected president, a post he combined with that of supreme army commander. His rise illustrated the renewal of the old colonial ruling class through the admission of a new elite of military caudillos, frequently of humble origins. The Venezuelan society and economy over which Páez presided essentially resembled the colonial social and economic order. The latifundio continued as the basic unit of economic activity; concentration of landownership increased after independence because of the rapid acquisition of royalist estates and public lands by a small group of military caudillos. A decree of October 15, 1830, compelling the sale of so-called uncultivated indigenous lands, gave the latifundists more opportunities to expand their landholdings. Labor relations in the countryside continued to rely heavily on slavery, peonage, and various forms of tenancy, including sharecropping and obligatory personal service.

Slavery in Venezuela, as in other parts of Latin America, had long been in decline. Enslaved Africans' defiant opposition to enslavement, either through passive forms of resistance, rebellions, or escape to *cumbes* (runaway slave settlements), had made slavery socially destabilizing and less economically efficient. Nonetheless, slave owners continued to insist on the protection of their property rights, which, under the terms of the 1821 law, would have required manumission of the first generation of free-born blacks in 1839. So the Venezuelan Constituent Congress of 1830 adopted a manumission law that extended their masters' control until the age of twenty-one. Thereafter, another decree established a mandatory "apprenticeship" program that prolonged the age of manumission from twenty-one to twenty-five and secured the patrón's control over his labor force. Continuing a tendency that began in the late colonial period, however, many slave owners found it more profitable to free their slaves voluntarily, because they generally remained on their former masters' land as tenants or peons bound by debts and other obligations. By 1841, fourteen thousand had been freed in this manner—one hundred fifty of them only because they had reached the age of manumission—but some forty thousand slaves remained in 1844.

The long revolutionary war had caused immense material damage and loss of life—the population declined by 262,000—and destroyed the fragile economic links between the country's different regions. By the 1830s, however, Venezuela experienced an economic boom, rooted in the switch from cacao to coffee as its principal export and the country's integration into the capitalist world market, which henceforth absorbed about 80 percent of Venezuela's exports of coffee, cacao, indigo, tobacco, and hides.

The high coffee prices that accompanied the 1830s boom made planters hungry for credit to expand production by obtaining new land. Foreign merchant capitalists, the Venezuelan export-import merchants who were their agents, and native moneylenders were happy to oblige, using coffee crops and the planters' estates as security, but colonial legislation that regulated interest rates and punished usury posed an obstacle. The Venezuelan congress removed this impediment by passing a credit law in 1834 that abolished all traditional Spanish controls on contracts; the state then enforced legally executed contracts, no matter how exorbitant the interest rates. By the late 1830s, with the world price of coffee in decline, the Venezuelan economy was in serious trouble. Creditors refused to refinance their debtors, plunging Venezuela into a severe depression.

The economic crisis caused a rift in the elite, with the emergence of factions that turned into political parties in the 1840s. One called itself Conservative, but opponents dubbed its members *godos* (Goths) to identify them with the unpopular Spanish colonial rule. Páez was its acknowledged leader, and it represented the views and interests of the export-import merchants and their foreign partners, the moneylenders, the high civil and military bureaucracy, and

some great landowners. The Liberal Party was led by Antonio Leocadio Guzmán and was a loose coalition of debt-ridden planters, the urban middle class, artisans, intellectuals seeking reform, and disaffected caudillos who resented Páez's long reign.

Guzmán's rhetorical press attacks on conservative economic policies contributed to the growing social tension. A series of popular uprisings and slave revolts between 1839 and 1852, which Páez described as open warfare against private property, terrified the Conservatives, who raised the specter of a general social race war waged by pardos and slaves. Although Conservatives blamed Guzmán's inflammatory propaganda, in fact the Liberals feared social revolution as much as their opponents and had no links to these popular revolts. Nonetheless, the government, determined to crush them at their supposed source, brought Guzmán to trial, found him guilty of instigating the revolutionary movements, and sentenced him to death.

By 1854, popular unrest, slave revolts, and passive resistance to slavery had dramatically raised its cost, which, combined with the downturn in global coffee prices, threatened planters' profits. Conservatives thereafter sought to assist their allies by supporting congressional passage of several laws designed to give relief to distressed planters. One of these laws abolished slavery in Venezuela, guaranteeing compensation to slave owners, some of whom already were voluntarily freeing their slaves to avoid paying their support.

In effect, abolition aimed to end an economically costly and socially destabilizing popular movement, but emancipation brought little change in the lives of most freedmen. In the absence of a modern factory system to provide alternative employment or any program for distributing land to them, most were doomed to remain on their former owners' estates as tenants burdened with heavy obligations. Others earned scanty wages paid in *vales* (tokens) redeemable only for goods purchased in the ***tienda de raya*** (estate store) at inflated monopoly prices.

Hard times continued in the late 1850s. Depressed coffee prices and elite fears of a social explosion persuaded Conservatives and Liberals to join forces momentarily, but the coalition soon fell apart. A group of extreme Conservatives seized power, installed a repressive government, and imprisoned or deported many Liberals, who responded with an uprising that began the Federal War (1858–1863).

The term *federal* as used here had different meanings for the liberal elite and its rank-and-file followers, most of whom were pardos or blacks who rallied to the federalist battle cry "Death to the whites." However, whereas Conservatives denounced the liberal elite for fomenting a "race war," the "colored population" saw it as a war of the poor majority against the wealthy, propertied elite. After their victory, liberal leaders gave the country a new constitution (1864) with many reforms, including universal male suffrage and increased autonomy for the twenty states. Nevertheless, without substantive social reform, these rights were virtually meaningless. Federalism under these conditions simply meant the continued supremacy of the local caudillo, who often was a great landowner.

However, for peasants and artisans who rose in spontaneous revolt against the conservative regime and rallied to the liberal leadership's slogan of federalism, the term had a different meaning. A manifesto by Ezequiel Zamora, a veteran guerrilla fighter, brilliantly captured their vague hopes for revolutionary change. Zamora supported the occupation of large estates by their former peons and tenants, creation of federal states, and election of local governments by the citizenry. Zamora's death by an assassin's bullet in 1860 cut short the life of a leader who represented a genuinely democratic, social revolutionary tendency in the Federal War.

Fearing the growing power of peasant revolutionists, Conservatives and Liberals agreed to a negotiated peace. The 1863 Treaty of Coche ended the war, which had cost some fifty thousand lives, inflicted immense damage on the economy, and destroyed many haciendas. The cattle herds of the llanos virtually had disappeared because of wartime depredations and neglect. Like the War of Independence, the Federal War produced limited social changes. The old conservative oligarchy disintegrated, and victorious liberal military officers, some of plebeian background, occupied their

estates. For the revolutionary rank-and-file, however, the war's end forced them to surrender the parcels of land and return as peons to the great estates that they once had occupied.

SANTANDER AND THE BIRTH OF A TWO-PARTY SYSTEM IN COLOMBIA, 1830–1850

Following the secession of Venezuela and Ecuador from Gran Colombia in 1830, the remaining territory went its separate way under the name of the Republic of New Granada (present-day Colombia plus Panama). Led by Bolívar's old ally Francisco de Paula Santander, New Granada adopted a constitution that provided for a president elected for four years, a bicameral Congress, and provincial legislatures. The constitution granted suffrage to all free males who were married or age twenty-one and were not domestic servants or day laborers. In practice, a small aristocratic ruling class dominated political life.

The geographic, economic, and social conditions of the new state posed even greater obstacles to the creation of a true national society. Dominated by the towering Andean cordillera, whose ranges, valleys, and plateaus were home to a million people, the country's difficult geography offered formidable barriers to communication and transport.

New Granadan industry displayed many precapitalist features. Working in their homes, women chiefly produced most industrial activity, including weaving and spinning, pottery making, and shoe manufacture. In Bogotá, many state-sponsored efforts to establish factories producing soap, glassware, textiles, and iron ended in failure. By the 1840s, sizable artisan groups had arisen in larger towns like Bogotá, Medellín, and Cali, but despite moderate tariff protections for local industries, they had difficulty competing with imported foreign goods. The backwardness of economic life was most apparent in transportation; in parts of the country, porters and pack mules typically dominated the local transport industry well into the twentieth century. Even after steamboat navigation became regular on the Magdalena River, it took between four and six weeks to make the voyage from Atlantic ports to Bogotá. The limited development of productive forces and the sluggish tempo of economic activity produced modest wealth even for the elite. In the first half of the nineteenth century, the income of Bogotá's upper class came to about $5,000 per capita, and the number of individuals whose capital exceeded $100,000 was exceedingly small.

The lack of a dynamic export base to stimulate the economy and provide resources for a strong nation-state was a major factor in Colombia's economic and political difficulties in its first half-century. Efforts to replace declining gold production with tobacco, cotton, and other export products generated a series of short booms that quickly collapsed because of shrinking markets, falling prices, and growing foreign competition. The absence of an export base and a nationally dominant elite helps explain the "economic archipelago" or regional isolation and self-sufficiency that developed. A corollary of this economic autarchy was political autarchy, an almost permanent instability punctuated by frequent civil wars or threats of war and even secession by hacendado-generals, who could mobilize private armies of peons to settle scores with rival caudillos or the weak central government.

The large hacienda or plantation, mainly dedicated to growing wheat, barley, potatoes, and raising cattle, dominated agriculture, the backbone of the economy. Their labor force usually consisted of mestizo peons or tenants who paid rent in labor or in kind for the privilege of cultivating their own small parcels of land; debts restricted their freedom of movement, and sometimes they owed personal service to their patrón.

Alongside these haciendas and on marginal lands and mountain slopes lived other peasants whose precarious independence came from subsistence farming and supplying food to nearby towns. The northwest region of Antioquia, with its rugged terrain and low population, had few haciendas and numerous small and midsize landholdings; a more independent peasantry had also arisen in neighboring Santander. The Spanish had enslaved thousands of Africans and their descendants to labor on plantations and in gold-mining districts in the western states and on the Caribbean coast. However, the institution, greatly weakened by independence wars, slave resistance, and Free Womb legislation, was in decline. Nonetheless, slave owners zealously defended their property rights and sought to limit both the pace of abolition and the rights of *libertos* (freedmen) born to slave mothers after 1821. To ensure their mothers' masters a plentiful supply of cheap labor, an 1842 law limited freedmen's mobility, enforced prison penalties for violation of vagrancy laws, and sanctioned *concertaje* (a mandatory "apprenticeship" program) that placed freedmen in a "trade craft, profession, or useful occupation" until age twenty-five.

Naturally, slaves and libertos resisted these efforts to control their labor by rebelling violently or running away. Moreover, they also joined together with merchants, artisans, peasants, and freedmen to create a cross-class, multiracial coalition dedicated to immediate emancipation. Some black freedmen even scandalized Liberals and Conservatives by their insistence upon what anthropologist Michael Taussig calls a "radical Catholic utopia, anarchist and egalitarian." Organized into Democratic Societies, this mass movement relentlessly pressured the liberal government of José Hilario López to abolish slavery, which he finally did in 1851, but not before quieting a slaveholders' rebellion by guaranteeing them full compensation. The measure, freeing about twenty-five thousand individuals, had its most severe impact on gold-mining areas, which generally relied heavily on slave labor.

The Liberals, however, always had equated emancipation with *mestizaje* (a homogenized mixed-race culture) that required the sacrifice of distinct African and indigenous ethnic identities and the invention of an idealized unified Hispanic national culture, perhaps best reflected in the Colombian motto of "one God, one race, one tongue." This secured the power and property of liberal elites, but it presumed the surrender of indigenous and African communal lands and their autonomous political traditions. Thereafter, the Liberals intensified the attack on *resguardos* (native communal lands), and land "liberated" by forced division often passed into the hands of neighboring hacendados by legal or illegal means. Natives made landless by such means often became peons forced to serve the hacendados.

To fashion a unified mestizo national identity, Liberals sought to distinguish themselves clearly from their conservative rivals. Until the late 1840s, the difference between the ideologies and programs of the two groups was far from absolute. Actually, both represented upper-class interests but accepted the formal democracy of representative, republican government; both had faith in social and technological progress, believed in the freedoms of speech and of the press as well as other civil liberties, and in economic policy accepted laissez-faire and liberal economics. Neither party cared about the agrarian problem or other problems of the rural and urban masses. The only genuine issue separating them was the relation between church and state and the church's role in education. The emergent Liberal Party was distinctly anticlerical, regarding the church as hostile to progress; however, they favored freedom of worship and separation of church and state. The nascent Conservative Party endorsed religious toleration but favored cooperation between church and state, believing that religion promoted morality and social peace.

In the struggle over emancipation, however, the ideological gap between Liberals and Conservatives widened, and three new political factions emerged: urban artisans, Gólgotas, and *Draconianos*, military from the lower officer ranks, who later aligned themselves with the artisans. Shaped by the rapid expansion of tobacco cultivation, the beginnings of the coffee cycle, and a resulting growth of foreign and domestic trade, the Gólgotas were the sons of a merchant class whose population increased to 2 million by 1850. Well-educated and influenced by antislavery agitation, French romanticism, utopian socialism, and the Revolution of 1848 in France, they developed a peculiar sentimental brand of liberalism that drew heavily on a romantic interpretation of Christianity in which Christ, described as the "Martyr of Golgotha," appeared as a forerunner of nineteenth-century secular reformism. This ideology's practical essence was its demand for the abolition of slavery, the ecclesiastical and military fuero, compulsory tithing, and all restraints on free enterprise.

Urban artisans, whose numbers also had increased in the preceding decade, faced growing competition from foreign imported manufactures, which caused serious unemployment. Attributing their distress to lower tariffs that benefited conservative slave owners and their plantations, these artisans readily identified with the language of freedom and equality that shaped the political struggle against slavery. In 1847, they created a network of Democratic Societies, beginning with the Democratic Society of Bogotá, which had almost four thousand members. These mutual-aid societies carried on education and philanthropic activities, but they also served as important political vehicles for the liberal leadership, enabling the new merchant elite, with large support from regional landed oligarchies, to seek the triumph of laissez-faire and modernity.

Clearly, struggles against slavery provided the historical context within which Brazil, Cuba, Peru, Colombia, and Venezuela defined their respective national identities, but the closely related issues of race and property played equally powerful roles. Ultimately, Liberals seized on the language of freedom and equality, always explicit in the abolitionist movements throughout the region, to insist on the emancipation of slaves. They also created a national discourse that demanded freedom from foreign domination and state regulation, conditions necessary to protect their class privileges and property. This language of nation sought to silence more radical demands for racial equality and mass democratic participation.

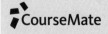 Go to the CourseMate website at **www.cengagebrain.com** for primary sources, additional study tools, and review materials—including audio and video clips—for this chapter.

The Triumph of Neocolonialism and the Liberal State, 1870–1900

11

FOCUS QUESTIONS

- What was neocolonialism, and what were its characteristic economic and political features? What role did the liberal state play in promoting national economic growth between 1870 and 1900?

- What were the policies of Mexico's Porfirio Díaz regarding indigenous communities, land, labor, trade, and foreign investment?

- What were the policies of Argentina's Julio Roca regarding indigenous communities, land, labor, and foreign investment?

- What were the major elements of Justo Rufino Barrios's liberal reform program in Guatemala?

- How did Antonio Guzmán Blanco's program in Venezuela compare with Rafael Núñez's plan in Colombia, and how did each affect national economic development?

- How did these liberal programs contrast with the developmental policies of José Manuel Balmaceda in Chile?

- How did liberal development programs affect subaltern social classes, especially peasants and workers?

BEGINNING ABOUT 1870, the quickening tempo of the Industrial Revolution in Europe stimulated a more rapid pace of change in the Latin American economy and politics. Responding to mounting demand for raw materials and foodstuffs, Latin American producers increased their output of those commodities. Increasing political stability, itself the result of the consolidation of the liberal state, facilitated the region's growing trade with Europe and the United States.

Encouraged by the increased stability and liberal economic policies, European capital flowed into Latin America, creating railroads, docks, processing plants, and other facilities needed to expand production and trade. Latin America became integrated into an international economic system in which it exchanged raw materials and foodstuffs for the factory-made goods of Europe and North America. Gradual adoption of free-trade policies by many Latin American countries, which marked the abandonment of efforts to create a native factory capitalism, hastened the area's integration into this international division of labor.

The New Colonialism

This "neocolonial" economic system fastened a new dependency on Latin America, with Great Britain and later the United States replacing Spain and Portugal in the dominant role. Despite its built-in flaws

1873–1885	Justo Rufino Barrios inaugurates liberal dictatorship in Guatemala
1876–1885	Rafael Zaldívar established liberal dictatorship in El Salvador
1879–1883	Chile wins the War of the Pacific and seizes mineral-rich lands from Peru and Bolivia, which becomes land-locked
1881	Revolt of the Comuneros in Nicaragua protests privatization of indigenous communal lands; Zaldívar abolishes communal land tenure in El Salvador
1883	*Ley de deslindes* privatizes public lands in Mexico; Chile expropriates Araucanian ancestral lands
1886–1891	President Balmaceda promotes national industrial and agricultural development in Chile despite opposition from latifundistas and foreign investors
1889	Benjamin Constant leads overthrow of Dom Pedro II in Brazil to create the First Republic
1891	Chilean oligarchy and foreign capitalists overthrow Balmaceda
1893–1910	José Santos Zelaya creates liberal dictatorhip in Nicaragua
1894	*Ley de terrenos baldíos* privatizes Mexican public lands
1896	Canudos Rebellion resists Brazil's oligarchic republic and abolishes private property
1899–1908	Cipriano Castro seizes dictatorial power in Venezuela
1906	Major labor strike at Cananea Copper Company in Mexico; Brazilian Labor Confederation protests oligarchic republic
1909	Rio Blanco strikes in Mexico close down textile production; Luis Emilio Recabarren organizes Chilean Workers' Federation
1912	Argentine oligarchy passes Sáenz Peña Law

and local breakdowns, the neocolonial order displayed a certain stability until 1914. By disrupting the markets for Latin America's exports and making it difficult to import the manufactured goods that Latin America required, World War I marked the beginning of a general crisis of neocolonialism and the liberal state.

Although the period from 1870 to 1914 saw rapid overall growth of the Latin American economy, the pace and degree of progress were uneven, with some countries (like Bolivia and Paraguay) joining the advance much later than others. A marked feature of the neocolonial order was its one-sidedness (monoculture). One or a few primary products became the basis of prosperity for each country, making it highly vulnerable to fluctuations in the world demand and price of these products. Argentina and Uruguay depended on wheat and meat; Brazil on coffee, sugar, and briefly rubber; Chile on copper and nitrates; Honduras on bananas; Cuba on sugar.

In each country, the modern export sector became an enclave that was largely isolated from the rest of the economy and that actually accentuated the backwardness of other sectors by draining off their labor and capital. The export-oriented nature of the modern sector shaped the pattern of national railway systems, which as a rule aimed to satisfy the transportation needs of export industries, rather than integrate each country's regional markets into a unified national network. In addition, the modern export sector often rested on extremely precarious foundations. Rapid, feverish growth, punctuated by slumps that sometimes ended in a total collapse, formed part of the neocolonial pattern; such meteoric rise and fall is the story of Peruvian guano, Chilean nitrates, and Brazilian rubber.

The triumph of neocolonialism in Latin America in the late nineteenth century was not inevitable or predetermined by Europe's economic "head start" or the area's past history of dependency. The leap from a feudal or semifeudal economy and society to an autonomous capitalist system, although difficult, is not impossible, as the case of Japan makes clear. Following independence, the new states had to choose between the alternatives of autonomy or dependency, or in the words of historian Florencia Mallon, "between focusing on internal production and capital formation, on the one hand, and relying increasingly on export production, foreign markets, and ultimately foreign capital, on the other." However, the formation of the dynamic entrepreneurial class and the large internal market required by autonomous capitalism could not be achieved without such sweeping reforms as the breakup of great estates, the abolition of peonage and other coercive labor systems, and the adoption of a consistent policy of supporting native industry. Such reforms required a powerful, activist nation-state committed to the regulation of market forces and the redistribution of material resources. Most sections of the elite, however, found them too costly and threatening. Instead, they embraced the liberal developmental creed that stressed the need to privatize public resources, reduce government expenditures, dismantle state bureaucracies, provide incentives to foreign investors, and encourage export trade. Most Latin American elites, therefore, chose the easier road of continued dependency, with first Great Britain and later the United States replacing Spain as the metropolis.

Latin America in the nineteenth century, however, produced some serious efforts to break with this pattern of dependence. We already described two such efforts. A remarkable and temporarily successful project for autonomous development was launched in Paraguay under the rule of Dr. Francia and the Lópezes, father and son. Their state-directed program of agrarian reform and industrial diversification transformed Paraguay from a backward country into a relatively prosperous and advanced state, but the disastrous Paraguayan War interrupted this progress and returned Paraguay to a state of backwardness and dependency. In Chile, in the 1850s, an alliance of mining capitalists, small farmers, and artisans attempted to overthrow the landed and mercantile oligarchy and implement a radical program of political and social reform; their "frustrated bourgeois revolution" was drowned in blood. In this chapter, we examine a second Chilean effort to achieve autonomous development under the slogan "Chile for the Chileans"; it too ended in defeat and in the death of the president who led it.

Expansion of the Hacienda System

The neocolonial order evolved within the framework of the traditional system of land tenure and labor relations. Indeed, it led to an expansion of the hacienda system on a scale far greater than the colonial period had known. As the growing European demand for Latin American products and the growth of national markets raised the value of land, the great landowners in country after country launched assaults on the surviving indigenous community lands. In part at least, this drive reflected an effort to eliminate indigenous competition in the emerging market economy. In Mexico, the Reforma laid the legal basis for this attack in the 1850s and 1860s; it reached its climax in the era of Porfirio Díaz. In the Andean region, similar legislation turned all communal property into individual holdings, leading to a cycle of indigenous revolt and bloody government repressions. However, not all native peoples opposed the nineteenth-century drive to dissolve the ancient communal landholding system. In both Mexico and the Andean regions, where market relations had induced significant socioeconomic differentiation within villages, indigenous leaders often willingly accepted privatization of communal lands, viewing it as a road to personal enrichment.

Seizure of church lands by liberal governments also contributed to the growth of the latifundio. Mexico again offered a model, with its Lerdo Law and the Juárez anticlerical decrees. Following the Mexican example, Colombian liberal governments confiscated church lands in the 1860s, the liberal dictator Antonio Guzmán Blanco seized many church estates in Venezuela in the 1870s, and Ecuadoran Liberals expropriated church lands in 1895.

Expansion of the public domain through railway construction and wars also contributed to the growth of great landed estates. Liberal states typically expropriated lands from the church or from indigenous communities and usually sold them to buyers in vast tracts at nominal prices. Concentration of land, reducing the cultivable area available to native and mestizo small landowners, accompanied a parallel growth of the *minifundio* (an uneconomical small plot worked with primitive techniques).

The seizure of indigenous community lands, to use immediately or to hold for a speculative rise in value, provided great landowners with another advantage by giving them control of the local labor force at a time of increasing demand for labor. Expropriated natives rarely became true wage earners paid wholly in cash, for such workers were too expensive and independent in spirit. A more widespread labor system was debt peonage, in which workers were paid wholly or in part with vouchers redeemable at the *tienda de raya* (company store), whose inflated prices and often devious bookkeeping created a debt that was passed on from one generation to the next. The courts enforced the obligation of peons to remain on the estate until they had liquidated their debts. The landowners' private armies, local police, or military authorities typically punished peons who protested low wages or the more intensive style of work demanded by the new order.

In some countries, the period saw a revival of the colonial repartimiento system of draft labor for indigenous peoples. In Guatemala, this system required able-bodied natives to work for a specified number of days on haciendas. The liberal president Justo Rufino Barrios issued instructions to local magistrates to see to it "that any Indian who seeks to evade his duty is punished to the full extent of the law, that the farmers are fully protected, and that each Indian is forced to do a full day's work while in service."

As we have seen, slavery survived in some places well beyond mid-century—for example, in Peru until 1855, in Cuba until 1886, and in Brazil until 1888. Closely akin to slavery was the system of bondage, under which contract labor companies imported some ninety thousand Chinese coolies into Peru between 1849 and 1875 to work on the guano islands and in railway construction. The term *slavery* equally applies to the system under which Mexican authorities sent political deportees and captured native rebels to labor in unspeakable conditions on the coffee, tobacco, and henequen plantations of southern Mexico.

More modern systems of agricultural labor and farm tenantry arose only in such regions as southern Brazil and Argentina, whose critical labor shortage required the offer of greater incentives to the millions of European immigrants who poured into those countries between 1870 and 1910.

Labor conditions were little better in the mining industry and in the factories that arose in some countries after 1890. Typical conditions were a workday of twelve to fourteen hours, miserable wages frequently paid in vouchers redeemable only at the company store, and arbitrary, abusive treatment by employers and supervisors. Latin American law codes usually prohibited strikes and other organized efforts to improve working conditions, and police and the armed forces commonly intervened to break strikes, sometimes with heavy loss of life.

FOREIGN CONTROL OF RESOURCES

The rise of the neocolonial order accompanied a steady growth of foreign corporate control over the natural and human-made resources of the continent. The process went through stages. In 1870, foreign investment was still largely concentrated in trade, shipping, railways, public utilities, and government loans; at that date, British capital enjoyed an undisputed hegemony in the Latin American investment field. By 1914, foreign corporate ownership had expanded to include most of the mining industry and had deeply penetrated real estate, ranching, plantation agriculture, and manufacturing; by that date, Great Britain's rivals had effectively challenged its domination in Latin America. Of these rivals, the most spectacular advance was made by the United States, whose Latin American investments had risen from a negligible amount in 1870 to more than $1.6 billion by the end of 1914 (still well below the nearly $5 billion investment of Great Britain).

Foreign economic penetration went hand in hand with a growth of political influence and even armed intervention. The youthful U.S. imperialism proved to be the most aggressive of all. In the years after 1898, a combination of "dollar diplomacy" and armed intervention transformed the Caribbean into an "American lake" and reduced

Cuba, the Dominican Republic, and several Central American states to the status of dependencies and protectorates of the United States.

THE POLITICS OF ACQUISITION

The new economy demanded new politics. Conservatives and Liberals, fascinated by the atmosphere of prosperity created by the export boom, the rise in land values, the flood of foreign loans, and the growth of government revenues, put aside their ideological differences and joined in the pursuit of wealth. The positivist slogan "Order and Progress" now became the watchword of Latin America's ruling classes. The social Darwinist idea of the struggle for survival of the fittest and Herbert Spencer's doctrine of "inferior races," frequently used to support racist claims of the inherent inferiority of the native, black, mestizo, and mulatto masses, also entered the upper-class ideological arsenal.

The growing domination of national economies by the export sectors and the development of a consensus between the old landed aristocracy and more capitalist-oriented groups caused political issues like the Federalist–Centralist conflict and the Liberal–Conservative cleavage to lose much of their meaning; in some countries, the old party lines dissolved or became extremely tenuous. A new type of liberal caudillo—Porfirio Díaz in Mexico, Rafael Núñez in Colombia, Justo Rufino Barrios in Guatemala, and Antonio Guzmán Blanco in Venezuela—symbolized the politics of acquisition.

As the century ended, dissatisfied urban middle-class, immigrant, and entrepreneurial groups in some countries combined to form parties, called Radical or Democratic, that challenged the traditional domination of politics by the creole landed aristocracy. They demanded political, social, and education reforms that would give more weight to the new middle sectors. But these middle sectors—manufacturers, shopkeepers, professionals, and the like—were in large part a creation of the neocolonial order and depended on it for their livelihood; therefore, as a rule they did not question its viability. The small nationalist, socialist, **anarchist**, and **syndicalist** groups that arose in various Latin American countries

in the 1890s challenged capitalism, neocolonialism, and the liberal state, but the full significance of these movements lay in the future.

These trends lend a certain unity to the history of Mexico, Argentina, Chile, Brazil, Central America, Venezuela, and Colombia in the period from 1870 to 1914. Each, however, presents significant variations on the common theme—variations that reflect distinctive historical backgrounds and conditions.

Mexican Politics and Economy

DICTATORSHIP UNDER DÍAZ

Gen. Porfirio Díaz seized power in 1876 with the support of disgruntled regional caudillos and military personnel, Liberals angered by the old regime's patronage politics, and indigenous or mestizo small landholders who believed that Díaz would protect them. He also owed his success to the open support of American capitalists, army commanders, and great Texas landowners who, regarding his predecessor as "anti-American," supplied Díaz with arms and cash. Thereafter, Díaz erected the *Porfiriato*, one of the longest personal dictatorships in Latin American history.

However, the construction of the dictatorship was a gradual process. During his first presidential term, Congress and the judiciary enjoyed a certain independence, and the press, including a vocal radical labor press, was free. The outlines of Díaz's economic and social policies, however, soon became clear. Confronted with an empty treasury, facing pressures from above and below, Díaz decided in favor of the great landowners, moneylenders, and foreign capitalists, whose assistance could ensure his political survival. In return, he assured these groups that he would protect their property and other interests. Díaz, who had once proclaimed that in the age-old struggle between the people and the haciendas, he was firmly on the side of the people, now sent troops to suppress peasant resistance to land seizures. Moreover, although he had denounced generous concessions to British capitalists before taking power, Díaz granted even more lavish subsidies for railway construction to North American companies a few years later. Economic growth had become for Díaz the great object, the key solution to his own problems and those of the nation.

Economic growth required political stability; accordingly, Díaz promoted a policy of conciliation, described by the formula *pan o palo* (bread or the club). This consisted of offering an olive branch and a share of spoils to all influential opponents, no matter what their political past or persuasion. A dog with a bone in its mouth, Díaz cynically observed, neither kills nor steals. In effect, Díaz invited all sections of the upper class and some members of the middle class, including prominent intellectuals and journalists, to join the great Mexican barbecue, from which he barred only the poor and humble. Opponents who refused Díaz's bribes—political offices, monopolies, and the like—suffered swift reprisal. His regime beat up, murdered, or arrested and imprisoned dissidents in the damp underground dungeons of San Juan de Ulúa or the grim Belén penitentiary, a sort of Mexican Bastille. An important instrument of this policy was a force of *rurales* (mounted police), originally composed of former bandits and vagrants who gradually were replaced by artisan and peasant recruits dislocated by the large social changes that took place during the Porfiriato. Aside from chasing unrepentant bandits, the major function of the rurales was to suppress peasant unrest and break strikes.

By such means, Díaz virtually eliminated all effective opposition. The 1857 constitution and the liberties it guaranteed existed only on paper. Elections to Congress, in theory the highest organ of government, were a farce; Díaz simply circulated a list of his candidates to local officials, who certified their election. The dictator contemptuously called Congress his *caballada* (stable of horses). Díaz appointed the state governors, usually from the ranks of local great landlords or his generals. In return for their loyalty, he gave them a free hand to enrich themselves and terrorize the local population. Under them were *jefes políticos* (district heads), petty tyrants appointed by the governors with the approval of Díaz; below the jefes were municipal presidents who ran the local administrative units. One feature of the Díaz Era was a mushrooming of the

coercive apparatus; government administrative costs during this period soared by 900 percent.

The army naturally enjoyed special favor. Higher officers received good salaries and enjoyed many opportunities for further enrichment at the expense of the regions in which they resided, but the Díaz army was pathetically inadequate for purposes of national defense. The regime appointed generals and other high officers for their loyalty to the dictator, not for their ability. Discipline, morale, and training were extremely poor. It recruited a considerable part of the rank-and-file from the dregs of society; the remainder included young native conscripts. These soldiers, often used for brutal repression of strikes and agrarian unrest, themselves endured harsh treatment and miserable pay: ranks below sergeant earned $0.50 a month.

The church became another pillar of the dictatorship and agreed to support Díaz in return for his disregard of anticlerical Reforma laws. Monasteries, nunneries, and church schools reappeared, and wealth again accumulated in the hands of the church. Faithful to its bargain, the church hierarchy ignored the complaints of the lower classes and taught complete submission to authorities.

The Díaz policy of conciliation targeted prominent intellectuals as well as more wealthy and powerful figures. A group of such intellectuals, professional men, and business leaders made up a closely knit clique of Díaz's advisers. Known as **Científicos**, they got their name from their insistence on "scientific" administration of the state and were especially influential after 1892. About fifteen men made up the controlling nucleus of the group. Their leader was Díaz's all-powerful father-in-law, Manuel Romero Rubio, and after his death in 1895, the position passed to the new minister of finance, José Yves Limantour.

For the Científicos, the economic movement was everything. Most Científicos accepted the thesis of the inherent inferiority of the native and mestizo population and the consequent necessity for relying on the native white elite and on foreigners and their capital to lead Mexico out of its backwardness. In the words of the journalist Francisco G. Cosmes, "The Indian has only the passive force of inferior

Beginning in the 1920s, with considerable support from the state, there arose in Mexico a school of socially conscious artists who sought to enlighten the masses about their bitter past and the promise of the revolutionary present. One of the greatest of these artists was David Alfaro Siqueiros, whose painting depicts with satire the former President Porfirio Díaz, who tramples on the constitution of 1857 as he diverts his wealthy followers with dancing girls.

races, is incapable of actively pursuing the goal of civilization."

CONCENTRATION OF LANDOWNERSHIP

At the opening of the twentieth century, Mexico was still predominantly an agrarian country; 77 percent of its population of 15 million still lived on the land. The laws of the Reforma already had promoted the concentration of landownership, and under Díaz, this trend greatly accelerated. The rapid advance of railway construction increased the possibilities of production for export and therefore stimulated both a rise in land values and the growth of land-grabbing in the Díaz period.

A major piece of land legislation was the 1883 *Ley de Deslindes* that provided for the survey of

public lands. The law authorized real estate companies to survey such lands, retain one-third of the surveyed area as compensation, and sell the remainder for low fixed prices in vast tracts, usually to Díaz's favorites and their foreign associates. The 1883 law opened the way for vast territorial acquisitions. One individual alone obtained nearly 12 million acres in Baja California and other northern states. Nonetheless, the acquisition of such lands did not satisfy the land companies. In 1894, the *Ley de Terrenos Baldíos* declared that a parcel of land without legal title was vacant land, opening the door to expropriation of untitled land cultivated by indigenous villages and other small landholders from times immemorial. If the victims offered armed resistance, Díaz sent troops against them and sold the vanquished rebels like slaves to labor on henequen plantations in Yucatán or sugar plantations in Cuba. This was the fate of the Yaquis of the northwest, defeated after a long, valiant struggle.

Another instrument of land seizure was an 1890 law designed to give effect to older Reforma laws requiring the distribution of indigenous village lands among the villagers. The law created enormous confusion. In many cases, land speculators and hacendados cajoled illiterate villagers into selling their titles for paltry sums. Hacendados also used other means, such as cutting off a village's water supply or simply brute force, to achieve their predatory ends. By 1910, the process of land expropriation was largely complete. More than 90 percent of the indigenous villages of the central plateau, the most densely populated region of the country, had lost their communal lands. Only the most tenacious resistance enabled villages that still held their lands to survive the assault of the great landowners. Landless peons and their families made up 9.5 million of a rural population of 12 million.

As a rule, the new owners did not use the land seized from indigenous villages or small landholders more efficiently. Hacendados let much of the usurped land lie idle, waiting for a speculative rise in value or an American buyer. By keeping land out of production, they helped keep the price of maize and other staples artificially high. The technical level of hacienda agriculture generally was extremely low, with little use of irrigation, machinery, and commercial fertilizer, although some new landowning groups—northern cattle raisers and cotton growers, the coffee and rubber growers of Chiapas, and the henequen producers of Yucatán—employed more modern equipment and techniques.

The production of foodstuffs stagnated, barely keeping pace with population growth, and per capita production of such basic staples as maize and beans actually declined toward the end of the century. This decline culminated in three years of bad harvests, 1907 to 1910, principally because of drought. As a result, the importation of maize and other foodstuffs from the United States steadily increased in the last years of the Díaz regime. Despite the growth of pastoral industry, per capita consumption barely kept pace, for a considerable

proportion of the livestock was destined for the export market.

The only food products for which the increase exceeded the growth of population were alcoholic beverages. The growth of bars in Mexico City from fifty-one in 1864 to fourteen hundred in 1900 reflected this increased consumption of alcohol. At the end of the century, the Mexican death rate from alcoholism—a common response to intolerable conditions of life and labor—was approximately six times that of France. Meanwhile, inflation, rampant during the last part of the Díaz regime, greatly raised the cost of the staples on which the mass of the population depended. Without a corresponding increase in wages, the situation of agricultural and industrial laborers deteriorated sharply.

THE ECONOMIC ADVANCE

Whereas food production for the domestic market declined, production of food and industrial raw materials for the foreign market experienced vigorous growth. By 1910, Mexico had become the largest producer of henequen, a source of fiber in great demand in the world market. Mexican export production increasingly catered to the needs of the United States, which was the principal market for sugar, bananas, rubber, and tobacco produced on foreign-owned plantations. U.S. companies dominated the mining industry, whose output of copper, gold, lead, and zinc rose sharply after 1890. The oil industry, controlled by U.S. and British interests, developed spectacularly, and by 1911 Mexico was third among the world's oil producers. French and Spanish capitalists virtually monopolized the textile and other consumer goods industries, which had a relatively rapid growth after 1890.

Foreign control of key sectors of the economy and the fawning attitude of the Díaz regime toward foreigners gave rise to a popular saying: "Mexico, mother of foreigners and stepmother of Mexicans." The ruling clique of Científicos justified this favoritism by citing the need for a rapid development of Mexico's natural resources and the creation of a strong country capable of defending its political independence and territorial integrity. Thanks to an influx of foreign capital, the volume of foreign trade greatly increased, a modern banking system arose, and the country acquired a relatively dense network of railways linking the interior to overseas markets. But these successes were achieved at a heavy price: a brutal dictatorship, the pauperization of the mass of the population, the stagnation of food agriculture, the strengthening of the inefficient latifundio, and the survival of many feudal or semi-feudal vestiges in Mexican economic and social life.

LABOR, AGRARIAN, AND MIDDLE-CLASS UNREST

The survival of feudal vestiges was especially glaring in the area of labor relations. Labor conditions varied from region to region. In 1910, forced labor and outright slavery, as well as older forms of debt peonage, were characteristic of the southern states of Yucatán, Tabasco, Chiapas, and parts of Oaxaca and Veracruz. The rubber, coffee, tobacco, henequen, and sugar plantations of this region depended heavily on the forced labor of political deportees, captured indigenous rebels, and contract workers kidnapped or lured to work in the tropics by a variety of devices.

In central Mexico, where a massive expropriation of village lands had created a large, landless native proletariat, tenantry, sharecropping, and the use of migratory labor had increased and living standards had declined. The large labor surplus of this area diminished the need for hacendados to tie their workers to their estates with debt peonage. In the north, the proximity of the United States, with its higher wage scales, and the competition of hacendados with mine owners for labor made wages and sharecropping arrangements somewhat more favorable and weakened debt peonage. In all parts of the country, however, agricultural workers endured hardships and abuses of every kind.

Labor conditions in mines and factories were little better than in the countryside. Workers in textile mills labored twelve to fifteen hours daily for a wage ranging from $0.11 for unskilled women and children to $0.75 for highly skilled workers. Employers found ways to reduce even these meager wages. They discounted wages for alleged carelessness in the use of tools or machines or for defective goods; they usually paid workers wholly or in part with vouchers good only in company stores, the prices of which were higher than in other stores. Federal and state laws banned trade unions and strikes. Troops shot down scores of workers, both men and women, and broke the great textile strike in the Orizaba (Veracruz) area in 1909 and the strike at the U.S.-owned Consolidated Copper Company mine at Cananea (Sonora) in 1906. Despite such repressions, the trade union movement continued to grow in the last years of the Díaz Era, and socialist, anarchist, and syndicalist ideas began to influence the still-small urban working class.

The growing wave of strikes and agrarian unrest in the last, decadent phase of the Díaz Era indicated an increasingly rebellious mood among even broader sections of the Mexican people. Alienation spread among teachers, lawyers, journalists, and other professionals, whose opportunities for advancement were sharply limited by the monolithic control of economic, political, and social life by the Científicos, their foreign allies, and regional oligarchies. In the United States in 1905, a group of middle-class intellectuals, headed by Ricardo Flores Magón, called for the overthrow of Díaz and advanced a radical program of economic and social reforms.

Even members of the ruling class soon joined the chorus of criticism. These upper-class dissidents included national capitalists, like the wealthy hacendado and business executive Francisco Madero, who resented the competitive advantages enjoyed by foreign companies in Mexico. They also feared that the static, reactionary Díaz policies could provoke the masses to overthrow the capitalist system itself. Fearing revolution, these upper-class critics urged Díaz to end his personal rule, shake up the regime, and institute modest reforms needed to placate popular protest and preserve the existing economic and social order. When their appeals failed, some of these bourgeois reformers reluctantly prepared to take the road of revolution.

The simultaneous advent of an economic recession and a food crisis sharpened this growing discontent. The depression of 1906–1907, which spread from the United States to Mexico, caused a wave of bankruptcies, layoffs, and wage cuts. At the same time, the crop failures of 1907–1910 provoked a

Striking workers at the Rio Blanco textile works in Mexico in 1909; the business was controlled by French capital. Troops broke up the strike, and much blood was shed.

dramatic rise in the price of staples like maize and beans. By 1910, Mexico's internal conflicts had reached an explosive stage. The workers' strikes, the agrarian unrest, the agitation of middle-class reformers, and the disaffection of some great landowners and capitalists all reflected the disintegration of the dictatorship's social base. Despite its superficial stability and posh splendor, the house of Díaz was rotten from top to bottom. Only a slight push was necessary to send it toppling to the ground.

Argentine Politics and Economy

Although the principal source of conflict in Argentina remained rivalry between provincial caudillos and Buenos Aires, Julio Roca and other oligarchs sought to unify the nation by forging stronger economic links between the port city and interior provinces. In Argentina, like Porfirian Mexico, the consolidation of a liberal state was the key to neocolonial economic growth.

CONSOLIDATION OF THE STATE

Julio Roca institutionalized this new unification by carrying out a long-standing pledge to federalize the city of Buenos Aires, which now became the capital of the nation, while La Plata became the new capital of the Buenos Aires province. The interior seemed to have triumphed over Buenos Aires, but that apparent victory was an illusion; the provincial lawyers and politicians who carried the day in 1880 had absorbed the commercial and cultural values of the great city and wished not to diminish but rather to share in its power. Far from losing influence, Buenos Aires steadily gained in wealth and power until it achieved an overwhelming ascendancy over the rest of the country.

The federalization of Buenos Aires completed the consolidation of the Argentine state, the new leaders of which closely identified with and often emerged from the ruling class of great landowners and wealthy merchants. The "generation of 1880," or the Oligarchy, as it was called, shared a faith in economic development and the value of the North American and European models, but it also reflected a deep cynicism, intense egotism, and a profound distrust for the popular classes. These autocratic Liberals prized order and progress above freedom. They regarded the gauchos, indigenous peoples, and the mass of illiterate European immigrants flooding Argentina as unfit to exercise civic functions. Asked to define universal suffrage, a leading oligarch, Eduardo Wilde, replied, "It is the triumph of universal ignorance."

The new rulers identified the national interest with the interest of the great landowners, wealthy merchants, and foreign capitalists. Regarding the apparatus of state as their personal property or as the property of their class, they used their official connections to enrich themselves. Although they maintained the forms of parliamentary government, they were determined not to let power slip from their hands and organized the *unicato* (one-party rule) to monopolize political control in their newly formed National Autonomist Party. Extreme concentration of power in the executive branch and systematic use of fraud, violence, and bribery were basic features of the system.

ECONOMIC BOOM AND INFLATION

Roca presided over the beginnings of a great boom that appeared to justify the oligarchy's optimism. Earlier, Roca had led a military expedition—the so-called Conquest of the Desert—southward against native peoples of the pampa in 1879–1880. This conquest added vast new areas to the province of Buenos Aires and to the national public domain. The campaign, devastating to the region's indigenous communities, had created an opportunity to implement a democratic land policy directed toward the creation of an Argentine small-farmer class. Instead, the Roca administration sold off the

area in huge tracts for nominal prices to army officers, politicians, and foreign capitalists.

Coming at a time of steadily mounting European demand for Argentine meat and wheat, the Conquest of the Desert triggered an orgy of land speculation that drove land prices ever higher and caused a prodigious expansion of cattle raising and agriculture. This expansion took place under the sign of the latifundio. Few of the millions of Italian and Spanish immigrants who entered Argentina in this period realized the common dream of becoming independent small landowners. Although some immigrants established agricultural colonies in the provinces of Santa Fe and Entre Ríos in the 1870s and 1880s, by the mid-1890s, with wheat prices now declining, small-scale farming shifted to extensive tenant farming. The traditional unwillingness of the estancieros to sell land forced the majority of would-be independent farmers to become ranch hands or tenant farmers, whose hold on the land was precarious. Because leases usually were limited to a few years, these immigrants broke the virgin soil, replaced the tough pampa grass with the alfalfa pasturage needed to fatten cattle, and produced the first wheat harvests but then had to move on, leaving the landowner in possession of all improvements.

As a result, the great majority of new arrivals settled in Buenos Aires, where the rise of meat-salting and meat-packing plants, railroads, public utilities, and many small factories created a growing demand for labor. True, the immigrant workers received very low wages, worked long hours, and crowded with their families into one-room apartments in wretched slums. In the city barrio, however, they lived among their own people, free from the loneliness of the pampa and the arbitrary rule of great landowners, and had some opportunity of rising in the economic and social scale. As a result, the population of Buenos Aires shot up from 500,000 in 1889 to 1,244,000 in 1909. The great city, which held the greater portion of the nation's wealth, population, and culture, grew at the expense of the interior—particularly the northwest—which was impoverished, stagnant, and thinly peopled. Argentina, to use a familiar metaphor, became a giant head set on a dwarf body.

Foreign capital and management played a decisive role in the expansion of the Argentine economy in this period. The creole elite obtained vast profits from the rise in the price of their land and the increasing volume of exports but showed little interest in plowing those gains into industry or the construction of the infrastructure required by the export economy, preferring a lavish and leisurely lifestyle to entrepreneurial activity. Just as they left to English and Irish managers the task of tending their estates, so too they left to English capital the financing of meat-packing plants, railroads, public utilities, and docks and other facilities. As a result, most of these resources remained in British hands. Typical of the oligarchy's policy of surrender to foreign interests was the decision of Congress in 1889 to sell the state-owned Ferrocarril Oeste, the most profitable and best-run railroad in Argentina, to a British company. Service on a growing foreign debt claimed an increasingly larger portion of the government's receipts.

Meanwhile, imports of iron, coal, machinery, and consumer goods grew much faster than exports. Combined with the unfavorable price ratio of raw materials to finished goods, the result was an unfavorable balance of trade and a steady drain of gold. New loans with burdensome terms brought temporary relief but aggravated the long-range problem. The disappearance of gold and the government's determination to keep the boom going at all costs led to the issue of great quantities of unbacked paper currency and a massive inflation.

The great landowners did not mind, for their exports earned French francs and English pounds, which they could convert into cheap Argentine pesos for the payment of local costs; besides, inflation caused the price of their lands to rise. The sacrificial victims of the inflation were the urban middle class and the workers, whose income declined in real value.

THE FORMATION OF THE RADICAL PARTY

In 1889–1890, just as the boom was turning into a depression, the accumulated resentment of the urban middle class and some alienated sectors of the elite over the catastrophic inflation, one-party rule, and official corruption produced a protest movement that took the name *Unión Cívica* (Civic Union). Although the new organization had a middle-class base, its leadership united such disparate elements as disgruntled urban politicians like Leandro Além, its first president; new landowners and descendants of old aristocratic families denied access to patronage; and Catholics outraged by the government's anticlerical legislation. Aside from the demand for effective suffrage, the only thing uniting these heterogeneous elements was a common determination to overthrow the government.

The birth of the new party in 1890 coincided with a financial storm: The stock market collapsed, bankruptcies multiplied, and in April the cabinet resigned. Encouraged by this last development, and counting on support from the army, the leaders of the Unión Cívica planned a revolt that ended in defeat for the rebels.

The oligarchy now showed its ability to maneuver and divide its enemies. It appeased disgruntled elements of the elite by revising the system of state patronage and sought to improve economic conditions by a policy of retrenchment that reduced inflation, stabilized the peso, and revived Argentine credit abroad. Thanks to these measures and a gradual recovery from the depression, popular discontent began to subside.

These reforms isolated Leandro Além and other dissidents, who now formed a new party committed to a "radical" democracy—the *Unión Cívica Radical*. The party knew that rigged voting made electoral victory impossible, so they prepared for another revolt—a move that effectively was squelched by the government's decision to deport Além and other Radical leaders.

On his return from exile, Além organized a third revolt in July 1893. The rebels briefly seized Santa Fe and some other towns, but after two and a half months of fighting, the revolt collapsed for lack of significant popular support. Depressed by his failures and the intrigues of his nephew, Hipólito Yrigoyen, to seize control of the Radical Party, Além committed suicide in 1896. Until 1910, the Radical Party, now led by Yrigoyen, proved unable to achieve political reform by peaceful or revolutionary means, as the reunited oligarchy consolidated its power.

In Yrigoyen, however, the Radicals possessed a charismatic personality and a masterful organizer who refused to admit defeat. Yrigoyen, a one-time police superintendent in Buenos Aires, was formerly a minor politician who used his official party connections to acquire considerable wealth, which he invested in land and cattle. As a Radical caudillo, Yrigoyen was the architect of a program whose vagueness was dictated by the party's need to appeal to diverse elements and by its wholehearted acceptance of the economic status quo. "Abstention," refusal to participate in rigged elections, and "revolutionary intransigence," the determination to resort to revolution until free elections were achieved, were the party's basic slogans.

The Radical Party represented a dependent bourgeoisie that did not champion industrialization, economic diversification, or nationalization of foreign-owned industries. Far from attacking the neocolonial order, the Radical Party proposed to strengthen it by promoting cooperation between the landed aristocracy and the urban sectors, which challenged the creole elite's monopoly of political power. The Radical Party went into eclipse after the debacles of 1890 and 1893 but gradually revived after 1900, in part because of Yrigoyen's charismatic personality and organizing talent. The most important factor, however, was the steady growth of an urban and rural middle class largely composed of immigrant children. The domination of the export sector, which limited the growth of industry and opportunities for entrepreneurial activity, increasingly focused middle-class ambitions on government employment and the professions, two fields dominated by the creole elite. Signs of growing unrest and frustration in the middle class included a series of student strikes in the universities, caused by efforts of creole governing boards to restrict enrollment of students of immigrant descent.

ELECTORAL REFORM AND THE GROWTH OF THE LABOR MOVEMENT

Meanwhile, a section of the oligarchy had begun to advocate electoral reform. These aristocratic reformers argued that the existing situation created a permanent state of tension and instability; they feared that eventually the Radical efforts at revolution would succeed. Therefore, they believed that the concessions demanded by the Radicals would open up the political system and gain for the ruling party—now generally called Conservative—the popular support and legitimacy it needed to remain in power. Moreover, the Conservative reformers, aware of a new threat from the labor movement and especially its vanguard—the socialists, anarchists, and syndicalists—hoped to make an alliance with the bourgeoisie against the revolutionary working class. They therefore supported a series of measures known collectively as the Sáenz Peña Law (1912). The new law established universal and secret male suffrage for citizens when they reached the age of eighteen. This law, which historian David Rock calls "an act of calculated retreat by the ruling class," opened the way for a dependent bourgeoisie to share power and the spoils of office with the landed aristocracy.

The principal political vehicle for working-class aspirations was the Socialist Party, founded in 1894 as a split-off from the Unión Cívica Radical by the Buenos Aires physician and intellectual Juan B. Justo, who led the party until his death in 1928. Despite its professed Marxism, the party's socialism was of the parliamentary reformist kind, appealing chiefly to highly skilled, native-born workers and the lower-middle class. The majority of workers, foreign-born noncitizens who still dreamed of returning someday to their homelands, remained aloof from electoral politics but readily joined trade unions that valiantly resisted deteriorating wages and working conditions; the government crushed a series of great strikes with brutal repression and deported the so-called foreign agitators. Despite these defeats, the labor movement continued to grow and struggle, winning such initial victories as the ten-hour workday and the establishment of Sunday as a compulsory day of rest.

Chilean Politics and Economy

NITRATES AND WAR

In 1876, the Liberal president Aníbal Pinto inherited a severe economic crisis (1874–1879). Wheat and copper prices dropped, exports declined, and unemployment grew. The principal offset to these unfavorable developments was the continued growth of nitrate exports from the Atacama Desert because of a doubling of nitrate production between 1865 and 1875. Nevertheless, nitrates, the foundation of Chilean material progress, also became the cause of a major war with dramatic consequences for Chile and its two foes, Bolivia and Peru.

The nitrate deposits exploited by the Anglo-Chilean companies lay in territories belonging to Bolivia (the province of Antofagasta) and Peru (the province of Tarapacá). In 1866, a treaty between Chile and Bolivia defined their boundary in the Atacama Desert as the twenty-fourth parallel, gave Chilean and Bolivian interests equal rights to exploit the territory between the twenty-third and twenty-fifth parallels, and guaranteed each government half of the tax revenues obtained from the export of minerals from the whole area. Anglo-Chilean capital soon poured into the region, developing a highly efficient mining–industrial complex. A second treaty of 1874 left Chile's northern border with Bolivia at the twenty-fourth parallel. Chile relinquished its rights to a share of the taxes from exports north of that boundary but received in return a twenty-five-year guarantee against increase of taxes on Chilean enterprises operating in the Bolivian province of Antofagasta.

Chile had no boundary dispute with Peru, but aggressive Chilean mining interests, aided by British capital, soon extended their operations from Antofagasta into the Peruvian province of Tarapacá. By 1875, Chilean enterprises in Peruvian nitrate fields employed more than ten thousand workers, engineers, and supervisory personnel. At this point, the Peruvian government, on the brink of bankruptcy because of an expensive program of public works, huge European loans, and the depletion of the guano deposits on which it had counted to service those loans, decided to expropriate the foreign companies in Tarapacá and establish a state monopoly over the production and sale of nitrates. Meanwhile, Peru and Bolivia had negotiated a secret treaty in 1874 providing for a military alliance in the event either power went to war with Chile.

Ejected from Tarapacá, the Anglo-Chilean capitalists intensified their exploitation of the nitrate deposits in Antofagasta. In 1878, Bolivia, counting on its military alliance with Peru, challenged Chile by imposing higher taxes on nitrate exports from Antofagasta, in violation of the treaty of 1874. When the Chilean companies operating in Antofagasta refused to pay the new taxes, the Bolivian government threatened them with confiscation. The agreement of 1874 provided for arbitration of disputes, but the Bolivians twice rejected Chilean offers to submit the dispute to arbitration.

In February 1879, despite Chilean warnings that expropriation of Chilean enterprises would void the treaty of 1874, the Bolivian government ordered the confiscation carried out. On February 14, the day set for the seizure and sale of the Chilean properties, Chilean troops occupied the port of Antofagasta, encountering no resistance, and proceeded to extend Chilean control over the whole province. Totally unprepared for war, Peru made a vain effort to mediate between Chile and Bolivia. Chile, however, having learned of the secret Peruvian-Bolivian alliance, charged Peru with intolerable duplicity and declared war on both Peru and Bolivia on April 5, 1879.

In this war, called the War of the Pacific, Chile faced enemies whose combined population was more than twice its own; one of these powers, Peru, also possessed a respectable naval force. Chile enjoyed major advantages, however. By contrast with its neighbors, it possessed a stable central government, a people with a strong sense of national identity, and a disciplined, well-trained army and navy. Chile also enjoyed the advantage of being closer to the theater of operations, because Bolivian troops had to come over the Andes and the Peruvian army had to cross the Atacama Desert.

All three powers had serious economic problems, but Chile's situation was not as catastrophic as that of its foes. Equally important, Chile had the support of powerful English capitalist interests, who knew that the future of the massive English investment in Chile depended in large part on the outcome of the war. The prospect of Chilean acquisition of the valuable nitrate areas of Antofagasta and

Tarapacá naturally pleased the British capitalists. British capital also invested in Bolivia and Peru; however, whereas the Chilean government had maintained service on its debt, Bolivia and Peru had suspended payment on their English loans. In addition, the Peruvian nationalization of the nitrate industry in Tarapacá had seriously injured British interests.

With British assistance, Chile won the war in 1883 and imposed its terms. By the Treaty of Ancón (October 20, 1883), Peru ceded the province of Tarapacá to Chile in perpetuity. The provinces of Tacna and Arica would be Chilean for ten years, after which a plebiscite would decide their ultimate fate. The plebiscite never occurred, however, and Chile continued to administer the two territories until 1929, when Peru recovered Tacna, and Arica went to Chile. An armistice signed in April 1884 by Bolivia and Chile assigned the former Bolivian province of Antofagasta to Chile, but for many years, no Bolivian government would sign a formal treaty acknowledging that loss. Finally, in 1904, Bolivia signed a treaty in which Chile agreed to pay an indemnity and to build a railroad that, by 1913, connected the Bolivian capital of La Paz to the port of Arica.

AFTERMATH OF THE WAR OF THE PACIFIC

Chile took advantage of the continued mobilization of its armed forces during the negotiations with Peru to settle scores with the Araucanians, whose struggle in defense of their land against encroaching whites had continued since colonial times. After two years of resistance against unequal odds, the Araucanians were forced to admit defeat and sign a treaty (1883) that resettled them on reservations but retained their tribal government and laws. The Araucanian campaign of 1880–1882, which extended the Chilean southern frontier into a region of mountain and forest, sparked a brisk movement of land speculation and colonization in that area.

The War of the Pacific shattered Peru economically and psychologically, and it left Bolivia more isolated than before from the outside world. However, Chile emerged the strongest nation on the west coast, in control of vast deposits of nitrates and copper, the mainstays of its economy. Nonetheless, the greater part of these riches soon passed into foreign hands. In 1881, the Chilean government made an important decision: It returned the nitrate properties of Tarapacá to private ownership—that is, to the holders of the certificates issued by the Peruvian government as compensation for the nationalized properties.

During the war, uncertainty as to how Chile would dispose of those properties had caused the Peruvian certificates to depreciate until they fell to a fraction of their face value. Speculators, mostly British, had bought up large quantities of these depreciated certificates. In 1878, British capital controlled some 13 percent of the nitrate industry of Tarapacá, and, by 1890, its share had risen to at least 70 percent. British penetration of the nitrate areas proceeded not only through formation of companies for direct exploitation of nitrate deposits but also through the establishment of banks, which financed entrepreneurial activity in the nitrate area, and through the creation of railways and other companies more or less closely linked to the central nitrate industry. An English railway company with a monopoly of transport in Tarapacá, the Nitrate Railways Company, controlled by John Thomas North, paid dividends of up to 20 and 25 percent, compared with earnings of from 7 to 14 percent for other railway companies in South America.

The Chilean national bourgeoisie, which had pioneered the establishment of the mining-industrial-railway complex in the Atacama, offered little resistance to the foreign takeover. Lack of strong support from the liberal state, the relative financial weakness of the Chilean bourgeoisie, and the profitable relations between Chilean oligarchs and British interests facilitated the rapid transfer of Chilean nitrate and railway properties into British hands. This transformed Chilean mine owners into a dependent bourgeoisie content to share the profits of British companies.

Elsewhere in Chile, the war had energized the national economy and mobilized local manufacturers and workers, who pressed for electoral reform; in 1884, a literacy test replaced the property qualification for voting. Because the great majority

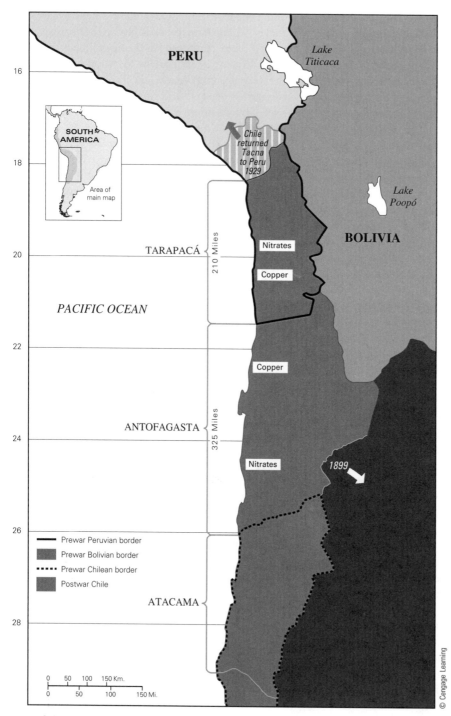

War of the Pacific

of Chilean males were illiterate *rotos* (seasonal farm workers) and inquilinos, this change did not materially add to the number of voters; as late as 1915, out of a population of about 3.5 million, only one hundred fifty thousand persons voted. However, it did secure the 1886 presidential victory of José Manuel Balmaceda, who took office with a well-defined program of state-directed economic modernization. By the 1880s, stimulated by the War of the Pacific, factory capitalism had taken root in Chile. In addition to consumer goods industries—flourmills, breweries, leather factories, furniture factories, and the like—foundries and metalworking enterprises served the mining industry, railways, and agriculture. Balmaceda proposed to consolidate and expand this native industrial capitalism.

BALMACEDA'S NATIONALISTIC POLICIES

Balmaceda came to office when government revenues were at an all-time high: They had risen from about 15 million pesos a year before the War of the Pacific to about 45 million pesos in 1887. The chief source of this government income was the export duty on nitrates. Knowing that the proceeds from this source would taper off as the nitrate deposits diminished, Balmaceda wisely planned to employ those funds for the development of an economic infrastructure that would remain when the nitrate was gone. Hence, public works figured prominently in his program. In 1887, he created a new ministry of industry and public works, which spent large sums to extend and improve the telegraphic and railway systems and to construct bridges, roads, and docks. Balmaceda also generously endowed public education, needed to provide skilled workers for Chilean industry. During his presidency, the total enrollment in Chilean schools rose in four years from some seventy-nine thousand in 1886 to more than one hundred fifty thousand in 1890. He also favored raising the wages of workers but was inconsistent in his labor policy; yielding to strong pressure from foreign and domestic employers, he sent troops to crush a number of strikes.

Central to Balmaceda's program was his determination to "Chileanize" the nitrate industry. In his inaugural address to Congress, he declared that his government would consider what measures it should take "to nationalize industries which are, at present, chiefly of benefit to foreigners," a clear reference to the nitrate industry. Later, Balmaceda's strategy shifted; he encouraged the entrance of Chilean private capital into nitrate production and exportation to prevent the formation of a foreign-dominated nitrate cartel whose interest in restricting output clashed with the government's interest in maintaining a high level of production to collect more export taxes. In November 1888, he scolded the Chilean elite for their lack of entrepreneurial spirit:

> Why does the credit and the capital which are brought into play in all kinds of speculations in our great cities hold back and leave the foreigner to establish banks at Iquique and abandon to strangers the exploiting of the nitrate works of Tarapacá? ... The foreigner exploits these riches and takes the profit of native wealth to give to other lands and unknown people the treasures of our soil, our own property and the riches we require.

Balmaceda waged a determined struggle to end the monopoly of the British-owned Nitrate Railways Company, whose prohibitive freight charges reduced production and export of nitrates. His nationalistic policies inevitably provoked the hostility of English nitrate "kings" like North, who had close links with the Chilean elite and employed prominent liberal politicians as their legal advisers.

Balmaceda had many domestic as well as foreign foes. The clerics opposed his plans to curb church powers. The landed aristocracy resented his public works program because it drew labor from agriculture and drove up rural wages. His proposal to establish a national bank with a monopoly of note issue angered the banks, which had profited from an uncontrolled emission of notes that fed inflation and benefited mortgaged landlords and exporters. The entire oligarchy, Liberals as well as Conservatives, opposed his use of the central government as an instrument of progressive economic and social change.

Meanwhile, the government's economic problems multiplied, adding to Balmaceda's political difficulties by narrowing his popular base. By 1890, foreign demand for copper and nitrates had weakened. Prices in an overstocked world market fell, and English nitrate interests responded to the crisis by forming a cartel to reduce production. Reduced production and export of nitrates and copper sharply diminished the flow of export duties into the treasury and caused growing unemployment and wage cuts even as inflation cut into the value of wages. The result was a series of great strikes in Valparaíso and the nitrate zone in 1890. Despite his sympathy with the workers' demands and unwillingness to use force against them, Balmaceda, under pressure from domestic and foreign employers, sent troops to crush the strikes. These repressive measures ensured much working-class apathy and even hostility toward the president in the eventual confrontation with his foes.

Indeed, Balmaceda had few firm allies at his side when that crisis came. The industrial capitalist group whose growth he had promoted ardently was still weak. The mining interests, increasingly integrated with or dominated by English capital, joined the bankers, the clericals, and the landed aristocracy in opposition to his nationalist program of economic development and independence. The opposition mobilized its forces in parliament, where Balmaceda lacked a reliable congressional majority, forcing him to abolish the system of parliamentary government and return to the traditional system of presidential rule established by the constitution of 1833. His rash act, made without any serious effort to mobilize popular forces, played into the hands of his enemies, who already were preparing for civil war.

On January 7, 1891, congressional leaders proclaimed a revolt against the president in the name of legality and the constitution. The navy, then as now led by officers of aristocratic descent, promptly supported the rebels, who seized the ports and customhouses in the north and established their capital at Iquique, the chief port of Tarapacá.

English-owned enterprises also actively aided the rebels. Indeed, by the admission of the British minister at Santiago, "our naval officers and the British community of Valparaíso and all along the coast rendered material assistance to the opposition and committed many breaches of neutrality." Many nitrate workers, alienated by Balmaceda's repression of their strike, remained neutral, or even joined the rebel army, organized by a German army officer, General Emil Korner. Politically isolated and militarily defeated, Balmaceda sought refuge in the Argentine embassy, and on September 19, 1891, the day on which his legal term of office ended, Balmaceda put a bullet through his head.

The death of Chile's first anti-imperialist president restored the reign of the oligarchy, a coalition of landowners, bankers, merchants, and mining interests closely linked to English capital. A new era began, the era of the so-called Parliamentary Republic. Taught by experience, the oligarchy now preferred to rule through a congress divided into various factions rather than through a strong executive. Such decentralization of government favored the interests of the rural aristocracy and its allies. A new law of 1892, vesting local governments with the right to supervise elections both for local and national offices, reinforced the power of the landowners, priests, and political bosses who had fought Balmaceda's progressive policies.

THE PARLIAMENTARY REPUBLIC, FOREIGN ECONOMIC DOMINATION, AND THE GROWTH OF THE WORKING CLASS

The era of the Parliamentary Republic accompanied a growing subordination of the Chilean economy to foreign capital, confirmed by a steady increase in the foreign debt and foreign ownership of the nation's resources. English investments in Chile amounted to 24 million pounds in 1890 and rose to 64 million pounds in 1913. Of this total, 34.6 million pounds formed part of the Chilean public debt. In the same period, North American and German capital began to challenge the British hegemony in Chile. England continued to be Chile's principal trade partner, but U.S. and German trade with Chile grew at a faster rate. German instructors also acquired a strong influence in the Chilean army, and the flow of German immigrants into southern Chile continued, resulting in the formation of compact colonies dominated by a Pan-German ideology. The revival of the Chilean economy from the depression of the early 1890s brought an increase of nitrate, copper, and agricultural exports, and further enriched the ruling classes, but it left inquilinos, miners, and factory workers as desperately poor as before. Meanwhile, the working class grew from one hundred twenty thousand to two hundred fifty thousand between 1890 and 1900, and the doctrines of trade unionism, socialism, and anarchism achieved growing popularity in its ranks.

Luis Emilio Recabarren (1876–1924), the father of Chilean socialism and communism, played a decisive role in the social and political awakening of the Chilean proletariat. In 1906, Recabarren won an election to Congress from a mining area, but state officials did not allow him to take his seat because he refused to take his oath of office on the Bible. In 1909, he organized the Workers Federation of Chile, the first national trade union movement. Three years later, he founded the Socialist Party, a revolutionary Marxist movement, and became its first secretary.

The growing self-consciousness and militancy of the Chilean working class found expression in a mounting wave of strikes. Between 1911 and 1920, almost three hundred strikes, involving more than three hundred thousand workers, took place, many of which the state crushed with traditional brutal methods that left thousands of workers dead.

Brazilian Politics and Economy

THE FALL OF THE MONARCHY

Abolition of slavery in 1888 sabotaged slavery's sister institution, the monarchy, which had long rested on the support of the planter class, especially the northern planters, who saw in it a guarantee of slavery's survival. Before 1888, the Republican Party had its principal base among the coffee interests, who resented the favor shown by the imperial government to the sugar planters and wished to achieve political power that corresponded to their economic clout. Now, angered by abolition and embittered by the failure of the crown to indemnify

them for their lost slaves, those planters who had opposed abolition joined the Republican movement. The monarchy that had served the interest of regional elites for the previous sixty-seven years had lost its reason for existence.

Republicanism and a closely allied ideology, positivism, also made many converts in the officer class, who were disgruntled by the imperial government's neglect and mistreatment. Many of the younger officers belonged to the new urban middle class or were of aristocratic descent but disagreed with the ways of their fathers. Positivism, it has been said, became "the gospel of the military academy," where a popular young professor of mathematics, Benjamin Constant Botelho de Magalhães, a devoted disciple of Auguste Comte, the doctrine's founder, taught. The positivist doctrine, with its stress on science, its ideal of a dictatorial republic, and its distrust of the masses, fit the needs of urban middle-class groups, progressive officers, and businessmen-fazendeiros, who wanted modernization but without drastic changes in land tenure and class relations. On November 15, 1889, a military revolt led by Benjamin Constant and Marshal Floriano Peixoto overthrew the government, proclaimed a republic with Marshal Deodoro da Fonseca as provisional chief of state, and sent Pedro II into exile in France.

Like the revolution that gave Brazil its independence, the republican revolution came from above; the coup d'état encountered little resistance but also inspired little popular enthusiasm. Representatives of the business, landed, and military elites monopolized political, economic, and social power.

The new rulers promptly promulgated a series of reforms, including a decree that ended corporal punishment in the army, a literacy test that replaced property qualifications for voting (because property and literacy usually went together, this measure did not significantly enlarge the electorate), and successive decrees that established a secular state and civil marriage.

THE NEW REPUBLIC

Two years after the revolt, a constituent assembly met in Rio de Janeiro to draft a constitution for the new republic. It provided for a federal, presidential

Fundação Maria Luísa e Oscar Americano, São Paulo

Allegory of the Departure of Dom Pedro II for Europe After the Declaration of the Republic. This romantic painting suggests the respect and affection many Brazilians, including supporters of the republic, felt for the ousted emperor.

form of government with the customary three branches: legislative, executive, and judicial. The principal debate was between the partisans of greater autonomy for the states and those who feared the divisive results of an extreme federalism. The coffee interests, which dominated the wealthy south-central region, sought to strengthen their position at the expense of the central power. The urban business groups, represented in the convention chiefly by lawyers, favored a strong central government that could promote industry, aid the creation of a national market, and offer protection from British competition.

The result was a compromise tilted in favor of federalism. The twenty provinces in effect became self-governing states with popularly elected governors,

the exclusive right to tax exports (a profitable privilege for wealthy states like São Paulo and Minas Gerais), and the right to maintain militias. The national government received control over the tariffs and the income from import duties, whereas the president obtained significant powers: He could designate his cabinet ministers and other high officers, declare a state of siege, and, in the event of a threat to their political institutions, intervene in the states with the federal armed forces. The constitution proclaimed the sanctity of private property and guaranteed freedom of the press, speech, and assembly.

If these freedoms had some relevance in the cities and hinterlands touched by the movement of modernization, they lacked meaning over the greater part of the national territory. The fazendeiros, former slave owners, virtually monopolized the nation's chief wealth: its land. The land monopoly gave them absolute control over the rural population. Feudal and semifeudal forms of land tenure, accompanied by the obligation of personal and military service on the part of tenants, survived in the backlands, especially in the northeast. Powerful *coronéis* (urban or rural bosses) maintained armies of *jagunços* (full-time private soldiers) and waged war against each other.

In this medieval atmosphere of constant insecurity and social disintegration, there arose messianic movements that reflected the aspirations of the oppressed *sertanejos* (inhabitants of the sertão) for peace and justice. One of the most important of such movements arose in the interior of Bahia, where the principal activity was cattle raising. Here, Antônio Conselheiro (Anthony the Counselor) established a settlement at the abandoned cattle ranch of Canudos. Rejecting private property, Antônio required all who joined his sacred company to give up their goods, but he promised a future of prosperity in his messianic kingdom. All would share in the division of hostile landowners' property and the treasure of the "lost Sebastian," the Portuguese king who had disappeared in Africa in 1478, but soon would return as a redeemer.

Despite its religious coloration, the existence of such a focus of social and political unrest was intolerable to the fazendeiros and the state authorities. When the sertanejos easily defeated state forces sent against them in 1896, the governor called on the federal government for aid. Four brutal military campaigns finally broke the epic resistance of the men, women, and children of Canudos, nearly all of whom perished in the national army's final assault. A Brazilian literary masterpiece, *Os sertões* (*Rebellion in the Backlands*) by Euclides da Cunha (1856–1909), immortalized the heroism of the defenders and the crimes of the victors. It also revealed to the urban elite another and unfamiliar side of Brazilian reality.

THE ECONOMIC REVOLUTION

An enormous historical gulf separated the bleak sertão—where the tragedy of Canudos played out—

from the cities, the scene of a mushrooming growth of banks, stock exchanges, and corporations. In Rio de Janeiro, writes Pedro Calmon, there was "a multitude of millionaires of recent vintage—commercial agents, bustling lawyers, promoters of all kinds, politicians of the new generation, the men of the day." Even the physical appearance of some of Brazil's great urban centers changed. The federal capital of Rio de Janeiro experienced the most marked changes, when Prefect Pereira Passos mercilessly demolished narrow, old streets to permit the construction of broad, modern avenues. At the same time, the distinguished scientist Oswaldo Cruz waged a victorious struggle to conquer mosquito-borne disease by filling in swamps and installing adequate water and sewage systems. Thus, Rio became a beautiful and healthful city between 1902 and 1906.

The economic policies of the new republican regime reflected pressures from different quarters: the planter class, urban capitalists, and the military. Many planters, left in a difficult position by the abolition of slavery, demanded subsidies and credits to enable them to convert to the new wage system. The emerging industrial bourgeoisie, convinced that Brazil must develop an industrial base to emerge from backwardness, asked for protective tariffs, the construction of an economic infrastructure, and policies favorable to capital formation. Within the provisional government, these aspirations had a fervent supporter in the minister of finance, Ruy Barbosa, who believed that the factory was the crucible in which an "intelligent and independent democracy" would be forged in Brazil. Finally, the army, whose decisive role in the establishment of the republic had given it great prestige and influence, called for increased appropriations for the armed services. These various demands far exceeded the revenue available to the federal and state governments.

The federal government initially tried to satisfy these competing demands by resorting to the printing press and allowing private banks to issue notes backed by little more than faith in the future of Brazil. In two years, the volume of paper money in circulation doubled, and the foreign-exchange value of the *milréis* (the Brazilian monetary unit) plummeted disastrously. Because objective economic conditions (the small internal market and the lack of an adequate technological base, among other factors) limited the real potential for Brazilian growth, much of the new capital served highly speculative purposes, including the creation of fictitious companies.

The resulting economic collapse brought ruin to many investors, unemployment and lower wages to workers, and a military coup that replaced President da Fonseca with his vice president, Marshal Floriano Peixoto. The urban middle-class sector thereafter briefly gained greater influence, and inflation continued unchecked. The rise in the cost of many imported items to almost prohibitive levels stimulated the growth of Brazilian manufactures: The number of such enterprises almost doubled between 1890 and 1895.

However, the suppression of a new revolt with strong aristocratic and monarchical overtones increased Peixoto's reliance on the financial and military support of the state of São Paulo, whose coffee oligarchy resolved to use its clout to end the ascendancy of the urban middle classes. The oligarchy distrusted their policies of rapid industrialization and blamed them for the financial instability that had plagued the first years of the republic. In 1893, the old planter oligarchies, whose divisions temporarily had enabled the middle classes to gain the upper hand in coalition with the military, reunited to form the Federal Republican Party, with a liberal program of support for federalism, fiscal responsibility, and limited government. Because they controlled the electoral machinery, they easily captured the presidency and again institutionalized the domination of the coffee interests, relegating urban capitalist groups to a secondary role in political life.

A succession of Liberal governments thereafter gave primacy to export agriculture and fully endorsed the international economic division of labor that rendered Brazil dependent on foreign manufactured imports. "It is time," proclaimed President Manuel Ferraz de Campos Sales (1898–1902), "that we take the correct road; to that end we must strive to export all that we can produce better than other

countries, and import all that other countries can produce better than we." This formula confirmed the continuity of neocolonialism from the empire through the early republic. Determined to halt inflation, the Liberals drastically reduced expenditures on public works, increased taxes, made every effort to redeem the paper money to improve Brazil's international credit, and secured new loans to cover shortfalls in government revenues.

Coffee was king. Whereas Brazil produced 56 percent of the world's coffee output from 1880 to 1889, it accounted for 76 percent from 1900 to 1904. Its closest competitor, rubber, supplied only 28 percent of Brazil's exports in 1901. Sugar, once the ruler of the Brazilian economy, now accounted for barely 5 percent of the nation's exports. Minas Gerais and especially São Paulo became the primary coffee regions, and Rio de Janeiro declined in importance. Enjoying immense advantages—the famous rich, porous *terra roxa* (red soil), an abundance of immigrant labor, and closeness to the major port of Santos—the *Paulistas* harvested 60 percent of the national coffee production.

The coffee boom from the late 1880s through the mid-1890s soon led to overproduction, falling prices, and the accumulation of unsold stocks after 1896. Because coffee trees came into production only four years after planting, the effects of expansion into the western frontier of São Paulo continued to be felt even after prices fell; between 1896 and 1900 the number of producing trees in São Paulo alone went from 150 million to 570 million. Large international coffee-trading firms controlled the world market, and they added to planters' difficulties by paying depressed prices during the height of each season and selling off their reserves in periods of relative shortage when prices edged up.

Responding to the planters' clamor for help, the São Paulo government took the first step for the defense of coffee in 1902, forbidding new coffee plantings for five years. Other steps soon proved necessary. Faced with a bumper crop in 1906, São Paulo launched a coffee price-support scheme to protect the state's economic lifeblood. With financing from British, French, German, and U.S. banks and the eventual collaboration of the federal government, São Paulo purchased several million bags of coffee and held them off the market in an effort to maintain profitable price levels. Purchases continued into 1907; from that date until World War I, the state gradually sold off the stocks with little market disruption. The operation's principal gainers were the foreign merchants and bankers, who, because they controlled the Coffee Commission formed to liquidate the purchased stocks, gradually disposed of them with a large margin of profit. The problem, temporarily exorcised, shortly returned in an even more acute form.

The valorization scheme, which favored the coffee-raising states at the expense of the rest, reflected the coffee planters' political domination. President Campos Sales institutionalized this ascendancy with the so-called *política dos governadores* (politics of the governors). Its essence was a formula that gave the two richest and most populous states (São Paulo and Minas Gerais) a virtual monopoly of federal politics and the choice of presidents. Thus, the first three civilian presidents from 1894 to 1906 came from São Paulo; the next two, from 1906 to 1910, came from Minas Gerais and Rio de Janeiro, respectively.

In return, the oligarchies of the other states enjoyed almost total freedom of action within their jurisdictions, with the central government usually intervening only when it suited the local oligarchy's interest. Informal discussions among the state governors determined the choice of president, whose election was a foregone conclusion because less than 2 percent of the population was eligible to vote. No official candidate for president lost an election before 1930. Similar reciprocal arrangements existed on the state level between the governors and the coronéis, who rounded up the local vote to elect the governors and thereby earned a free hand in their respective domains.

Despite the official bias in favor of agriculture, industry continued to grow. By 1908, Brazil could boast of more than three thousand industrial enterprises. Foreign firms dominated the fields of banking, public works, utilities, transportation, and the export and import trade. On the other hand, native Brazilians and permanent immigrants almost exclusively engaged in manufacturing. This national industry concentrated in the four states of São Paulo, Minas Gervais, Rio de Janeiro, and Rio Grande do Sul. Heavy industry did not exist; more than half of the enterprises were textile mills and food-processing plants. Many of these "enterprises" were small workshops that employed only a few artisans or operated with archaic technology, and Brazilians in the market economy continued to import most quality products. Semifeudal conditions prevailing in the countryside, the extreme poverty of the masses (which sharply limited the internal market), the lack of a skilled and literate labor force, and the hostility of most fazendeiros and foreign interests to industry all limited the quantitative and qualitative development of industry.

Together with industry, a working class arose destined to play a significant role in the life of the country. The Brazilian proletariat formed partly from sharecroppers and minifundio peasants fleeing to the cities to escape dismal poverty and the tyranny of coronéis, but above all, it relied on the flood of European immigrants, who arrived at a rate of one hundred thousand to one hundred fifty thousand each year. Working and living conditions of the working class were often intolerable. Child labor was common, for children could legally seek employment from the age of twelve. The workday ranged from nine hours for some skilled workers to more than sixteen hours for various categories of unskilled workers. Wages were pitifully low and often paid in vouchers redeemable at the company store. Legislation was totally absent to protect workers against the hazards of unemployment, old age, or industrial accidents.

Among the European immigrants, many militants with socialist, syndicalist, or social-democratic backgrounds helped organize the Brazilian labor movement and gave it a radical political orientation. National and religious divisions among workers, widespread illiteracy, and quarrels between socialists and **anarcho-syndicalists** hampered the rise of a trade union movement and a labor party.

Nonetheless, trade unions grew rapidly after 1900, and the first national labor congress, representing the majority of the country's trade unions, met in 1906 to struggle for the eight-hour workday. One result of the congress was the formation of the first national trade union organization, the Brazilian Labor Confederation, which organized a number of strikes that authorities and employers tried to suppress by arresting labor leaders, deporting immigrants, and sending dissidents to forced labor on a railroad under construction in distant Mato Grosso. The phrase "The social question is a question for the police" was often used to sum up the labor policy of Brazil's liberal state.

Central American Politics and Economy

In the last third of the nineteenth century, the three Central American countries selected for special study—Guatemala, Nicaragua, and El Salvador—underwent major economic changes in response to growing world demand for two products the area produced in great quantity: coffee and bananas. The changes included a liberal reform that sought to promote economic growth but left intact existing class and property relations. This liberal program also led to a new dependency on the export of one or two products, foreign control of key natural resources, and acceptance of U.S. political hegemony. Throughout Central America, these changes accompanied concentration of landownership, intensified exploitation of labor, and contributed to a growing gulf between the rich and the poor.

GUATEMALA, 1865–1898

Six years of continuous liberal political and military challenge to Guatemala's conservative rule followed Rafael Carrera's death in 1865. The Liberals responded to changes in the world economy, in particular to the mounting foreign demand for coffee and the adjustments this required in Guatemala's economic and social structures. In 1871, they seized power, and two years later the energetic Justo Rufino Barrios became president. Barrios and his successors were determined to consolidate state power, subjugate relatively autonomous indigenous communities, and create a unified national market for land, labor, and commodities.

Their liberal reform program included major economic, social, and ideological changes. The ideological reform introduced doctrines of white supremacy then current in Europe and the United States to justify racist immigration policies designed to "whiten" the population. It also rejected clerical and metaphysical doctrine in favor of a firm faith in science and material progress. This called for the secularization and expansion of education. The shortage of public funds, however, greatly limited public education; as late as 1921, the Guatemalan illiteracy rate was more than 86 percent. Seeking to reduce the power and authority of the church, the Liberal governments nationalized its lands, ended its special privileges, and established freedom of religion and civil marriage.

The economic transformation encompassed three major areas: land tenure, labor, and infrastructure. A change in land tenure was necessary for the creation of the new economic order. Thousands of small and midsize producers had grown the old staples of Guatemalan agriculture, indigo and cochineal; coffee, however, required significant accumulations of capital and large expanses of land concentrated in relatively few hands. Barrios began an agrarian reform designed to make such land available to the coffee growers. He confiscated Church and monastery lands, indigenous communal lands, and uncultivated state holdings, which he divided and either sold cheaply or granted freely to private interests. Legislation requiring titles to private property provided the legal basis for this expropriation. The principal native beneficiaries of this process were small and midsize coffee growers who could purchase or otherwise obtain land from the government. However, foreign immigrants, warmly welcomed by the Liberal regimes, also benefited from the new legislation. By 1914, foreign-owned (chiefly German) lands produced almost half of Guatemala's coffee. By 1926, concentration of land ownership had reached a point at which only 7.3 percent of the population owned land.

The land reform helped achieve another objective of the liberal program: the supply of a mass of cheap labor to the new group of native and foreign coffee growers. Many highland natives who had lost their land migrated to the emerging coffee-growing areas near the coast. The most common labor system was debt peonage—legal under Guatemalan law—in which hereditary debts bound indigenous workers to the *fincas* (plantations). Export agriculture also depended on the recruitment of native peoples who came down from the mountains to work as seasonal laborers on haciendas and plantations to supplement their meager income from their own tiny landholdings. Barrios also revived the colonial system of *mandamientos* (a system of coerced indigenous labor), which required indigenous people to accept offers of work from planters. Local officials maintained registers for this purpose and also used them to conscript natives for military service or public works. Those who could not pay the two-peso head tax—the great majority—had to work two weeks per year on road construction.

Constituting 70 percent of the nation's 1 million people in the late nineteenth century, indigenous peoples naturally resisted this liberal onslaught, occasionally through overt acts of localized rebellion. However, in the face of a ruthless military state prepared to obliterate them, they more commonly survived by deploying "weapons of the weak," modes of resistance designed to limit the risk of annihilation. In rural Guatemala, these indigenous communities relied on *guachibales* (independent religious brotherhoods rooted in colonial Catholic traditions) to maintain their cultural identities, defend their autonomy, and preserve communal customs, ancestral languages, and religious rituals against the homogenizing power of liberalism's unfettered market forces.

NICARAGUA, 1870–1909

A struggle between Liberals and Conservatives also dominated the history of Nicaragua for two decades after the collapse of the Central American federation in 1838. The Liberals' responsibility for inviting William Walker to assist them, followed by Walker's attempt to establish his personal empire in Central America, so discredited them that the Conservatives ruled Nicaragua with little opposition for more than three decades thereafter (1857–1893).

Although coffee was grown commercially as early as 1848, the principal economic activities in Nicaragua until about 1870 were cattle ranching and subsistence agriculture. Indigenous communities still owned much land, a class of independent small farmers lived on public land, and peonage was rare. On the Atlantic coast, however, the autonomous Kingdom of Mosquitia, controlled by the British since 1678, was home to traditional Miskitos, Sumus, and Afro-creoles, who labored at low wages on thriving British- and U.S.-owned banana plantations, timberlands, gold mines, and commercial port facilities. But the sudden growth of the world market for coffee induced the Nicaraguan elite to demand additional land suitable for coffee growing and an expanded supply of cheap labor.

Beginning in 1877, a series of laws required indigenous villages to sell their communal lands and effectively drove the indigenous and mestizo peasants off their land, gradually transforming them into a class of dependent peons or sharecroppers. The passage of vagrancy laws and laws permitting the conscription of native peoples for agricultural and public labor also ensured the supply of cheap labor needed by the coffee growers. These laws provoked a major indigenous revolt, the War of the Comuneros (1881), which ended in defeat for indigenous communities and thereafter unleashed a ferocious repression that took five thousand lives.

The new class of coffee planters was impatient with the traditional ways of the conservative cattle ranchers who had held power in Nicaragua since 1857. In 1893, the planters staged a revolt that brought the Liberal José Santos Zelaya to the presidency. A modernizer, Zelaya ruled for the next seventeen years as dictator-president. He undertook to provide the infrastructure needed by the new economic order through the construction of roads, railroads, port facilities, and telegraphic communications. He reorganized the military, separated church and state, and promoted public education. Like other Latin American Liberal leaders of his time, he believed that foreign investment was necessary for rapid economic progress and granted large concessions to foreign capitalists, especially U.S. firms. By 1909, North Americans controlled much of the production of coffee, gold, lumber, and bananas—the principal sources of Nicaragua's wealth.

El Salvador, 1876–1911

By the mid-nineteenth century, El Salvador already had passed through two economic cycles. The first was dominated by cacao, the prosperity of which collapsed in the seventeenth century; the second by indigo, which entered a sharp decline in the latter half of the nineteenth century, first as a result of competition from other producing areas and then as a result of the development of synthetic dyes. The search for a new export crop led to the enthronement of coffee. Coffee cultivation began at about the time of independence, but it did not expand rapidly until the 1860s. As elsewhere in Central America, expropriation and usurpation of native lands—carried out in the name of private property and material progress—accompanied the rise of coffee because indigenous communities owned most of the land best suited to coffee cultivation.

Unlike indigo, which was planted and harvested every year, coffee trees did not produce for three years. Producers, therefore, had to have capital or credit, and the people with capital or access to credit were the hacendados who had prospered from the growing of indigo. To help these hacendados in their search for land and labor, a government decree of 1856 declared that, if a pueblo did not plant two-thirds of its communal lands in coffee, ownership would pass into the hands of the state. Later, the Liberal president and military strongman, Rafael Zaldívar, directly attacked native landholdings with passage of an 1881 law that ordered the division of all communal lands among the co-owners. This division of land opened the way for the expanding coffee growers to acquire their land by legal or illegal means. Thirteen months later, Zaldívar decreed the abolition of all communal land tenure. The new legislation harmed these communities and **ladino** (mestizo) small farmers. These farmers often relied on municipal **tierras comunes** (the free pasture and woodlot where they could graze their stock) for an important part of their subsistence. In 1879, 60 percent of the people depended on communal properties, which composed 40 percent of arable lands.

The result of this new legislation was a rapid concentration of landownership in the hands of a landed oligarchy often referred to as "the fourteen families." The number, although not an exact figure, expressed symbolically the reality of the tiny elite that dominated the Salvadoran economy and state. Throughout most of the nineteenth century, the great landowners used their own private armies to deal with the problem of recalcitrant peasants. Government decrees of 1884 and 1889 made these private armed forces the basis of the public Rural Police, later renamed the National Police. In 1912 the *Guardia Nacional* (National Guard), modeled after the Spanish National Guard, was established. Like the National Police, the National Guard patrolled the countryside and offered police protection to haciendas.

For the rural poor, the social consequences of the coffee boom were disastrous. A few of the dispossessed peasants were permitted to remain on the *fincas* (new estates) as *colonos*—peons who received a place to live and a *milpa* (garden plot) where they could raise subsistence crops in exchange for their labor. Unlike the old indigo or sugar latifundia, however, which required a large permanent labor force, the need for labor on the coffee plantations was seasonal, so for the most part planters relied on hired hands. This circumstance determined the pattern of life of most Salvadoran campesinos. They might farm a small plot as squatters or as colonos on a plantation, but their tiny plots usually did not provide sufficient subsistence for their families. They therefore tended to follow the harvests, working on coffee fincas during the harvest season, moving on to cut sugar cane or harvest cotton during August and September, and finally returning to their milpas, hopeful that the maize had ripened. This unstable migratory pattern created many social problems.

Venezuelan Politics and Economy

Turmoil in the aftermath of the Federal War ended in 1870 when Antonio Guzmán Blanco, the ablest of Venezuela's nineteenth-century rulers, seized power. Like his father, Guzmán Blanco was a master of demagogic rhetoric. He was a self-proclaimed Liberal and foe of the oligarchy, an anticlerical and devout believer in the positivist creed of science and progress, whose ambition was to create a "practical republic" of "civilized people." To secure this vision, he forged pacts with the Conservative merchant class of Caracas, regional caudillos, and foreign economic interests who profited from his ambitious program to construct roads, railroads, and telegraph systems. In the end, Guzmán Blanco's dream of a developed capitalist Venezuela proved to be a mirage; after two decades of his rule, Venezuela remained rural, monocultural, and dependent, a country in which caudillos again ran rampant as they struggled for power.

Guzmán or "the illustrious American," as his sycophantic Congress and press called him, presided over a system of government that Venezuelan historians often describe as "a national alliance of caudillos." The supreme caudillo replaced the constitution of 1864 with a succession of new constitutions that reinforced the centralization of power. Although Guzmán's dictatorship was mild by comparison with some others in Venezuelan history, he did not hesitate to use repressive measures against his foes.

By his pact with the caudillos, Guzmán secured a relatively stable peace (though several large-scale revolts erupted against him between 1870 and 1888, and local uprisings were common throughout the period). Soon after coming to power, he established a *compañía de crédito* with a powerful group of Caracas merchants. This group gave him the resources needed to initiate a program of public works designed to improve transportation and communication. Between 1870 and 1874, he began fifty-one road-building projects, but local funding did not suffice. Although Guzmán solicited the cooperation of foreign capital, other countries were reluctant to invest in a country where recurrent episodes of civil war had marked its recent history. In 1879, he secured his first foreign contract with a group of British investors for the construction of a railroad to connect Caracas with its major port, La Guaira. By the time he left office, Venezuela had eleven railroad lines completed or under construction, all designed to serve the export-import trade by connecting Caracas and the major agricultural and mining areas with the ports. Given Venezuela's unfavorable terms of trade—the long-term

tendency for the prices of its exports to decline and those of its manufactured imports to rise—the net result was to reinforce Venezuela's economic dependency, promote decapitalization, and leave the country a legacy of large unpaid foreign debt that in time posed a threat of foreign intervention and loss of sovereignty.

Guzmán Blanco's anticlerical policies led to a further weakening of the church. Liberals already had abolished tithing as "an excessive tax burden" on the citizenry, but Guzmán Blanco ended the priestly fuero, established civil marriage and registration of births and deaths, and closed convents and seminaries. His government forbade the church to inherit real estate and seized many church estates. Guzmán Blanco also tried to prohibit black and Asian immigration, even as he enticed Europeans with generous subsidies. Ultimately, this failed, and Venezuela remained a society in which a small, self-proclaimed white wealthy minority ruled a black majority.

For the rest, Guzmán Blanco's development programs caused little change in the country's economic and social structures. In 1894, the population, numbering some 2.5 million, was overwhelmingly rural; only three cities had a population of more than ten thousand. Most of the laboring population worked in agriculture; what little modern industry existed was limited to light industry, such as food processing and textiles. Artisan shops, employing some fifty thousand workers, were economically much more important.

After a chaotic decade following the demise of Guzmán Blanco, Cipriano Castro, an energetic young caudillo from the Andean state of Táchira, seized power with his *compadre* (buddy) Juan Vicente Gómez, a prosperous cattle raiser and coffee grower. Castro's rise reflected the growing economic importance of the Andean coffee-growing region. Although he tried to continue Guzmán Blanco's policy of centralization by establishing a strong national army to replace the old-time personal and state militias, declining coffee prices reduced state revenues and handicapped his program of military reform. This led to a series of caudillo revolts repressed at heavy cost and a major conflict with foreign powers whose blockade of Venezuelan ports deprived the government of a vital source of income: custom duties.

Castro presided over a country in ruin because of devastating civil wars and a prolonged depression. The German and British governments demanded immediate settlement of their nationals' claims for unpaid debts and damages suffered in civil wars, but the government could not pay. In December 1902, despite Castro's offer to negotiate, the two powers sent an Anglo-German squadron of twelve warships into Venezuelan waters with orders to seize or destroy Venezuela's tiny fleet and blockade its ports. The powerful guns of the Anglo-German squadron soon silenced the answering fire of Venezuelan coastal batteries, and the aggressors occupied several Venezuelan ports. The unequal nature of the struggle, the catastrophic economic impact of the Anglo-German blockade, and the continuing internal revolts in some areas of the country made a settlement necessary. Accordingly, Castro asked the U.S. ambassador to mediate in negotiating a settlement. The terms required Venezuela to allocate 30 percent of its customs duties to the payment of claims, provided for an end to the blockade, and reestablished diplomatic relations between the parties, but the settlement denied Venezuela compensation for its losses.

Castro's last years in power were troubled by new clashes with foreign states—France, Holland, the United States—usually caused by his insistence that foreign nationals were subject to Venezuelan courts and laws. As Castro's health declined, Juan Vicente Gómez, with support of foreign powers, notably the United States, ended the Castro regime and launched a new Liberal dictatorship.

Colombian Politics and Economy

Dominating the presidency and Congress in 1853, the Liberals in Colombia authored a new constitution that provided for universal male suffrage, a provision that troubled some Liberals, who feared that illiterate proclerical peasants might vote Conservative. Actually, because in most areas peasants

continued to vote the wishes of the local *gamonales* (bosses), the new electoral law did not significantly change anything.

In economics, the Liberals sought a decisive break with the colonial tradition of restriction and monopoly. They abolished the state tobacco monopoly and ceded to the provinces revenues from tithes (hitherto collected by the state but used for support of the church), the quinto tax on gold and other precious metals, and other traditional sources of national state revenue. They also empowered the provinces to abolish these taxes. To compensate for the resulting loss of national revenues, Congress adopted a tax on individuals.

Having achieved these objectives with artisan support, the Liberal elite now ignored their allies' demands for tariff protection. This triggered a new political crisis in 1854 when a coup, supported by artisans who formed workers' battalions to defend the revolution, briefly installed Gen. José María Melo. However, Liberal and Conservative generals, putting aside their differences, raised private armies and defeated Melo in a short campaign. They subsequently imprisoned his artisan allies and deported three hundred to Panama. The economic, political, and military rout of the artisans was complete.

In 1860, Liberals carried their religious and political reforms to their extreme and logical conclusions. They abolished compulsory tithes and ecclesiastical fueros, suppressed all religious orders, closed all convents and monasteries, and seized church wealth. However, the resulting transfer of massive amounts of church land into private hands produced little or no change in the land tenure system; clerical latifundia simply became lay latifundia, contributing to a further concentration of landownership. The principal buyers were Liberal merchants, landowners, and politicians, but Conservatives also participated in the plunder of church land.

In 1863, Liberal political reform reached its climax when a new constitution carried the principle of federalism to great lengths. The nine sovereign states became, in effect, independent nations, each with its own armed forces and possessing all the legislative powers not explicitly granted to the weak central government. The Liberals remained in power until 1885 in a political climate that approximated institutionalized anarchy, as the central government was powerless to intervene against the local revolutions that toppled and set up state governments.

The economic movement and its quest for the export base that could firmly integrate Colombia into the capitalist world economy continued. By the 1870s, tobacco exports were down sharply, but exports of coffee, quinine, and other products made up for this decline. Coffee emerged as the country's major export product, but its development lagged behind that of Brazil, which relied increasingly on European immigrant free labor. In Colombia, coffee production in its principal centers of Santander and Cundinamarca relied on traditional haciendas worked by peons and tenants who lived and labored under oppressive conditions. A more satisfactory situation existed in Antioquia and Caldas, characterized by a mix of haciendas with more enlightened forms of sharecropping and smallholdings, operations marked by high productivity. In these states, the twentieth-century takeoff of the Colombian coffee industry occurred.

The development of coffee as the major export, the growing ties between foreign and domestic merchants and coffee planters, and the stimulus that expropriation of church lands gave to trade and speculation created economic interests that required a new political model. Its principal characteristic was a strong state that could impose order, construct a railroad network, and create the financial infrastructure needed to expand the coffee industry. The Liberal reform had removed many obstacles to capitalist development, but its federalist excesses had created others. By the early 1880s, Conservatives and many moderate Liberals agreed that political and social stability required the consolidation of a centralized nation-state, a project initiated by Rafael Núñez in 1879.

RAFAEL NÚÑEZ, THE "REGENERATION," AND THE WAR OF A THOUSAND DAYS, 1880–1903

Núñez began political life as a radical Liberal and spent thirteen years in the consular service in Europe. He returned home in 1875 and won the presidential election in 1879, governing with a coalition of Liberal and Conservative Parties. Re-elected in 1884, he swiftly crushed a radical Liberal revolt and announced that the 1863 constitution had "ceased to exist." In 1886, he presented the country with a new constitution that replaced the sovereign states with departments headed by governors appointed by the president, extended the presidential term to six years, established literacy and property qualifications for voting for representatives, and provided for indirect election of senators. Under that constitution, personally or through surrogates, Núñez ruled Colombia until his death in 1894.

The foundations of Núñez's authoritarian republic were a strong standing army and a national police force. Earlier regimes had virtually dismantled the regular army; private armies, formed by the great landowners with their tenants and peons, had fought the revolts and civil wars of the federal period. The existence of these regional private armies and militias was incompatible with Núñez's unitary project. The 1886 constitution created a permanent army and reserved to the central government the right to possess arms and ammunition. The national police, organized in 1891, kept a watchful eye on political suspects and disrupted most plots against the government.

Núñez was responsible for two major economic innovations. Claiming that free trade or low tariffs were the cause of economic decadence and poverty, which had caused civil war, he proposed to use tariff protection to stimulate the growth of certain industries. He believed this would create a new middle class that would form a buffer between the governing social class and the unlettered multitude. His implementation of this program was timid and inconsistent. The new policy succeeded, however, in providing a modest level of protection for domestic industry.

Núñez's other innovation was the creation in 1881 of a national bank designed to relieve the financial distress of a government always on the verge of bankruptcy. The bank had the exclusive right to issue money; managed prudently until 1890, this monopoly enabled the state to provide for its needs. Thereafter, its uncontrolled emissions of paper money caused a galloping inflation. An expensive civil war in 1899 provoked the emission of paper money on such a scale that the printers could not keep up with demand, and millions of pesos of depreciated currency flooded the country.

The "Regeneration," as the Núñez Era is known, represented an effort to achieve national unification from above; it was comparable to Bismarck's project for German national unification, a compound of feudal and capitalist elements. Under Núñez, the conditions for the rise of a modern, capitalist state began. An important step in this direction was his creation of a permanent army and the state's monopolistic exercise of force. His removal of internal barriers to trade and his policy of tariff protection, however modest, contributed to the formation of an internal market; his national bank, despite its later scandalous mismanagement, represented an initial effort to create a national system of credit; and he gave impulse to the construction of internal improvements, especially railroads. Finally, he sought to give private enterprise access to frontier lands by formally denying the existence of ethnic Afro-Colombian and indigenous communities, voiding their proprietary claims. These policies, combined with the coffee boom, created national markets in land, labor, and commodities and contributed to a growth of capitalism in Colombia.

When he died, corruption, flagrant rigging of elections, division over freedom of the press and electoral reform, and an economic slump caused by a sharp decline of coffee prices produced a political crisis, followed by a resort to arms. Confident of victory over a thoroughly unpopular government, the Liberals launched a revolt in 1899 that ushered in the disastrous War of a Thousand Days. It raged for three years, caused an estimated loss of one hundred thousand lives, and created immense material damage. It ended in a government victory.

During the last third of the nineteenth century, liberal economic policies shaped the development of the various nations of Latin America. This typically included encouragement of exports, foreign investment, and privatization of public resources like land and subsoil rights. But it also relied on the consolidation of forceful, often brutal, dictatorships that used their monopoly of state power to create a unified national market, control labor, subordinate local caudillos, and conquer indigenous lands. The liberal dictatorships consolidated political authority and promoted economic growth, but they failed to sustain an authentic national development that benefited a broad cross-section of the population. Thus, they bequeathed a legacy of social instability and political discontent that frequently combined to produce violent movements for social reform.

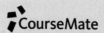 Go to the CourseMate website at **www.cengagebrain.com** for primary sources, additional study tools, and review materials—including audio and video clips—for this chapter.

INDEX